1956

Copyright, 1955, 1948, By Row, Peterson and Company
International and Imperial Copyright secured
All rights reserved for all countries, including the right of translation

4862

THE NEW

Building Better English 12

JOHN J. DE BOER

Illustrations by Muriel and Jim Collins

ROW, PETERSON AND COMPANY

Evanston, Illinois   White Plains, New York

PREFACE

In the years since the first edition of this book was written, a number of new emphases have appeared in high school language arts instruction. Among these are especially the current interest in improving the use of the mass media of communication—newspapers and magazines, radio and television, and motion pictures; the semantic approach to language study, in which the understanding of grammatical structure is supplemented by the exploration of problems in the communication of meaning; and the mastery of effective techniques in group discussion. *The New Building Better English* has undertaken to reflect these and other new emphases.

A large section of the book is again devoted to the systematic study of English grammar. The author earnestly hopes that teachers will regard this section as reference material except in the case of those students who elect to study language as a subject of interest in itself. Superior students frequently find such study challenging and satisfying. Grammar studied in isolation, however, is not likely to be effective in the improvement of language expression among average or below-average students.

In recognition of the increased emphasis on speech, the chapter on spoken English has been completely rewritten. The chapter on vocabulary is essentially new. The concern about reading skills and the mass media of communication has resulted in a new chapter entitled "Reading, Looking, and Listening." Creative writing has been given greater attention than before. Other parts of the book, which seem as useful today as they were at the time that they were first published, remain almost unchanged.

Grateful acknowledgement is made to the *Illinois English Bulletin* for permitting us to quote from two of its issues. Appreciation is expressed to Professor Kenneth Burns, of the Speech Department of the University of Illinois, for writing the chapter on spoken English.

John J. De Boer

TESTS

The tests to accompany the mechanics section of this text are contained in a test booklet that may be purchased for each pupil. The tests also appear in the *Teacher's Manual*. Schools not wishing to buy the booklets may mimeograph the tests. (See page 6 for instruction about taking tests.) Following are the titles of the tests. The page numbers, which refer to the text, indicate when the tests should be given.

	PRETEST *(To precede instruction)*	CHECK TEST *(To follow instruction)*	MASTERY TEST *(To follow review)*
The Parts of Speech	7	81	84
The Parts of the Simple Sentence	7	81	84
The Sentence	7	99	99
Verbs and Verb Usage	7	24	25
Noun and Pronoun Usage	25	50	51
Adjectives and Adverbs	51	71	71
Prepositions and Conjunctions	71	80	81
Punctuation	134	161	162
Capitalization	156	161	162

CONTENTS

SECTION I *Handbook of Language Mechanics*

CHAPTER 1. REVIEWING THE ELEMENTS OF GRAMMAR	3
What Is Correct English?	4
The Testing Program	6
What Grammar Includes	6
CHAPTER 2. BUILDING THE SIMPLE SENTENCE	7
How the Verb Helps to Build the Sentence	7
Properties of Verbs	10
Using Verbs Correctly	14
Review Practice	24
How the Noun and the Pronoun Help to Build the Sentence	25
How the Gerund and the Infinitive Help to Build the Sentence	35
Using Nouns and Pronouns Correctly	38
Making Verbs Agree with Their Subjects	46
Review Practice	50
How the Adjective Helps to Build the Sentence	51
Classification of Adjectives	51
Using Adjectives Correctly	57
How the Adverb Helps to Build the Sentence	60
Types of Adverb Modifiers	60
Using Adjectives and Adverbs Correctly	64
Review Practice	71
How Prepositions and Conjunctions Help to Build the Sentence	71
Using Prepositions and Conjunctions Correctly	73
Review Practice	80
The Interjection	81
Bringing Together All Parts of Speech and Their Uses	81

CHAPTER 3. BUILDING COMPOUND, COMPLEX, and COMPOUND-COMPLEX
SENTENCES 85
   The Compound Sentence 85
   The Complex Sentence 89
   The Compound-complex Sentence 97

CHAPTER 4. EXPRESSING IDEAS IN EFFECTIVE SENTENCES 100
   1. Avoiding Fragments and Run-on Sentences 100
   2. Showing Relations between Statements within Sentences . . . 106
   3. Establishing Clear Reference in Sentences 110
   4. Making Sentences Forceful and Interesting 116

CHAPTER 5. PHRASING IDEAS CLEARLY 120

CHAPTER 6. PROOFREADING WHAT YOU WRITE 133
   1. Punctuation 134
   2. Capitalization 156
      Review Practice 161
   3. Spelling 163
   4. Syllabication 169
   5. Manuscript Form 170
   6. Corrections and Insertions 172

SECTION II *Using Language to Communicate*

CHAPTER 7. EXPLORING THE MAGIC OF WORDS 175
   1. English—A World Language 175
   2. English—A Changing Language 177
   3. The Uses of the Dictionary 185
   4. Figurative Language 189
   5. Word Sounds 193
   6. Careful Word Usage 194
      Denotation and Connotation 194
      Faulty or Confused Expressions 196
      Idiomatic Usage 204
      Trite Expressions 206
      Wordiness 208
      General Review of Diction 209

CHAPTER 8. WRITING GOOD PARAGRAPHS 211

   The Topic Sentence 212
   Development of Paragraphs 215
   Relations within and between Paragraphs 219
   Concluding the Paragraph 221
   Single-Sentence Paragraphs 222
   Do Your Sentences Really Communicate? 222

CHAPTER 9. GAINING SKILL IN CREATIVE EXPRESSION 223

   1. What Shall I Write About? 223
   2. Being a Good Observer 226
   3. Creative Personal Letters 228
   4. Writing Letters of Opinion 229
   5. Evaluating What Others Have Written 231
   6. Other Types of Original Writing 236
      Writing Description 237
      Writing Exposition 237
      Writing Essays 237
      Writing Short Stories 238
      Writing Argumentation 239
      Writing Poetry 240
   Glossary of Terms Used in Creative Writing 242

CHAPTER 10. GAINING SKILL IN RESEARCH 245

   Step 1. Selecting the Subject 247
      Defining the Problem 249
      The Preliminary Outline 249
   Step 2. Finding the Facts 250
      Personal Observation or Experience 251
      Personal Interviews 251
      Current Documents and Reports 252
      The Resources of the Library 253
         The Card Catalogue 254
         Arrangement of Books in the Stacks of a Library 256
         Reference Books 257
         The *Readers' Guide* 261
         Other Guides to Periodicals 262
      Compiling a Working Bibliography 263

CHAPTER 10. GAINING SKILL IN RESEARCH — Continued

Step 3. Organizing the Facts 267
    The Working Outline 268
    Taking Notes as You Read 268
    The Final Outline 270
    Arranging the Note Cards to Fit the Outline 273
Step 4. Reporting the Facts 273
    The First Draft 273
    Footnotes 274
    The Bibliography 276
    Making the Final Draft 277
    Supplementary Pages 278

CHAPTER 11. SPEAKING EFFECTIVELY 279

1. Speech—A Learned Activity 279
2. Speech as a Means of Communication 280
    The Body as a Tool of Communication 280
    The Voice as a Tool of Communication 283
3. Informal Speaking Activities 290
    How to be a Good Conversationalist 291
    What to Remember in Telephoning 291
    How to Conduct an Interview 292
    How to Make a Good Impression in a Job Interview 292
    What to Remember in Appearing on Radio or Television . . 293
4. Discussion 294
    Discussion Defined 294
    The Discussion Outline 295
    Types of Discussion 295
    Leading a Discussion 297
    Participating in the Discussion 297
5. Making a Speech 298
    Types of Speeches 298
    Choosing a Subject 299
    Collecting Material 300
    Making an Outline 301
    Planning the Introduction and the Conclusion 301
    Rehearsing 301
6. Introducing a Speaker 302
7. Evaluating a Speech 302

CHAPTER 12. READING, LOOKING, AND LISTENING 304
  Learning through Reading 304
    Taking Inventory 305
    Developing Good Reading Habits 305
    Recognizing New Words 308
    Increasing Reading Speed 311
    Understanding What You Read 313
    Reading Newspapers and Magazines 314
  Enjoying Radio and Television 319
  Enjoying Motion Pictures 324
  The Art of Listening 326

CHAPTER 13. USING ENGLISH IN BUSINESS 328
  Writing Business Letters 329
    General Appearance of Letters 330
    Standard Forms for Letters 330
    Types of Letters 340
      The Letter of Application 341
      The Letter of Order 345
      The Letter of Adjustment 347
      The Letter of Payment 348
      The Letter of Request 348
  Telegrams 350
  Advertisements 352
  The Job Interview 352

APPENDIX 356
  Conjugation of the Verb TO TAKE 356
  Conjugation of the Verb TO BE 357

INDEX 359

SECTION I

Handbook of Language Mechanics

CHAPTER 1 *Reviewing the Elements of Grammar*

CHAPTER 2 *Building the Simple Sentence*

CHAPTER 3 *Building Compound, Complex, and Compound-complex Sentences*

CHAPTER 4 *Expressing Ideas in Effective Sentences*

CHAPTER 5 *Phrasing Ideas Clearly*

CHAPTER 6 *Proofreading What You Write*

Reviewing the Elements of Grammar

CHAPTER 1

The first and most difficult requirement in language learning is that you must have something to say. Saying nothing, even if you say it correctly, is not communication. You must therefore extend the range of experience on which you may draw in speaking and in writing. Visiting new places; meeting new people; reading increased numbers of books, magazines, and newspapers; and pursuing new hobbies or games will provide the raw material for expressing yourself.

If you are to have something to say about this raw material, you must (1) learn to observe widely and carefully, (2) learn to take a real interest in people, (3) learn to reflect upon what you observe, and (4) learn to ask questions. Only thus can you become an interesting person; only thus can you become an interesting writer and speaker!

A second requirement in language learning is that you must apply common sense and straight thinking to the language that you use. Remember, the primary purpose of language is to *communicate;* that is, to convey meaning, and not to confuse it. You must learn to build sentences and to choose words that say clearly what you mean.

A third requirement for language growth is that you must develop sensitivity to language and language forms. You must learn to *listen*—not only to the language of others, but also to your own. You must learn to note carefully the language constructions used in good books and periodicals. You must learn to be able to criticize your own language.

A fourth requirement is that when you discover usage errors in your speech or writing, you must strive to make the correct forms habitual. You cannot usually take time, in the midst of a conversation or a report, to recall a rule or to debate a grammatical construction with yourself. Especially in animated conversation, you will fall back upon language *habits*. If some of them are unacceptable, those language habits can betray you in embarrassing ways.

What Is Correct English?

Dictionary makers are not the ones who determine what is the correct meaning or use of a word. Neither are textbook writers the ones who determine what is good English. No lawmaking body rules whether one may use "ain't" or "light-complected," or where the accent is to be placed in the word "grimace." The idea may be new to you, but even under a dictatorship, *the people who speak a language* are the ones who decide its usage.

A confusing thing about language is that it has a way of changing even while you are writing or talking about it. In Shakespeare's day, double and triple negatives were acceptable in the most exclusive circles. New words are constantly appearing, and old ones are dying out. What is doubtful usage today may be good usage fifty years from now. New meanings for old words are constantly coming into existence. Just when, for example, did a "ceiling" come to mean the altitude of a cloud formation?

The purpose of such a textbook as this is to report, as accurately as possible, what the prevailing standards of usage are. Good unabridged dictionaries and scholarly reports on the English language furnish the information on which the description of the standards is based.

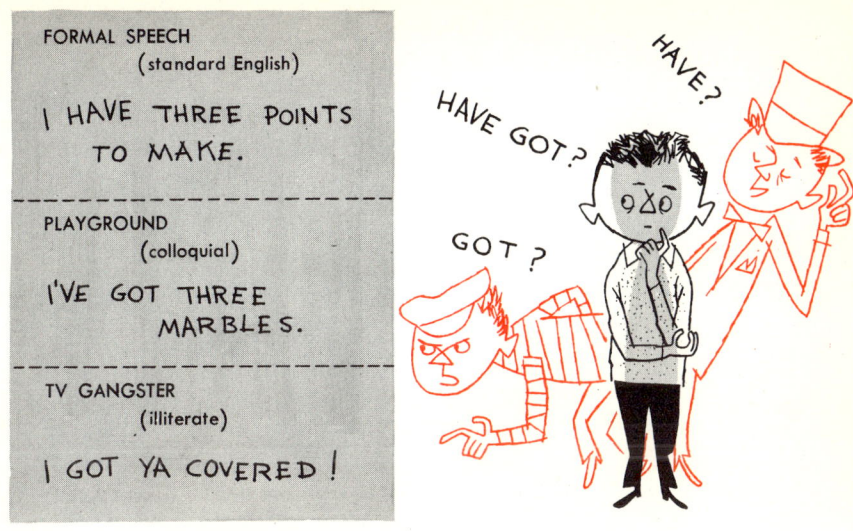

You should realize that language has "levels of usage." *Standard* English is the careful usage adapted to such things as a secretary's report, a commencement speech, or business correspondence. There is *colloquial* usage, suited, for example, to informal letters and conversation. There is *illiterate* usage, avoided by good speakers and writers except when they use it knowingly and deliberately for a special effect. The important thing for you to understand is that these levels of usage do exist; that what may be good usage in one situation may be wrong or unsuitable usage in another. Just as you would not wear an overcoat on the basketball court, or gym shoes with a formal gown, so you should suit your language to the time and place in which you are expressing yourself. In an informal telephone call, you might say, "*I'll phone* you tomorrow," but in a business letter you should say, "*I shall telephone* you tomorrow." Each expression represents a different level of usage; each is good in its place.

GUIDES FOR STUDYING THIS SECTION

There are at least two ways in which you may use this section.
1. Use it simply as a reference section, to help you investigate a point that you do not understand, or to look up a topic assigned by your teacher in connection with an error that you have made.
2. Investigate to see which parts of the section you need; then study only those parts.

The Testing Program[*]

To determine your needs, your teacher may wish you to take the diagnostic tests that are available. These tests are intended to avoid waste of time and effort for you. If you can score 95 per cent or better on any one test, it probably is unnecessary for you to study the part of this section dealing with the topic of that test. If your score on any test falls below 95 per cent, you should turn to the appropriate part of this section, study it, do the practice exercises, take the check test, do any additional practice needed, and then take the mastery test.

The first three diagnostic tests cover *parts of speech* and *syntax*. If you fail to score 95 per cent or better on any one of these, you should study all of chapters 2–4. They discuss, in turn, each part of speech and its use in building a simple sentence; then they proceed to a study of the compound sentence, the complex sentence, and the compound-complex sentence.

In connection with the study of each part of speech, there are tests covering problems in usage peculiar to that part of speech. Even though you score high on the diagnostic tests that deal with parts of speech and syntax, you should take the diagnostic tests in correct usage.

WHAT GRAMMAR INCLUDES

1. *Grammar* is the science of language. It deals with the *parts of speech, inflection,* and *syntax*.

2. The term *parts of speech* indicates the classification of words with reference to the functions that they perform in the sentence. The parts of speech are *verbs, nouns, pronouns, adjectives, adverbs, prepositions, conjunctions,* and *interjections*. Most words may be used as more than one part of speech. The word *fast,* for example, may be used as a noun, a verb, an adjective, or an adverb; which part of speech it is in a particular sentence will be determined by the way that it is used there.

3. *Inflection* is a change in the form of a word to show some change in meaning or in relationship to some other word or group of words. The inflection of verbs is called *conjugation;* of nouns and pronouns, *declension;* of adjectives and adverbs, *comparison*.

4. *Syntax* indicates the relation that a word or a sentence part bears to the rest of the sentence. To give the syntax, then, is to name the parts of a sentence, telling how they are used and how they are related.

---

[*] The tests to accompany this text are contained in a test booklet that may be purchased for each pupil. The tests also appear in the *Teacher's Manual*. Schools not wishing to buy the booklets may mimeograph the tests.

Building the Simple Sentence

CHAPTER 2

How the Verb Helps to Build the Sentence

1 A *verb* expresses condition (being or state of being) or action. The verb is essential to the sentence. **It serves as the** *simple predicate,* **which is the part of the sentence that (1) makes a statement, (2) asks a question, or (3) gives a command.** Since it is the word around which the idea of the sentence is built, you should master first the use of this part of speech.

1a A verb may consist of only one word.

>John *hit* the ball. (*action*)   He *is* our captain. (*condition*)

1b A *verb phrase* is a group of words used as one verb.

>John *had hit* the ball to right field. (*action*)
>John *should have hit* the ball to left field. (*action*)
>He *has been* our captain. (*condition*)

A *verb phrase* combines one or more *auxiliary,* or *helping,* **verbs with a verb of action or condition.** There are twenty-three auxiliary verbs: *is, am, are, was, were, be, being, been, has, have, had, do, does, did, shall, will, should, would, may, might, must, can, could.*

Eight of the auxiliaries may also be used as *linking,* or *copulative,* **verbs.** They are *is, am, are, was, were, be, being, been.* Other linking verbs are *seem, appear, look, feel, become, grow* (when it means *become*), *remain, taste, smell, sound.* **Linking verbs are so called because they join predicate nominatives or predicate adjectives to the subject.** A predicate nominative renames the subject; a predicate adjective describes it.

>James *is* my brother. (*predicate nominative*)
>James *seems* ambitious. (*predicate adjective*)

7

1c **The parts of a verb phrase may be separated in a sentence.**

    John *does* not always *hit* to right field. (*action*)
    John *doesn't** always *hit* to right field. (*action*)
    We*'ve* often *been* much *impressed* by his hitting. (*action*)
    Has he ever *been* captain? (*condition*)

1d **A verb may be compound.**

    The sun *shone* brightly and *gave* us new courage.

FOR PRACTICE AND APPLICATION

A. To see how much the basic sentence idea depends upon the choice of the verb, do this activity.

Here are two sentences from which the verb has been omitted.

    The man .... at me.   He .... my friend.

For each blank, list five action verbs. Go over your lists in class. Note how many utterly different sentence ideas are expressed simply by a change of verb.

B. Copy the following sentences. Draw two lines under each verb or verb phrase. Do not overlook any auxiliaries. Exchange papers for checking.

1. In the last quarter of the game, we increased our lead.
2. This is news to me. Don't repeat it to anyone else.
3. Have those two girls ever been elected to the honor society?
4. All evening long that radio has been blaring. May I shut it off?
5. They've not lost a game on their home field in five years.
6. Have you two boys always been rivals? Can't you be friends?
7. Just then the man turned around and glared at me. I didn't know why.
8. I should know you. Aren't you related to Oscar Peterson?
9. I shall be there at five. Will you wait for me?
10. At that time I had never traveled outside my home state.
11. Weren't you being considered for a promotion? Would you have taken it?

VERBALS

2 **Do not mistake verbals for verbs.** *Verbals* **are verb forms used as adjectives, nouns, or adverbs.** Verbals cannot serve as the predicate of a sentence. There are three types: *participles, gerunds,* and *infinitives.*

2a **A** *participle* **(except when it is part of a verb phrase) is a verb form used as an adjective; that is, it modifies a noun or a pronoun.**

                    v.   *part.*
    Our town **is surrounded** by **rolling** hills.
               part.   *v.*
    Elmer, **having grown** sleepy, **had lost** interest.

---

* NOTE: The contraction *n't* is not a part of the verb.

2b A *gerund* is a verbal noun. It, or its auxiliary, always ends in *ing*.

ger.   *v.*   *ger.*   *v.*
Eating rapidly **is** a bad habit.   **Being elected was** a thrill.

2c The *infinitive* is a verbal noun, adjective, or adverb. It consists of the preposition *to*, expressed or understood, and a verb or a verb phrase. The *to* of an infinitive is often understood after such verbs as *feel, make, dare, see, let, hear,* or *help.*

    inf.   *v.*
To go now **is** the best plan. (*noun use*)

          inf.   *v.*
The game **to be played** tonight **will decide** the title. (*adjective use*)

v.   *inf.*
Help me **to lift** this box. (*adverb use*)

v.   *inf.*
Let me (to) **help** you. (to *understood*)

FOR PRACTICE AND APPLICATION

A. (1) Copy the following sentences. (2) Draw two lines under each verb. Be sure that you find the complete verb. (3) Circle each verbal. (Some sentences have more than one.) Exchange papers for checking.

1. Suddenly we heard the screeching of brakes.
2. Will you help me persuade the following people to contribute?
3. Swimming has long been Jean's favorite sport.
4. Digby was booed loudly, having been called out on strikes again.
5. To take defeat well is often hard to do.
6. Bill, proceeding deliberately across the fallen log, crossed the creek without taking a ducking.
7. A parcel wrapped in brown paper was lying on the desk.
8. Flown successfully in three test flights, the plane was pronounced ready to resume service.
9. Let me tell you how to avoid becoming confused on this road.
10. Having been invited to attend the party, Mavis began to feel happier.

B. Study the following groups of words. Some of these word groups are not sentences, because they contain no verb. Find these incomplete sentences. Rewrite them so that each one contains a verb.

Example: Fred lying in the grass and dreaming of vacation. (*incomplete*)
           Fred **was** lying in the grass, dreaming of vacation. (*complete*)

1. Alfred having been stationed here during the war.
2. The time certainly has been dragging lately.
3. Our team having won by a wide margin.
4. Joining forces seems a logical step toward improving matters.
5. The family cut off completely from the outside world.

6. Typing really wrecks my fingernails.
7. My report, based upon reading and experience.
8. The car sped on.
9. The Sox continuing their winning streak for another day.
10. To tell the truth, I am annoyed.

PROPERTIES OF VERBS

3 Verbs have five properties: *person, number, tense, voice,* **and** *mood.*

PERSON

4 *Person* refers to the change in form of a verb to show its agreement with the person of the subject, which may be the speaker (*first person*), the person spoken to (*second person*), or the person spoken of (*third person*).

NUMBER

5 *Number* refers to the change in form of a verb to show its agreement with the number (*singular* or *plural*) of the subject.

TENSE

6 The word *tense* comes from the Latin word meaning *time.* The tense of a verb indicates the *time* of the action, condition, or state of being expressed. There are six tenses.*

1. PRESENT TENSE: Jimmy *eats* slowly. (*present or habitual action*)

2. PAST TENSE: Dick *ate* rapidly.

3. FUTURE TENSE: Joe *will eat* with us.   I *shall eat* lunch.

   Shall **and** *will* **are the signs of the simple future.** Future time may also be indicated in other ways, but in such cases the idea of future time is not expressed by the verb. Some other word or expression in the sentence indicates the future.

   I *shall go* with you. (The main verb gives the idea of future time.)
   I am going *tomorrow.* (Here the verb itself—*am going*—shows only present time; *tomorrow* gives the idea of future time.)
   I plan *to go.* (The main verb is in the present; the speaker is planning *now.* The action of *going,* expressed by the infinitive, is the future action indicated.)

   Note the difference in meaning in the preceding sentence if the main verb is put into the simple future.

   I *shall plan* to go.

   Now *both* the main verb and the infinitive refer to future actions.

---

* For the complete conjugation of a verb, see pages 356–58.

4. PRESENT PERFECT TENSE: (1) Ethel *has eaten*.
(2) Ethel *has eaten* here often.

The *present perfect tense* **indicates (1) action begun in the past and now completed or (2) repeated or habitual action in the past.** This tense is formed with the present tense of *have* and the perfect (past) participle.

5. PAST PERFECT TENSE: Jimmy *had eaten* before he left home.

The *past perfect tense* **indicates an action begun in the past and completed before some later event in past time.** This tense is formed with the past tense of *have* and the perfect (past) participle.

6. FUTURE PERFECT TENSE: Jimmy *will have eaten* before he leaves.

The *future perfect tense* **expresses action that will have been completed by some future time.** This tense is formed with the future tense of *have* and the perfect (past) participle.

6a *Progressive* **verbs show action continued over a space of time. In the active voice, they combine the tense forms of** *to be* **with the present participle of an action verb. In the passive voice, they contain the auxiliary** *being*.

Bob *is reading* the book. (*act*.)   The book *is being read*. (*pass*.)

6b *Emphatic* **forms of verbs may be used in the present and the past in the active voice. The auxiliaries are** *do, does, did*.

I *do care* about this. (*pres*.)   I *did care* about this. (*past*)

7 **Various shades of meaning can be given by use of the auxiliaries** *should, would, may, might, must, can, could*.

He *should* (*would, may, might, must, can, could*) help me.

8 **All forms of a verb are derived from the** *principal parts* **of the verb—the** *present tense*, **the** *past tense*, **and the** *past participle*.*

8a **Regular verbs, such as** *fill*, **form the past tense and the past participle by adding** *d* **or** *ed* **to the present:** *fill, filled, filled*.†

8b **Irregular verbs follow no rule to form the past and the past participle.** One must learn the forms of such verbs. (See page 14 for a list of the principal parts of some troublesome verbs.)

FOR PRACTICE AND APPLICATION

A. Copy the following sentences, putting in the forms of verbs called for in parentheses. The conjugation on page 356 will help you.

1. She (know, *pres. act*.) that we (wait, *pres. prog. act*.) for her.
2. We (stop, *past pass*.) by a roadblock that (throw, *past perf. pass*.) up.
3. He never (come, *pres. emph*.) before he (expect, *pres. perf. pass*.).

---

* The *past participle* is also called the *perfect participle* because it is used with forms of the auxiliary verb *have* to form the *perfect tenses*.

† See page 165 for spelling changes that may occur.

4. That man (punish, *fut. pass.*) for what he (do, *pres. perf. act.*).
5. Dick (say, *past act.*), "Yes, I (go, *past emph.*) to the game."
6. We (find, *fut. act.*) out how well the work (do, *pres. prog. pass.*).
7. The game (end, *past perf. act.*), and the spectators (leave, *past prog. act.*).
8. We (drive, *fut. prog. act.*) to Denver on May 6. Our damaged car (repair, *fut. perf. pass.*) by then.

B. Here is a sentence: *Cary will go with you.* By using the auxiliary verbs *can, should, may,* and *must,* express the four ideas that follow. Make this a written or an oral exercise.

(1) He ought to go. (2) Perhaps he will go.
(3) It is necessary that he go. (4) He is able to go.

VOICE

9 *Voice* is the change in the form of a transitive verb to show whether the subject is the *doer* or the *receiver* of the action. A *transitive verb* is one that shows action going over to some other word in the sentence.

9a *Active* voice shows the subject as the doer of the action.

Dan *won* the prize.

9b *Passive* voice shows the subject as the receiver of the action.

The **prize** *was won* by Dan.

Note that in the *active* voice the emphasis is on the *doer* of the action; in the *passive* voice, on the *receiver* of the action.

Verbs neither transitive active nor transitive passive are *intransitive*. They are of two kinds: (1) *complete* and (2) *linking,* or *copulative.*

(1) He *was waiting* for me.   (1) We *looked* for you.
(2) He *was* our leader.   (2) We *looked* busy.

NOTE: Many verbs may be either transitive or intransitive, depending upon the way that they are used.

You *should turn* at the next corner. (*intransitive*)
You *should turn* the **pages** carefully. (*transitive*)

FOR PRACTICE AND APPLICATION

A. Turn back to practice *B* on page 8. Classify the verbs as *transitive active, transitive passive, intransitive complete,* or *intransitive linking.* Make this an oral or a written exercise.

B. Write sentences using some form of the following verbs both transitively and intransitively: *begin, blow, eat, ring, climb.* Underline each verb and label its use. Go over your sentences in class.

  Example: I *began* my work. (*trans.*)   You *must begin* here. (*int.*)

MOOD

10 *Mood* shows the manner of the action expressed by the verb. There are three moods: *indicative, imperative,* and *subjunctive.*

10a The *indicative mood* states a fact or asks a question.

   I *attended* the lecture.   *Have* you *seen* Henry?

10b The *imperative mood* gives a command or makes a request. Its only forms are in the second person, present tense.

   Throw the paper away.   Kindly *close* the window.

10c The *subjunctive mood* represents an action or idea still in the mind; that is, one that is not yet an accomplished fact. (See also page 18.)

   I wish that he *were* here. [*He isn't.*]
   I move that a committee *be* appointed. [*One hasn't been.*]

Note the use of the auxiliaries *were* and *be.* See the conjugation on page 357.

FOR PRACTICE AND APPLICATION

A. (1) Copy the following sentences. (2) Draw two lines under each verb or verb phrase. (3) Circle the number before each sentence that illustrates subjunctive mood. (4) Put a check mark before the number of each sentence that illustrates imperative mood. Exchange papers for checking.

1. Chief Hancock has ordered that these men be released.
2. Have you changed your mind about buying that sweater?
3. Look for me about nine o'clock tomorrow night.
4. I certainly wish that this were my watch.
5. There are several matters to be decided at this meeting.
6. Jerry moved that the treasurer's report be accepted.
7. What else could anyone have done about the matter?
8. Just follow my advice.
9. If I were Harry, I'd look for another position.
10. At the end of the first quarter, we were leading by ten points.

B. Write sentences to illustrate the three moods. Read your sentences in class.

USING VERBS CORRECTLY: I

11a Use no auxiliaries with the *past tense* form of an irregular verb; always use auxiliaries with the *past participle*.

The following verbs are often troublesome.

Present Tense	Past Tense	Past Participle	Present Tense	Past Tense	Past Participle
become	became	become	ride	rode	ridden
begin	began	begun	ring	rang,†	rung
bite	bit	bitten		rung	
blow	blew	blown	rise	rose	risen
break	broke	broken	run	ran	run
bring	brought	brought	see	saw	seen
burst	burst	burst	set	set	set
buy	bought	bought	shake	shook	shaken
catch	caught	caught	shine ‡	shone	shone
choose	chose	chosen	shrink	shrank,†	shrunk
climb *	climbed	climbed		shrunk	
come	came	come	sing	sang,†	sung
do	did	done		sung	
drag *	dragged	dragged	sink	sank,†	sunk
draw	drew	drawn		sunk	
drink	drank	drunk	sit	sat	sat
drive	drove	driven	speak	spoke	spoken
drown*	drowned	drowned	spring	sprang,†	sprung
eat	ate	eaten		sprung	
fall	fell	fallen	steal	stole	stolen
fly	flew	flown	swear	swore	sworn
freeze	froze	frozen	swim	swam	swum
give	gave	given	take	took	taken
go	went	gone	tear	tore	torn
grow	grew	grown	throw	threw	thrown
know	knew	known	wear	wore	worn
lay	laid	laid	write	wrote	written
lie	lay	lain			

11b Do not confuse the verbs *sit* and *set*.

Sit, sat, (has) *sat, sitting.*§ *Sit* means "to occupy a seat"; an intransitive verb, needing no object.

The baby *sits* in a high chair.

---

* This verb is conjugated regularly, but wrong forms often are used in the past and the past participle.
† The first form is preferred.
‡ When *shine* means *polish*, the parts are *shine, shined, shined.*
§ The present participle is included because it, unlike most present participles, is often used incorrectly.

14

Set, set, (has) *set, setting. Set* means "to place something"; usually a transitive verb, needing an object.

> He *set* the **glass** on the tray.

11c **Do not confuse the verbs** *rise* **and** *raise.*

Rise, rose, (has) *risen, rising. Rise* means "to move upward"; intransitive, needing no object.

> Soon smoke *rose* from the chimney.

Raise, raised, (has) *raised, raising. Raise* means "to lift something up"; transitive, needing an object.

> He *raised* the **window.**

11d **Do not confuse the verbs** *lie* **and** *lay.*

Lie, lay, (has) *lain, lying. Lie* means "to recline"; intransitive, needing no object.

> I must *lie* down now.   Dan *lay* in the sun for an hour yesterday.
> The book *is lying* on the desk.   It *has lain* there all week.

Lay, laid, (has) *laid, laying. Lay* (present tense) means "to place something"; almost always a transitive verb, needing an object.

> *Lay* your **work** aside.   Last night I *laid* new **plans.**
> I *have laid* my **books** aside.   He *is laying* a **trap** for me.

IS THE HEN LAYING OR LYING?

FOR PRACTICE AND APPLICATION

A. *Irregular Verbs.* Supply the correct form of each verb listed in parentheses. If you write the activity, go over the sentences orally.

1. Yesterday when our class (go) on a skating party, Ned (break) through the ice and almost (freeze) his legs.
2. Has the bell (ring)? I must have (fall) asleep.
3. This shirt has been (tear); I should not have (wear) it.
4. Had the game (begin) when you arrived? You should have (come) early.
5. A weasel had (spring) the trap and (take) the bait.
6. At first the moon had (shine), but soon it had (steal) under a cloud.
7. Jack had (ride) in a plane but had never (fly) one.
8. Last year Bert (run) the mile and (throw) the javelin. He (do) very well.

9. We've (sing) that song so often that I've (become) tired of it.
10. When we (see) the levee, the water had (burst) through one small gap. As we watched, it (grow) rapidly larger.
11. If he hadn't (eat) and (drink) so fast, Fred would feel better.
12. Don sighed, "This suit must have (shrink) since I (buy) it."
13. We (begin) our trip secretly, but someone must have (see) us.
14. The first race had been (run) before we (come).

B. *Irregular Verbs.* Use the correct form of each verb in parentheses. Your instructor may ask you to write these sentences. If so, be sure to read them aloud afterward. Listen for the correct forms.
1. Had James (know) the circumstances, he would have (speak).
2. When the whistle had (blow), we (swim) ashore.
3. Though the ship had (sink), no one had (drown).
4. If I had not (climb) that tree, your dog would have (bite) me.
5. Young Ames (bring) the dog in as soon as he had (catch) it.
6. Although she had not (choose) it, they (give) Ann the prize.
7. Have you (write) Mother about what we (do) last Sunday?
8. As I (draw) near, a voice said, "We've (do) it! We've (shake) them off!"
9. He had (drag) the fallen tree away and (drive) on.
10. Have you (see) Bob? I (know) that he'd be late, even though he had (swear) to come on time.
11. Last night the wind (blow) so hard that I (begin) to worry.
12. When he (come) in, Tim asked, "Have you (draw) lots yet?"
13. He (drink) the milk and then said, "I've (grow) to like this!"

C. If you know that you habitually misuse certain irregular verbs, or if any wrong forms in the preceding activities sound right to you, write original sentences using those verbs correctly. Use your sentences for class drill.

D. *Sit, set; rise, raise; lie, lay.* In each sentence, choose the correct verb or verbs. Read the sentences aloud to hear the correct sounds.
1. Have you (lain, laid) your work aside?
2. Jack should have (lain, laid) his glasses in a safer place.
3. When you (set, sit) the table, (lay, lie) only five places.
4. Because the yeast was old, the dough did not (rise, raise).
5. It is hard for me to (set, sit) still.
6. His voice (raising, rising) angrily, he shouted, "(Set, Sit) down!"
7. You've (set, sat) up long enough. (Lie, Lay) down now.
8. Had the moon (raised, risen) when you finally (lay, laid) down?
9. Their farm (lays, lies) next to ours.
10. Hand me my glasses. They're (laying, lying) on the desk.
11. Who is (setting, sitting) where I used to (sit, set)?
12. Since prices had (risen, raised) greatly, we (set, sat) up a new budget.

E. Write sentences using correctly *lie, lay* (past of *lie*), *lain, lying, laid, rose, raised, rising.* Exchange papers for checking. After corrections have been made, read the sentences in class.

USING VERBS CORRECTLY: II

11e (*Tense sequence and other tense uses*) **Verbs in sentences should show proper time relation to one another:** if events told in a sentence happened at different times, the verb forms used should indicate the time order.

(1) **Suit the tense of dependent clauses and of verbal phrases to the time expressed by the verb in the main clause.**
We sold the house that we *had built* [not *built*]. (The building of the house preceded the selling; *had built* indicates that fact.)
I planned to *go* [not *have gone*] to the reunion. (At the time of planning, the reunion had not taken place.)
Having hurried [not *Hurrying*] home, I ate lunch. (The hurrying preceded the eating.)

(2) **When indirect discourse follows a past tense, use the auxiliaries** *could, should, would,* **and** *might,* **not** *can, shall, will,* **and** *may.**
John declared that he *would* [not *will*] help us.

(3) **Express in present tense the verb in a noun clause that states a generally accepted truth or a fact that is true for all time.**†
I forgot that light *travels* [not *traveled*] faster than sound.
Shakespeare *is* [not *was*] the author of *The Tempest*.

(4) **Keep in the same tense any verbs that are parallel in use.**
He *slipped* past his guard and *made* [not *makes*] a long shot.

(5) **Avoid using** *says* **for** *said.*
I *said* [not *says*] to him, "What do you want?"

FOR PRACTICE AND APPLICATION

A. Complete the following sentences by filling the blanks with verb forms that show the correct sequence of tenses. Be sure to go over your sentences orally.

1. Jim called to say that he .... be late.
2. She smiled and ...., "We hoped to .... you at home."
3. He turned and .... away. "Well," I .... to myself, "that is that!"
4. I knew that air pressure .... lower at high altitudes.
5. Dick announced that he .... change his mind.
6. .... this game, we concentrated on the next one.
7. The day after I .... you, I called Elmer.
8. Jill planned to .... her vacation in October.

*An exception is made if the idea is one of present action continued into the future: He said that he *is* still waiting for a reply.
†Current usage tends to disregard this rule, though logically it makes good sense.

17

9. The whistle blew, and our team .... onto the field.
10. We finally found the man who .... the bank.
11. I believe that Kipling .... the author of *Kim*.

B. Write sentences to illustrate the rules in *11e*. In pairs or in small groups, go over your sentences. From the sentences, make a good practice exercise similar to *A*. Give it to your teacher for use by any students who need the practice.

USING VERBS CORRECTLY: III

11f Use *subjunctive* **forms to express the following:**

(1) *Condition contrary to fact.* This idea may be a wish or a supposition.
      I wish that I *were* taller. (*wish*)
      If this *be* the case, I'll call you. (*supposition**)

(2) *Command.* I order that he *leave* at once.

(3) *Necessity.** It is essential that you *be* here.

(4) *Desirability.** It is best that she *wait* for you.

(5) *Demand.** I insist that someone *help* me.

(6) *Formal motion.* Kay moved that the rules *be* suspended.

FOR PRACTICE AND APPLICATION

A. The following sentences would be better if stated in the subjunctive mood. Reword them; then read them aloud.
1. I wish that I was in Honolulu.
2. The doctor insisted that his orders are carried out at once.
3. That horse looks as if it was ill.
4. It is desirable that this information is kept a secret.
5. I move that he is given complete authority.
6. If I was wealthy, I should need a lawyer.
7. I move that the motion is laid on the table.
8. It is important that you are on time tomorrow.
9. If I was you, I should accept the offer.
10. Probably Jane wishes that she was taking your place.

B. The commonest error in the use of the subjunctive is with the pronoun *I*. Form the habit of saying, "If I *were* ..." and "I wish that I *were* ..." Practice now by writing five sentences to complete each of those expressions. Read your sentences aloud to get used to the sound of these forms.

C. If your teacher wishes, write sentences to illustrate each use of the subjunctive. When you read your sentences in class, identify each use.

* Colloquial usage favors the indicative form.

USING VERBS CORRECTLY: IV

11g **Learn when and how to use certain troublesome auxiliary verbs.** The following four rules cover errors that you should avoid both in your speech and in your written work.

(1) **Use *had better*, not *better*, as a synonym for *ought to*.**
RIGHT: I *had better* go now.   WRONG: I *better* go now.

(2) **Use no auxiliary verbs with *ought*. Avoid the use of *oughta*.**
RIGHT: You *ought* to leave.   WRONG: You *had ought* to leave.
WRONG: You *oughta* leave.

(3) **Do not make one verb both a main verb and an auxiliary. Repeat it.**
RIGHT: Your work *is* good and *is* preparing you for promotion.
WRONG: Your work *is* good and preparing you for promotion.

(4) **Avoid using *would have*, *would of*, *had of*, and their corruptions *woulda* and *hada* for *had* in "if" clauses.**

RIGHT: If you *had* come . . .   WRONG: If you *would have* come . . .
                                 WRONG: If you *would of* come . . .
                                 WRONG: If you *woulda* come . . .
RIGHT: If I *had* seen . . .   WRONG: If I *had of* seen . . .
                                 WRONG: If I *hada* seen . . .

11h Note the distinction in meaning between the verbs in the following pairs. Learn to use these verbs accurately.

(1) **Borrow, lend**
Borrow means "to obtain temporary use of from someone."
Lend means "to grant temporary use of to someone."
   I *borrowed* a quarter.   Will you *lend* me your knife?

(2) **Bring, take**
Bring implies motion *toward*; *take* implies motion *away from*.
   Bring me your report; then *take* it back to your office.

NOTE: Another good word to add to your vocabulary is *fetch*. This word, less often used than it deserves, means "go, get, and bring."
   Fetch me a hammer. (Go where the hammer is, get it, and bring it to me.)

(3) **Imply, infer**
Implying is done by a speaker or a writer; *inferring*, by the hearer or the reader.
   His remarks *imply* that he will go.
   From his remarks I *infer* that he will go.

(4) **Learn, teach**
To *learn* means "to get knowledge"; to *teach* means "to impart knowledge to someone."
   My father *taught* me to fish. At first I *learned* slowly.

19

(5) **Let, leave**

Let means "permit"; *leave* means "to go away from" or "to allow to remain behind."

Let [not *Leave*] me wait for you.   *Leave* this house!

(6) **Rear, raise**

In popular usage, these two verbs are interchanged. In standard English, however, *rear* applies to children and *raise* to crops or livestock.

I was *reared* in a happy home.   My father *raised* cattle in Texas.

11i **Repeat a verb needed to make clear the sentence meaning.**

CONFUSING: I know Charles better than Sam.
CLEAR: I know Charles better than Sam *does*.
CLEAR: I know Charles better than *I know* Sam.

CONFUSING: When a youngster, my uncle often visited us.
CLEAR: When *I was* a youngster, my uncle often visited us.

11j **Be accurate in your use of the verbs** *allow, calculate, expect, guess,* **and** *reckon*. In standard English they are not acceptable substitutes for the verbs *think, suppose, believe, assume, gather*. When they are so substituted, those five verbs are usually classed as dialectal expressions.

RIGHT: *Allow* me to help you.   WRONG: I *allow* that you're wrong.
RIGHT: *Calculate* the cost.   WRONG: I *calculate* that he'll go.
RIGHT: We *expect* company.   WRONG: I *expect* you're right.
RIGHT: Can you *guess* why?   WRONG: I *guess* I'll go home.
RIGHT: I *reckoned* the cost.   WRONG: I *reckon* you're angry.

11k **Do not omit the** *ed* **from the past tense of such verbs as** *ask*.

RIGHT: He *asked* me to help.   WRONG: He *ask* me . . .
RIGHT: He *risked* his life for me. WRONG: He *risk* his . . .
RIGHT: We *husked* corn last week. WRONG: We *husk* corn . . .

11l **Within a sentence, avoid careless shifts of voice and of subject.**

POOR: **He** *lives* here in summer, but his **winters** *are spent* in Florida.
BETTER: **He** *lives* here in summer but *spends* his winters in Florida.

FOR PRACTICE AND APPLICATION

A. The following paragraphs contain 18 errors covered by rules 11g–11l. Make all needed corrections, either in an oral activity or in writing. If you write them, go over the paragraphs orally.

Yesterday my father decided that he would learn me to play golf. If he would of known what would happen, I guess he would have brought my brother Sam to the golf course, and not me. I don't mean to infer that he likes me less than Sam, but Sam is naturally athletic and planning to be a coach. I'm different; I like music.

USING VERBS CORRECTLY: IV

11g **Learn when and how to use certain troublesome auxiliary verbs.** The following four rules cover errors that you should avoid both in your speech and in your written work.

(1) **Use** *had better*, **not** *better*, **as a synonym for** *ought to*.
RIGHT: I *had better* go now.   WRONG: I *better* go now.

(2) **Use no auxiliary verbs with** *ought*. **Avoid the use of** *oughta*.
RIGHT: You *ought* to leave.   WRONG: You *had ought* to leave.
WRONG: You *oughta* leave.

(3) **Do not make one verb both a main verb and an auxiliary. Repeat it.**
RIGHT: Your work *is* good and *is* preparing you for promotion.
WRONG: Your work *is* good and preparing you for promotion.

(4) **Avoid using** *would have, would of, had of,* **and their corruptions** *woulda* **and** *hada* **for** *had* **in "if" clauses.**

RIGHT: If you *had* come . . .   WRONG: If you *would have* come . . .
                                  WRONG: If you *would of* come . . .
                                  WRONG: If you *woulda* come . . .
RIGHT: If I *had* seen . . .   WRONG: If I *had of* seen . . .
                                  WRONG: If I *hada* seen . . .

11h **Note the distinction in meaning between the verbs in the following pairs.** Learn to use these verbs accurately.

(1) **Borrow, lend**
Borrow means "to obtain temporary use of from someone."
Lend means "to grant temporary use of to someone."
   I *borrowed* a quarter.   Will you *lend* me your knife?

(2) **Bring, take**
Bring implies motion *toward;* *take* implies motion *away from.*
   Bring me your report; then *take* it back to your office.

NOTE: Another good word to add to your vocabulary is *fetch*. This word, less often used than it deserves, means "go, get, and bring."
   Fetch me a hammer. (Go where the hammer is, get it, and bring it to me.)

(3) **Imply, infer**
Implying is done by a speaker or a writer; *inferring*, by the hearer or the reader.
   His remarks *imply* that he will go.
   From his remarks I *infer* that he will go.

(4) **Learn, teach**
To *learn* means "to get knowledge", to *teach* means "to impart knowledge to someone."
   My father *taught* me to fish. At first I *learned* slowly.

(5) **Let, leave**

Let means "permit"; *leave* means "to go away from" or "to allow to remain behind."

Let [not *Leave*] me wait for you.   *Leave* this house!

(6) **Rear, raise**

In popular usage, these two verbs are interchanged. In standard English, however, *rear* applies to children and *raise* to crops or livestock.

I was *reared* in a happy home.   My father *raised* cattle in Texas.

11i **Repeat a verb needed to make clear the sentence meaning.**

CONFUSING: I know Charles better than Sam.
CLEAR: I know Charles better than Sam *does*.
CLEAR: I know Charles better than *I know* Sam.

CONFUSING: When a youngster, my uncle often visited us.
CLEAR: When *I was* a youngster, my uncle often visited us.

11j **Be accurate in your use of the verbs** *allow, calculate, expect, guess,* **and** *reckon.* In standard English they are not acceptable substitutes for the verbs *think, suppose, believe, assume, gather.* When they are so substituted, those five verbs are usually classed as dialectal expressions.

RIGHT: *Allow* me to help you.   WRONG: I *allow* that you're wrong.
RIGHT: *Calculate* the cost.   WRONG: I *calculate* that he'll go.
RIGHT: We *expect* company.   WRONG: I *expect* you're right.
RIGHT: Can you *guess* why?   WRONG: I *guess* I'll go home.
RIGHT: I *reckoned* the cost.   WRONG: I *reckon* you're angry.

11k **Do not omit the** *ed* **from the past tense of such verbs as** *ask.*

RIGHT: He *asked* me to help.   WRONG: He *ask* me . . .
RIGHT: He *risked* his life for me.   WRONG: He *risk* his . . .
RIGHT: We *husked* corn last week.   WRONG: We *husk* corn . . .

11l **Within a sentence, avoid careless shifts of voice and of subject.**

POOR: **He** *lives* here in summer, but his **winters** *are spent* in Florida.
BETTER: **He** *lives* here in summer but *spends* his winters in Florida.

FOR PRACTICE AND APPLICATION

A. The following paragraphs contain 18 errors covered by rules 11g–11l. Make all needed corrections, either in an oral activity or in writing. If you write them, go over the paragraphs orally.

Yesterday my father decided that he would learn me to play golf. If he would of known what would happen, I guess he would have brought my brother Sam to the golf course, and not me. I don't mean to infer that he likes me less than Sam, but Sam is naturally athletic and planning to be a coach. I'm different; I like music.

I expect that I could have done better if Dad woulda had more patience with me. Maybe it would have helped, too, if I had of ask some questions. As it was, I did everything wrong, and probably the high-scoring record for the course was broken that afternoon.

When we finally started home, Dad grunted, "I didn't raise my son to be a piccolo player, but I better get used to having one in the family!"

He hasn't left me play golf with him since. I've been thinking, though. Hitting that ball down the fairway might be fun, at that. If Sam will borrow me his clubs and will help me, I reckon I'll see whether I can surprise Dad one of these days. I'll learn him he hadn't ought to look down on piccolo players!

B. Write sentences to illustrate rules 11g–11l. Go over your sentences orally with a partner or in your small groups.

C. Try writing an exercise similar to *A*. Exchange papers with a classmate. After the corrections have been made, have the paragraphs read in class.

FOLLOW-UP

Some of the preceding rules probably give you more trouble than others. Choose one or two errors that you know you make often. Concentrate on them. Learn to listen for those errors; correct yourself every time that you make one of them. Ask a friend or someone at home to help you break yourself of these particular mistakes. When you have really learned to use the right forms, choose other errors on which to work. Hit-and-miss attempts at improving your use of English will not help you much. Concentrated effort on a few usages at a time will bring results.

USING VERBS CORRECTLY: V

11m **Certain verb usages are not yet acceptable English.**

(1) **Avoid using** *ain't* **for** *is not* [*isn't*], *are not* [*aren't*], *am not*, *has not* [*hasn't*], *have not* [*haven't*].

There is no good contraction for *am not*. **Use the complete expression, or word your sentence differently. Avoid** *aren't I*.

Right: I'm next, *am I not?*   Right: I believe that I'm next.

(2) **Avoid using** *didn't go to* **for** *didn't mean to, didn't intend to*.
Right: I *didn't mean to do it*   Wrong: I *didn't go to do it*.

(3) **Avoid using** *disremember* **for** *forget*.
Right: I *forget* when he came.   Wrong: I *disremember* when . . .

21

(4) **Avoid using** *invite, recommend* **as nouns.**
   RIGHT: Send her an *invitation* to the party.
   WRONG: Send her an *invite* ...
   RIGHT: *Invite* her to the party.

   RIGHT: He gave me a *recommendation*.
   WRONG: He gave me a *recommend*.
   RIGHT: I *shall recommend* you for the job.

(5) **Avoid using** *say, listen, look* **as introductory words.**
   POOR: *Say*, what time is it?   *Listen*, I can't stay.   *Look*, it's like this.
   BETTER: What time is it?   I can't stay.   It's like this.

(6) **Avoid using** *suspicion* **for** *suspect.*
   RIGHT: I *suspect* that he is guilty.   WRONG: I *suspicion* that ...
   RIGHT: My *suspicion* was correct.

(7) **Avoid the expressions** *take and* **or** *took and.*
   WRONG: He *took and followed* me.   RIGHT: He *followed* me.

(8) **Avoid using** *take* (or *took*) *sick* **for** *become* (or *became*) *ill.*
   RIGHT: He *became ill* last night.   WRONG: He *took sick* ...

(9) **Avoid the expression** *used to could.*
   RIGHT: I *used to be able to* remember names.
   RIGHT: I *formerly could* remember names.
   WRONG: I *used to could* remember names.

FOR PRACTICE AND APPLICATION

A. The following "halves" of telephone conversations are filled with errors covered under Rule 11m. Rewrite these conversations correctly; then go over them in class.

1. Hello, Fred? ... Say, did you get your invite to Helen's party? ... You did? ... Look, it ain't going to be held this Friday. ... Helen's mother took sick last night. She's better today, but the party is off. ... Helen asked me to call you. ... Listen, Fred, I'll have to go now. Somebody wants in. I suspicion that it's Dad. ... Good-by, Fred.

2. Hello. Is this Mrs. Burton? ... Listen, this is Jane Stanley. ... Look, I need a recommend as a baby sitter; so I took and called you. ... You don't remember me? ... Say, you used to could! I disremember myself the last time I stayed with the twins, but I suspicion it probably was over a year ago. They took sick that night, and I had to call you. I didn't go to upset you, but I ain't forgotten how you rushed home. ... Remember now? Hello? ... Hello? ... (She hung up on me!)

B. Write sentences to illustrate correct usage of these parts of Rule 11m: (1), (2), (3), (4), (6), (8), and (9). Go over your sentences in class.

USING VERBS CORRECTLY: VI

11n The following points deal with minor problems in the use of verbs and with forms that were once felt to be wrong but that are now rather generally accepted as good colloquial English.

(1) **Avoid misuse and overuse of the verb** *get*. **Never use** *gotta*.

    POOR: You'll *get it* for this!   BETTER: You'll *be punished* ...
    COLLOQUIAL: I *didn't get* to go. (*was not permitted* to go? or *was not able?*)
    CLEAR: I *was not allowed* to go.   I *was unable* to go.
    WRONG: You *gotta* help me.   COLLOQUIAL: You've *got to* help me.
    STANDARD: You *must* help me.

(2) **Present usage tends to make little distinction between** *shall* **and** *will*, **between** *should* **and** *would*, **between** *may* **and** *can* (in asking permission). Most careful writers and speakers, however, like to distinguish between the words in these pairs.

Shall, will

With first person, use (1) *shall* to show simple future and (2) *will* to show determination or a promise. For second and third persons, reverse the rule.

    (1) **I** *shall* be waiting.   (2) **I** *will* try harder.
    (1) **They** *will* expect us.   (2) **He** *shall* not go!

Should, would

Use *should* like *shall* and *would* like *will* except as follows:

(a) Use *would* in all persons, both singular and plural, to indicate *habitual action*.

    We *would* sit there talking for hours.

(b) Use *should* in all persons, both singular and plural, to express an *obligation* or a *duty*.

    You *should* have called me.

May, can

Use *may* in asking *permission*; use *can* for indicating *ability to do*.

    May I leave now?   *Can* you lift this box?

(3) **Express a repeated verb if a different form of it is needed.**

    RIGHT: Then the door *was* locked and the windows *were* barred.
    WRONG: Then the door *was* locked and the windows barred.
    RIGHT: I *study* now more than I ever have *studied*.
    WRONG: I *study* now more than I ever have. (have *what?* *study?*)

(4) **Avoid** *is* [or *are*] *done with, is* [or *are*] *through with*. **Say** *has* [or *have*] *finished*.

    Have you finished [not *Are you done with*] that book?

(5) **The verb forms** *contact, enthuse,* **and** *proven* **have established themselves in popular usage. It still is a good idea, however, to avoid them in formal expression.**

Colloquial	Standard
Contact me at my office.	*Get in touch with* me ...
He *enthused* about the plan.	He *is enthusiastic* ...
Can this be *proven*?	Can this be *proved*?

FOR PRACTICE AND APPLICATION

A. The speaker in the following paragraph is in the "get" rut. Wherever you can, improve what he has to say by substituting other expressions for *get* or *got*. If you write this exercise, go over your work orally.

> When I got home from school yesterday, I found that our dog had got out of the yard. Lately my little brother Billy has got a bad habit of leaving the gate open. This habit really gets me. I haven't got time to go into details of our hunt for Prince, but I'll tell you this—we didn't get to eat supper until eight o'clock!

B. Assume that the following sentences are to be used in business letters. Make any corrections or improvements suggested by the points under *11n*.

1. We will contact you when the plans are complete and the money collected.
2. If you like, you can return the unused part.
3. I would appreciate hearing what you have got to suggest.
4. Our dealers have enthused about this product.
5. By the end of the week, I will be done with this project. I would have been through sooner if I hadn't got sick.
6. The value of this product may be proven by trying it.

REVIEW *Review practice*

VERB USAGE

A. Change to standard English all verb errors or colloquialisms in these sentences. If you write the sentences, be sure to go over your work orally.

1. After everyone else had rose, Barry still lay in bed.
2. Jim hurried out the door and shouts, "The roof has fell in!"
3. Mother said that she may have took the wrong road.
4. Have you saw Harry? I hoped to have run into him today.
5. Yesterday Lee swum too far out and nearly drownded. He better be careful.
6. You had ought to slow down. You've always drove too fast.
7. He drawed a deep breath and says, "I have did my best."
8. When she run in and seen Bert laying there, she busted into tears.
9. The moon shined into the room where we were setting.
10. My parents raised six children. Every one of us was learned to work.

11. Say, if I would have knew you'd be here, I'd have wore my new hat.
12. I guess that you have not rode on this bus lately. Fares have raised again.
13. He give me a closer look and come toward me. I growed nervous.
14. If I was you, I'd not set in that draft. You might take sick.
15. Say that again. Are you inferring that I must bring you there with me?

B. Follow the directions given in *A*.
1. The wind that had sprung up blowed hard for an hour.
2. I suspicion that she sees Elaine oftener than Eleanor.
3. Time really has flew since you first brung me here.
4. Then I ask him why he had neither eaten nor drunk for days.
5. Have you broke the watch that Uncle Chris give you?
6. The nights have became colder, but our plants have not froze.
7. A thief took and clumb through that window and stoled my coat.

How the Noun and the Pronoun Help to Build the Sentence

CLASSIFICATION OF NOUNS

12 A *noun* is a word that is used to name a person, place, or thing. A *thing* may be a real object, an idea, or an action.

12a A *common noun* names any one of a class of persons, places, or things: *man, city, rock, truth, election.*

12b A *proper noun* is a name applied to a specific person, place, or thing. Proper nouns begin with capital letters: *William, Dr. Smith, the United States, Central High School.*

12c A *collective noun* is a name applied to a group: *navy, orchestra, club, band, class.*

12d A *concrete noun* is a name applied to something that can be perceived by one or more of the senses: *water, boy, river, table, wind.*

12e An *abstract noun* is a name applied to a quality or a general idea: *smoothness, foolishness, love, hate, beauty.*

12f A *compound noun* is one made up of two or more words: *father-in-law, race truck, schoolhouse, looker-on, Indo-China.*

12g A noun or any word or group of words used as a noun is called a *substantive*. Thus, a *gerund* is a substantive, and an *infinitive* may be one.

CLASSIFICATION OF PRONOUNS

13 A *pronoun* is a word used in place of a noun.

13a *Personal pronouns* indicate (1) **the speaker** (first person); (2) **the one spoken to** (second person); (3) **the one spoken of** (third person).

First person pronouns: I, my, mine, me, we, our, ours, us
Second person pronouns: you, your, yours
Third person pronouns: he, his, him, she, her, hers, it, its, they, their, theirs, them *

13b *Interrogative pronouns* **ask questions. Interrogative pronouns are** *who, whose, whom, which, what.*

Who went with you?   With *whom* did you go?

13c *Relative pronouns* **are both pronouns and connectives. As** *connectives* **they introduce dependent, or subordinate, clauses and refer to an antecedent in the independent clause. Relative pronouns include** *who, whom, whose, which,* **and** *that.* **Some relative pronouns may be compounded:** *whoever, whomever, whichever.*

The theory *that* he explained is new to me.
The man *whom* you introduced spoke well.

13d *Demonstrative pronouns* **point out. They are** *this* (plural, *these*) **and** *that* (plural, *those*).

Those are my books.   What is *this*?

13e *Indefinite pronouns* **do not point out so definitely as demonstratives do. There are many indefinite pronouns, including** *another, any, anybody, anyone, anything, both, each, either, everybody, everyone, everything, many, neither, nobody, none, no one, one, others, some, somebody, someone, such.*

Some have already gone.   *No one* brought his hat.

13f *Compound personal pronouns* (**the** *self* **pronouns**) **have two uses: (1) as** *intensive pronouns* (to emphasize) **or** (2) **as** *reflexive pronouns* (to refer to the subject).

(1) He did the work *himself.*   (2) She hurt *herself.*

PROPERTIES OF NOUNS AND PRONOUNS

NUMBER

14 There are two numbers, *singular* and *plural. Singular* **number denotes** *one* **person, place, or thing.** *Plural* **number denotes** *more than one* **person, place, or thing.**†

---

* The declension of pronouns appears on page 38.
† For the formation of plural nouns, see pages 164–65.

PERSON

15 *Person* **denotes the speaker** (*first person*); **the person spoken to** (*second person*); **or the person spoken of** (*third person*).

First person singular:	*I*, Harry Jones, can help you.
First person plural:	*We*, the men on the team, support him.
Second person singular:	Richard, *you* will be next.
Second person plural:	*You* students in the first row, rise.
Third person singular:	Betty said that *she* sent it to him.
Third person plural:	*They* refused to give it to the members.

GENDER

16 *Gender* indicates sex: *masculine, feminine, neuter*.
    Masculine, male: The *man* has completed *his* work.
    Feminine, female: Jane must call *her* friend.
    Neuter, inanimate objects: The *paint* has lost *its* sheen.

NOTE: *Common gender* is a term sometimes applied to nouns and pronouns that may refer either to males or to females: *player, musician, dog*.

CASE

17 The form of a noun or a pronoun that shows its relation to the rest of the sentence is called *case*. The cases are *nominative, possessive, objective*.

Nouns change their form only in one case, the *possessive*.

Some personal, relative, and interrogative pronouns change their form in all three cases.*

THE NOMINATIVE CASE

18a A noun or a pronoun is in the *nominative case* when it is the *subject* of a verb.

To find the subject of a verb, first find the verb. Then ask the question *who* or *what* of the verb.

    Ed *caught* a large trout. (*Who* caught? *Ed*, the subject.)
    Has she *gone* home? (*Who* has gone? *She*, the subject.)
    One row of trees *had died*. (*What* had died? *Row*, the subject.)
    There *was* no need for us. (*What* was? *Need*, the subject.)

A verb may have a *compound subject;* that is, it may have more than one subject.

    Beth and *she* collect stamps. (*Who* collect? *Beth* and *she*.)

---

* For the formation of possessive nouns, see page 150. For the declension of pronouns, see page 38.

18b A noun or a pronoun is in the *nominative case* when it is used as a *predicate nominative*.

    The girl is *Betty*. (*predicate noun*)   This is *she*. (*predicate pronoun*)

A *predicate nominative* (predicate noun or pronoun) is so called because it completes the predicate verb and names the same person or thing as the subject. Predicate nominatives complete *linking verbs,* which are so called because they link the subject and the word that completes the meaning of the subject: *girl—Betty; This—she.* *

    Predicate nominatives may be compound:

        The tennis players were *Ray, Vern, Harold,* and *I.*

18c A noun or a pronoun is in the *nominative case* when it is *in apposition with another noun or pronoun in the nominative case.*

    That man is Carl Jones, our *agent.* (*apposition with predicate noun*)

    We, *Bud* and *I,* are the committee. (*apposition with subject*)

18d A noun or a pronoun is in the *nominative case* when it is used in *direct address*. This construction is called a *nominative of address,* or a *vocative.*

    Now, *Gary,* move over here.   *Men,* you must play harder tonight.

Note that the nominative of address is set off by a comma or commas.

FOR PRACTICE AND APPLICATION

A. List all the nouns and pronouns in the following sentences. After each noun or pronoun in the nominative case, state why it is in the nominative case. Refer to rules 18a–18d.

Remember: To find the subject, find the verb first; then ask the question, "Who or what . . . ?"

1. Jane, I shall leave for camp in July. Ellen is going with me.
2. Has she ever attended camp before?
3. One group of boys was playing baseball.
4. Otto was their pitcher and their star.
5. August and he, their best hitters, scored three runs.
6. There weren't many members present.
7. That was he. Didn't anyone recognize him?
8. Not long ago I saw him and Elsie at the store.
9. This animal must be a lizard. Do you agree, Jim?
10. After a long year of hard work, with no vacation whatever, John finally left for the country.

*See page 7 for the list of linking verbs.

B. Write original sentences containing the following:
1. A compound subject made up of a noun and a pronoun
2. A nominative of address and a predicate pronoun
3. A compound predicate nominative made up of a noun and a pronoun
4. An appositive to a predicate noun
5. An introductory *there*. Use a compound subject.
6. A collective noun and an abstract noun
7. A demonstrative pronoun and an indefinite pronoun

C. *Remember:* To be a sentence, a group of words must have a verb (simple predicate) and a subject.

Copy the numbers of the following groups of words. If a group of words is a sentence, write the verb and the subject after the corresponding number. If it is only a sentence fragment, write *F*. Change the fragments to sentences; then compare your sentences in class.

1. Harry, having visited the zoo innumerable times and being thoroughly tired of spending hours at the snake pit.
2. The lamp on that table beside the couch is made of china.
3. In the winter Harriet spends most of her time on skis.
4. Running madly down the lane, Elroy was yelling like a maniac.
5. We may never again see such a display of fireworks.
6. That crowd of people, wearing clothes of every color in the rainbow, stretching from one end of the stadium to the other.
7. Sharpened to pin-point fineness, the pencil lay invitingly on the clean sheet of paper.
8. That was he, the short man disappearing behind that tent.
9. Those shrubs, flowering so gaily, were planted only three years ago.
10. The referee blowing his whistle and pointing to Al Evers, our captain.

Using Diagrams to Analyze Sentence Structure (The Nominative Case)

A sentence diagram gives a picture of the relationship of words within a sentence. Many students find that this diagrammatic picture helps them to see sentence structure more clearly.

At this time, you will diagram only (1) verbs and (2) nouns and pronouns in the nominative case. As you study other sentence elements, you will learn how to diagram those elements also.*

---

*Throughout this book, the diagramming of sentence elements follows complete instruction on those sentence elements. The instructor, if he wishes, may omit diagramming without disturbing to any degree the sequence of instruction.

THE STEPS IN DIAGRAMMING

Sentence: Bud Smith caught three large catfish.

1. Draw a horizontal line. This horizontal line is called the base line, because the basic sentence elements appear upon it.

    _____

2. Find the verb and place it on the right half of the line. Always find the verb first; it is the most essential sentence element.

    _____ caught _____

3. To the left of the verb, draw a vertical line that cuts through the horizontal line. This line serves to separate the predicate verb and the subject, the two chief sentence elements.

    _____|_caught _____

4. Place the subject to the left of the vertical line. To find the subject, ask yourself, "Who or what caught?"

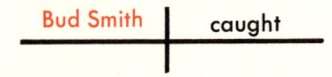

    Bud Smith|_caught_____

The following diagrams illustrate constructions in the *nominative case* (Rules 18a–18d). The diagrams omit sentence parts not yet studied, except for the conjunction joining compound parts.

Subject of a Verb
Has she gone to school?

    she | Has gone

Compound Subject
Beth and she collect stamps.

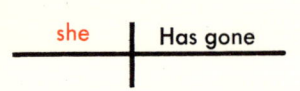

    Beth ╲
       and ⟩— collect
    she ╱

Compound Verb
They sang and cheered for hours.

          sang
They —⟨ and
          cheered

*Introductory "There"**
There was no need for us.

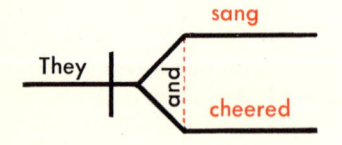

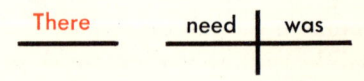

    There   need | was

---

* An introductory *there*, called an *expletive*, has no relation to the other parts of the sentence; therefore it appears on a separate line of the diagram. Such a word is called an *independent element*.

Predicate Noun
The girl in the red hat is Betty.

Predicate Pronoun
This is she.

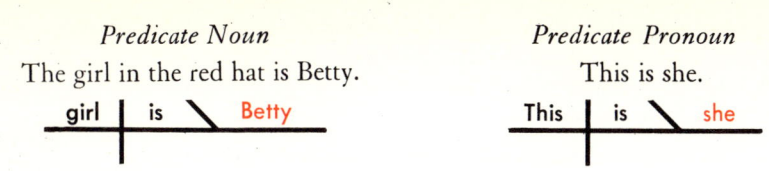

Notice that a predicate nominative is separated from the verb by a slanting line pointed toward the subject to show that the predicate nominative refers to it. Because the predicate nominative is part of the complete predicate, this line reaches the base line but does not cross it.

Compound Predicate Nominative
The members of the tennis team were Raymond, Vernon, Harold, and I.

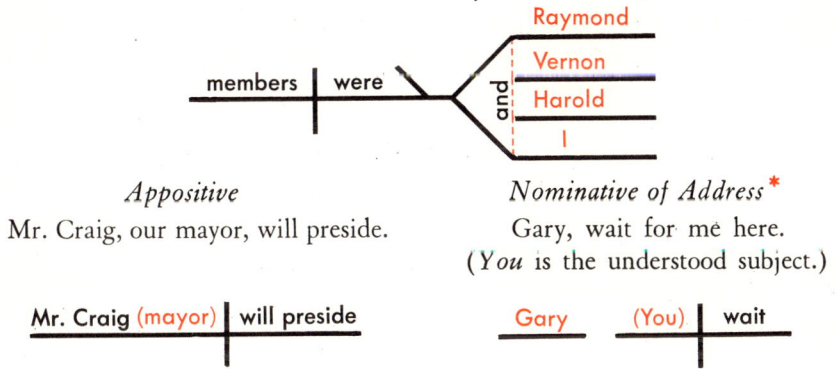

Appositive
Mr. Craig, our mayor, will preside.

*Nominative of Address**
Gary, wait for me here.
(*You* is the understood subject.)

FOR PRACTICE AND APPLICATION

A. Diagram the verb, the subject, and any other nouns and pronouns in the nominative case in the following sentences. Go over your diagrams orally.

1. The final game of the tournament was the most exciting one of all.
2. Did you see it, Jack?
3. It was played between Horton and Bellville.
4. There were two overtime periods in this game.
5. At the end of the first half, Horton was leading by two points.
6. In the third quarter, Dick Barr, Horton's star forward, fouled out.
7. The lead changed hands several times in the second half.
8. The fans groaned and cheered alternately for their teams.
9. In the first overtime period, two Horton players and three Bellville players were removed for having too many fouls.
10. Then in the last seconds of the final overtime, Ted Barton of Bellville tried a thirty-foot shot and made it.

B. If your instructor so directs, diagram the sentences in *A*, page 28, as you did the preceding activity.

---

*A nominative of address, like the expletive *there*, is an independent element; therefore it is diagrammed apart from the rest of the sentence.

THE POSSESSIVE CASE

19 A noun or a pronoun is in the *possessive case* when it denotes *ownership, possession,* or *connection.* *

> *Ownership or possession:* Bob's clothes, *his* room
> *Connection:* a *day's* work, two *days'* delay, a *dime's* worth

THE OBJECTIVE CASE

20a A noun or a pronoun is in the *objective case* when it is the *object of a verb* (*direct object*).

> Scott **threw** the *ball* to first base.
> Father **took** *Bill* and *me.* (*compound direct object*)

In the sentences above, the verbs *threw* and *took* are *transitive verbs.* (See page 12.) They show action passing from a doer to a receiver. In the first sentence above, *ball* receives the action of the verb *threw;* in the second sentence, two words, *Bill* and *me,* receive the action of the verb *took. Ball, Bill,* and *me* are direct objects.

A direct object answers the question, "*To whom* or *what* was something done by the subject?"

20b A noun or a pronoun is in the *objective case* when it is the *object of a preposition.* †

> Mark is traveling **through** *Kansas.*   Elizabeth called **to** *her.*
> Irene went **with** *Sue* and *me.* (*compound objects*)

20c A noun or a pronoun is in the *objective case* when it is the *indirect object* of a verb.

> Father bought my *brother* a calf.
> Give *him* and *me* a chance. (*compound indirect objects*)

In the first sentence, *bought* is the verb. *Who* bought? *Father,* the subject. Father bought *what? calf,* the direct object. *To* or *for whom* did he buy a calf? for *brother,* the indirect object. (The prepositions *to, for,* or *of* can always be inserted before an indirect object.)

In the second sentence, the verb is *Give;* the subject, *You* (understood); the direct object, *chance;* the indirect objects, *him* and *me.*

20d A noun or a pronoun is in the *objective case* when it is the *subject* or the *object* of an *infinitive.*

> Don asked the *girls* to come. (subject of *to come*)
> We asked *Jane* and *her* to sing. (compound subjects of *to sing*)
> James taught me to like *them.* (object of *to like*)

---

*For the formation and spelling of possessive nouns, see page 150. For possessive pronouns, see page 150.
†For further discussion of prepositional phrases and a list of common prepositions, see pages 71–72.

20e A noun or a pronoun is in the *objective case* when it is the *predicate complement* after the infinitive *to be* if the subject of the infinitive is expressed.

> Charles thought me to be *her*.

In this sentence, *me* (objective case) is the subject of the infinitive *to be*. Therefore the objective pronoun *her*, not the nominative *she*, is needed as the predicate complement.

If the subject of the infinitive *to be* is not expressed, the complement is in the nominative case: "It proved to be *she*."

20f A noun or a pronoun is in the *objective case* when it is the *objective complement*.

> They called the boy *Jock*.

In this sentence, *boy* is the direct object; *Jock*, the objective complement.

20g A noun or a pronoun is in the *objective case* when it is a *retained object;* that is, when it completes a passive verb.

> Dick **was given** the *prize*.

20h A noun or a pronoun is in the *objective case* when it is in *apposition with another noun or pronoun in the objective case*.

> He needs two boys, *Si* and *me*. (apposition with *boys*, direct object)

FOR PRACTICE AND APPLICATION

A. In the following sentences, list each noun and each pronoun. After each, state whether it is in the nominative, the possessive, or the objective case; then tell why. Check your work by rules 18a–20h.

Remember, to find any direct object, say the subject and the verb, followed by *whom* or *what*.

1. James drew five books from the library.
2. He brought Lola the biographies of two famous inventors.
3. The other books contained stories of Indian scouts.
4. One of these books was titled *Apache Trail*.
5. James read them and told Susan and me some of the stories.
6. Then she and I took the books back to the library.
7. We didn't allow ourselves enough time, however.
8. The library door was locked.
9. There went our plans for a visit inside the library!
10. We pushed the books through the slot in the door and started gloomily for home.

B. For more practice, list all nouns and pronouns in the objective case in the sentences in *A*, page 28. Tell why each one is in the objective case.

C. Write original sentences containing pronouns used as the following:

1. A compound direct object
2. A compound indirect object
3. A compound object of a preposition
4. A compound subject of an infinitive

Using Diagrams to Analyze Sentence Structure
(The Objective Case)

The following examples show how to diagram nouns and pronouns in the objective case.* Elements not yet studied are ignored in these diagrams.

Direct Object
The ball hit him.

Compound Direct Objects
Father took Bill and me.

Because the direct object is part of the complete predicate, the vertical line between the verb and the direct object meets the base line but does not go through it.

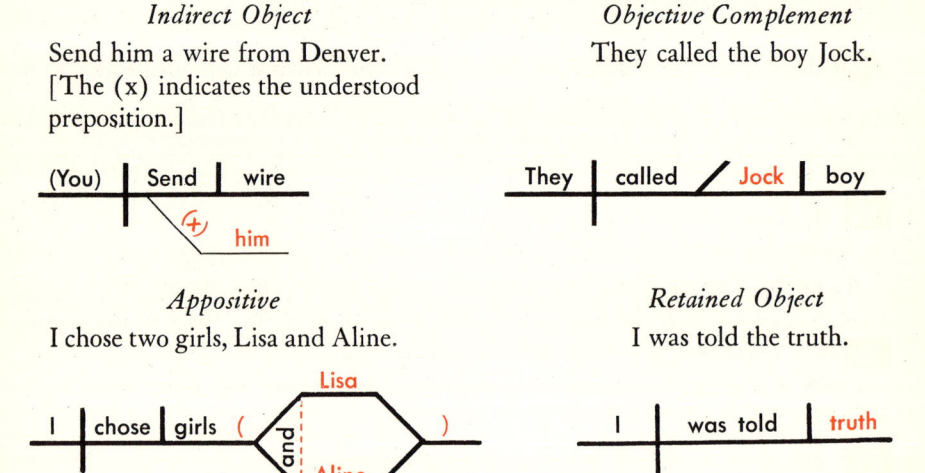

Indirect Object
Send him a wire from Denver.
[The (x) indicates the understood preposition.]

Objective Complement
They called the boy Jock.

Appositive
I chose two girls, Lisa and Aline.

Retained Object
I was told the truth.

FOR PRACTICE AND APPLICATION

A. Diagram verbs, subjects, and all nouns and pronouns in the objective case in the following sentences. Put your diagrams on the board; then go over them orally. Be specific in explaining them. *Example:* I chose two girls, Lisa and Aline. In this sentence the verb is *chose*. The subject is the pronoun *I*. There is a direct object, the noun *girls*. *Lisa* and *Aline* are proper nouns used in apposition with the direct object.

1. This book has certainly given me some exciting moments.
2. Tell me the latest developments.
3. Has Miss Bates named you temporary chairman?
4. Yesterday Mr. Akers made us, George and me, a tempting offer.

*The diagramming of prepositional phrases is omitted here. It is covered under adjectives, page 55 and adverbs, page 63.

5. The Forestry Club has just postponed its April meeting.
6. Last night I saw two television shows, a play and a boxing match.
7. Your entry has been given a special award.
8. Coach Rayburn taught us some new plays yesterday.
9. Have you met my cousin, Ralph Elliott?
10. We have elected Frank and Fritz co-captains.

B. For more practice, use the sentences in *A*, page 33. Omit prepositional phrases. Follow instructions for the preceding activity.

HOW THE GERUND AND THE INFINITIVE HELP TO BUILD THE SENTENCE

21a The *gerund*, a verbal noun, can be used as any of the following:
1. *Subject: Walking* is good exercise.
2. *Direct object:* He enjoys *attending* school.
3. *Appositive:* This sport, *rowing*, has developed my shoulders.
4. *Indirect object:* The speaker paid our *debating* a compliment.
5. *Predicate nominative:* His chief pleasure is *watching* games.
6. *Object of preposition:* Father scolded him for *chasing* the cows.

21b A gerund keeps certain verb characteristics; that is, it may have *complements* and *modifiers*.

>Cleaning *silver* is a tedious task. (*silver*, object of *Cleaning*)
>*Fast* thinking prevented an accident. (*Fast*, modifier of *thinking*)

21c A *gerund phrase* is made up of a gerund and its complements or modifiers. In the examples above, *Cleaning silver* and *Fast thinking* are gerund phrases.

22a The *infinitive* can be used as a noun.
1. *Subject: To go* immediately is the best solution.
2. *Direct object:* He planned *to leave* at once.
3. *Predicate nominative:* The only solution is *to speak* to him.
4. *Appositive:* His plan, *to travel* in June, is satisfactory.
>It is difficult *to decide*. (It, to decide, is difficult.)
5. *Object of preposition:* I can do nothing except *to wait*.

22b After such verbs as *let, help, make, see,* and *hear*, the *to* of the infinitive usually is omitted.

>Will you let me (*to*) go with you?

22c An *infinitive*, like a gerund, keeps certain verb characteristics; that is, it may have *complements* and *modifiers*. Further, an infinitive used as a noun may have a subject.

>To keep your *friendship* is my aim. (*friendship*, object of *To keep*)
>You need to work *harder*. (*harder*, modifies *to work*)
>I shall ask *Clyde* to help you. (*Clyde*, subject of *to help*)

22d An *infinitive phrase* is made up of an infinitive and its complements or modifiers. In the first two examples, *To keep your friendship* and *to work harder* are infinitive phrases.

FOR PRACTICE AND APPLICATION

A. Explain how each infinitive and each gerund in the following sentences is used. Make this an oral or a written exercise.
1. Fishing is my father's favorite sport.
2. He hopes to spend his vacation at Catfish Lake.
3. Will you be changing your mind?
4. To take them by surprise is our only hope.
5. Pauline has never learned to stroke a good backhand shot.
6. Comparing oneself with others is an unfortunate habit.
7. Did you see me make that last shot?
8. This weakness, losing my temper, gets me into trouble.
9. It is not easy to understand you.

B. By using a gerund or a gerund phrase, combine each of the following sentence pairs into one good sentence. Exchange papers for checking. Read the revised sentences in class.
Example: I kept a record of my reading. That record proved useful.
Keeping a record of my reading proved useful.
1. In emergencies I lose my head. This habit causes me trouble.
2. We should leave at once. Then we shall be sure to arrive in time.
3. In the last quarter we used a new offense. In this way we won the game.
4. That night we slept in the woods. This was a new experience for me.
5. Jim has two hobbies. He collects stamps and builds model planes.

C. Write original sentences using the infinitive *to agree* in these ways: (1) as a sentence subject, (2) as a predicate nominative, (3) as a direct object. Go over your work as in *A*.

Diagramming Gerunds and Noun Infinitives

Subject
To go immediately is the best solution.

Object
He enjoys playing golf.

Predicate Nominative
My hobby is modeling in clay.

Appositive
It is not easy to apologize.

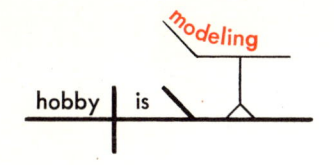

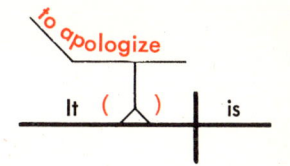

Compound Form
I expect to live and to learn.

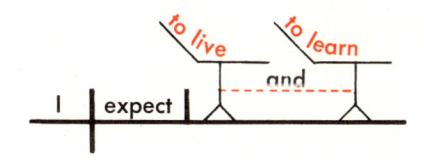

Subject of an Infinitive
Dad made us eat lunch.

Predicate Complement after To Be
When To Be *Has a Subject*
Charles thought me to be her.

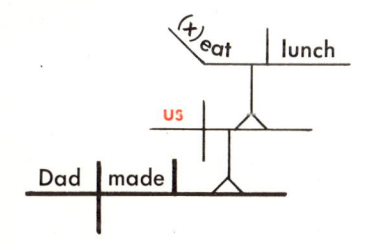

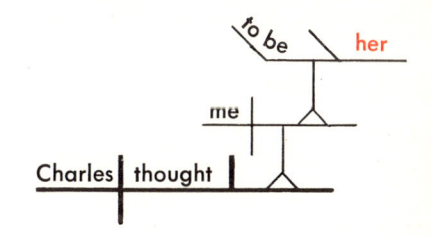

FOR PRACTICE AND APPLICATION

A. Diagram verbs, subjects, predicate nominatives, direct objects, indirect objects, and appositives in these sentences. Go over all diagrams orally. Be specific.

1. Weeping and wailing will not help matters.
2. I need you to do an errand for me.
3. It is difficult to understand you.
4. His chief interests are reading mysteries and writing them.
5. I saw him open the package.
6. Have you tried keeping an account of your expenses?
7. You have discovered my weakness, mislaying my keys.
8. We do not plan to change anything.
9. To redecorate this room will be expensive.
10. Blaming others will never win friends.

B. For further practice, use the sentences in *A,* page 36. Treat as in *A.*

USING NOUNS AND PRONOUNS CORRECTLY

USING CORRECT CASE

One difficulty in using pronouns correctly is that certain pronouns change their form, depending upon their use. The following declensions give the forms of personal, relative, and interrogative pronouns.

THE PERSONAL PRONOUN

	Nominative Case	Possessive Case	Objective Case
First person, singular	I	my, mine	me
First person, plural	we	our, ours	us
Second person, singular	you	your, yours	you
Second person, plural	you	your, yours	you
Third person, singular	he, she, it	his, her, hers, its	him, her, it
Third person, plural	they	their, theirs	them

RELATIVE AND INTERROGATIVE PRONOUNS

	Nominative Case	Possessive Case	Objective Case
Singular	who	whose	whom
Plural	who	whose	whom
Singular	which	whose	which
Plural	which	whose	which
Singular	what	.....	what
Plural	what	.....	what

The compound forms *whoever* and *whomever* are used like *who* and *whom*.

The following rules will guide you in using correct case.

23 Use the *nominative case* for (1) *subjects* and (2) *predicate nominatives*. (See *18a–18d*.)

    (1) *He* went fishing.   (2) The one to blame is *I*. *   (2) This is *she*.

24 Use the *objective case* for *objects*. (See *20a–20h*.)

    Helen asked *me* for my report. (*direct object*)
    They gave *me* two tickets. (*indirect object*)
    Send this note to *them*. (*object of a preposition*)

25 Most errors occur when a pronoun is part of a compound. To help decide which form to use, eliminate the other member of the compound.

    Jim chose *Ed* and (*I, me*).
    Jim chose (*I, me*). [Now the choice is easy: "Jim chose *me*."]

26 Keep an *appositive pronoun* in the same case as the word with which it is in apposition. (See *18c* and *20h*.)

    We three—John, *she*, and *I*—went. (*apposition with subject*)
    They took *us*, Jean and *me*. (*apposition with direct object*)

27 Use *who* and *whoever* as subjects or predicate nominatives; *whom* and *whomever* as objects. The insertion of such expressions as "do you think" does not affect the rule.

    Who is going? (subject of *is going*)
    Who do you think is going? (subject of *is going*)
    Whom did you call? † (object of *did call*: You did call *whom*.)
    Whom did you say you saw? † (object of *saw*: You did say you saw *whom*.)
    Give this to *whoever* comes first. (subject of *comes*; the object of the preposition *to* is "whoever comes first.")
    Choose *whomever* you like. (object of *like*)

28 Use *objective case* for (1) the subject of an infinitive and (2) the object of one. (See *20d*.)

    (1) He asked *me* to help.   (2) Would you like to help *me*?

29 When a form of the infinitive *to be* links two pronouns, use the same case for both pronouns.

    I should like to be *she*. (*nominative*)   He took *me* to be *her*. (*objective*)

30 Use *we* in combination with *nominative nouns* and *us* in combination with *objective nouns*.

    We girls helped. (*subject*)   Don't neglect *us* four *men*. (*direct object*)
    The guides are *we* boys. (*predicate nominative*)

31 Use *possessive case* before a gerund if you wish to show ownership.

    His (not *Him*) coming is news.   Don't mind *my* complaining.

---

* There is growing acceptance of *me* as good usage in informal expression. This form is another example of what is known as "levels of usage."
† *Who* is frequently used in informal expressions, especially if the object begins the sentence. This use is another example of levels of usage.

32a **Never use an apostrophe in possessive personal pronouns.**

Write *its, hers, ours, yours, theirs*. Avoid confusing possessive pronouns with contractions that sound like them: *it's* (*it is* or *has*), *you're* (*you are*), *who's* (*who is* or *has*).

RIGHT: Is this like our book?   Yes, *it's* just like *ours*.
RIGHT: Whose book has *its* cover torn? Is it *yours*?
RIGHT: *Who's* there?   *You're* early again.

32b **Use an *apostrophe* and *s* to form the possessive of indefinite pronouns. If, however, the indefinite pronoun is followed by *else*, add the apostrophe to that word instead.**

RIGHT: Here is *someone's* notebook.
RIGHT: His ideas are like no one *else's*.
WRONG: His ideas are like no *one's* else.

33 **Let sentence meaning guide your choice of case after *than* or *as*.**

 I help her oftener *than* **him.** (*Him* is the object of *help* understood; the meaning is "... than *I help* him.")

 I help her oftener *than* **he.** (*He* is the subject of *help* understood; the meaning is "... than *he helps her*.")

34 **Do not use a possessive noun as the antecedent of a pronoun.**

WRONG: I grew up on my *uncle's* ranch *who* lives in Texas.
RIGHT: I grew up on the ranch of an *uncle who* lives in Texas.

FOR PRACTICE AND APPLICATION

A. List the correct pronouns for the following sentences, or write each entire sentence correctly, as your instructor directs. Exchange papers for checking. Then read the sentences aloud to hear the correct sound. In each instance give the reason for your choice of pronoun.

1. Bill and (he, him) have been assigned to the guard posts.
2. Nobody knew but you and (I, me). (Who, Whom) do you suppose told?
3. He depends on me more than (Jerry, Jerry depends on me).
4. He is a talented boy (who, whom) I believe will succeed.
5. Dismiss (whoever, whomever) has completed his work.
6. Carl has invited (we, us) boys. Do you mind (our, us) going?
7. (Whose, Who's) ready for dessert? Have you eaten (yours, your's)?
8. (It's, Its) a fact; John is shorter than Ted and (I, me).
9. Help Doris and (I, me) sort these papers.
10. I've called to interview Mrs. Robbins. Are you (her, she)?
11. We have his permission. Do we need (anyone's else, anyone else's)?
12. John is older than (he, him) or (I, me).
13. Mary gave tickets to (whoever, whomever) attended.
14. (Who, Whom) do you think they called? It was (we, us) two.
15. Everyone applauded except John and (I, me).

16. I wonder (who, whom) she asked. Was it (him, he)?
17. They did not know about (us, our) leaving.
18. Mr. Banks offered Fred and (I, me) a summer job.
19. This is (my sister's picture, a picture of my sister) who is engaged.
20. He often takes me to be (her, she). I'd like to be (her, she), too!

B. Correct any pronoun errors in the following sentences. Read the sentences correctly aloud to hear the right sound. In each instance give the reason for your correction.

1. The boy who they say will win the title is Bob.
2. These plans must be kept a secret among we three.
3. He praised the student who his classmates called "The Brain."
4. Barton is younger than her, but he is as tall as she.
5. I'll stay at my aunt's house who lives in Akron.
6. We were surprised to hear of him flying to New York.
7. This is him speaking. Who did you think it was?
8. At the ball game Ted bought Helen and I a program.
9. Do you want Joe and I to wait for you?
10. Your advice is just like everybody's else.
11. I should like to be him for just one week.
12. Between you and I, there will have to be some changes made.
13. Was that her who you saw last night?
14. Kenneth plans to give exactly as much as him.
15. No one except Jake and me had come. Us two haven't missed a meeting.
16. Let Fritz and I help you.
17. Whom do you think is going with us?
18. They've really given you and I too much credit.
19. Did anyone call for we boys?
20. Give this copy to whomever needs it.

C. From the results in *A* and *B*, make a list of errors common to your class. Write sentences to use for class practice in improving your usage.

FOLLOW-UP

In your notebook, list the case uses that give you most trouble, with a correct example of each. If any of the wrong sentences in *B* sounded right to you, include in your list the case uses covered by those sentences, even though you may have corrected them properly. Check by this list all papers that you write for your various classes.

MAKING PRONOUNS AGREE WITH THEIR ANTECEDENTS

35 **A pronoun should agree in person, number, and gender with its antecedent. The antecedent is the noun (or other substantive) to which the pronoun refers.**

35a Certain indefinite pronouns are *singular*. They include *another, anybody, anyone, each, either, everybody, everyone, neither, nobody, no one, somebody, someone.** Unless you know that the antecedent is feminine, use singular masculine pronouns to refer to these indefinite pronouns.† (See also Rule 51, page 45.)

>   *Everyone* needs *his* [not *their*] health.
>   *Each* of the workers does *his* [not *their*] share.
>   *Each* of the women does *her* share.
>   *Everyone* should keep *himself* [not *themselves*] healthy.

35b The indefinite pronouns *many* and *both* are plural. Use a plural pronoun to refer to them.

>   *Many* have changed *their* politics.   *Both* have risked *their* lives.

AVOIDING MISCELLANEOUS FAULTS WITH NOUNS AND PRONOUNS

36 Do not use the illiterate pronoun forms *hisself, theirself, theirselves.*

37 Avoid the double subject.

>   RIGHT: The weather was hot.   WRONG: The *weather it* was hot.

38 Avoid use of *this here, that there, these here, those there.*

>   *That* (not *That there*) is a fine horse.   *These* (not *These here*) are mine.

39 As a rule, use *who* or *whom* to refer to persons, and *which* to refer to animals or things. *That* may refer to persons, animals, or things.

>   The boy *whom* [not *which*] you saw plays the trombone.

40 Be sure that the reference to an antecedent is clear.

>   CONFUSING: Kenneth's uncle said that he knew *his* friend.
>   CLEAR: Kenneth's uncle said, "I know your friend."

41 Avoid using a singular noun of measurement or amount where a plural form is needed.

>   We swam in six *feet* [not *foot*] of water.
>   This field produced only twenty *bushels* [not *bushel*] per acre.

42 Never use *them* as a demonstrative; it is not a pointing-out pronoun.

>   *Those* [not *Them*] are my shoes.
>   My shoes are *those* [not *them*] in the corner.

---

* Sometimes *everybody* and *everyone* are used to mean *all*. In such cases a plural pronoun may be used to refer to them: *Everyone* came early, for *they* were eager to hear the speaker. Some authorities, however, would substitute "all" for "they."

† If the antecedent implies a mixed group containing both masculine and feminine members, a masculine pronoun is better than the clumsy combination of masculine and feminine forms.

>   AWKWARD: Every citizen in the land should exercise his or her right to vote.
>   BETTER: Every citizen in the land should exercise his right to vote.

43 **Avoid using redundant (unnecessary) pronouns.**
Right: *Let's* leave now.
Wrong: *Let's us* leave now. (*Let's* means *Let us*.)
Right: These two are alike.   Wrong: These two are *both* alike.

44 **Use *what* as a relative pronoun only when it means *that which*.**
He is a man *that* [not *what*] you can trust.
I forget *what* [*that which*] he said.

45 **To keep meaning clear, avoid using *which*, *that*, or *it* to refer to the whole idea of a clause or sentence.**
Poor: We are short of money. *It* worries me.
Better: It worries me that we are short of money.
We are short of money, a fact that worries me.

46 **In compounds, put second person before first and third, and third before first.**
You, she, and *I* must help.   He and *I* are friends.

FOR PRACTICE AND APPLICATION

A. In all but one of the following sentences, pronouns fail to agree with antecedents. Correct the sentences, reading them aloud in class.
1. Everyone must make their own choice.
2. Neither Joe nor Walt had combed their hair.
3. Each of the students must present their activity ticket.
4. Another of the forwards has sprained their ankle.
5. Each of the delegates must pay part of their own expenses.
6. Either of the boys may be called on to give their speech.
7. Everybody who comes must show their pass.
8. Each of the girls wore their newest dress.
9. Both of them forgot their notebooks.
10. Does everybody have their gloves?
11. Somebody must have placed their books in my locker.
12. Nobody can leave before their locker is neat and clean.
13. Every player must provide their own shoes.
14. Has everyone here written their report?

B. Write original sentences to illustrate each example given under rules 35a and 35b. Check the sentences in an oral class drill.

C. Improve the poor or incorrect uses of pronouns in the following sentences. Make this a written exercise; then exchange papers for checking. Read the sentences aloud.
1. That there is the man which hired me.
2. Let's us not wait for the bus. That will make us late.

3. I and he found the knife what was lost.
4. Are them Ed's boots? He should polish them hisself.
5. How many gallon of gas did you buy?
6. Orville he is over six foot tall.
7. Pete found the man, but he refused to talk with him.
8. Our cat, who is really spoiled, has expensive tastes in food.
9. I've bought two pairs of shoes. I like these here better than those.
10. The twins are both taller than I am.
11. Which earrings shall I wear? Do you like them that I bought today?

FOLLOW-UP

If you are like most people, you probably have a tendency to use *their*, not *his* or *her*, in referring to a singular indefinite pronoun. To break the habit, you must learn to listen for this error, both in your own expression and in that of others. Ask a friend to watch for this error in your speech; then make a conscious effort to avoid it.

LEARNING MORE ABOUT GOOD USE OF NOUNS AND PRONOUNS

The following points cover minor or disputable items in pronoun usage. Most of the expressions or constructions given here are accepted colloquial English. As a rule, they should be avoided in what you write.

47 **Avoid careless use of** *you, it, they* **as indefinite pronouns.**
COLLOQUIAL: Nowadays *you* don't see many men with beards. (*Who* don't?)
STANDARD: Nowadays one doesn't see many men with beards.
COLLOQUIAL: *They* have many beautiful spots in the Ozarks. (*Who* have?)
STANDARD: There are many beautiful spots in the Ozarks.
POOR: In this report *it* tells about the mining of zinc.
BETTER: This report tells about the mining of zinc.

48 **Use compound personal pronouns as** *intensives* **or** *reflexives*. (See page 26.)
I *myself* will come. (*intensive*) I blame *myself*. (*reflexive*)

In colloquial speech, compound personal pronouns sometimes replace personal pronouns. Even here, however, avoid using them as the subject of a sentence.
COLLOQUIAL: He chose Don and *myself*. STANDARD: He chose Don and *me*.
POOR: Tom and *myself* went. STANDARD: Tom and *I* went.

49 **To show possession by or connection with nonliving things, use a phrase with** *of* **instead of a possessive noun. Expressions of time and measurement are exceptions.**
The cover *of the book* is soiled.
We had an *hour's* wait.   I bought a *dime's* worth of paper.

50 Use *either* **to refer to one of** *two;* **use** *any one* **to refer to one of** *more than two.* (Consult your dictionary to find the basis for this rule.)

> *Either* of these two plans is good.   *Any one* of the four will do.

51 Use either *one's* or *his* **in referring to the indefinite pronoun** *one.* Some authorities, however, consider *one's* the better usage.

> One should try to profit by *one's* [or *his*] mistakes.

52 Avoid confusing or unnecessary shifts of person.

Poor: The *driver* should know the road, or *you* may lose your way.
Better: The *driver* should know the road, or *he* may lose his way.

53 Use *one another* **in referring to** *more than two;* **use** *each other* **in referring to** *two.*

> All the guests know *one another*.   Jim and I looked at *each other*.

54 Avoid weak reference of pronouns.

Weak: I like riding horseback but have never owned *one*.
Improved: I like riding horseback but have never owned *a horse*.

55 Do not use *same* as a substitute for personal pronouns.

Poor: Thank you for your suggestion. *Same* will be adopted.
Better: Thank you for your suggestion. *It* will be adopted.

FOR PRACTICE AND APPLICATION

A. The following sentences contain expressions that do not conform to rules 47-55. Change these expressions to standard English. If you write this exercise, go over your sentences orally in class.

1. They need new traffic laws in this town.
2. You don't see many horses on farms in this part of the country.
3. In this story it tells about life on a large ranch.
4. Jean and myself are on the committee.
5. Did either of those four boys make the team?
6. This is an expensive machine. Same should receive special care.
7. The two boys glared at one another.
8. The knife's handle is made of bone.
9. Yourself and Jack have done a good day's work.
10. I bought a book on magic, but I still don't know how they do their tricks.

B. Bring a daily newspaper to class. Examine these sections: (1) letters to the editor, (2) comic strips, (3) interviews with people in the news, (4) editorials. What examples or violations of rules 47-55 can you find? What other examples of faulty usage do you notice? of colloquial usage? Do some sections conform more closely to standard English usage than do the others? If so, how do you account for that fact? Discuss your findings in class.

REVIEW — *Brush up!*

The following conversation contains twenty-four errors in the use of verbs, nouns, and pronouns. Probably none of you would make all these errors in a brief conversation, but this exercise will give you concentrated practice in finding and correcting common mistakes. Since this is informal speech, do not change good colloquial usage. Rewrite the conversation; then read your revised versions in class. Be ready to give the reason for each change that you have made.

"Bill, I seen Tom last night. He's selling tickets for Friday's game. He told me that I and you better buy our tickets right away. If I would have had enough money with me, I'd have bought them the first thing this morning, but all I have is two dollars. This here is a game we don't want to miss, you know. By the way, I hope you ain't spent that money your dad give you yesterday."

"No, not yet—but it's a good thing you come along just now, because Bob Boyd asks me in gym class to borrow him a dollar. If I would of had my money with me, I'd have left him have it. You know me—I'm the kind which can't say no even when I had ought to. . . . How much are the tickets?"

"Well, I ask Tom, and he said that them on the fifty-yard line are two dollars apiece. We can set in the bleachers for fifty cents, but in the bleachers it's everyone for themselves, if you know what I mean."

"I know, all right! The bleachers would do for you and I, but if us boys plan to bring Betty and Jean, we better try to get grandstand seats. How much will they cost us?"

"A dollar, Tom said. Is that all right with you?"

"Well, I hate to tell Dad tonight that I've ran out of money again, but he had ought to realize by now that girls are expensive!"

MAKING VERBS AGREE WITH THEIR SUBJECTS

56 **A verb should agree in person and number with its subject.** Rules 56a–56p cover verb-subject situations that cause difficulty.

56a Use *is, was, has,* and their contractions with subjects in the *third person singular.* Use *are, were, have,* and their contractions with all *plural* subjects. If the subject is *I,* use *am, was, have,* and their contractions.

        He *is* here.   The **boys** *aren't* here.   **I** *am* here.

56b Always use a plural verb with the pronoun *you.*

        Roger, **you** *are* excused.   Boys, **you** *are* excused.

56c Use *don't* with the subject-pronoun *I;* use *doesn't* with subjects in the *third person singular.* Use *don't* with all *plural* subjects.

        I *don't* know the answer.   These **dishes** *don't* look clean.
        She *doesn't* know me.   *Doesn't* **Kay Wright** live here?

"DO YOU SAY, 'THE ENEMY IS APPROACHING,' OR, 'THE ENEMY ARE APPROACHING'?"

56d Do not be misled by a phrase that follows the subject. Phrases beginning with such expressions as *accompanied by, as well as, together with* are especially troublesome. Such a phrase does not affect the number of the subject. Once you have found the subject, pay no attention to phrases following it. (Rule 56e contains exceptions.)

> A long **line** of men *was* waiting. (*Line* is the subject; the singular *was* is needed.)
>
> **Roy**, as well as his sisters, *is* here. (*Roy* is the subject; the singular *is* is needed. If the singular verb sounds awkward to you, recast the sentence: Roy is here, as are his sisters.)

56e If the subject is *all, more, most, part, some;* a *fraction;* or a *per cent* and is followed by an "of" phrase, use a verb that agrees with the object in that phrase.

> **More** of this *matter* **needs** explaining. **More** of my *friends* **have left** me.
> **All** of *it* **is** mine.   **All** of *these* **are** mine.
> **Most** of this *day* **has been** rainy. **Most** of these *days* **have been** rainy.
> **Part** of this *page* **is missing.** **Part** of these *people* **are going.**
> **Some** of the *loaf* **has been** eaten. **Some** of the *loaves* **have been** eaten.
> **Two thirds** of our *time* **was** wasted. **Two thirds** of the *voters* **were** women.
> **Ten per cent** of the *farm* **is** pasture. **Ten per cent** of the *farms* **are** small.

56f Do not be misled by an introductory *there*. It is not the subject.

> *There* are no errors. (*Errors*, the plural subject, needs the plural *are*.)

56g If a predicate nominative differs in number from the subject, be sure that the verb agrees with the subject, not the predicate nominative.

> My favorite **gift** *is* flowers.   **Flowers** *are* my favorite gift.

56h Use a *singular* verb with a collective-noun subject if you think of a group as a *unit*.

>Our **team** *has* won twelve games.

Use a *plural* verb if you mean the *individual members* of a group.

>Our **team** *have* been arguing about this play.

As a rule, use a singular verb after *the number;* use a plural verb after *a number.*

>**The number** of accidents *is* alarming.   **A number** of accidents *have* occurred.

56i As a rule, use *singular* verbs with these subjects: *civics, economics, gallows, mathematics, measles, molasses, mumps, news, United States, whereabouts;* plural verbs with *acoustics, ashes, assets, athletics, clothes, fireworks, gymnastics, hysterics, oats, pincers, proceeds, riches, scissors, shears, slacks, statistics, suds, tactics, thanks, tongs, trousers, tweezers.*

56j Use a *singular* verb with any subject that is plural in form but singular in its meaning.

>*Brave Men* **was** written by Ernie Pyle. (*one* book title)
>*Two dollars* **is** a generous allowance. (*one* sum of money)

56k Use *plural* verbs with compound subjects joined by *and,* unless the subjects form a unit.

>**Eggs, butter,** and **cheese** *are* nourishing foods. (*separate items*)
>**Chicken and dumplings** *is* my favorite dish. (*one item*)

56l When two or more *singular* subjects are joined by *or* or *nor,* use a *singular* verb; if the subjects are *plural,* use a *plural* verb; if the subjects *vary* in number, use a verb that agrees with the *nearest* subject.

>Either **Tim** or his **brother** *is* usually at the meetings.
>Neither the **teams** nor their **coaches** *have* seen today's paper.
>No **galoshes, hat,** or **coat** *was* left here.

56m If *one* subject is *affirmative* and *another negative,* use a verb that agrees with the *affirmative* subject.

>**Bill,** not the other players, *was* responsible for the victory.

56n Use a *singular* verb with these indefinite pronouns: *another, anybody, anyone, anything, each, either, everybody, everyone, everything, neither, nobody, no one, one, somebody, someone.*

>**Neither** of us *was* ready.   **Everybody** *has* left.

Use a *plural* verb with *many* * or *both.*

>**Many** of you *are* strangers.   **Both** of us *are* needed.

Use *either* a *singular* or a *plural* verb with *any, such,* or *none,* depending upon their meaning in the sentence.

>*Has* **any** of the mail been opened?   *Have* **any** of the letters been opened?

---

*But the expression *many a* calls for a singular verb: *Many a* famous man has been buried here.

56o Use a *singular* verb with compound subjects modified by a singular indefinite adjective.

> *Each* day and hour *is* important.   *Every* boy and girl *was* there.

56p If a verb has a relative pronoun as its subject, the verb should agree with the antecedent of the pronoun.

> She is one of the girls **who** *help*. (The antecedent of *who* is *girls*, third person plural: girls help.)
>
> It is I **who** *demand* a change. (The antecedent of *who* is *I*, first person singular: I demand.)

FOR PRACTICE AND APPLICATION

A. Choose the correct verb for each sentence that follows. Read the sentences correctly aloud. Explain why you chose each verb.

1. Joe and Tom (is, are) absent. (Was, Were) either here yesterday?
2. The scissors (is, are) lying on the table.
3. Twenty per cent of the residents (own, owns) two cars.
4. Dick, as well as his sisters, (has, have) an album of recordings.
5. (Don't, Doesn't) Marty live near you?
6. (Was, Were) you at the meeting? The club (has, have) won a prize.
7. One of the members (has, have) been awarded a contract.
8. We (was, were) an hour late. Time (don't, doesn't) mean much to us.
9. It (don't, doesn't) seem right. Ten dollars (are, is) too much.
10. There (is, are) never too many hard workers in this world.
11. Each of the sons (was, were) presented with a watch.
12. She is one of those people who (is, are) naturally gifted.
13. Edward, not his brothers, (work, works) after school.
14. My first choice (is, are) those red sandals.
15. Neither the singers nor the accompanist (expect, expects) a fee.
16. His whereabouts (are, is) a secret. Even his family (haven't, hasn't) been told.
17. (Have, Has) anyone in your classes lost a notebook?
18. Some of the boys usually (helps, help) me.
19. Bread and milk (make, makes) a good bedtime snack.
20. Three fourths of our farm (were, was) flooded.

B. In most of the following sentences, a verb fails to agree with its subject. Correct the sentences, reading them aloud in class. In each instance give a reason for your choice of verb.

1. Each of the players have agreed to contribute to the fund.
2. John said, "It is I who demands an explanation."
3. Jane, as well as two of her friends, has been invited.
4. Either the vice-president or the secretary check the roll.
5. Those girls, not that boy, is responsible.

6. There go one of the leaders of the band.
7. The greatest weakness of these girls is rich desserts.
8. She is one of those students who are welcome at any gathering.
9. That bunch of bananas seem green. The last ones wasn't ripe, either.
10. Not one of you look ready. Most of your shirts need changing.
11. Mathematics is easy for me. So is most of my other subjects.
12. Neither James nor his sisters is going East this summer.
13. It don't matter much now. You and Bill have spoiled everything.
14. Everything in these lockers are to be removed.
15. Three yards of material are not enough. Wasn't you told to get more?

C. Write at least one original sentence to illustrate each of the rules numbered 56b–56p. Give right and wrong choices for each verb. Exchange papers; then read the sentences correctly aloud.

D. Choose those rules for agreement of verb and subject that you most often abuse. Write original sentences illustrating those rules and submit them to someone else for checking.

FOLLOW-UP

A. Put into your notebook the list of rules mentioned in activity D. As you write papers for any of your classes, use the list to check verb-subject agreement in those papers.

B. From the members of the class, choose a partner with whom you converse often outside the classroom. Decide upon one or two errors in agreement that you often make. Have a little contest to see which of you can first eliminate these errors from his speech. The best feature of this plan is that it requires you to listen closely, for learning to hear wrong forms is a necessary step toward eliminating them from your daily expression.

REVIEW *Review practice*

USING PRONOUNS CORRECTLY

Copy the following sentences, choosing the correct form from those in parentheses. Exchange papers for checking as the sentences are read aloud. Give the reason for each choice.

1. Don and (me, I) are going to the game today.
2. (Those, Those there) are men (which, who) volunteered.
3. It was (we, us) they saw at the theater.
4. You are certainly more ambitious than (me, I).
5. Harold wrote Ed and (I, me) a letter.
6. (Them, Those) are not good plays for a real game.
7. Father bought Sarah and (I, me) a new camera.

8. (Him, His) coming so late inconvenienced us.
9. Save those tickets for John and (they, them).
10. (Who, Whom) do you think will win the election?
11. For that one hour I should like to be (him, he).
12. She didn't say (who, whom) she would invite.
13. (Whom, Who) did you say went with you?
14. The (coach, coach he) asked Jim and (I, me) to keep score.
15. Has anybody in the class finished (their, his) report?
16. Neither of the girls brought (her, their) hat.
17. I need six more (foot, feet) of wire.
18. Somebody placed (his, their) books on my glasses.
19. (We, Us) three—Paul, Dean, and (I, me)—sold tickets at the game.
20. (I and you, You and I) aren't needed. (Let's, Let's us) not stay.
21. Jim says he went to the game all by (hisself, himself).
22. I've lost my book. May I use (someone's else, someone else's)?

MAKING VERBS AGREE WITH SUBJECTS

Follow the instructions for the preceding activity.
1. This coat, as well as my shoes, (is, are) new.
2. (Was, Were) you looking for me?
3. There (was, were) very few of my friends at the party.
4. The biggest problem (is, are) the absentees.
5. Our group (has, have) won the prize three times.
6. News (is, are) scarce.
7. Either those girls or this boy (volunteer, volunteers) each time.
8. That (don't, doesn't) make any difference in this case.
9. Each of these bushes (has, have) different blossoms.
10. He is one of those boys who (is, are) always asking questions.
11. A number of changes (have, has) taken place.
12. Dick's attitude, not yours, (is, are) the one I criticize.

How the Adjective Helps to Build the Sentence

CLASSIFICATION OF ADJECTIVES

57 *Adjectives* **are words that modify nouns or pronouns by describing or limiting them.** Thus adjectives are highly useful in making more vivid or exact what you have to say. Your study of adjectives, then, should have a real purpose: to help you to build better sentences.

57a *Descriptive* **adjectives describe. They may be either** *common* **or** *proper:* a *small* village, an *English* village.

NOTE: Both proper nouns used as adjectives and adjectives made from proper nouns are called *proper* adjectives: an *Iowa* farm, a *Spanish* city.

57b *Limiting* **adjectives point out or tell how many, either definitely or indefinitely.**

(1) **The articles** *a, an,* **and** *the* **are one type of limiting adjective.** *The* is *definite* in its pointing out: *the* child, *the* idea; *a* and *an* are *indefinite:* *a* child, *an* idea.

(2) *Pronominal* **adjectives are pronouns** (personal, demonstrative, indefinite, relative, or interrogative) **used to limit nouns or pronouns:** *his* hat, *that* man, *every* day, *which* tree, *whose* coat.

(3) *Numeral* **adjectives may be either cardinal or ordinal numbers.** *Cardinal* numbers (one, two, . . .) tell how many: *six* rooms, *ten* men. *Ordinal* numbers (first, second, . . .) tell which: *sixth* row, *tenth* man.

(4) *Possessive* **nouns may serve as limiting adjectives:** *Mary's* mother.

57c **Adjectives are sometimes classified according to their position.**

(1) *Attributive* **adjectives precede the words that they modify.**

    Three large trees grow on our lawn.

(2) *Predicate* **adjectives complete the meaning of linking (copulative) verbs and describe their subjects.***

  Your idea is excellent. He seems capable.

(3) *Appositive* **adjectives follow the words that they modify. They are set off by commas.**

    Mother, tired and anxious, was waiting for me.

57d **An adjective used as an** *objective complement* **follows the direct object that it modifies.**

    This promotion should make you happy.

57e *Prepositional phrases* **may be used as adjectives.**

    The door behind me opened.

(The phrase *behind me* tells *which* door. Since it modifies a noun, it is used as an adjective.)

Every prepositional phrase has two essential parts: an introductory word called a *preposition,* **and a noun or pronoun** *object.* The object may be compound, and it may have adjectives modifying it.

    Wait for *Jerry* and *me.* (*compound object*)
    Buy the paper with the blue border. (*object with modifiers*)

---

* See *1b*, page 7, for a list of linking verbs.

57f *Infinitives* and *participles* **may be used as adjectives.** These verbals help to condense sentences.

> The car *to drive* is the convertible.

(*To drive*, an infinitive, modifies the noun *car* and is therefore used as an adjective. *To drive* replaces a clause, such as *that one should drive*.)

> The *wrecked* car was hauled away.

(The participle *wrecked* modifies the noun *car*. *Wrecked* replaces an adjective clause, *that had been wrecked*.)

A *participial phrase* consists of a participle and the complements or modifiers that complete its meaning.

> The company *lending me the money* is well established.

(The participial phrase *lending me the money* modifies the noun *company*. *Money* is the direct object of the participle *lending*. *Me* is the indirect object of the participle *lending*.)

> *Having walked rapidly*, I reached school early.

(The participial phrase *Having walked rapidly* modifies the pronoun *I*. *Rapidly* is an adverb modifying the participle *Having walked*.)

FOR PRACTICE AND APPLICATION

A. (1) Find each adjective modifier in the following sentences. (2) Name the word that it modifies. Make this an oral or written exercise. If you try omitting the adjectives from the sentences, you will see how much these modifiers affect the basic sentence idea.

1. His searching glance terrified the timid boy.
2. Whose car has a deep dent in the left door?
3. My parents attend the large church on the corner of Main and Elm.
4. Having eaten lunch, I answered that letter from my brother.
5. You should buy a purse to match those shoes.
6. Decayed and crumbling, that old mansion at the edge of town is the scene of many secret meetings.
7. The team winning the title will receive a bronze plaque.
8. Twenty wild geese crossed the woods bordering the south pasture.
9. That little brown kitten is vicious and quarrelsome.
10. Can you understand Willie's failing in mathematics and science?

B. Write original sentences using all the types of adjective modifiers discussed in *57b–57f*. Exchange papers in class. On the paper that you receive, point out the adjectives and the words modified.

C. Condense the following sentences by changing the italicized words to a participial phrase or an infinitive phrase used as an adjective. Exchange papers for checking; then read the sentences in class. Note the usefulness of these phrases in condensing or otherwise improving expression.

1. *Since I had worked hard,* I needed a rest.
2. The method *that should be used* is described here.
3. *Because I was afraid of rain,* I carried an umbrella.
4. The man *who is talking to Mr. Ellis* is our coach.
5. A new road, *which will be built soon,* should ease traffic.
6. *I do not know all the facts; therefore* I hesitate to criticize.

D. In the following quotation from Washington Irving's "The Legend of Sleepy Hollow," notice how much the italicized adjectives and adjective phrases add to the effectiveness of the description.

> The animal Ichabod bestrode was a *broken-down* plow horse that had outlived almost everything but his viciousness. He was *gaunt* and *shagged,* with a *ewe* neck and a head *like a hammer;* his *rusty* mane and tail were *tangled* and *knotted with burrs;* one eye had lost its pupil and was *glaring* and *spectral,* but the other had the gleam *of a genuine devil* in it.

Bring your literature books to class. Take ten minutes to skim through one or more selections as you search for effective use of adjective modifiers. At the end of the ten minutes, read to the class a sentence or a paragraph that you think is effective because of its use of adjectives. Point out those vivid expressions.

E. The following paragraph would give a better picture if it contained some vivid and exact adjective words and phrases. Rewrite the paragraph, inserting such expressions where they seem helpful. Do not overdo your use of adjectives, however; too many are as bad as too few. Read your paragraphs in class. Note how the choice of adjectives affects the picture that you see.

> The house stands on a hill a mile west of the village of Ashley. It is set well back, and the lawn slopes sharply to the road. Behind the house is a grove of trees, and on the lawn there are other trees, as well as bushes. The house itself has two stories. Two wings extend forward from the main center section, which has a porch with pillars.

F. As you know, a participle cannot serve as the verb (simple predicate) of a sentence. Without a verb, a group of words is only a sentence fragment.

If a group of words below is a sentence, write the verb and its subject after the corresponding number. If the group of words is only a sentence fragment, write *F* after the corresponding number. Then, by changing participles to verbs, make the fragments into good sentences. Go over your work in class.

1. The baby, spending all day in a small buggy, lying on her back and staring into the sky.
2. No one, looking at that statue, and failing to be impressed.
3. Jameson, having peered around the corner, finally emerging.
4. The whole crowd chanting in unison.
5. Hurled from the swerving jeep, Mike rolled over and over.
6. Having served the luncheon in the garden far from her kitchen, Irene sank exhausted into a chair.
7. Favored with a steady wind, the yacht beating the storm into port.

Diagramming Adjective Words and Phrases

The relation of adjective modifiers to the words that they modify can be pictured clearly by diagrams. Note the following diagrams, which illustrate various types of adjective modifiers.

Direct Adjective Modifiers
My sister's hat is the red one.

Compound Adjectives
The last candidate gave a clear and honest speech.

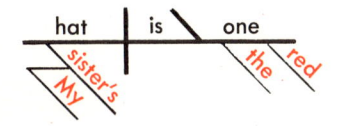

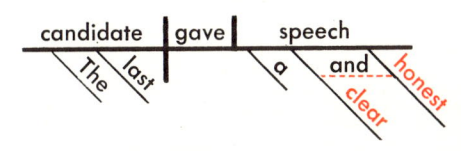

Notice that each adjective is suspended beneath the noun or pronoun which it modifies. *Sister's* modifies *hat*, but *My* modifies *sister's*.

Prepositional Phrases as Adjectives
Fields of corn and oats dotted the landscape to our right.

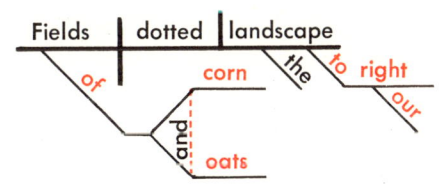

Notice that the first phrase has a compound object.

Compound Prepositional Phrase as Adjective
A home in the country but near the city is the right kind for someone like me.

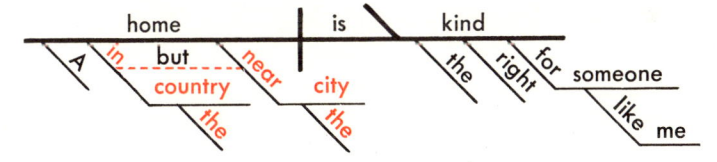

Notice that the phrase *like me* modifies *someone,* the object of another adjective phrase.

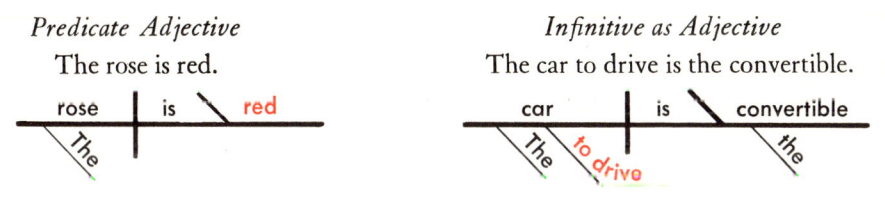

Predicate Adjective
The rose is red.

Infinitive as Adjective
The car to drive is the convertible.

Notice that a predicate adjective is diagrammed like a predicate nominative.

55

Participial Phrase as Adjective
The company providing the money has a good reputation.

Adjective as Objective Complement
I found the room empty.

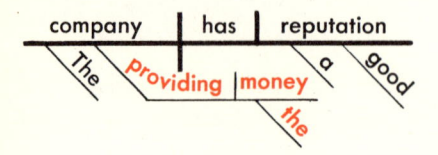

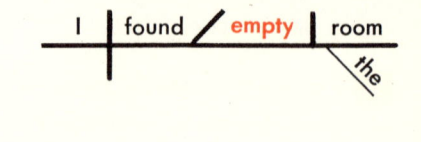

Prepositional Phrase with Verbal Object
Your success in building team spirit is a credit to you.

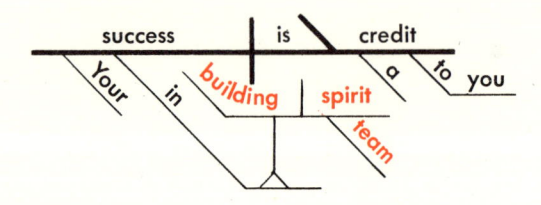

FOR PRACTICE AND APPLICATION

A. Diagram the following sentences. These sentences contain only grammatical elements that you have studied. As you go over your diagrams in class, be sure to do so in an orderly and specific way. For example, in explaining the last sample diagram, you might say: "In this sentence the verb is a linking verb, *is;* the subject is the noun, *success; credit* is a predicate noun; *Your* is a possessive pronoun used as an adjective to modify the subject; *in building team spirit* is a prepositional phrase used as an adjective to modify the subject; the object of the preposition *in* is a gerund, *building,* which has an object, the noun *spirit; team* is an adjective modifying *spirit; a* is an adjective modifying the predicate noun; and *to you* is a prepositional phrase also used as an adjective modifying the predicate noun." This specific oral analysis will do more than anything else to make grammatical terms a part of your working vocabulary.

1. Two weak hitters on our team made most of the hits in this game.
2. Forgetting her promise, Aline borrowed her mother's watch.
3. The boys, alone and leaderless, felt anxious.
4. One way to improve is odd but practical.
5. I have no plan except to consult your parents.
6. The present tenants have kept the house neat.
7. Our flight through the woods and across the river saved us.
8. Having changed his mind, Dick wrote a note of apology.

B. If you need further practice, use the sentences in *A,* page 53. Go over your diagrams as in the preceding activity.

USING ADJECTIVES CORRECTLY

Many errors in the use of adjectives are errors in comparison. To build good usage habits, study and apply the following rules, of which 58–58c deal with comparison.

58 **Use special adjective forms to show differences in** *degree.* **Adjectives have three degrees of comparison:** (1) **the** *positive,* (2) **the** *comparative,* **and** (3) **the** *superlative.*

Positive degree: expressing a quality (*not a comparison*), as *good, bad, short*

Comparative degree: expressing a higher degree than the positive; used in a comparison of *two,* as one is *better, worse, shorter* than another

Superlative degree: expressing the highest degree of quality; used in a comparison of *more than two,* as *best, worst, shortest* of all

REGULAR FORMS FOR ONE-SYLLABLE ADJECTIVES AND
SOME TWO-SYLLABLE ADJECTIVES

Positive	*Comparative*	*Superlative*
wise	wiser	wisest
small	smaller	smallest
slim	slimmer	slimmest
happy	happier	happiest

NOTE: Some compound adjectives are compared by adding *er* and *est* to the first word of the compound: *kindhearted, kinderhearted, kindesthearted.*

REGULAR FORMS FOR LONG ADJECTIVES AND THOSE
HARD TO SAY WITH -ER AND -EST

Positive	*Comparative*	*Superlative*
joyous	more joyous	most joyous
interesting	more interesting	most interesting

IRREGULAR ADJECTIVES

Positive	*Comparative*	*Superlative*
good, well	better	best
bad, ill	worse	worst
much, many	more	most
little (*quantity*)	less	least

In a literal sense, certain adjectives, because of their meaning, cannot be compared. They include such words as *perfect, correct, immortal, dead, final, round,* and *square.* To indicate a difference in degree, use *more nearly.* Popular usage, however, makes frequent use of *rounder, squarest,* and so on.

Webster's New International Dictionary gives the comparison of all adjectives formed irregularly, of those in which there may be doubt about the spelling, and often of ones compared simply by adding *er* and *est.*.

Inverted comparison uses *less* and *least: helpful, less helpful, least helpful.*

58a Use the *comparative* **degree in comparing** *two;* **the** *superlative,* **in comparing** *more than two.*

> That is the *prettier* [not *prettiest*] hat of the two.
> Which of those three boys is the *oldest* [not *older*]?

58b **Avoid double comparison.**

RIGHT: Yours is the *prettiest* hat of all.
WRONG: Yours is the *most prettiest* hat of all.

58c **In making comparisons within a group, say** *any other,* **not** *any.*

ILLOGICAL: Joe, our center, is taller than any player on the team.
  (Joe is on the team. If you say that Joe is taller than any player on the team, you are saying that he is taller than himself; therefore you are stating an impossibility.)
RIGHT: Joe, our center, is taller than any other player on the team.
RIGHT: Joe, our center, is the tallest player on the team.

59 **Use** *less* **for quantity;** *fewer* **for number.**

> Myron has *less* responsibility and *fewer* worries now.

60 **Use the article** *a* **before consonants and consonant sounds; use** *an* **before vowels (***a, e, i, o, u***) and vowel sounds.**

> It is *an* honor and *a* pleasure to call you *an* ally.

61 **Repeat the article before separate items if it might not otherwise be clear that they are separate items.**

CONFUSING: He hired *a* file clerk and typist. (Did he hire *one* person or *two?*)
CLEAR: He hired *a* file clerk and *a* typist. (*two persons*)

62 **Do not use the objective pronoun *them* as an adjective.**

Those [not *Them*] books belong on this shelf.

63 *Kind, sort,* **and** *type* **are** *singular* **nouns. Use** *this* **and** *that,* **not** *these* **and** *those,* **to modify them.**

RIGHT: I like *this* kind of shoes.   WRONG: I like *these* kind of shoes.

64 **Use** *his* **or** *her* **to refer to an antecedent limited by the pronominal adjectives** *each, every, either,* **or** *neither.*

RIGHT: *Each* girl likes *her* job.   WRONG: *Each* girl likes *their* job.
RIGHT: *Neither* man has *his* own car.   WRONG: Neither man has *their* . . .

65 **Avoid the expression** *complected;* **use** *complexioned* **instead.**

He is a dark-*complexioned* [not dark-*complected*] man.

66 **Do not omit the** *ed* **from a past participle used as an adjective.**

I like *whipped* [not *whip*] cream.   I ate a *baked* [not *bake*] potato.

FOR PRACTICE AND APPLICATION

A. Choose the correct adjective expressions from those in parentheses in the following sentences. Make this an oral or a written exercise. If you write it, be sure to read your work aloud in class. Explain your choices.

1. Have you ever before seen (these, this) kind of sheep?
2. Don't buy any more of (them, those) (small-sized, small-size) oranges.
3. I bought a vanilla and (chocolate, a chocolate) soda. (*two sodas*)
4. There must be (a, an) earlier bus than this one.
5. From now on I shall eat (fewer, less) pieces of candy.
6. Each boy must be responsible for (his, their) own expenses.
7. Greenland is larger than (any, any other) island in the world.
8. The (oldest, older) one of those two girls is a senior.
9. I know that he is (a, an) honest man.
10. Neither man has changed (their, his) mind.
11. Which of these two samples do you like (better, best)?
12. I try to avoid (those, that) type of people.
13. I am too (dark-complexioned, dark-complected) to wear that color.

B. Copy the following sentences, filling each blank with the adjective form called for in parentheses. Read the sentences aloud.

1. This is the .... paper I've ever written. (superlative of *good*)
2. The .... answer came from my uncle. (superlative of *unsatisfactory*)
3. She is the .... girl of the two. (comparative of *pretty*)
4. Dick's .... height will help us. (comparative of *great*)

59

5. Use the .... paper that you can find. (superlative of *thin*)
6. The .... one of those three boys is Charles. (superlative of *busy*)
7. Bob has .... corn to plant than John. (comparative of *little*)
8. I have the .... work of all. (superlative of *little*)

C. Write original sentences to illustrate rules 58a–66. Exchange papers for checking; then go over your sentences orally in class.

D. Go over papers that you have written or are writing for other classes. Check them carefully to see whether you have made any errors in adjective usage.

FOLLOW-UP

Choose one or two errors that you know now you make in adjective usage. Break yourself of the habit by following the plan in *B* on page 50.

How the Adverb Helps to Build the Sentence

TYPES OF ADVERB MODIFIERS

67 *Adverbs* **are words used to modify or limit the meaning of** *verbs, adjectives,* **or other** *adverbs*. Well-chosen adverbs can help you in building good sentences.

The old man proceeded *slowly* and *shakily*. (*Slowly* and *shakily*, compound adverbs, modify the verb *proceeded*.)

That was a *really* heavy rain. (*Really*, an adverb, modifies the adjective *heavy*.)

James walks *too* rapidly. (*Too*, an adverb, modifies the adverb *rapidly*.)

Adverbs tell *manner* (how), *time* (when), *place* (where), *degree* (how much), **and sometimes** *cause* (why). Typical examples are given here.

Adverbs of manner: angrily, carefully, not, lazily, roughly
Adverbs of time: now, then, soon, lately, early, often, before, immediately
Adverbs of place: here, there, near, forward, outside, where
Adverbs of degree: very, so, much, too, extremely, rather
Adverbs of cause: why, therefore, hence

Adverbs, useful as they are, often are less effective when combined with a weak verb than is a more vivid verb used alone.

Weak: Something *went rapidly* past my head.
Better: Something *whizzed* past . . .

68a *Adverbial objectives* (called also *adverbial nouns*) **are nouns used as adverbs. Usually they indicate** *amount, weight, time, distance, direction,* **or** *value.*

> We walked a *mile.*   He waited two *days.*   It weighs a *ton.*
> This model costs five *dollars.*   I hurried *home.*

68b *Prepositional phrases* **may be used as adverbs.**

> *In the afternoon* Bruce went *to the zoo.*

> (*In the afternoon* and *to the zoo* are prepositional phrases used as adverbs to modify the verb *went;* they tell *when* and *where* Bruce went.)

68c An *infinitive* **may be used as an adverb.**

> This problem is easy *to solve.*

> (*To solve* is an infinitive used as an adverb to modify the adjective *easy.*)

68d *Indirect objects* **really are the objects in adverbial prepositional phrases in which the preposition is understood.**

> I have told [to] *him* the truth.   Mother bought [for] *me* a coat.

69 **Adverbs and adverb phrases may modify participles or infinitives.**

> Crying *loudly,* the child ran on.   Would you like to go *with me?*

FORMING AND COMPARING ADVERBS

70 **Many adverbs are formed by adding** *ly* **to descriptive adjectives.** *

> He is an *eager* student. (*adj.*)   Many watched him *eagerly.* (*adv.*)

71 **Often adjectives and adverbs have the same form. As with every other part of speech, you must identify adverbs by their use in the sentence.**

> We took the *fast* train. (*adj.*)   He ran *fast.* (*adv.*)

72a **Most adverbs can be compared.**† **For adverbs ending in** *ly,* **use** *more* **and** *most* **to form the comparative and the superlative degrees.**

Positive	*Comparative*	*Superlative*
easily	more easily	most easily
carefully	more carefully	most carefully

72b **For some adverbs that are not formed from adjectives, use** *er* **and** *est* **to form the comparative and the superlative:** *soon, sooner, soonest.*

72c **Use** *irregular* **forms in comparing certain adverbs.**

Positive	*Comparative*	*Superlative*
badly, ill	worse	worst
much	more	most
well	better	best

* Rules 173o-p, page 165, apply to the spelling of these adverbs.
† Adverbs that cannot be compared include the following: *now, then, very, not, too, already, always, again, almost, never.*

FOR PRACTICE AND APPLICATION

A. In the following sentences, classify the italicized words as verbs, nouns, adverbs, or adjectives. Name the words modified by the adjectives and adverbs. Make this an oral or a written exercise.

1. You must pay your *back* rent. My patience will not *last* much longer.
2. Tom has done well in *past* meets. As a rule, I come in *last*.
3. In the *past* we have always had *enough* help.
4. John came *back* early. He went *past* an hour ago.
5. I have had *enough* of your excuses. You felt *well enough last night*.
6. During the *night* one of our cows fell into that old *well*.

B. Find all adverbs and adverb phrases in the following sentences. Name the words modified. Make this an oral or a written exercise, as your teacher directs.

1. Our team swept smoothly and rapidly down the field.
2. Having swum out to the float twice, I felt rather tired.
3. Sometimes I need to work more slowly.
4. The already cloudy sky grew even darker.
5. During my early childhood, we lived three miles west of town.
6. That man in the blue suit must have been caught in the rain.
7. I almost always fail on this type of problem.
8. In the morning and in the late afternoon, Don lies in the sun.
9. Surreptitiously slipping the note across the aisle, Jack innocently turned his eyes toward the ceiling.
10. Why don't you want to go to the dance with me?
11. One never becomes too old to learn.
12. In the ninth inning of that game, we gained a one-run lead as the result of an error by the shortstop.

C. Write sentences to illustrate the constructions discussed in *68a–72c*. Exchange papers in class. Name the adverb modifiers and the words modified.

D. The following sentences would be improved by the use of well-chosen adverbs. Rewrite the sentences, supplying such adverb modifiers as will express the basic sentence ideas more vividly and exactly. Compare sentences in class.

1. The man watched me. (*how?*)
2. Frowning, the man moved toward us. (*how?*)
3. I'll meet you tomorrow. (*where? when?*)
4. Rain continued to fall. (*how? when?*)

E. In the following sentences, substitute vivid verbs for the italicized verbs and adverbs. Compare sentences in class. Be sure that the substitute verbs express accurately the sentence idea.

1. The sun *shone warmly* down upon us.
2. The boat *went smoothly* over the water.
3. We *ate* our lunch *hastily*.
4. I *walked softly* down the dark hallway.
5. Somewhere in the distance, we heard a gun *go off*.

Diagramming Adverb Words and Phrases

As you will note by the following examples, adverb modifiers are diagrammed like adjective modifiers, except that they modify verbs, adjectives, or other adverbs. Note how clearly the diagrams show the relationship of the various sentence parts.

Simple Adverb Modifiers
Too often he gives one an entirely wrong impression.

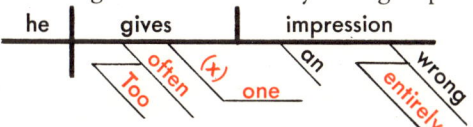

Adverbial Objective
I waited an hour.

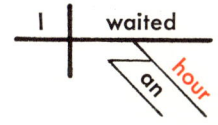

Notice that the adverb *often* modifies the verb; that it itself has an adverb modifier, *too;* and that the adverb *entirely* modifies the adjective *wrong*. Notice, too, the diagramming of the indirect object *one*.

Adverb Phrases
You are without doubt able to help him.

Compound Adverb Modifiers
Leave here and now, with me or without me.

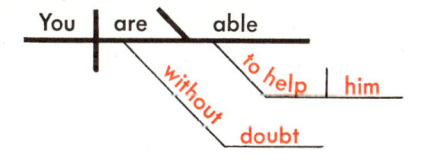

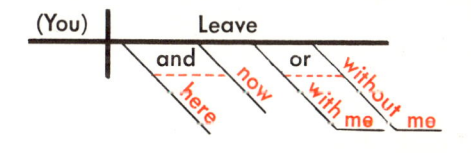

Without doubt is a prepositional phrase modifying the verb; *to help him* is an infinitive phrase modifying an adjective.

Adverb Modifying a Phrase
We arrived almost on time.

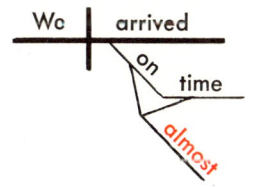

Adverb Modifying a Preposition
You rank slightly above Earl.

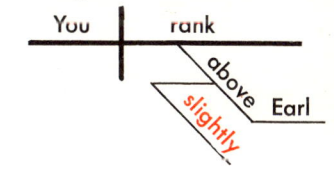

FOR PRACTICE AND APPLICATION

A. Diagram the following sentences; then put your diagrams on the board for oral analysis. Be sure that you explain all diagrams in a specific, orderly manner, as in the example on page 56. Diagramming requires that you understand exactly what you are doing.

1. Briefly but clearly he told me the bad news.
2. Louise certainly is not too busy to help us with the drive for funds.
3. He comes here only in the morning.
4. I could never believe the highly improbable story.

5. Far below us the lights of many ships swept across the bay.
6. This machine is easy to use and to repair.
7. We waited two years for word about the expedition.
8. Where did you go to look for clues to the crime?
9. Luckily, we hadn't locked the door before leaving for the game.
10. Long after that day, I brooded bitterly and selfishly over John's action.

B. For additional practice, diagram the sentences in *B*, page 62. Go over your diagrams as in the preceding activity.

USING ADJECTIVES AND ADVERBS CORRECTLY: I

Rules 73–80i cover errors that you should avoid in all that you say. Many of them are illiterate expressions; others cause confusion in meaning.

73 Avoid using adverbs where adjectives are needed, and vice versa.

73a Use predicate adjectives, not adverbs, to complete linking verbs.

Your plan sounds *wise* [not *wisely*].   The milk tastes *sour* [not *sourly*].

73b Do not use the adjective *most* for the adverb *almost*.

RIGHT: We are *almost* there.   WRONG: It is *most* three o'clock.

73c Do not use the adjective *awful* for such adverbs as *very, really, extremely*.*

RIGHT: You look *very* tired.   WRONG: You look *awful* tired.

73d Use *badly* as an adverb; use *bad* as an adjective.

RIGHT: Don't feel *bad*. (*predicate adjective,* completing a linking verb)
RIGHT: He dances *badly*.

73e Use *good* as an adjective. Use *well* either as an adjective or as an adverb, depending upon the sentence meaning. In speaking of one's health or appearance, *well* is an adjective; in other uses, an adverb.†

This pie tastes *good*. (*predicate adjective*)
Do you feel *well*? (*adj.*)   I don't drive very *well*. (*adv.*)

73f Do not use the adjective *real* for such adverbs as *really* or *very*.

I am *very* [not *real*] sorry.   Today is *really* [not *real*] cold.

73g Do not use the adjective *some* for such adverbs as *rather* or *somewhat*.‡

He is *somewhat* [not *some*] older than I.

73h Do not use the adjective *sure* for the adverb *surely*.

I *surely* [not *sure*] am tired.

---

* Informal expression permits the use of *awful* and *awfully* in such expressions as these: I have an *awful* headache. I'm *awfully* sorry. It is better usage, however, to avoid these expressions.

† Colloquially, one may say, "A day like this makes me feel *good*."

‡ Acceptable, though not recommended, is such usage as this: "You have grown *some*."

FOR PRACTICE AND APPLICATION

Rewrite the following sentences, correcting all errors in the use of adjectives and adverbs. Exchange papers for checking. Read the sentences aloud, telling why each correction is needed.

1. Mr. Smith always speaks real quiet, but he sure gets results.
2. Our car still runs good, but Dad has most decided on a new one.
3. I sure won't vote for him. He speaks too sarcastic.
4. Are you feeling badly again? I'm awful sorry.
5. I'm some thinner now, but I was real fat for a while.
6. She looks beautifully in red. I sure wish I could wear that color!
7. I always sleep bad before a test.
8. Drive real careful around these curves. They're awful sharp.
9. Mother sure felt bad yesterday, but she is some better today.
10. Doesn't that bacon smell good! I'm most starved!

FOLLOW-UP

If you habitually misuse *real* and *sure,* concentrate for a time on correcting your usage. Follow the plan suggested on page 50. If you prefer, choose one or more of the other errors covered by rules 73a–73h.

USING ADJECTIVES AND ADVERBS CORRECTLY: II

74 **Avoid the singular form of adverbial objectives needing the plural.**

He lives five *miles* [not *mile*] away.
We had two *feet* [not *foot*] of snow.
We burned six *tons* [not *ton*] of coal.

75 **Do not use** *ways* **or** *piece* **for** *distance* **or** *way.*

I live a long *way* [not *ways*] from here.
His house is just a short *distance* [not *piece*] down the road.

76 **Avoid the use of redundant (unneeded) modifiers.**

76a **Do not repeat** *a* **or** *an* **unnecessarily.**

Right: *a* half hour, half *an* hour   Wrong: *a* half *an* hour

76b **Avoid** *this here, these here, that there, those there.*

Right: *This* book is mine.   Wrong: *This here* book is mine.

76c **Do not say** *seldom ever, rarely ever.* **Simply omit** *ever,* **or change** *seldom* **and** *rarely* **to** *hardly.*

Right: I *seldom* go there.   Wrong: I *seldom ever* go there.
Right: I *rarely* eat here.   Wrong: I *rarely ever* eat here.
Right: I *hardly ever* see him.   Wrong: I *seldom ever* see him.

65

76d Avoid the unnecessary use of such adverbs as *back, up, with, over, again.*
Wrong: *Return back* at once.   Right: *Return* at once.
Wrong: I *paid up* my debts.   Right: I *paid* my debts.
Wrong: He *met up* with a stranger.   Right: He *met* a stranger.
Wrong: *Redo* this paper *over*.   Right: *Redo* this paper.

77a Avoid the *double negative;* that is, two negative expressions applied to the same idea. These words convey a negative meaning: *no, not, nothing, none, no one, never, hardly, scarcely, only* (when it means *no more than*), *but* (when it means *only*), *nowhere, nobody, neither.*
Right: I did*n't* see *anyone*.   Wrong: I did*n't* see *no one*.
Right: We have *hardly* seen you.   Wrong: We have*n't hardly* ...
Right: I have *but* one sister.   Wrong: I have*n't but* one sister.
Right: I have *only* enough for today.   Wrong: I have*n't only* enough ...
Right: *No*, I have*n't* seen him. (*No* is purely introductory.)

77b Avoid using *but* after negative ideas expressed by such words as *doubt* and *fear*. Complete *cannot* (or *could not*) *help* by a gerund, not by *but* and an infinitive.
Right: I don't *doubt* that you're right.   Wrong: I don't *doubt but* that ...
Right: I can't help *worrying*.   Wrong: I can't help *but worry*.

FOR PRACTICE AND APPLICATION

Rewrite the following sentences, correcting each violation of rules 74–77b. Exchange papers for checking; then read the sentences aloud in class.

1. That there rocket ascended up to a record height.
2. I can't help but think you still owe me a half a dollar.
3. We seldom ever drive a long ways in one day.
4. You haven't none of the right answers. Rework the problems over.
5. I don't doubt that you've met up with some odd people.
6. Jim is almost six foot tall, but I'm half a foot taller.
7. He rarely ever returns back from lunch on time.
8. We haven't burned scarcely five ton of coal this winter.
9. This here man you want lives just a short piece from me.
10. Nobody didn't miss him until a half an hour ago.

FOLLOW-UP

If one type of error—the double negative, for example—gives you particular trouble, train yourself to listen for it in your own speech and that of others. Ask a friend to call each wrong use to your attention. Once you learn to hear a wrong usage, you will be amazed that you could ever have been deaf to the sound of that expression.

USING ADJECTIVES AND ADVERBS CORRECTLY: III

78 Avoid the use of *dangling modifiers;* that is, modifiers not related logically to some other word in the sentence.

DANGLING PARTICIPLE: Listening closely, no sound was heard. (*Who was listening?*)

BETTER: Listening closely, *we* heard no sound.

DANGLING GERUND: By leaving now, the rush can be avoided. (*Who will do the leaving?*)

BETTER: By leaving now, *I* can avoid the rush.

DANGLING INFINITIVE: To make faster time, the load was lightened. (*Who wanted to make faster time?*)

BETTER: To make faster time, *we* lightened the load.

DANGLING ELLIPTICAL EXPRESSION: While eating dinner, the bell rang. (*Was the bell eating?*)

BETTER: While *we* were eating dinner, the bell rang.

79 Place modifiers where they will keep meaning clear and sensible. Your readers should not have to puzzle out your meaning.

MISLEADING: I have almost read all these books. All are not mine.
CLEAR: I have read almost all these books. Not all are mine.
MISLEADING: I spent an hour cracking walnuts with my little brother.
CLEAR: With my little brother, I spent an hour cracking walnuts.
MISLEADING: I watched the parade pass the house leaning out an upstairs window.
CLEAR: Leaning out an upstairs window, I watched the parade pass the house.
MISLEADING: I put the billfold into my pocket that I had just bought.
CLEAR: I put into my pocket the billfold that I had just bought.
PUZZLING: She told me *before she left* she had locked the door.
  (The italicized clause is a "squinting" modifier; that is, it is a modifier that could modify either *told* or *had locked*.)
CLEAR: She told me that she had locked the door before she left.
CLEAR: Before she left, she told me that she had locked the door.

"HANGING ON A HOOK IN THE CLOSET, I FOUND MY NECKTIE."

80 Avoid various miscellaneous errors in the use of adjectives and adverbs.

80a Do not use such expressions as *all the farther, all the faster* in place of *as far as, as fast as.*
WRONG: This is *all the farther* I read.   RIGHT: This is *as far as* . . .
WRONG: Is that *all the faster* he can run?   RIGHT: Is that *as fast as* . . .

80b Say *anyway,* **not** *anyways.*
WRONG: *Anyways,* Jim told me so.   RIGHT: *Anyway,* Jim told me so.

80c Do not use *considerable* as an adverb.
He is *much* [not *considerable*] older than I am.

80d Do not use *leave* for the adverb *lief.*
I'd as *lief* [not *leave*] go as stay.

80e Avoid using *nowhere near* or *nowheres near* for *not nearly.*
RIGHT: I have *not nearly* enough.   WRONG: I have *nowhere near* enough.

80f Add no *s* to the words *anywhere, nowhere, somewhere, everywhere.*
My watch must be here *somewhere* [not *somewheres*].

80g Avoid the expression *nohow.*
WRONG: I don't like it *nohow.*   RIGHT: I don't like it *at all.*

80h Do not use *right* as an adverb of degree.
WRONG: He seems *right* friendly.   RIGHT: He seems *very* friendly.

80i Avoid using *worse* to mean *more,* **and** *the worst way* or *in the worst way* to mean *very much.*
POOR: I need help *worse* than ever.   BETTER: I need help *more* than ever.
POOR: I need it *in the worst way.*   BETTER: I need it *very much.*

FOR PRACTICE AND APPLICATION

A. Improve the use of modifiers in the following sentences. Get rid of all dangling modifiers; move all misleading or squinting modifiers. Go over your work in class.

1. Waiting there in the cold, the time really dragged.
2. He agreed after the meeting he would write the letter.
3. I spent the day mending fence with my uncle.
4. You have almost eaten all these pears.
5. All the pupils are not girls. I just know a few of them.
6. I told you when you left you should call me.
7. While talking to my brother, a black cat shot across our path.
8. That boy owns the dogs wearing hip boots.
9. By springing a surprise play, the winning touchdown was scored.
10. To be considered for this position, certain steps are necessary.
11. She was wearing the ring on her little finger that I had bought in Italy.

B. Correct all errors in the use of modifiers in these sentences. If you write this exercise, be sure to go over your work orally.

1. I'd as leave go somewheres else. I'm not right sure where.
2. He is nowhere near old enough, but he wants to go in the worst way.
3. This is all the farther I'll go. I don't like this trip nohow.
4. I've been looking for you everywheres. We need you worse than ever.
5. That is as fast as he has driven, or so he says, anyways.

C. If you need the practice, write sentences to illustrate correct usage of the items in Rule 80. Use your sentences for class drill.

CORRELATING ENGLISH WITH YOUR OTHER CLASSES

Go over papers that you have written or are writing for any of your classes. If you find any dangling, misleading, or squinting modifiers, rewrite the sentences so that you correct the faults. Ask a partner or the class to criticize your handling of these sentences.

FOLLOW-UP

Make a conscious effort to eliminate from your expression any of the errors covered by rules 78–80i. Follow the plan suggested on page 66.

LEARNING MORE ABOUT ADJECTIVE AND ADVERB USAGE

The following rules deal chiefly with expressions that are acceptable at the colloquial level but that are not yet generally regarded as standard English.

81 Use *as–as* in *affirmative* constructions; *so–as,* in *negative.* This rule is often disregarded in informal expression. It is, however, one of the niceties of style that you should know.
STANDARD: I am *as* sure *as* I can be.   He is not *so* fat *as* he was.

82 Except in informal expression, avoid the use of *badly* to mean *very much* or *greatly* after such verbs as *want* and *need.*
I need a change *very much* [not *badly*].

83 Avoid the use of *poorly* to describe how one is feeling or looking.
DOUBTFUL: I've been feeling *poorly.*   BETTER: I've *not* been feeling *well.*

84 Use *rather* or *somewhat* in preference to *kind of* or *sort of.* **Never say** *sorta* **or** *kinda.*
ILLITERATE: Today is *sorta* chilly.   COLLOQUIAL: Today is *sort of* chilly.
STANDARD: Today is *rather* chilly.

85 **Do not use** *a great deal of* **as a substitute for** *many*.

        We saw *many* [not *a great deal of*] sailors on the train.

86 **Avoid the use of** *never* **for** *did not*. ***Never***, **meaning** *not ever*, **should be used only of** *more than a single instance. Helpful hint:* **Use** *never* **only when** *not* **would change the meaning.**

    CORRECT: I *never* eat breakfast. (*I did not eat breakfast* would give a different meaning.)
    FAULTY: I *never* ate breakfast this morning. (*a single instance*)
    BETTER: I *did not* eat breakfast this morning.

87 **Do not add** *a* **or** *an* **to such expressions as** *this* [or *that*] *kind of, sort of, type of.*

    POOR: I like this kind of *a* day.   BETTER: I like this kind of day.
    POOR: This type of *a* player wins.   BETTER: This type of player wins.

88 **Avoid using** *very* **or** *too* **to modify past participles.**

    DOUBTFUL: I was *very* impressed.   BETTER: I was *really* impressed.
    DOUBTFUL: I wasn't *too* annoyed.   BETTER: I wasn't *too much* annoyed.

89 **Do not use** *way* **as a substitute for** *away*.

    DOUBTFUL: I've stayed here *way* too long.
    BETTER: I've stayed here *away* too long.

90 **Avoid careless use of** *lots* **or** *a lot* **in the sense of** *very much* **or** *many*.

    COLLOQUIAL: *Lots of* strangers came.   STANDARD: *Many* strangers came.
    COLLOQUIAL: I like him *a lot*.   STANDARD: I like him *very much*.

91 **Avoid the use of** *mighty* **to mean** *very, really, extremely*.

    DOUBTFUL: That pie was *mighty* good.   BETTER: That pie was *really* good.

FOR PRACTICE AND APPLICATION

A. In the following sentences, change to standard English any expressions not in accord with rules 81–91. Exchange papers for correction and oral practice.

1. This type of an error is made by lots of writers.
2. A great deal of critics are very excited about this play.
3. Mother still feels poorly, but she is not as weak as she was.
4. A vacation would be mighty welcome. I need one badly.
5. Sue never called me tonight. I'm kinda worried.
6. This kind of a story takes me way back to my childhood.
7. It may seem sorta strange, but I'm not too interested in him.
8. This sort of idea might bring us a great deal of customers.
9. Unlike a lot of our other employees, James is never late.

B. If you feel the need, write original sentences covering any of the preceding rules. Practice reading your sentences aloud.

Review practice

REVIEW

ADJECTIVES AND ADVERBS

A. (1) Copy the following sentences. (2) Underline all adjectives and all adjective phrases. Omit the articles (*a, an,* and *the*). (3) Circle all adverbs and all adverb phrases. (4) Draw arrows to the words modified.

1. That dirt road to Linwood hasn't been passable for weeks.
2. Feeling the cold, I pulled my coat more closely around me.
3. Three men besides me will be ready to go with you.
4. Unfortunately I now have no money to invest.

B. Write a paragraph telling what happens at your house between the time that you wake up in the morning and the time that you leave for school. Use vivid adjective and adverb words or phrases. Underline these to show that you have used them deliberately. Read your paragraphs in class. Listen closely as the paragraphs are read; then comment upon the effectiveness of the modifiers.

C. Correct any faulty expressions in the following sentences. If you make it a written exercise, be sure to go over the sentences orally.

1. I'm real glad to see you. You're sure looking good.
2. It's awful late for the youngest of them two boys to be out.
3. The team is not as heavy as that there one last year.
4. I should eat less rich desserts, but I can't hardly resist them.
5. Dad bought a new car and truck. I couldn't help but feel surprised.
6. My sister Jean is more busier than any member of our family.
7. I've seldom ever traveled anywheres by myself.
8. I'd as leave lend you the money. You can repay it back easy.
9. Tonight I never ate much dinner. I didn't even want no pie.
10. Use this here wrench. It works real good.
11. Give me a idea of your plans. I'm very interested.

How the Preposition and the Conjunction Help to Build the Sentence

92 A *preposition* is a word that shows the relation between a noun or a pronoun, called its *object*, and some other word in the sentence.

> The first score *of* the game came *in* the second quarter.
>
> (*Of* shows the relation between *game* and *score*. *In* shows the relation between *quarter* and *came*.)

As the examples show, the object of the preposition may have modifiers.

A preposition and its object, with or without modifiers, constitute a *prepositional phrase*. **Prepositional phrases modify other words.** *Of the game* is an adjective phrase, and *in the second quarter* is an adverb phrase. (See also Rule 57e, page 52, and Rule 68b, page 61.)

Frequently used prepositions are listed below.

about	behind	down	off	till
above	below	during	on	to
across	beneath	except	out	toward, towards
after	beside	for	outside	under
against	besides	from	over	underneath
along	between	in	past	until
amid, amidst	beyond	inside	regarding	up
among	but (except)	into	round	upon
around	by	like	since	with
at	concerning	near	through	within
before	despite	of	throughout	without

Sometimes two or more words are used together as a preposition and are called a *phrasal preposition.* Examples are *according to, apart from, as to, because of, by means of, in place of, in spite of, instead of, out of.*

Do not confuse prepositions with other parts of speech. A preposition must have an object that answers the question *whom* or *what*. Remember, the way that a word is used determines what part of speech it is.

    Maynard drove *past* the house without seeing us. (*preposition*)
    Maynard had just driven *past*. (*adverb*)
    Some people live only in the *past*. (*noun*)
    I have been here for the *past* hour. (*adjective*)

93 A *conjunction* **is a word that connects words, phrases, or clauses.**

93a *Co-ordinate* **conjunctions join words, phrases, or clauses of** *equal* **value. Simple co-ordinate conjunctions are** *and, or, nor, but,* **and sometimes** *for*. **Co-ordinate conjunctions that go in pairs, like** *both-and, either-or, neither-nor, not only-but also,* **are called** *correlative* **conjunctions.**

    He *and* I went. (*simple*)   Either he *or* I can go. (*correlative*)

93b *Subordinate* **conjunctions connect dependent (subordinate) clauses with independent (main) clauses. Subordinate conjunctions include** *since, before, after, while, than, if, although, though, when, where, as, until, unless,* **and** *because*. Their use is to build complex sentences, discussed on pages 90–91.

    I shall wait [*ind. cl.*] **until** he comes [*dep. cl.*].

93c **Do not confuse conjunctions with prepositions, adverbs, or other parts of speech. Remember,** *prepositions* **introduce** *phrases; conjunctions* **introduce** *clauses; adverbs* **introduce neither.**

    Call me *before* you leave. (*conjunction*)
    Call me *before* noon. (*preposition*)
    I have seen him *before*. (*adverb*)

FOR PRACTICE AND APPLICATION

A. Determine the part of speech of each italicized word in the following sentences. Make this an oral or a written activity.

1. *Before* you leave, check the thermostat. The heat may be turned *off*.
2. I *like* to get *outside* on a day *like* this.
3. Do you *still* want to stay *behind*? I shall worry *about* you.
4. *Before* noon most of the snow had slid *off* the roof.
5. *About* fifteen minutes ago, he drove *up outside* our house.
6. Come *on!* We should leave *while* the wind is *still*.
7. *After* a *while*, I'll introduce you to the man *behind* this project.
8. *After* you leave the bus, you will have a long walk *up* the hill.

B. Write sentences using the following words as indicated: *inside* as noun, preposition, adverb; *since* as adverb, preposition, conjunction; *either* as pronoun, adjective, conjunction. Exchange papers for checking or for reading aloud.

USING PREPOSITIONS AND CONJUNCTIONS CORRECTLY: I

Rules 94–100 cover errors that you should avoid in all your expression, oral or written.

94 **Avoid the use of** *as, as how, where* **for** *that, who,* **or** *whether.*

> I do not know *whether* [not *as* or *as how*] I can go.
> I read *that* [not *where*] the Senate has passed a new tax law.
> You are the only one *who* [not *as*] wants a change.

95 **Say** *different from,* **not** *different than. Than* **is a conjunction, not a preposition.**

> Your answers are *different from* [not *than*] mine.

96 **Do not use the preposition** *like* **for the conjunctions** *as* **or** *as if.**

> Those children look *as if* [not *like*] they have a holiday.
> Just do *as* [not *like*] I do.

97 **Never use** *of* **or its corruption** *a* **as an auxiliary verb.**

> You should *have* [not *of*] called me.   He *must have* [not *musta*] left.

98 **Do not confuse the prepositions in the following pairs or groups.**

At, to. Use *to* for *motion toward*.

RIGHT: Did you go *to* school today?   Were you *at* school?
WRONG: Were you *to* school today?   I stayed *to* home.

Beside, besides. *Beside* refers to *position. Besides* means *in addition to.*

RIGHT: He sat down *beside* her.   Who else is going *besides* you?
WRONG: Have you told anyone *beside* me?

---

* In informal usage, some authorities accept the use of *like* for *as,* though not for *as if.*

Between, among. *Between* usually refers to *two* objects or persons; *among*, to *three or more.*

Right: *Between* you and me, this is a dull party.
Right: They passed the candy *among* all the boys.

If each member of a group is being considered separately in relation to each other member, use *between.*

How are the roads *between* Stanwood, Clarence, and Lowden?

By, at, with. Do not use *by* as a substitute for *at* or *with*.

Right: My grandmother lives *with* us. She lives *at* our house.
Wrong: My grandmother visited *by* our house last week.
Right: The plan is all right *with* me.
Wrong: It's all right *by* me.

In, into. *In* should be used for *place* or *position* with respect to enclosure; *into* should be used for *direction.*

Right: He sat there *in* the boat.   He stepped *into* the boat.
Wrong: He opened the door and ran *in* the house.*

On, for. Do not use *on* as a substitute for *for.*

Right: We are leaving. We can't wait *for* you any longer.

99 Do not use *off* or *off of* as a substitute for *from.*

Wrong: I borrowed this pencil *off of* Don.
Right: I borrowed this pencil *from* Don.

100 Omit redundant [unnecessary] prepositions.

Right	Wrong
Where is he?	Where is he at?
He fell off the wall.	He fell off of the wall.
Come inside the house.	Come inside of the house.
Is the storm over?	Is the storm over with?
I want you to help me.	I want for you to help me.
Wait outside my office.	Wait outside of my office.
Where did he go?	Where did he go to?
If I had known, I'd have gone.	If I had of known, I'd have gone.

FOR PRACTICE AND APPLICATION

A. Choose the correct word from the pairs or groups listed in parentheses. If you write this exercise, be sure to read the sentences aloud in class.

1. I borrowed this magazine (off, from, off of) Bill.
2. Why don't you wear your hair (like, as) she does?
3. He should (have, of) invited me. If he (had, had of), I'd have gone.
4. Don't wait (for, on) me. I'll be late.
5. We must (cover, cover over) those tomato plants tonight.

---

* Some authorities approve this form in informal expression.

6. Mother called, "Take the lid (off, off of) that kettle!"
7. Was John (to, at) the game today?
8. My cousin lives (by, at) our house.
9. These apples are different (from, than) those.
10. No one (as, who) knows you would doubt your word.
11. Divide these names (among, between) all the members.
12. I'm not sure (that, as, as how) I understand your meaning.
13. Jim is staying (by, at) his aunt's house.
14. Where is (he, he at)? Is he (to, at) home?
15. Did you read (where, that) the strike has finally been settled?
16. Don't you want to (continue, continue on) with the plan?
17. The robin hopped (off, off of) its perch. Where did it (go, go to)?
18. Tom (could of, coulda, could have) finished his work on time.
19. He jumped (in, into) the car and drove away.
20. It looks (like, as if) it is poison ivy. I don't know (as, that) it is, though.

B. Correct any errors in the following sentences. Read the corrected sentences aloud.

1. Is the game over with? It must of been a fast one.
2. Was Elmer to the meeting? I feel about that club like he does.
3. It seems as how I have made a mistake.
4. Put these papers inside of your desk. I borrowed them off Dick.
5. Please take my name off of the list. You should of done it before.
6. It looks as if we don't know where we are at.
7. I'm sorry to be late. Have you been waiting on me?
8. The Smiths must of gone away. Their house has been closed up.

C. For each error that you made in *A* and *B*, write an original sentence to illustrate the correct usage. After each sentence, write the number of the rule that applies. Exchange papers. Let the class judge the sentences as you read them.

USING PREPOSITIONS AND CONJUNCTIONS CORRECTLY: II

Rules 101–109 cover additional rules for using prepositions and conjunctions correctly. You should learn to apply them in all your expression.

101 Do not use *and* or *but* where they are not needed.

WRONG: I have a new coat *and which* I like very much.
RIGHT: I have a new coat *which* I like very much.
RIGHT: I have a new coat which I like, *but which* needs to be altered slightly. (Here the conjunction joins two adjective clauses; it does not come between a main clause and a dependent clause, as in the example labeled *Wrong.*)
WRONG: Write the consonants in order—b, c, d, f, *and etc.*
RIGHT: Write the consonants in order—b, c, d, f, *etc.*

102 **Do not use** *where* **or** *when* **to introduce a definition.**

RIGHT: A blood bank is *a place* in which blood for transfusions is stored.
WRONG: A blood bank is *when* blood is stored for transfusions.

103 **Do not use** *being as, being that, beings as, beings that* **for** *as* **or** *since*.

WRONG: *Beings as* you're here, you may stay.
RIGHT: *Since* you're here, you may stay.

104 **Avoid incomplete comparisons.**

RIGHT: Melvin is as young as, or younger than, Harold.
RIGHT: Melvin is as young as Harold, or younger.
WRONG: Melvin is as young or younger than Harold.

105 **Do not omit a needed preposition.** The italicized prepositions in the following sentences are needed.

When did you graduate *from* high school?
Be here *at* the same time as before.
I have no time *for* or interest in this project.

106 **Do not use** *on account of* **to introduce a clause or to complete "The reason was…" or "The cause was…"**

I'm helping you only *because* [not *on account of*] I like you.
The reason for the accident *was* [not *was on account of*] icy roads.

107 **Keep in parallel structure grammatical elements joined by co-ordinate conjunctions.**

WRONG: Tell me his *name* and *where he lives*. (*word and clause*)
RIGHT: Tell me his *name* and *address*. (*two words*)
RIGHT: Tell me *what his name is* and *where he lives*. (*two clauses*)
WRONG: I like *fishing* and *to hunt*. (*gerund and infinitive*)
RIGHT: I like *fishing* and *hunting*. (*two gerunds*)
RIGHT: I like *to fish* and *to hunt*. (*two infinitives*)
WRONG: He is *tall, sandy,* and *with freckles*. (*one-word modifiers and a prepositional phrase*)
RIGHT: He is *tall, sandy,* and *freckled*. (*all one-word modifiers*)

108 **Do not use** *till* **or** *until* **for** *when*.

I had hardly arrived *when* [*not till* or *until*] he called.

109 **Do not use the prepositions** *without* **or** *except* **for the conjunction** *unless*.

WRONG: I'll not go *except* you go, too.   *Without* I'm ill, I'll be there.
RIGHT: I'll not go *unless* you go, too.   *Unless* I'm ill, I'll be there.

FOR PRACTICE AND APPLICATION

A. Correct any errors in the sentences that follow. Read the corrected sentences in class.

1. The reason for the higher price is on account of our costs have risen.
2. Beings that you're here, you may as well help us.

3. Eddie won't stay here without you do, too.
4. The green suit fits as well or better than the blue one.
5. This plan will fail except it has your support, and which I hope it has.
6. We canceled our picnic on account of the twins couldn't come.
7. A free throw is where a player gets an unguarded shot.
8. I don't want to see him without you are there with me.
9. I had scarcely opened my mouth until he interrupted me.
10. My hobbies are baseball and to collect stamps.
11. We'll have to hurry, on account of a storm is coming.
12. He graduated high school last year.
13. A *faux pas* is when you make an embarrassing mistake.
14. List the days of the week: Sunday, Monday, and etc.
15. I have no knowledge or interest in his plans.

B. Which rules are new to you or difficult for you? Write original practice sentences to fix them in your mind. Go over these sentences in class.

CORRELATING ENGLISH WITH YOUR OTHER CLASSES

Go over papers that you have written or are writing for other classes. Make suitable corrections wherever you find violations of rules 94–109.

USING PREPOSITIONS AND CONJUNCTIONS CORRECTLY: III

Rules 110–114 cover two types of usages: (1) those that are acceptable in colloquial, but not in standard, use and (2) those about which there is some disagreement among authorities.

110 In standard usage, distinguish between the following prepositions.

About, around. Avoid using *around* in the sense of *not far from*.

POOR: He came *around* noon.   BETTER: He came *about* noon.

At, in. One arrives *at* his home, his office, etc.; one arrives *in* town, *in* a city, etc.

We arrived *in* [not *at*] Dallas late that night.

Behind, in back of. Say *behind*, not *in back of*.

POOR: Stay *in back of* me.   BETTER: Stay *behind* me.

Inside or **inside of, within.** Avoid *inside* or *inside of* for *within* in expressions of time.

POOR: I'll leave *inside of* an hour.   BETTER: I'll leave *within* an hour.

Outside of, except or **except for.** Do not use *outside of* for *except* or *except for*.

POOR: No one *outside of* you knows.   BETTER: No one *except* you knows.

111 **Do not use** *at about* **for** *at* **or** *about.*

Poor: He came *at about* ten o'clock.
Better: He came *about* [or *at*] ten o'clock.

112 **Avoid the use of** *also* **as a conjunction.**

Poor: I am tired, *also* hungry.   Jean came, *also* Jerry.
Better: I am tired *and* hungry.   *Both* Jean *and* Jerry came.

113 **Avoid saying** *blame on* **or** *blame it on* **for** *blame.*

Poor: Don't put the *blame on* him.   Better: Don't *blame* him.

114 **Say** *consensus,* **not** *consensus of opinion.*

The *consensus* of the members is that we should lower our dues.

FOR PRACTICE AND APPLICATION

A. Rewrite the following sentences, changing to standard English any faulty or colloquial expressions. Exchange papers for checking as the sentences are read aloud.

1. We should arrive at Austin inside an hour.
2. Bill has seen every team outside of the Braves.
3. We need butter, also cream.
4. We should leave at about four o'clock.
5. About midnight we heard a shout, also a scream.
6. If I'm not back inside of two days, blame it on the weather.
7. The consensus of our class is that we can spend around ten dollars.
8. Tell no one except Mary that I shall be at Denver.
9. Look in back of you. There is the one to put the blame on.
10. The consensus of opinion among the members is favorable.
11. Light the oven about five. I should be back around that time.

B. Write an original sentence to illustrate standard usage as covered by rules 110–114. Have a partner check your paper.

USING PREPOSITIONS AND CONJUNCTIONS CORRECTLY: IV

Rules 115–124 cover additional usages that are disputable or that are acceptable only in colloquial expression.

115 **Place** *correlative conjunctions* **immediately before the elements joined.**

Poor: You may *either* decide **now** *or* **later.**
Better: You may decide *either* **now** *or* **later.**

Poor: I like **Ed** *and* **Al** *both.*   Better: I like *both* **Ed** *and* **Al.**

116 Avoid use of *due to* for *because of*. *Due to* may follow a linking verb; it should not introduce an adverb phrase.

> We came late *because of* [not *due to*] a heavy fog.
> Our lateness was *due to* a heavy fog.

117 Feel free to end a sentence with a preposition if such a construction makes the sentence read more smoothly. Be sure, however, that the final preposition has an object.

Good: I wonder **what** he is waiting *for*.
Awkward: I wonder *for* **what** he is waiting.

118 Do not use *following* as a substitute for the preposition *after*.

> *After* [not *Following*] the storm, we continued our trip.

119 Use the conjunction *if* to state a condition, not to take the place of *whether*.

Right: Do you know *whether* you can go?
Right: *If* you can go, meet us at ten o'clock.
Colloquial: I wonder *if* he will meet us.

120 Use *than* after such negative expressions as *no sooner;* use *when* after such expressions as *hardly* or *scarcely*.

> **No sooner** had I spoken *than* I was sorry.
> We had **scarcely** arrived *when* the storm began.

121 Do not use *providing* for the conjunction *provided*.

> He will go *provided* [not *providing*] he can find time.

122 Avoid "The reason is because . . ." Say, "The reason is that . . ."

> His reason for leaving is *that* [not *because*] he is ill.

123 Say *try to,* not *try and*.

Standard: *Try to* meet me.   Colloquial: *Try and* meet me.

124 Use *while* to denote duration of time, not to take the place of *but, although,* or *whereas*.

Standard: William likes cantaloupe, *but* Fred prefers watermelon.
Standard: Wait here *while* I call the office.
Colloquial: I enjoy football, *while* Ed does not care for it.

FOR PRACTICE AND APPLICATION

Tell whether the italicized expressions in the following sentences represent *standard* or *colloquial* usage. Make this an oral activity.

1. No sooner had he left *when* our bad luck began.
2. Ronald swims well, *whereas* Don cannot swim a stroke.
3. *Try and* have your report ready tomorrow.
4. The reason I am late is *because* I overslept.
5. This experiment should tell us *if* our theory is sound.
6. We had scarcely arrived *than* the storm became worse.

7. The men *either want* more money *or a shorter work week*.
8. Tell me what you are looking *for*.
9. We can help you, *providing* you are not in a hurry.
10. His poor marks are *due to* illness.
11. We need *time and money both*.
12. *While* I am not an expert, I believe that I can help you.
13. Will you call me *following* the game?
14. *Due to* a storm, our plane was delayed.
15. I do not know *if* I understand you.

CORRELATING ENGLISH WITH YOUR OTHER CLASSES

Study a report that you have written for science or some other class. Change to standard English any colloquial usage of prepositions or conjunctions. Explain changes to the class.

Review practice

A. In the following sentences, tell how the italicized words are used. Make this an oral or a written exercise.

1. He went *by after* lunch. *Where* is he now?
2. *By* this time tomorrow, I shall have gone *where* I told you.
3. *After* you have eaten, you may run *along*.
4. *Below,* men were pushing carts *along* the narrow street.
5. The temperature has stayed *below* zero *since* last Friday.
6. Prices have gone *up since* you were here *last*.
7. At noon he hurried *up* those stairs. I have not seen him *since*.

B. Write sentences using *before* as a conjunction, a preposition, and an adverb; *in* as a preposition and an adverb; *after* as a preposition and a conjunction; *since* as a preposition, a conjunction, and an adverb. Exchange papers for checking and reading in class.

C. Correct each error in preposition or conjunction usage in the following sentences.

1. Joe should of known where we had gone to.
2. I can't decide as how you're right without you tell me the whole story.
3. Doesn't Pat live by your house? Why did she stay to home today?
4. On the map, it looks like the paving continues on to Avoca.
5. Has anyone beside you found an answer different than mine?
6. Just between the three of us, the change is all right by me.
7. Don't wait any longer on him. He just went in the house.
8. If I had of thought, I might have borrowed that book off of Joe.
9. Do you want for me to label these angles *a, b, c,* and etc.?

10. A tornado is when a whirling wind accompanied by a funnel-shaped cloud sweeps across a strip of country.

D. Identify as such all colloquial or doubtful usages in the following sentences. Make this an oral activity.

1. The consensus of opinion among the committee was that we should not put the blame on these boys, but on the other two. No sooner had this conclusion been reached when there was a protest from John and Charles both.
2. I'm not sure if I can meet you following the game. The reason is because I promised to do an errand for Mother. While I can't say for certain, I'll try and be there. I can make it, providing nothing goes wrong.

THE INTERJECTION

125 An *interjection* **is a word that expresses** *emotion* **or** *feeling* **and has no grammatical relation to the other words in the sentence.***

Wow! Fire! Police! (*Strong emotion; followed by exclamation point*)
Oh, I didn't mean that one. (*Mild emotion; followed by comma*)

BRINGING TOGETHER ALL PARTS OF SPEECH AND THEIR USES

1. CLASSIFYING SENTENCES ACCORDING TO MEANING

126 **Sentences are classified according to meaning as** *declarative, interrogative, imperative,* **and** *exclamatory.*

(1) **A** *declarative* **sentence is one that makes a statement.**

>The wind howled through the trees.

(2) **An** *interrogative* **sentence is one that asks a question.**

>Where are you going?

(3) **An** *imperative* **sentence is one that expresses a command or a request.**

>Do exactly as I tell you.   Please raise the window.

(4) **An** *exclamatory* **sentence is one that expresses strong feeling or surprise.**

>We've won! What do you know about that!

---

* Like the introductory *there* (see page 30), the interjection is known as an *independent element,* or an *expletive.* It is diagrammed as is *there.*

2. ANALYSIS OF THE SENTENCE

Syntax is that phase of grammar which deals with the relationship of words within a sentence. You have studied separately each part of speech and its use in building the simple sentence. All these elements are brought together here for purposes of review.

127 A *simple sentence* contains only one verb (predicate) and one subject, either or both of which may be compound. It expresses one main idea.

128 The *simple predicate* is the verb alone. The *complete predicate* is the verb plus all its modifiers or complements.

> The truck crossed the busy intersection at Vine Street.

The simple predicate is *crossed*. The complete predicate is *crossed the busy intersection at Vine Street*. It includes the verb *crossed;* the object of the verb, *intersection;* and the modifiers of *intersection: the, busy, at Vine Street.*

129 The *simple subject* is the noun or pronoun (or *substantive*) about which something is said. The *complete subject* is the simple subject plus all its modifiers.

> The fat little boy in the middle lives next door to us.

Boy is the simple subject. *The fat little boy in the middle* is the complete subject. *The, fat,* and *little* are simple adjectives; and *in the middle* is an adjective phrase. All are used as modifiers of the simple subject.

130 **In normal sentence order, the subject is near the beginning, as in the preceding examples.** Sometimes sentences are formed in inverted order; that is, the verb or a part of the complete predicate may precede the subject. In the following examples the complete predicate is set in boldface (heavy black) type, and the complete subject is set in regular (Roman) type. Note what parts of the predicate precede the subject.

EXAMPLES

(1) **Are** you **going to the dance?** (The verb, or simple predicate, is *Are going*. It has a modifier, *to the dance,* to form the complete predicate. The simple subject is *you*. Having no modifiers, it is also the complete subject.)

(2) **What reason for the theft did** he **give?** (The verb, or simple predicate, is *did give*. It has an object, *reason,* modified by the adjective *What* and the prepositional phrase *for the theft*. *He* is the simple subject, but, because it has no modifiers, it is also the complete subject.)

(3) *There* **are** five candidates for the office. (The verb, or simple predicate, is *are*. It is also the complete predicate, because it has no modifiers. *Candidates* is the simple subject. It is modified by the adjective *five* and the prepositional phrase *for the office*. The expletive *There* is printed in italics because it belongs neither to the complete predicate nor to the complete subject; it has no grammatical relation to any of the other words that are in the sentence.)

(4) **Open the door.** (The verb, or simple predicate, is *Open*. This verb with its object, *door*, and a modifier of *door, the*, forms the complete predicate. *You*, the simple and complete subject, is understood.)

(5) **Silently,** crawling with extreme caution on hands and knees, Pat **made his way through the tangled underbrush.** (*Made* is the verb, or simple predicate. What complements does the verb have? *Way*, the direct object, with its modifier, *his: Through the tangled underbrush* is an adverb phrase modifying the verb because it tells *where* Pat made his way; *silently*, an adverb telling *how* Pat made his way. *Silently made his way through the tangled underbrush* is the complete predicate. *Pat* is the simple subject. It is modified by a participial phrase made up of the participle *crawling* and two adverb phrases, *with extreme caution* and *on hands and knees*. The complete subject is *Pat crawling with extreme caution on hands and knees*.)

This sentence is diagrammed as follows:

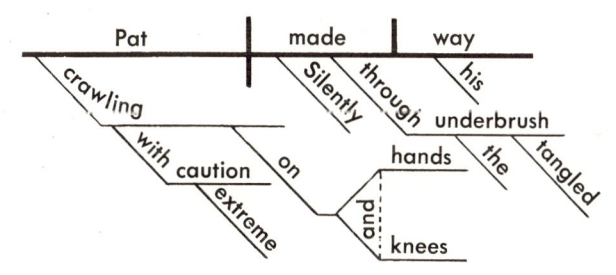

Note that the vertical line which crosses the horizontal base line separates the complete predicate from the complete subject.

GUIDES TO SOLVING PROBLEMS IN SYNTAX

To solve a problem in syntax, follow this procedure:

1. Read the complete sentence to understand its meaning.
2. Look for the verb to see *what happened*.
3. Look for the subject of this verb to see *who* or *what* did it.
4. Look to see whether there is a *direct object, an indirect object, a predicate nominative*, or *a predicate adjective*.
5. Look for any simple *modifiers* and decide what they modify.
6. Determine the relationship of word groups that belong together in meaning (*prepositional phrases, verbal phrases, dependent clauses*).
7. Remember that the use of a word in relation to the other words in the sentence determines its part of speech.

FOR PRACTICE AND APPLICATION

A. Using the preceding steps, give the syntax of the parts in the following sentences. If your instructor so directs, name also the complete subject and the complete predicate. Here is an example for the sentence diagrammed on page 83.

v.—made
subj.—Pat
d. o.—way
adj.—crawling, extreme, his, the, tangled
adv.—Silently
adj. phr.—crawling with extreme caution on hands and knees (*participial phrase*)
adv. phr.—with extreme caution; on hands and knees; through the tangled underbrush

1. John felt exceedingly tired by the end of the day.
2. That girl in the blue dress is a fine soprano.
3. Yesterday we made plans to celebrate.
4. In the early morning that man wearing the brown suit takes a walk along the river.
5. Has Bert apologized or offered any excuses?

B. If you made any errors in analyzing the sentences in *A,* be sure that you discover why. Then, if your instructor wishes, analyze the sentences below, following the same procedure as in *A*.

1. The picture hanging on that wall came to us from a friend in Europe.
2. Soldiers and sailors, weary of war, were relaxing on the beach.
3. He plans to return after the election.
4. Singing has brought Elizabeth many happy experiences.
5. Majestic elm trees, planted by some unknown early settler, formed a Gothic arch down the length of Lincoln Avenue.

C. If your instructor so directs, analyze sentences 2, 3, 4, 5, 7 on page 73 in the same way as those in *A* and *B;* then diagram them. Explain orally.

D. If you want practice in identifying the parts of speech, copy the eight sentences on page 73 and those in exercises *A* and *B* above, leaving a blank line between the lines that you write. Then, above each word, write its part of speech as used in the sentence. Use these symbols:

v.—verb   *adv.*—adverb
n.—noun   *prep.*—preposition
pro.—pronoun   *conj.*—conjunction
adj.—adjective *int.*—interjection

Example

adv.   adj.   prep.   adj.   n.   prep.   n.   conj.
Silently, crawling with extreme caution on hands and
n.   n.   v.   adj.   n.   prep.   adj.   adj.   n.
knees, Pat made his way through the tangled underbrush.

Building Compound, Complex, and Compound-complex Sentences

CHAPTER 3

The Compound Sentence

According to their structure, sentences are classified as *simple, compound, complex,* or *compound-complex.* You have studied how the various parts of speech are used to build the simple sentence. Now note these definitions:

131 A *clause* is a group of words containing a verb and a subject.

132 An *independent clause* contains a verb and a subject and expresses a complete idea. The independent clause can "stand alone" and "make sense."

133 A *dependent (subordinate) clause* contains a verb and a subject but does not express a complete idea. It is used as a part of speech.

INDEPENDENT CLAUSE: The sun is shining. (This group of words contains a verb, *is shining,* and a subject, *sun.* It expresses a complete idea and is, therefore, an independent clause.)

DEPENDENT CLAUSE: While the sun is shining.
Unless the sun is shining.
(These groups of words contain a verb and a subject, but they do not express a complete thought, therefore they are dependent clauses. One naturally asks, "What happens *while* the sun is shining, or what is it that fails to happen *unless* the sun is shining?")

85

134 **A *compound sentence* consists of two or more independent clauses.**

(1) The horse pricked up its ears, *but* Dan heard nothing.
(Here the two independent clauses are connected by a co-ordinate conjunction.)

(2) *Either* Albert did not know the signals, *or* the quarterback called the wrong play.
(Here the independent clauses are connected by correlative conjunctions.)

(3) That beam is weak; it may break.
(The two independent clauses here have no joining conjunction; they are separated by a semicolon.)

(4) That beam is weak; *therefore* we shall have to replace it.
(The two independent clauses are connected by a *conjunctive adverb*. A conjunctive adverb, as the name indicates, is an adverb used as a conjunction. Common conjunctive adverbs are *moreover, indeed, in fact, however, nevertheless, so, consequently, accordingly, thus, therefore, besides, also, furthermore, hence, likewise, otherwise, still, then, yet.*

(5) The alert horse pricked up its ears, but Dan heard nothing; his thoughts were far away.
(Three independent clauses form this compound sentence.)

135 **Only closely related and equally important ideas should be combined to make a compound sentence.**

136 **In using compound sentences, the conjunctions should express the proper relationship between the clauses.**

(1) **To join two clauses the second of which adds a related thought, use** *and, in addition, likewise, moreover, besides, furthermore, nor* (adds a negative thought).

(2) **To join two clauses the second of which gives an explanatory idea, use** *that is, for instance, for example.*

(3) **To join two clauses the second of which is a consequence of the first, use** *hence, therefore, accordingly, thus.*

(4) **To join two clauses the second of which is a contrast or an objection to the first, use** *but, yet, however, instead, nevertheless, still, on the contrary, whereas, on the other hand.*

(5) **To join two clauses the second of which gives an alternative, use** *or, otherwise, else.*

(6) **To join two clauses both of which need to be emphasized, use the correlatives** *either-or, neither-nor, not only-but also.*

137 **Do not confuse a compound sentence with a simple sentence that has a compound verb.** Divide the sentence before and after the conjunction. If it is a compound sentence, each part will make sense by itself.

George left, |and| I went with him. (*compound* sentence)
George left soon |and| did not return. (*simple* sentence)

"MY MOTHER LIKES TO READ IN THE EVENING; MY FATHER WATCHES TELEVISION; AND I STUDY MY LESSONS."

FOR PRACTICE AND APPLICATION

A. Tell whether each of the following sentences is simple or compound. Give the subjects and the predicates of each clause. Make this an oral activity.

1. Over the week end, Bill and I swim, play tennis, or hike.
2. Never before had I played badminton, and never before had I suffered such embarrassment.
3. The sun was setting, causing white clouds in the west and north to reflect many beautiful tints.
4. Paper and pencil lay there before me, but my mind was a blank.
5. The principal had spoken to us about our plans and had cautioned us to submit a full report.
6. Joe loves dogs; Elsie prefers cats.
7. Women shopped with frantic eagerness; some became very inconsiderate, but others kept their self-possession.
8. In that final semester Bob earned a letter in basketball, served as president of the student council, and ranked near the top in his studies.
9. Father likes variety in the weather; nevertheless, he dislikes rain to spoil his weekly golf game.
10. There was never a more disappointed crowd; nor was there ever a more unhappy team.

B. (1) Make single sentences of the pairs below. Use conjunctions that show proper relationship of ideas. (2) In parentheses after your sentences, using the numbers under *136,* name the relationship. (3) Punctuate properly.

1. Something must be done about finances. We may have to disband.
2. He has some constructive ideas. We should listen to him.
3. Our team lost the first game. The second was another story.
4. I needed help with the cleaning. I called Luella.
5. Dean does not care for ice cream. Dave likes it at every meal.
6. The house was broken into. Considerable damage was done.

Diagramming Compound Sentences

Each clause of a compound sentence is diagrammed in the same way a simple sentence is diagrammed.

Compound Sentence, Two Independent Clauses

Either Albert did not know the signals, or the quarterback called the wrong play.

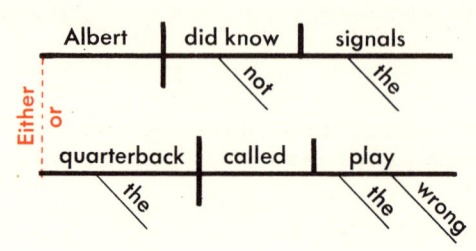

Compound Sentence, Three Independent Clauses

The alert horse pricked up its ears, but Dan heard nothing; his thoughts were far away.

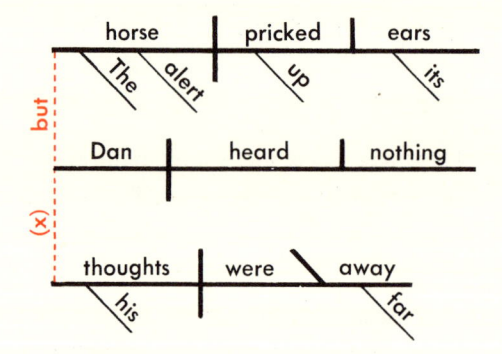

FOR PRACTICE AND APPLICATION

A. Diagram the following sentences. Not every one is a compound sentence. Put the diagrams on the board for class analysis and discussion.

1. I opened the door and stood there, but nothing moved in the shadowy room facing me; suddenly I heard a low moan.
2. You must not have mailed that letter, or we should have had a reply.
3. Rabbits stole into our garden and nibbled the plants down to the ground.
4. Nobody has called me, nor do I expect any news.
5. Prospects for our team look gloomy; however, we are not yet giving up hope.
6. After breakfast, cut the grass; then trim the hedge and the other shrubbery.
7. Have you bought your ticket to the banquet, or do you have a date for it?
8. Jack made no reply but stood there with clenched fists and angry eyes.

B. For more practice, diagram and explain the sentences in *A*, page 87.

The Complex Sentence

138 **A** *complex sentence* **consists of one independent clause and at least one dependent (subordinate) clause.**

You have read that a dependent clause does not express a complete idea and that it is used as a part of speech. The dependent clause may be used as an *adjective,* as an *adverb,* or as a *noun.*

USING DEPENDENT CLAUSES AS ADJECTIVES

139 **The** *adjective clause,* **like the adjective, modifies a noun or a pronoun. It is introduced by a relative pronoun,** *who, whose, whom, which, that,* **or by the subordinate conjunctions** *where* **or** *when.*

Examples of Dependent Clauses Used as Adjectives

1. The boy who is speaking is my brother.
2. Give it to him who needs it.
3. The racket that I bought has nylon strings.
4. This is the place where we had a flat tire.
5. The boy who caught the fish that are displayed here is ten years old.
6. Tom Nelson, who arrived today and who is a fine tennis player, will teach us the game. (*compound adjective clauses*)

The relative pronoun is an important part of the adjective clause. It may be a subject, a direct object, an object of a preposition, or a possessive modifier. *When* or *where* in an adjective clause modifies the verb in that clause.

139a **The main idea of a complex sentence should be put into the independent clause.** An adjective clause, in other words, should never express the chief sentence idea.

139b **Adjective clauses that are not essential to sentence meaning should be set off by commas.** Such clauses are called "nonrestrictive." (Why is that a good name?) Clauses that are essential to sentence meaning are called "restrictive." Adjective clauses beginning with *that* are always restrictive.

    The man *that you saw* came back again. (*restrictive*)
    Mr. Smith, *whom you have met,* called today. (*nonrestrictive*)

FOR PRACTICE AND APPLICATION

A. By turning one or more sentences into adjective clauses, combine the following into good complex sentences. Be sure that the important idea is in the independent clause. Punctuate carefully. Exchange papers and read your sentences aloud.

1. I walked to school with Dave Evarts. He lives next door.
2. This game was our first victory. We had not expected to win it.
3. Bring me the pliers. They are lying on the kitchen table.
4. My birthday fell on a Saturday this year. As usual, it was a real occasion.
5. For dessert we had pecan pie. It is my favorite.
6. Mr. Briggs leads an interesting life. He is an FBI agent.
7. Read the instructions carefully. They are printed on the label.
8. The road grew narrower and narrower. It was very rough.
9. Dick will be elected. He is popular. His record is excellent.
10. The wind had been howling mournfully. Suddenly it stopped.

B. Write two sentences containing restrictive adjective clauses and two containing nonrestrictive clauses. Punctuate them correctly. Exchange papers for checking.

CORRELATING ENGLISH WITH YOUR OTHER CLASSES

Bring into English class a report or other paper that you are writing for one of your classes. Go over it carefully to see where you can improve it by using adjective clauses to turn simple sentences into complex ones.

USING DEPENDENT CLAUSES AS ADVERBS

140 The *adverb clause,* like the adverb, modifies a verb (including the verb form in an infinitive), an adjective, or an adverb.

140a Adverb clauses are introduced by subordinate conjunctions, such as *although, though, as, since, than, unless, whereas, whether, in order that, so that, provided that, as if, as though, as soon as, even if, where, when.*

Examples of dependent clauses used as adverbs to modify (1) *verb,* (2) *adjective,* (3) *adverb,* (4) *infinitive,* (5) *participle* are these:

1. When the bell rings, everyone hurries into the building.
2. Today is warmer than yesterday was.
3. The boys come here oftener than they came before.
4. He wishes to leave before the rain begins.
5. Grumbling as he did so, Don retraced his steps.

140b Sometimes an adverb clause is *elliptical;* that is, certain words are understood.

>The green dress is newer *than the red one.*
> (The complete clause is *than the red one is new.*)
>*Although annoyed with me,* Father kept his temper.
> (The complete clause is *Although he was annoyed with me.*)

140c For variety, a sentence may begin with an adverb clause. Generally, such an arrangement is desirable only if meaning is the same as when the sentence is in normal order.

INVERTED ORDER: While we waited, night began to fall.

NORMAL ORDER: Night began to fall while we waited.

Note that sentence meaning is the same in both cases.

Watch sentence arrangement particularly if a pronoun and its antecedent are involved, as in this example:

GOOD: When *he* saw me, *Dick* began to run.

>If the sentence is put into natural order, the sense remains the same:
>>Dick began to run when he saw me.

DOUBTFUL: When *Dick* saw me, *he* began to run.

>If the sentence is put into natural order, the sense is no longer the same:
>>He began to run when Dick saw me.

140d Do not mistake the *nominative absolute* **for an adverb clause.** It is an expression made up of a noun followed by a participle or a participial phrase. It is so named because it has no connection with the rest of the sentence; that is, it is an *independent element.* It is never an adverb clause, although it has the force of one.

>*My foot having slipped,* I tumbled down the muddy bank.
> (*My foot having slipped* has the force of *Because my foot had slipped.*)

FOR PRACTICE AND APPLICATION

A. Decide whether the following sentences containing adverb clauses would be better with their subjects reversed. For any that you think should be changed, be ready to tell why.

1. When the man had eaten, he returned to work.
2. As she passed me, the girl turned her face away.
3. Although Jake was angry, he kept his temper.
4. Before the timid child could answer, he was sent from the room.
5. When Mother called me again, she sounded annoyed.
6. After they had argued briefly, the boys reached an agreement.

B. Write three sentences containing introductory adverb clauses. Begin them with the subordinate conjunctions *when, as, before.* Read your sentences aloud. The class will decide whether you have written them correctly.

CORRELATING ENGLISH WITH YOUR OTHER CLASSES

As you write papers for any class, check to see that you follow Rule 140c.

USING DEPENDENT CLAUSES AS NOUNS

141 The noun clause may be used within the sentence in the various ways that a noun is used; that is, as *subject, appositive, predicate nominative, direct object, indirect object, objective complement, object of the preposition,* **or** *retained object.*

To identify a noun clause, try substituting the pronoun *it* for what you think is the clause. (If the clause definitely refers to a *person*, substitute the correct form of the pronouns *he* or *she*.)

141a Noun clauses, unlike adjective and adverb clauses, are a part of the independent clause.
1. *What he has done* does not concern us. (*subject*)
2. He believes *that John told the truth*. (*direct object*)
3. My theory is *that he will refuse*. (*predicate nominative*)
4. He may ask for *what he wants*. (*object of preposition*)
5. It is a fact *that he is late*. (*apposition with subject*)
6. He made me *what I am today*. (*objective complement*)
7. Give *whomever you find* a share. (*indirect object*)
8. He was given *what he had earned*. (*retained object*)

141b Many of the words that introduce adjective and adverb clauses may introduce noun clauses. Such words include *that, whether, who, whom, what, how, when, where, whoever,* **and** *whomever.*

FOR PRACTICE AND APPLICATION

(1) Supply a noun clause to fill the blank in each of the following sentences. (2) After each sentence, tell how the clause is used. Compare your work in class or in your small groups.
1. I have decided ....
2. Do not judge a person by ....
3. It is true ....
4. .... has not been announced.
5. I have told you ....
6. Tell .... the facts in the case.
7. We were told ....
8. Hard work has made Mr. Lucas ....

PRACTICE IN TYPES OF SENTENCES ACCORDING TO FORM

A. (1) Copy the following complex sentences. (2) Underscore each independent clause with two lines and each dependent clause with one line. (3) State whether the dependent clause is used as an adjective, as an adverb, or as a noun. (4) If it is used as an adjective or an adverb, name the word modified. (5) If it is used as a noun, state whether it is a subject, an object, a predicate noun, an object of a preposition, or an appositive. As you go over the sentences in class, be prepared to give the reason for your analysis.

Remember: To determine clauses, find the verbs first; then find the subject for each verb.

1. The boy who plays center is president of the senior class.
2. Those who come first will receive souvenirs.
3. The large house that stands on the corner has been vacant for a year.
4. That is the root over which I tripped.
5. Tod, who tried to hit when he should have bunted, was fined.
6. Although you may not care for it, I like this one.
7. Your report is far better than mine.
8. When the sun shines, my canary sings.
9. What he has said sounds interesting.
10. I thought that you had left for Louisiana.
11. The trouble is that we lack reserve strength.
12. I have looked everywhere for a coat that I can afford.
13. All who were within shouting distance hurried to the spot.
14. It seems certain that Tom will be elected.

B. State whether each of the following sentences is simple, compound, or complex. In each instance give the reason for your statement. Tell how the dependent clauses in the complex sentences are used, as you did in exercise *A*. Make this an oral activity.

Remember: Find the verbs and their subjects first.

1. No one who had heard the speech questioned its truth.
2. The trees growing in that gully have begun to die.
3. You may be right, but I have serious doubts about the matter.
4. Lee has always said exactly what he thinks.
5. Although strangers to each other, the men soon became friends.
6. His actions are a good clue to what he really believes.
7. The younger boys played ball, but the older ones fished.
8. The younger boys played ball while the older boys fished.
9. A narrow iron stairway led to a roof where many people dozed in the sunshine.
10. Alternately reading and dozing, one man in a pair of bright blue trunks occasionally emitted a long groan which he invariably ended with a staccato grunt.
11. Do you know where Mother had gone?
12. Have you read any novel written by this author?

C. Tell whether or not each of the following groups of words is a sentence. *Remember:* A dependent clause, even though it has a verb and a subject, cannot be a sentence if it stands alone. In each instance tell why the group of words is or is not a sentence. Make this a written or an oral activity.

1. A large dog running up a stairway is a picture of smooth motion.
2. One time when I saw a large dog running up a stairway.
3. The man twirling a rope over the top of his head and occasionally lassoing one of us spectators.
4. There stood a man in a top hat, twirling a rope over his head and occasionally lassoing one of us spectators.
5. Even though their car had a bad knock and they seemed to have not a care.
6. Even though their car had a bad knock, they seemed to have not a care.
7. After the boy had been tied securely to a chair, like a Houdini, he extricated himself.
8. After the boy had been tied securely to a chair and, like a Houdini, had extricated himself.
9. Because they had never seen a large circus, we invited them to go; and they, in turn, offered to drive us there in a car.
10. After a perfect take-off and after all the usual precautions had been carefully observed.

D. Here are three simple sentences. Turn each one into three different complex sentences containing (1) an adjective clause, (2) an adverb clause, and (3) a noun clause.

Example: I questioned the man.
> *After he had eaten,* I questioned the man. (*adverb*)
> I questioned the man *who had been captured.* (*adjective*)
> I questioned the man about *what he had said.* (*noun*)

1. This man seems honest.
2. The farm has been sold.
3. The stranger told an interesting story.

Diagramming Complex Sentences

Dependent Clauses Used as Adjectives

The boy who is speaking is my brother.

This is the place where we had the flat tire.

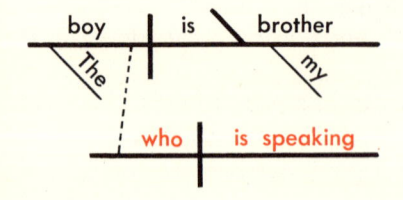

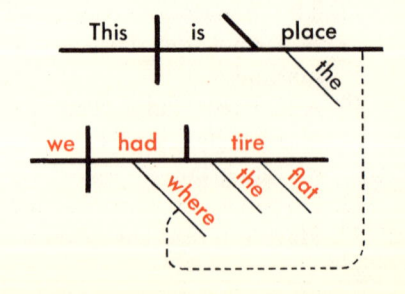

Compound Adjective Clauses

Tom Nelson, who arrived today and who is a fine tennis player, will teach us the game.

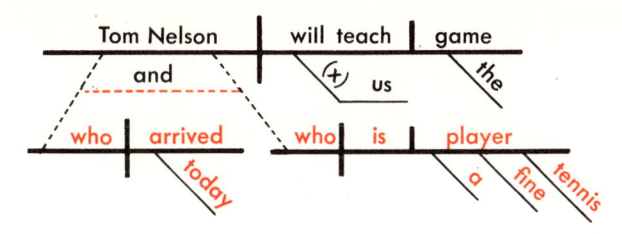

Dependent Clauses Used as Adverbs

When the bell rings, we hurry into the building.

The boys come here oftener than they came before.

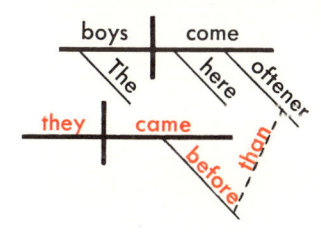

Modifying an Infinitive

He wishes to leave before the rain begins.

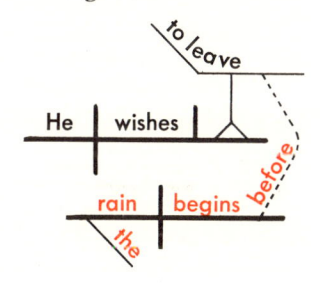

Modifying a Participle

Grumbling as he did so, Don retraced his steps.

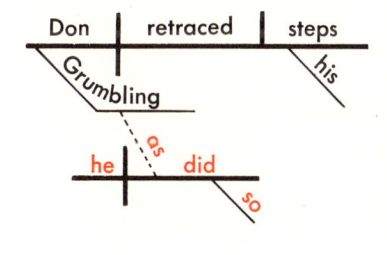

Elliptical Clauses

The green dress is newer than the red one.

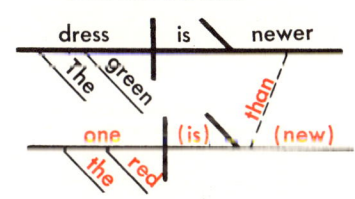

Although sorry for you, I can do nothing now.

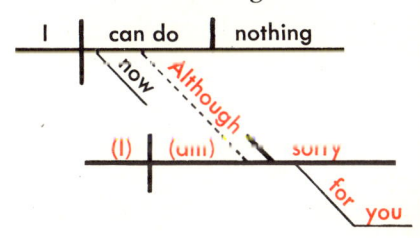

Nominative Absolute
My foot having slipped, I tumbled down the muddy bank.

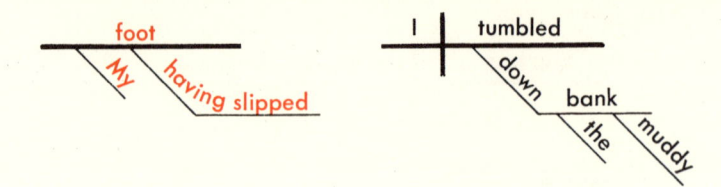

Dependent Clauses Used as Nouns

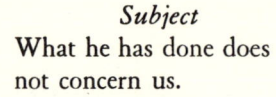

Subject
What he has done does not concern us.

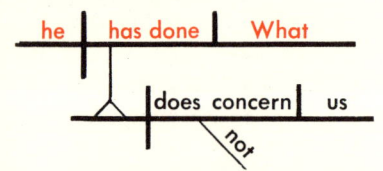

Direct Object
He believes that John told the truth.

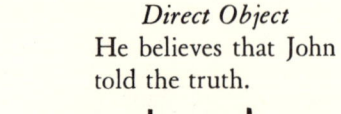

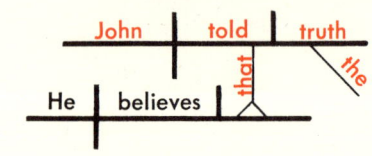

Predicate Nominative
My theory is that he will refuse.

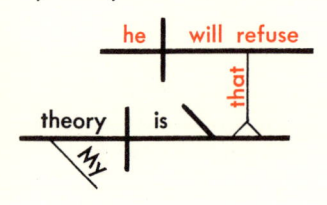

Object of Preposition
He may ask for what he wants.

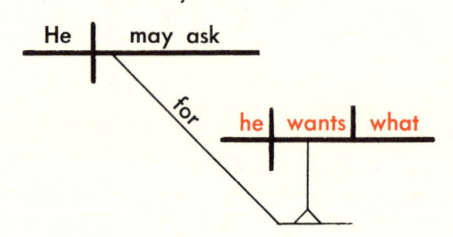

Apposition
It is a fact that he is late.

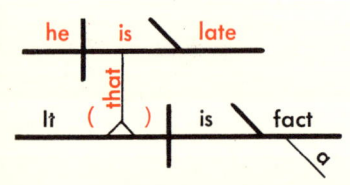

Objective Complement
He made me what I am today.

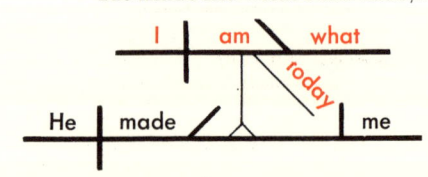

Indirect Object
Give whomever you find a share.

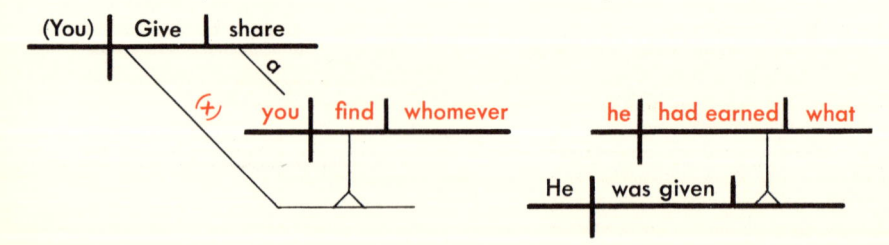

Retained Object
He was given what he had earned.

FOR PRACTICE AND APPLICATION

A. Diagram the following sentences containing adjective, adverb, and noun clauses. Put diagrams on the board and explain them orally. Begin with the independent clause; name its parts in a specific, orderly way; then do the same for the dependent clause. Diagramming is a useless skill if you do not know exactly what you are doing. *Warning:* There is one nominative absolute.

1. When I looked around, the tall stranger had disappeared.
2. Tell me what is worrying you.
3. Has anyone seen the camera that I left on my desk?
4. He should be careful about what he does in this matter.
5. It seems strange that no one notified me about your arrival.
6. The house where I was born was torn down recently.
7. Where we shall spend our vacation has not been decided.
8. Is Lester older than you?
9. Although new, this suit already looks shabby.
10. The sun having set, darkness came quickly.

B. For more practice, diagram the sentences in *A* and *B*, page 93. (Not all those in *B* are complex.) Put the diagrams on the board for oral analysis.

The Compound-complex Sentence

142 The *compound-complex* sentence consists of two or more independent clauses and one or more dependent (subordinate) clauses. In other words, it is simply a combination of the compound sentence and the complex sentence.

You should have no difficulty in recognizing or in using compound-complex sentences if you find all verbs and their subjects first. That procedure will tell you how many clauses there are. Then you determine whether the clauses are dependent or independent.

independent   *independent*   *dependent*
John went to school, but Arthur stayed at home because he had a cold.

dependent   *independent*
If he changes his mind, we shall know beyond a doubt

dependent   *independent*
that Henry has learned his lesson; but time will tell.

FOR PRACTICE AND APPLICATION

A. Copy the following compound-complex sentences. Underline each independent clause with two lines, and each dependent clause with one line. Then explain the use of each dependent clause, as you did in *A,* page 93.
1. After the tornado had struck, Jackson's garage was a complete wreck, and Simpson's barn had no doors.
2. The plans can be changed, but I know one man who will object strongly.
3. When the half ended, we were trailing by three touchdowns; the gloom in our dressing room was thick, because we had been confident of victory.
4. His suit was new; his shoes were new; and he had bought a new hat that he tilted jauntily over one eye.
5. I heard the noise again, and the sound was one that gave me cold chills.
6. James answered, "That was all that could be done," and everyone agreed.

B. Label each of the following sentences as *simple, compound, complex,* or *compound-complex.* In each instance give the reason for your label.
1. Stanley and his brother, Robert, planned to go with Sam on his trip.
2. Although he searched for hours, Tom could find no trace of his pen.
3. Luella wrote the original story, but Sue revised it.
4. Timothy built the wall of stones gathered on his rambles to the quarry.
5. It is easy to understand his reason for calling this valley the most beautiful spot that he has ever seen.
6. Neither of my friends asked me to change my mind.
7. They built the house; then, after they had planted a beautiful garden, they sold their property and moved to Florida.
8. That he is a thief cannot be denied.
9. Betty and Sally whispered and giggled.
10. Did you say that it was this dog that barked the warning?
11. The simple truth is that he does not like fishing.
12. A vacation should be restful, but many people do not get rest until they return to their work.
13. Looking from a tall building over a small city of many trees is a sight that I always enjoy.
14. Although the rabbits apparently were scurrying around aimlessly, closer observation revealed that they were having a well-organized game.
15. Shadows cast by the moon are somehow softer than those cast by the sun.
16. Don went fishing, but Ronnie went to the tennis matches, because his friend was playing in the finals.
17. Entrusted with responsibility, Edgar assumed a new attitude; he was no longer the practical joker.

C. Write compound-complex sentences containing (1) an adjective clause, (2) an adverb clause, (3) a noun clause, (4) two dependent clauses. Indicate verbs, subjects, and the kinds of clauses as in the examples on page 97. Have sentences put on the board for class evaluation.

Diagramming Compound-complex Sentences

The clauses of a compound-complex sentence are diagrammed just as they would be in a compound or a complex sentence. Note these examples.

Two Independent Clauses and One Dependent Clause
John went to school, but Arthur stayed at home because he had a cold.

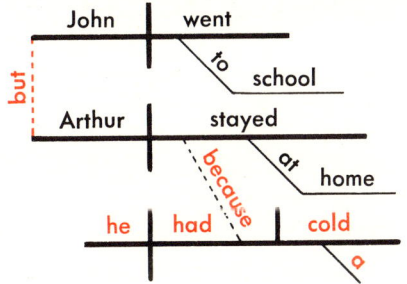

Two Independent Clauses and Two Dependent Clauses
If he changes his mind, we shall know beyond a doubt that Henry has learned his lesson; however, time will tell.

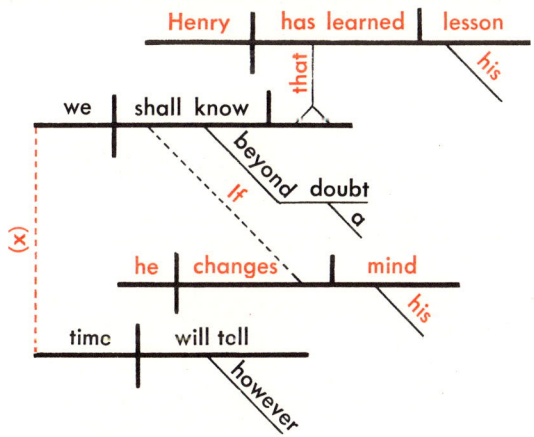

FOR PRACTICE AND APPLICATION

A. Diagram the following compound-complex sentences. Put them on the board and explain them orally.

1. Those clouds promise snow; we should return before we are caught in a blizzard.
2. Although we have gone only a mile from camp, darkness will soon fall, and we might lose our way.
3. Were you ever in a storm that struck suddenly, or don't you remember?
4. Here is the money that I owe you; I am glad to have finished the payments.

B. For additional practice, diagram and explain the sentences in *A*, page 98.

CHAPTER 4

Expressing Ideas in Effective Sentences

The material in the preceding chapters was designed to help you not only in speaking and writing correctly, but also in recognizing sentence elements and sentences. This chapter goes more definitely into sentence recognition and the writing of effective sentences. Some of the points stressed in this chapter have been covered under various rules for correct usage, but they are worth repeating here.

1. Avoiding Fragments and Run-on Sentences

143a **Complete the sentence!**

You have learned that a sentence is a group of words that makes an assertion or statement about something or someone. Groups of words that do not meet this requirement are known as *fragments*.

In conversation, fragments are often properly used as answers.

    Where do you live?
        At Hinman and Woodlawn.
    Are you happy in your work?
        Yes, very happy.
    When do you plan to leave?
        Tomorrow or the day after.

There are other occasions when fragments may be correctly used. Often, however, a writer unintentionally uses fragments instead of complete sentences. Developing "sentence sense" (that is, a feeling for the complete assertion) is essential to good writing.

A good test to determine whether a group of words is a sentence or a fragment is to take the group by itself and read it aloud. If it seems to make a statement that is understandable, it is probably a sentence—containing a predicate, and a subject about which the predication is made.

There are many types of sentence fragments, but basically each fragment falls into one of these classifications:

1. *A group of words without a verb or predicate*
   The boys working hard to complete their project.

2. *A group of words without a subject*
   Certainly did not say much.

3. *A group of words lacking both predicate and subject*
   Depending upon the weather and the condition of the roads.

4. *A group of words forming a dependent clause*
   After he had finally won a match.

FOR PRACTICE AND APPLICATION

A. Which of the following groups of words are sentences? Which are fragments? Tell what is lacking in each fragment. Make this an oral activity.

1. Shooting free throws and other shots from a standing position.
2. Once he "gets set," Dick has a deadly eye.
3. Practices by the hour at a basket in his back yard.
4. Underhand shots more easily guarded than others.
5. The coach likes each man to have his own style, but he doesn't encourage underhand shooting.
6. Insists upon the ability to shoot left-handed.
7. Dribbling low to the floor but shooting while at the top of a jump.
8. Although he has never taught us a delayed offense.
9. Fast-breaking teams, running up high scores, are usually more interesting to watch.
10. Small, fast men, especially a team of good dribblers, drawing slower, taller men completely out of position.
11. There was such a team in our league last year.
12. Only after they had reached the semifinals.
13. In four games, averaging forty-five points a game, and placing every one of their men in the scoring column.
14. They were the most popular team.
15. Finally defeated by a tall, fast team, which controlled the rebounds at both baskets.

B. If your instructor so directs, make complete sentences of the fragments in *A*. Read your complete sentences aloud in class. Note how your interpretations of the sentence fragments vary.

C. Which of the following groups of words make complete assertions? Which do not? Rewrite those that contain fragments. Exchange papers for checking.

1. The guests have left.
2. Depending on the weather, which looks threatening.
3. He will return in the spring. When the ships can sail again.
4. On one condition, that the president resign.
5. There are two ways of doing it. The wrong way and the right way.
6. She decided that she would go, after all. For his sake.
7. The work has all been done. Ages ago.
8. For one whole day, fearing that the heavy sea would tear the ship to pieces and that the cargo would be lost.
9. Christmas came none too soon. For Billy and Lois.
10. The new plane is faster and stronger.

D. Write the following paragraph, correcting all sentence fragments. You may have to add words in some places. Compare paragraphs in class.

A beach-rest chair is a strange object. And an entertaining one. It consists of two rows of wooden slats. One end of one row is attached to one end of the other row with a sort of hinge. Which is really a spring. This spring holds one row upright to form a back rest. The other resting directly upon the ground. The beach-rest is not entirely to be trusted. It may throw the sitter over backwards, letting him land on the base of his skull. If he suddenly moves his legs, which act as a lever for the back rest. It is possible, too, that all the slats may start a simultaneous, gradual, sliding movement in one general direction. As a result, the sitter's body in a strange position diagonal to itself. Then he seems at odds with the world and wonders why the originator called the thing a beach-*rest*.

FOLLOW-UP

Proofread every paper for every class to make sure that you avoid unintentional sentence fragments.

143b   Do not overload the sentence!

You have probably waited at a railroad crossing while a long freight train went by. Perhaps you counted the cars and wondered how one engine could pull so many cars so fast. Your teacher has wondered, in the same way, how one of your sentences could drag so many ideas along.

Railroad cars have couplings. New cars can be added to a train until the engine's load capacity has been reached. Students sometimes use their *and*'s and *but*'s as couplings, adding one thought to another until they are out of breath or until they fill the page. But a sentence is not like a train. *It must have only one primary thought, and all its parts must relate to that thought.*

FOR PRACTICE AND APPLICATION

The following four sentences are overloaded. Break them down into shorter sentences so that each will contain but one main thought. Recombine all elements that belong together. You may use compound, complex, or compound-complex sentences, but be sure that each sentence has *unity*. Sentences of not more than twenty-five words are usually most effective.

1. When the plane landed at Cleveland, weather conditions had become very bad, but Jerry insisted on taking off again because he was eager to see his mother, since it was her birthday, the first one since Jerry had entered the air service, and she was very proud of him.

2. Roslyn knew then that she was in love with Ben, so much in love that she could think of nothing or no one else, and she resolved to call him up at once even though it would cost a great deal and her mother had frequently warned her against extravagance, which had been one of her chief weaknesses in college.

3. Mathematics is a very hard subject, at least it is for me, and I had hoped I would not have to take it, but that attractive young instructor to whom I went for counseling told me that I would need it if I planned to take a degree, and of course I do want a degree because my parents have their hearts set on my getting one.

4. I saw Clark Gable in his new movie yesterday, and I found him more charming than ever; he was playing the role of a bomber pilot on his first mission, and he was frightened at first, but after he ran into antiaircraft fire he seemed to forget his fears and really inspired the other members of the crew to do their best.

143c Avoid running together two or more sentences. Such a blunder results in a *run-on sentence*.

(1) **Do not use a comma to join two sentences.** This error is the *comma fault*. It can be corrected in several ways.

WRONG: The circus is in town, I plan to go.
RIGHT: The circus is in town. I plan to go. (*two sentences*)
RIGHT: The circus is in town; I plan to go. (*compound sentence with semicolon*)
RIGHT: The circus is in town, and I plan to go. (*compound sentence with co-ordinate conjunction*)
RIGHT: As the circus is in town, I plan to go. (*complex sentence*)
WRONG: I am tired, however, it is too early to go to bed.
    (Here the fault is in placing a comma before a conjunctive adverb between two clauses.)
RIGHT: I am tired; however, it is too early to go to bed.
RIGHT: I am tired. However, it is too early to go to bed.
RIGHT: Although I am tired, it is too early to go to bed.

(2) **Do not make the even more serious error of running sentences together with no punctuation between.**

WRONG: The girl boarded the bus she didn't notice the number.
(This error may be corrected in the same ways as shown in the examples illustrating the comma fault.)

(3) **Do not string sentences together by the use of a succession of *and*'s or *and so*'s.**

POOR: Dick is taking Jean to the dance *and* I am taking Lois *and so* we plan to go together *and* we should have a good time.

BETTER: Dick is taking Jean to the dance; I am taking Lois. We plan to go together and should have a good time.

FOR PRACTICE AND APPLICATION

A. Combine the following pairs of statements into single sentences. Be sure to avoid the comma blunder. Compare papers in class or in your small groups to see what different methods were used.

1. Sylvia had made an excellent record in school. Therefore the store officials felt no hesitation about employing her.
2. The train had been late in starting. However, it soon made up for lost time.
3. Sheridan had a great deal of faith in his men. Nevertheless, he decided to make one final inspection.
4. The leader of the gang had been arrested, and all the loot recovered. In other words, the story had a happy ending.
5. Barry wanted very much to go to college. On the other hand, the prospect of a trip to Europe seemed very attractive to him.

B. Find the comma blunders in the following sentences and correct them. Which of the sentences are not in need of correction? Explain why.

1. Frances, by the way, was not enthusiastic about her new job, in fact, she thoroughly disliked it.
2. One member of the crew was hurt, however, according to my information the injury was not serious.
3. Clara, whom you met tonight, joined the club last year, therefore she is eligible for the position.
4. The neighbors objected to the disturbance, and therefore, contrary to the original plan, the party disbanded early.
5. The problem was difficult, one had to study it a long time.
6. The gas supply was low, moreover, it was rapidly getting dark.
7. Preparations have been completed, the guests have come, and we can begin.
8. The foghorn had given warning, nevertheless, the tug crashed into us.
9. We have great confidence in our statesmen, we shall however, overlook no precaution.
10. The whistles were blowing, the crowds were cheering, and the bands were playing, in short, the town was agog.

C. The following paragraphs contain comma blunders, run-on sentences, and overloaded sentences. Write the paragraphs in correct sentences. Exchange papers and evaluate the paragraphs.

Living in the North Woods hundreds of miles from any settlement is not easy it's hard work. Many times it snows for days and nights and all the air is white and falling, falling, falling so that one can't even see out the window and it feels as if the whole world were filled except for the small clear space in the cabin and it is stifling for one who has a tendency toward claustrophobia. When the temperature drops to forty below, the burning of two whole trees may keep the cabin warm for twenty-four hours. Keeping supplied with firewood is a problem in itself, however, cutting down trees in snow five feet deep is no task for a weakling.

There are compensations, of course, for instance, one can be assured that an evening's reading will not be interrupted, and the orchestration of a wolf pack can be far more thrilling than the best boogiewoogie a radio disc jockey might offer, furthermore when every living thing is fighting for existence birds become closer companions than they could ever be under any conditions back in civilization.

D. The following paragraph contains sentence fragments, comma blunders, run-on sentences, and overloaded sentences. Rewrite the paragraph, correcting all the sentence errors. Add words if necessary. Compare versions in class.

The Ozarks offer many inviting spots for camping. Swimming in clear streams, fishing, boating, and hiking, all interesting pastimes. There are resorts, they offer a vacation with the companionship of many people. We prefer to carry packs far into the woods and set up tents. Where no one else is seen for days and where there are no open fields or farmhouses. One time two of us set out. We wanted to hike to a small crossroads store about three miles from camp and we were talking and looking, we missed our trail although we did not realize it at once and all of a sudden we knew we were lost. We sat down. To take our bearings. Then we began again. Every cluster of trees looked alike, every open glade was the same, no vantage point revealed familiar landmarks. We slept out. That night. Finally, about noon of the next day, we stumbled upon an old road. And, eventually, upon an amused farm boy who was on his way to the store, it did not seem very funny to us.

CORRELATING ENGLISH WITH YOUR OTHER CLASSES

Proofread a paper that you are now preparing for this or for another class. Be sure that you have used in the paper no run-on sentences, comma blunders, or overloaded sentences.

2. Showing Relations between Statements within Sentences

Closely related statements, as you have seen, may frequently be combined into a single sentence. Now examine some ways in which the exact nature of the relationship between statements may be indicated.

144a Use *co-ordinate conjunctions* to join statements of equal rank or importance. Be sure to choose the conjunction that indicates clearly the relationship between the clauses.

1. Scrooge was a miserly man. Everybody detested him.
1. Scrooge was a miserly man, *and* everybody detested him. (The conjunction shows a *plus* relationship.)
2. Jefferson believed in the people. Hamilton felt they could not be trusted.
2. Jefferson believed in the people, *but* Hamilton felt they could not be trusted. (The conjunction shows *contrast*.)
3. You get complete satisfaction. You get your money back.
3. *Either* you get complete satisfaction, *or* you get your money back. (The conjunctions show *choice* or an alternative.)

FOR PRACTICE AND APPLICATION

Combine the following pairs into single sentences. Show the relationship of the statements by using the appropriate co-ordinate conjunction.

1. They lost the battle. They won the war.
2. Having seen the effects of the new plan, Harvey could not deny its usefulness. He could not bring himself to support it.
3. The shock proved too much. The old man was forced to retire.
4. You go. I shall resign.
5. The examinations were over. The students prepared to go home.
6. The light was too dim. The type was too small.

In one of the preceding pairs, the meaning may be changed by using different conjunctions. Find the pair and supply the different conjunctions.

144b Use subordinate conjunctions to join statements or ideas of unequal value.

Relationships between some independent statements may be indicated by converting one of the statements into a subordinate clause and combining it with the other. This process is known as *subordination*. The less important statement of two should be subordinated to give the reader an exact idea of the meaning.

One way to achieve subordination is to use adverbial clauses which are introduced by subordinate conjunctions. *

1. Move your arms rapidly back and forth. Pretend that you are rowing a boat.
1. Move your arms rapidly back and forth *as if* you were rowing a boat.
2. The weather has been cold for several days. Nevertheless the water in the pond has not frozen.
2. *Although* the weather has been cold for several days, the water in the pond has not frozen.
3. The new junior college may open soon. The legislature must first pass the educational appropriations bill.
3. The new junior college may open soon *if* the legislature passes the educational appropriations bill.

FOR PRACTICE AND APPLICATION

Combine each of the following pairs of statements into a single sentence by means of a subordinate conjunction. Make any other change that may be needed. Subordinate the less important idea. Exchange papers for criticism.

1. The applicant will sign his name to each of the documents. The documents should be signed immediately after the ceremony.
2. The appropriations bill probably will not become law. The President does not like it. He thinks it is a pork-barrel bill. He is expected to veto it.
3. The new building will be ready in time for the fall term. Some of the laboratory equipment will not arrive until February.
4. Sheldon defended the backboards well in yesterday's basketball game. He has a disadvantage in height.
5. Dad said that the lawn had to be mowed. It must be done before Jack went fishing with Bill and Jerry.
6. The shorter winter trail was impassable. They took the longer trail around Gooseneck Lake.
7. We must do proper research work on this paper. All our efforts will otherwise have been wasted.
8. Eugene demanded that he be given sole authority. Then he agreed to direct the efforts of the group.
9. Ed had made three hits and had raised his batting average considerably. Ed would rather have had his team win the game.

144c Use relative pronouns to subordinate ideas. Turn the less important ideas into adjective clauses.

1. The funeral train finally arrived at Springfield. Springfield had been Lincoln's home for many years.
1. The funeral train finally arrived at Springfield, *which* had been Lincoln's home for many years.

*See page 72 for a list of subordinate conjunctions.

2. The speaker, overcome with emotion, turned to the chairman. The chairman quickly handed him a glass of water.
2. The speaker, overcome with emotion, turned to the chairman, *who* quickly handed him a glass of water.
3. Benedict finally called upon the old family lawyer. He had relied upon the lawyer's advice even as a child.
3. Benedict finally called upon the old family lawyer, upon *whose* advice he had relied even as a child.

FOR PRACTICE AND APPLICATION

Combine each of the following pairs of sentences into a single sentence by means of a relative pronoun. Make any other changes that may be needed. Exchange papers for checking.

1. Suddenly Frances remembered that she had not done her homework. The homework had been assigned several days before.
2. Not long ago, Mrs. Fairchild received a visit from her cousin. Mrs. Fairchild had spent many happy days in this cousin's home.
3. These are the candidates who made the best scores. They will be given the jobs.
4. During our trip we spent a week in Atlanta. It is a wonderful place to visit.
5. Some birds are able to withstand the coldest weather. They have heavy layers of fat and oily feathers. The feathers repel water and snow.
6. The papers were piled high on Roger's desk. They had to be read before Roger left for his vacation.
7. The breaks of the game often determine the winner. They are made by the more alert team.
8. The chairs were placed in two long, straight rows. It made the room look stiff.
9. The hill had been taken over by an army of mosquitoes. Claire used to sit on that hill and gaze across the valley.

144d Subordinate or condense ideas by the use of words and phrases.

By using a *word*

My uncle owned a fine dog. It was a collie.
My uncle owned a fine *collie*.

By using a *prepositional phrase*

The children enjoy playing croquet. They play on the front lawn.
The children enjoy playing croquet *on the front lawn*.

By using an *appositive*

P. R. Ross is our new coach. He lettered in four sports at Duke.
P. R. Ross, *our new coach,* lettered in four sports at Duke.

By using a *participial phrase*
>The children cleared the table. Then they began to play games.
>*Having cleared the table,* the children began to play games.

By using a *nominative absolute*
>The storm had ended; therefore we proceeded on our way.
>*The storm having ended,* we proceeded on our way.

By using an *infinitive phrase*
>The road that you should take is this one.
>The road *to take* is this one.
>I do not know what I should do.
>I do not know what *to do.*

FOR PRACTICE AND APPLICATION

Rewrite the following sentences, subordinating or condensing ideas by the use of words and phrases. Go over your papers in class.

1. The team had a hard scrimmage. Afterward each player had to make three baskets from the twenty-foot line.
2. Marian was elected president. She immediately appointed committees for important projects.
3. Patricia received a fine present from her father. It was a lapel watch.
4. Bruce has a favorite place in the library. He always sits near the unabridged dictionary.
5. Don had played first base all season. He was surprised when the coach asked him to play third.
6. Dinner was ready. We hurried to our places at the table.
7. Gerry repeatedly ran to the window. She was obviously expecting someone whom she really wanted to see.
8. Larry hopes that he will be able to help us.
9. Harold had visited every museum in town. He began to look farther afield to carry on his research.
10. Dollar Lake is shallow but clear. It takes its name from its shape.
11. The price of tickets has gone up. I shall probably see fewer movies.
12. The directions that you should follow are on the board.

CORRELATING ENGLISH WITH YOUR OTHER CLASSES

Check a paper that you are now writing or have recently written for one of your classes. Examine every sentence to see whether you can subordinate or condense some statements to give a more exact picture of your idea.

3. Establishing Clear Reference in Sentences

145a **Avoid faulty reference of pronouns.**

In formal writing, a pronoun should refer to a definite antecedent. When the antecedent is ambiguous (doubtful), the reader cannot determine definitely to what word the pronoun refers.

Poor: The train was delayed, *which* caused the speaker to arrive late at the meeting. (A pronoun should not refer to a whole clause.)
Good: The train was delayed, with the result that the speaker arrived late at the meeting.
Good: The train being delayed, the speaker arrived . . .
Good: Because the train was delayed, the speaker arrived . . .

Poor: Eggs are eighty cents a dozen. *This* is one of the reasons so few are sold here. (A pronoun should not refer to a whole clause.)
Better: Since eggs are eighty cents a dozen, very few are sold here.

Confusing: The lawyer told his client that *he* must pay the court costs. (*Who* must pay? Ambiguous antecedent.)
Better: The lawyer told his client, "You must pay the court costs."

Poor: Farmer Brown sold the old mare to his neighbor, *which* had given him so much trouble. (The relative pronoun is too far from the word that it modifies.)
Better: Farmer Brown sold his neighbor the old mare *which* had given him so much trouble. *

FOR PRACTICE AND APPLICATION

Rewrite the following sentences so that any pronoun references are clear and definite. In some cases you can apply what you have learned about subordinating ideas. Read your sentences in class or in your small groups to see what different changes were made.

1. The landlord told the tenant that he was required to decorate the apartment.
2. I looked around the office and found no one there. This made me wonder whether I had come to the right place.
3. Ferguson claimed that his grandfather had fought in the Revolution and that he belonged to one of the leading families.
4. Sam introduced Ray to the guard and to his father and his sister.

*The reference of pronouns is often less definite in conversation than in formal writing. For example, "I called at the Bronsons' house yesterday, but *they* weren't at home," would be quite acceptable in informal speech, but less desirable in a formal letter or a report.

5. I received my commission just as the war ended, which pleased me very much.
6. Fitzhugh informed the prince that he was becoming unpopular.
7. The father of the new recruit regretted his rash words.
8. Is this the place where they sell school supplies?
9. I went to the barbershop, but he was too busy to cut my hair.
10. I couldn't decipher the cryptogram, which is the reason I did not win the prize.
11. The color was beautiful that I chose.
12. John's father knew that he was defeated.
13. The bat is in the box with which I hit a home run.
14. Today I saw the fox near the river which I saw in the grove yesterday.
15. I could find no fruit in the store which was not green.

145b **Avoid faulty reference of verbals.**

Participles and infinitives lacking clear and logical reference are known as *dangling elements*. Such expressions may obscure the meaning or produce a ridiculous effect.

BAD: *Looking* through his binoculars, a great *liner* greeted the captain's eyes. (*Looking* should refer to *captain,* not *liner.*)

BETTER: *Looking* through his binoculars, the *captain* sighted a great liner.

BAD: *Skimming* the tops of the trees, *I* saw a hummingbird. (*Who* or *what* was skimming?)

BETTER: I saw a *hummingbird skimming* the tops of the trees.

BAD: *To enjoy* poetry, *it* should be read aloud. (*To enjoy* should not modify *it.*)

BETTER: *To be enjoyed, poetry* should be read aloud.

BETTER: *To enjoy* poetry, [*you*] read it aloud.

"I CAN SEE THE LIBRARY LOOKING THROUGH MY LIVING ROOM WINDOW."

FOR PRACTICE AND APPLICATION

Rewrite the following sentences to secure clear and logical reference of the verbals. Exchange papers for judging.

1. Failing to secure approval of his plan, despair took possession of the young inventor.
2. Having moved frequently before, the new surroundings did not disturb the little kitten.
3. To graduate early, extra credits must be earned.
4. For making an exceptional record, the honor roll included Joseph's name.
5. To open the lock, the combination must be kept in mind.
6. Pursuing the culprit, one important clue escaped the detective's eye.
7. Singing in the treetops, I saw a bird.
8. Digging in the orchard, some Spanish gold pieces were found.
9. That storm was a severe blow to the people, destroying crops, ruining lives, and causing death and destruction.
10. Having many points of interest, we enjoyed the trip thoroughly.
11. I enjoyed lazily watching the shifting cloud formation, lying on the lawn.
12. James managed to stop the bull, wildly waving his dinner pail and jumping up and down.

CORRELATING ENGLISH WITH YOUR OTHER CLASSES

Bring to class reports or papers that you have written for any class. Exchange papers for critical reading to see whether they contain dangling elements. Mark such elements for correction.

145c Avoid misplaced modifiers.

You have often seen such humorous want ads as this one, though they seldom appear in real newspaper columns:

> WANTED—A used car by a traveling salesman with a convertible top.

The phrase "with a convertible top" should, of course, be placed near the word *car,* which it modifies. In general, a modifier, whether word, phrase, or clause, should be placed as near as possible to the word modified.

Special care should be taken to place such adverbs as *only, not only, nearly, just,* and *also* where they will not cause confusion in meaning. Notice in the following quotations that the meaning intended determines the location of *only:*

> I *only* saw him. (*I did not speak to him.*)
> *Only* I saw him. (*No one else saw him.*)
> I saw *only* him. (*I saw no one else.*)

When meaning is not affected, the position of such adverbs is optional, especially in colloquial (conversational) use.

FOR PRACTICE AND APPLICATION

Find the misplaced modifiers in the following sentences.
1. The cashier only returned thirty cents.
2. We stopped to pitch camp in view of the approaching storm.
3. We nearly earned a thousand dollars last month.
4. Just lift the lid, not the whole box.
5. The doctor only suggested that I take a walk before dinner.
6. The speaker declared that we only can have peace by co-operating with other nations.
7. He testified that the discovery could not be kept secret before the committee.
8. The crowd hailed the returning general, who was waving to them with a great shout.
9. After the game John maintained that he had not hacked his guard in the locker room.

145d Avoid awkward and illogical constructions.

Common sense will often help you to detect flaws in the construction of a sentence. Ask yourself, "Does the thought flow smoothly and logically?"

AWKWARD: Actually, the cause of your catching cold so often does not seem to me to be your failure to wear a coat outdoors.

IMPROVED: Actually, your failure to wear a coat outdoors is not, it seems to me, a cause of your catching cold so often. (This is a more direct statement.)

ILLOGICAL: The *reason* that he went is *because* he did not like to leave the patient alone. (*Reason* and *because* express the same idea. Only one of these words is needed.)

MORE LOGICAL: The reason that he went is *that* he did not like to leave the patient alone.

ILLOGICAL: *Stalemate* is *where* a chess player cannot move without moving into check. (*Stalemate* is not a place; it is an event or a situation.)

MORE LOGICAL: *Stalemate* is a *situation* in which a chess player cannot move without moving into check.

ILLOGICAL: Margaret is brighter than any of the girls in her class. (Margaret is not brighter than she herself is.)

MORE LOGICAL: Margaret is brighter than any *other* girl in her class.

FOR PRACTICE AND APPLICATION

Improve the awkward or illogical construction in the following sentences. Read your revised versions aloud for comparison and criticism.

1. Arbitration is when a neutral party is called in to settle a dispute.
2. The temperature this July 4 was higher than any day this summer.
3. He simply signs the application, is all.
4. The reason Sherlock Holmes is a popular character is because he is so colorful.
5. For vacating the apartment before the lease indicated that the tenant was obliged to do so, Stuyvesant received the landlord's thanks.
6. The defendant testified he could not think of what the new medicine consisted.
7. He still had to go to town to buy one thing another.
8. The thing is he just doesn't know.
9. John said that he had not taken the opposing end out of the play because the wrong signal had been called.
10. A squeeze play is when the batter bunts to score a man from third.

145e Maintain consistency in sentences.

Do you know what it means to be consistent? When he applies one rule of conduct to himself and another rule to others, a man is inconsistent. When he follows one principle on Sundays and another on weekdays, he is inconsistent.

Sentences can be inconsistent, too. If a sentence begins with one construction and suddenly shifts to another, it is inconsistent or lacking in *parallel structure*. Undesirable shifts may occur in the *person, number, voice,* or *tense of verbs,* or in the *kind of verbal* or the *type of modifier* employed.

INCONSISTENT: To maintain a peaceful world, *we* must recognize the rights of other nations, *and it* is necessary to follow a policy of give and take. (shift in *person*)
CONSISTENT: To maintain a peaceful world, *we* must recognize the rights of other nations, *and we* must follow a policy of give and take.

INCONSISTENT: To *accept* inferior goods, explained the consumers' counselor, *is cheating* oneself. (shift from *infinitive* to *gerund*)
CONSISTENT: To *accept* inferior goods, explained the consumers' counselor, *is to cheat* oneself.

INCONSISTENT: In this story, the old lady *operates* a small store. She *was* able to make a scant living by this method. (shift in *tense*)
CONSISTENT: In this story, the old lady *operates* a small store. She *is* able to make a scant living by this method.

INCONSISTENT: The senior class *wrote* the script, and the costumes *were made* by the art department. (shift in *voice*)
CONSISTENT: The senior class *wrote* the script, and the art department *made* the costumes.

INCONSISTENT: My swimming instructor taught me *to stay* near the shore and *that I should* always observe the safety rules. (shift from *infinitive* to *subordinate clause*)
CONSISTENT: My swimming instructor taught me *to stay* near the shore and always *to observe* the safety rules.

FOR PRACTICE AND APPLICATION

Revise the following sentences to eliminate inconsistencies.
1. Go to the next corner, and then you turn right for two blocks.
2. The great vessel entered port with her flags flying, and all her lights were ablaze.
3. Leaving at this hour is to show discourtesy to our hostess.
4. He was annoyed at hearing the news and decides to leave at once.
5. The store sent the package by mail instead of a messenger.
6. One can usually get provisions at the general store, but you will do well to bring your own fuel.
7. The columnist approved of the Congressman's speech, but his voting record was condemned.
8. Lucius faced the choice of enrolling at the state university or taking a job.
9. Carol said that she loved driving and to visit old shrines.
10. They built the house, and then they sell it.
11. The boy stamped out of the room, and the door bangs behind him.
12. Best of all, Maude enjoyed keeping house and to cook.
13. They must soon decide either on going or to stay.
14. He declared grumpily, "I am there for almost two hours."
15. Buck had been here for five minutes before he notices the sign.
16. It would be inhuman to send him back to Italy without a penny, no clothes, and when he cannot even speak Italian.
17. Ronald quickly called signals, and then he tries a quarterback sneak. This play fails because he had called the wrong signal.
18. They tried fishing in swift streams and to seine quiet backwaters, but they caught nothing.

CORRELATING ENGLISH WITH YOUR OTHER CLASSES

Bring to English class a paper that you are preparing for social studies or science class. Check carefully to see whether any sentences in the paper lack parallel structure. Correct any faulty sentences that you find.

4. Making Sentences Forceful and Interesting

A forceful and interesting style depends first of all upon good observation, clear thinking, and original ideas. Correctly written sentences in themselves, without vigorous and colorful thoughts, have little value. You must have something worth while to express if you are to write well.

There are no rules or recipes that will guarantee beauty or power of expression. If you write what is truly your own—what you have seen or heard or felt or strongly believed, however simple or commonplace the experience seems—you may be assured of an appreciative audience.

Although no one can give you a sure-fire recipe for writing forcefully and vividly, certain mechanical suggestions can be set down. Do not follow them too closely; use them if they seem to help.

146a **Use strong verbs and nouns in preference to weak verbs or nouns combined with adjectives or adverbs.**

Weak: "You should never have gone," Father *said angrily*.
More Expressive: "You should never have gone," Father *stormed*.
Weak: The *miserly old man* finally died.
More Expressive: The *old Scrooge* finally died.

146b **Use vivid adjectives and adverbs where they add to the total impression that you wish to give.** You will not overuse these modifiers if you remember that verbs and nouns are the real heart of the sentence. The following lines from "The Fall of the House of Usher" illustrate the skillful selection of descriptive words which contribute to a total effect:

> During the whole of a dull, dark, and soundless day in the autumn of the year, when the clouds hung oppressively low in the heavens, I had been passing alone, on horseback, through a singularly dreary tract of country, and at length found myself, as the shades of evening drew on, within view of the melancholy House of Usher.
>
> —Edgar Allan Poe

146c **Begin sentences with picturesque, vigorous words that introduce the reader at once to the thought.**

Whenever possible, avoid such weak beginnings as "There are . . ." "It is said . . ." "To tell the truth, . . ." "With regard to . . ." unless the thought particularly demands their use.

Weak: There is a strong wind blowing across the plains.
Stronger: A strong wind is blowing across the plains.

Weak: It is said that more than half of the American people are living in substandard houses.
Stronger: More than half of the American people, according to reports, are living in substandard houses.

146d **Wherever possible, use the active voice. It is in most cases more forceful than passive voice.**

WEAK: The petition was signed by every member.
STRONGER: Every member signed the petition.

Use *passive voice*, however, in these cases:

(1) To emphasize the action or the receiver of the action rather than the doer
> My eyes were blinded by the light.

(2) To avoid naming the doer of the act
> Several complaints have been registered.

(3) To eliminate the indefinite *you* as the subject
POOR: You don't see many strangers here.
BETTER: Not many strangers are seen here.

146e **Use the principle of suspense in the construction of your sentences; that is, make effective use of *periodic* sentences.** These are sentences that do not complete the essential thought until the very end. They are the opposite of loose sentences, which give a statement and then add details. Periodic sentences should not be used exclusively, but they add force to one's style.

LOOSE: Langley walked slowly toward the ranch, looking up at the sky, speculating about the weather, and wondering what adventures the day would bring. (Note that this sentence could end after each of the commas.)

PERIODIC: Baker thought that since sales had gone down steadily for three years, he would find it necessary to prepare the staff for a fundamental reorganization. (The main thought is not complete until the very end.)

146f **Use the principle of climax when you have a series of items in a sentence; that is, go from the least important to the most important.**

WEAK: We need your dollars, pennies, and dimes.
STRONGER: We need your pennies, dimes, and dollars.

FOR PRACTICE AND APPLICATION

A. Increase the emphasis in the following sentences by making them periodic. Read your work aloud for comparison.

1. We shall have to operate if the patient's condition continues to grow worse.
2. The keel of the ship was laid after many hardships and disappointments and after much delay and expense.
3. Let us press on to the goal, forgetting the things that lie behind, and looking forward to the prize.
4. Horace could not understand why he had not been promoted, in view of the great effort that he had put forth.
5. Dr. Fergus decided to accept the position, after much thought.

B. Improve the arrangement of the series in the following sentences to secure the effect of climax. Exchange papers for checking.
1. Misfortunes seemed to come to him all at once—the death of his son, his own failing health, and financial ruin.
2. Among the great problems that confronted the new administration were the threat of war, unemployment, and the reorganization of government bureaus.
3. For the defeated candidate there remained nothing but humiliation, despair, and poverty.
4. The people of this little country deserve our help, our affection, and our interest.

146g **Aim at variety in the type and structure of your sentences.**

Every baseball enthusiast knows what is meant by "change of pace." A pitcher may throw several fast balls, and then a very slow "teaser." The batter is thrown off balance and has difficulty in timing his swing at the ball.

This element of surprise, like the element of suspense or climax in the sentence, may give vitality to a paragraph. A speaker who drones through his speech, seldom changing his tone, may put his audience to sleep. A writer who uses the same cadence and pattern in every sentence may put the reader to sleep. By frequently varying the pattern, the writer arrests the attention of the reader.

Sometimes, of course, a series of short sentences, or a series of longer sentences of similar structure, may pound away at a single idea until the reader listens and understands. Usually, however, variety is more effective.

Mix some short sentences with the longer ones. Use some loose sentences as well as periodic sentences. Begin some sentences with the subject, others with a subordinate clause, a phrase, a gerund, a participle, . . .

FOR PRACTICE AND APPLICATION

A. Examine the sentences in the following paragraph and tell in what ways they differ from one another. Make this a class activity.

In my early journalistic days, I served upon a paper, the forerunner of many popular periodicals of today. Our boast was that we combined instruction with amusement. We gave advice to people about to marry—long, earnest advice that would, had they followed it, have made our readers the envy of the whole married world. We told our subscribers how to make fortunes by keeping rabbits, giving facts and figures. The thing that must have surprised them was that we ourselves did not give up journalism and start rabbit farming. Often and often have I proved conclusively how any man starting a rabbit farm with twelve selected rabbits and a little judgment must at the end of three years be in receipt of an income of two thousand pounds a year, rising rapidly. He simply could not help himself. He might not want the money. He might not know what to do with it when he had it. But there it was for him.*

B. Revise the following paragraph, making any changes necessary to secure greater variety of sentence structure. Compare your versions in class.

The students assembled at the appointed hour in the great assembly hall. A buzz of voices greeted the principal, who was already standing on the rostrum. The principal called the assembly to order to get the program under way. He introduced the speaker by telling a funny story about the time when they were boys together. The speaker responded by telling a joke about the principal.

C. Select one of the following writing exercises to test your ability to use words economically and to make your sentence structure reflect your thought. Proofread your paper carefully to catch thoughtless errors in form. Exchange papers for evaluation. Have good work read to the class.

1. Write a letter to a radio station approving of or criticizing a recent broadcast that you heard.
2. Describe an athletic contest that you have recently witnessed or a motion picture that you have seen.
3. For a local newspaper, write an announcement, imaginary or real, about a forthcoming school or community event.
4. Prepare a brief news account for the school newspaper about an incident that occurred in school.
5. Explain for the average reader the meaning of a principle or process which you learned in a science class or in your reading.

FOLLOW-UP

Examine every sentence of every paper that you write for any course. Have you used words economically? Does your sentence structure exactly reflect your thought? Make a conscious effort to improve your work by applying the helps in this chapter.

* From *Three Men on Wheels* by Jerome K. Jerome.

CHAPTER 5

Phrasing Ideas Clearly

The expression of ideas depends first of all upon careful sentence structure, but what one says or writes may fail of its purpose if the meaning is cloudy or misleading. This chapter offers ten aids to making meaning clear. Several of the ten overlap, but all are worth studying and applying.

147 **Give a direct explanation of a word.** Sometimes the most convenient and natural way to make a word, a phrase, a name, an idea, or a technical term clear to the reader is to insert an explanatory statement or definition.

A corpsman, *who is an enlisted man trained to give first aid and to perform various other medical services,* sometimes risks his life in the performance of his duties.

A panel discussion differs from a forum, *which consists chiefly of a series of lectures or talks followed by audience participation.*

FOR PRACTICE AND APPLICATION

A. Amplify the following sentences, explaining the meaning of the italicized words.
1. The glass industries of the United States and Canada are the chief market of *nephelite*.
2. One of the most interesting activities began when the pupils secured a *light meter* from the local health department.
3. The students devoted much time to the fundamentals of English composition and *rhetoric*.
4. She worked for six months as a *carhop*.
5. The statements made in this editorial are *platitudes*.

B. Write five sentences using words or phrases that are explained by means of a definition or an explanatory statement. Discuss your sentences in class.

120

CORRELATING ENGLISH WITH YOUR OTHER CLASSES

In your science or social studies textbook, or in required references in some other subject, find examples of sentences in which new terms are explained as in the preceding examples. See also whether you can find sentences containing words that need defining. In class, read and talk over the sentences that you found.

148 **Use substitute words,** such as *synonyms* (words with similar meanings) **and** *antonyms* (words with opposite meanings). When a single word of explanation will suffice, do not use more.

> We shall need to blow up, or *enlarge*, this snapshot. (*synonym*)
> Our plan applies to the disaffected, not the *loyal*, troops. (*antonym*)

FOR PRACTICE AND APPLICATION

Explain the italicized words in the first five of the following sentences by using synonyms; in the second five, by using antonyms. Compare work in class or in your small groups.

1. I appreciate your *candor* in explaining this matter.
2. He has been *coddled* far too long.
3. Try to avoid a *belligerent* attitude.
4. He gave me a *bland* smile.
5. What we need in our group is more *camaraderie*.
6. This change should *expedite* matters.
7. She has a *petulant* disposition.
8. His way of life is marked by *frugality*.
9. It seems that you always *nettle* him.
10. You should *spurn* his offer.

CORRELATING ENGLISH WITH YOUR OTHER CLASSES

In one of your other textbooks, find three synonyms or antonyms that are used to explain new terms. Present these sentences in class.

149 **Use comparisons.** Meanings can often be made more clear and vivid by comparing the unfamiliar with something that is like it. This type of comparison differs from a figurative comparison, which compares *unlike* things. (See page 190.)

> Attached to this board are two metal arches *similar to those in a loose leaf notebook*.
> This bird is *about the size of a robin*.

FOR PRACTICE AND APPLICATION

Make clearer the picture in each of the following sentences by completing it with an actual comparison. Read your sentences in class, noting how much the picture is affected by the different comparisons chosen.

1. This traveling elevator cage runs on rails like . . .
2. In the side of the ship was a hole about the size of . . .
3. Alan recognized a huge electric generator nearly as tall as . . .
4. This was a giant tree with huge leaves shaped like . . .
5. He was leading a pony no larger than . . .
6. The mixture should have the consistency of . . .

150 **Use mechanical aids.** Often you can make a point clear by inserting an explanatory word or phrase in parentheses, by supplying a footnote, by using quotation marks or underscoring to call special attention to something or to emphasize it.

1. He must put the selected parts together so that they are "in sync" (pronounced "sink") or properly synchronized.
2. He saw the embolus * that obstructed the circulation of the blood.

   *embolus (from the Greek *embolus,* a plug), a floating clot which wedges itself into a small blood vessel.

3. I don't really know what is good copy and what is not.
4. Among other terms, he defined mucosa, ligature, antipyretic.

FOR PRACTICE AND APPLICATION

Increase the clarity of the following sentences by any of the preceding means. Exchange papers for comparison.

1. Huxton explained that it was not the intensity of the sound, but its duration, that disturbed him.
2. The old doctor suggested that Elizabeth might enjoy the game more with the aid of binoculars.
3. The secretary of the Mental Hygiene Society reported that there was an alarming increase in the number of neurotics.
4. The schools in this town are of three types: public, private, and parochial.
5. At the end of the story, we discover that it was Frank, not the butler, who committed the crime.
6. These are bit players, those who have only a few lines to say.
7. This was an exhibit of parasol ants, each of them carrying a bit of green leaf over its head.
8. This address should read Street instead of Avenue.
9. They work hard, but sometimes I wonder what they really know.

151 **Use interpolated expressions.** Often you can make your meaning clear by inserting, between commas or dashes, an expression that throws light on an unfamiliar word or idea. Those expressions may be nonrestrictive clauses or phrases, appositives, or independent expressions.

>Two of the men, *it appeared,* had been Boy Scouts. (*nonrestrictive clause*)
>
>Frequently, fossil tree trunks—*called "bellmounds"*—are embedded in the coal. (*nonrestrictive phrase*)
>
>Alfonso was obliged to exile Don Pedro—*formerly his trusted advisor*—to the colonies. (*appositive*)
>
>Juarez performed miracles, *considering the obstacles in his path,* in rallying the people to his cause. (*independent expression*)

FOR PRACTICE AND APPLICATION

A. In the following sentences, tell which of the interpolated expressions are appositives, which are nonrestrictive clauses or phrases, and which are independent elements.

1. Once the collection is made, traveling employees of the dealers—expert and sympathetic keepers—place the animals on ships.
2. One day a sailor, on leave from active duty, came to school to tell of his experiences.
3. The police authorities, who had failed to solve forty murders that year, seized the first suspect that they could find.
4. He must know that even the deer, the favorite animal of the national forests, must be kept in check.
5. "Electric mules"—that is, motors—are replacing the live ones.
6. Presently a file of men, nine in all, appeared on the other side of the river.
7. Some of the men—in fact, most of them—failed to report.
8. If only there were no smugglers—forever trying to land goods without paying duty—there would be no need to watch the coast.
9. Everything needed by the adventurers—food, clothing, tools—had to be carried on their backs.
10. Those early settlers, many of whom were skilled artisans, had no thought of raising cotton.
11. It was, in its best forms, a good way of life.
12. The Jenkins family, like hundreds of thousands of other young farm couples, cannot afford to buy a farm.
13. The sunburnt farmer, his face a blank, watched me silently.
14. First came the Old South—also known as the Deep South—where the plantation system had its beginnings.
15. Progress, considering the difficulties to be overcome, has been encouraging.

B. Write five sentences in which you use an interpolated expression to make your meaning clearer. Put some of the sentences on the board and identify the kinds of interpolated expressions used.

152 **Use pictures, diagrams, cartoons, or graphs.** Often a simple illustration can convey an idea much more quickly than long explanations can. "A good picture is worth a thousand words." A sketch, drawing, diagram, or graph may tell the reader at a glance the facts or ideas which the writer is trying to convey.

The following graphs include a *bar* graph, a *line* graph, a *circle* or *pie* graph, a *picture* graph, and a *map* graph. Observe that in the illustrations the drawings are accompanied by exact figures, an informative heading, the sources of the data, and the notation of the scales.

Bar Graph

Estimated mileage death rate by time of day

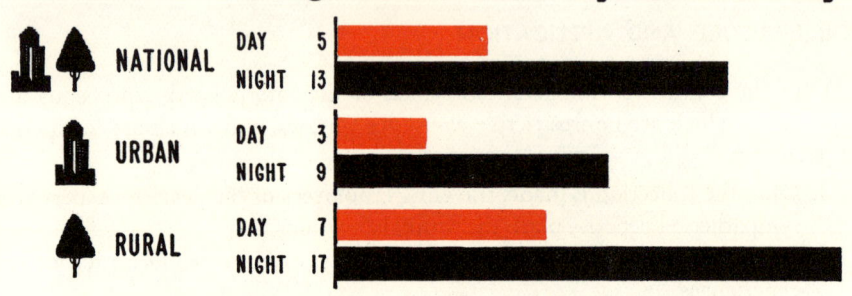

NATIONAL	DAY	5
	NIGHT	13
URBAN	DAY	3
	NIGHT	9
RURAL	DAY	7
	NIGHT	17

Line Graph

Seasonal variations in deaths 1936-41, 1946-51

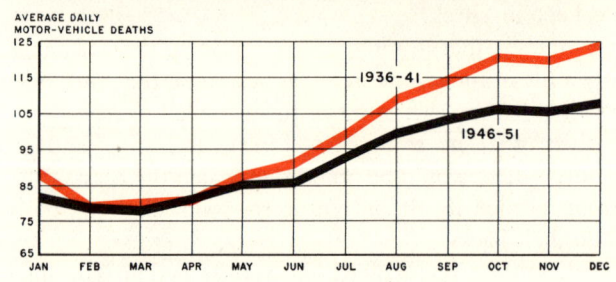

AVERAGE DAILY MOTOR-VEHICLE DEATHS

1936-41
1946-51

JAN FEB MAR APR MAY JUN JUL AUG SEP OCT NOV DEC

Circle (Pie) Graph

Student injuries by location

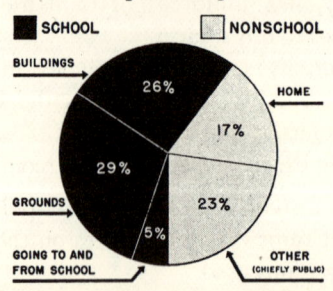

■ SCHOOL ▫ NONSCHOOL

- BUILDINGS 26%
- HOME 17%
- GROUNDS 29%
- GOING TO AND FROM SCHOOL 5%
- OTHER (CHIEFLY PUBLIC) 23%

Picture Graph

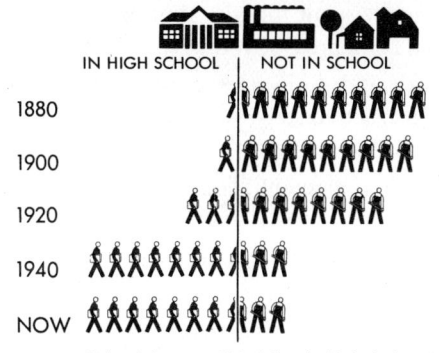

GROWTH IN HIGH SCHOOL ENROLLMENT*

IN HIGH SCHOOL | NOT IN SCHOOL

1880

1900

1920

1940

NOW

Each symbol represents 10% of all youth of high school age (14-17 inclusive)

Map Graph

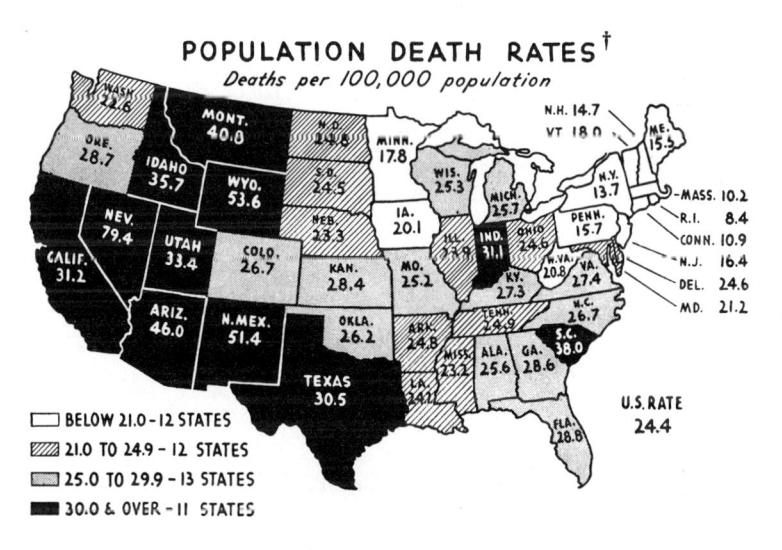

POPULATION DEATH RATES†
Deaths per 100,000 population

WASH. 22.6
MONT. 40.8
N.D. 14.8
MINN. 17.8
N.H. 14.7
VT 18.0
ME. 15.5
ORE. 28.7
IDAHO 35.7
WYO. 53.6
S.D. 24.5
WIS. 25.3
MICH. 25.7
N.Y. 13.7
MASS. 10.2
NEV. 79.2
UTAH 33.4
COLO. 26.7
NEB. 23.3
IA. 20.1
ILL. 31.9
IND. 31.1
OHIO 24.6
PENN. 15.7
R.I. 8.4
CONN. 10.9
CALIF. 31.2
KAN. 28.4
MO. 25.2
KY. 20.8
W.VA. 27.3
VA. 27.4
N.J. 16.4
DEL. 24.6
MD. 21.2
ARIZ. 46.0
N.MEX. 51.4
OKLA. 26.2
ARK. 24.8
TENN. 24.9
N.C. 26.7
S.C. 38.0
TEXAS 30.5
LA. 24.1
MISS. 23.2
ALA. 25.6
GA. 28.6
FLA. 28.8

U.S. RATE 24.4

☐ BELOW 21.0 - 12 STATES
▨ 21.0 TO 24.9 - 12 STATES
▦ 25.0 TO 29.9 - 13 STATES
■ 30.0 & OVER - 11 STATES

FOR PRACTICE AND APPLICATION

A. Explain briefly the significance of each of the preceding graphs.

B. From a science or social studies textbook, a newspaper, a magazine, an encyclopedia, an almanac, or other reference book, gather information on some topic like one of the following, and present in a short report the facts that you have discovered, using a graph to illustrate your findings.

  1. The number of immigrants entering this country in each decade since 1870, and the countries that they came from

---

* Reproduced by permission of Graphic Syndicate, Inc.
† The map, bar, line, and circle graphs are reproduced by permission of the National Safety Council.

2. The amount of money spent for education in the United States during any recent year compared with the national cost of crime, liquor, or tobacco
3. The amount of money spent for education per child in some of the richest states of the Union compared with that spent in some of the poorest
4. What this country could do in one year for public health, housing, education, and other constructive activities if it spent the equivalent of one year's war budget on peacetime projects of various types
5. The growth or decline of population in your state by decades since 1870, unless it became a state after that year
6. The position of the various players on a football field or a basketball court
7. Price trends of various consumer products during a given ten-year period
8. How your favorite major league baseball team has ranked the last twenty years

C. If you have some skill in drawing cartoons, write an anecdote from your childhood, illustrating it with one or more simple pencil sketches. (For help in writing the story, see pages 238–39.)

D. Give a floor talk accompanied by blackboard or chart illustrations. (See pages 298–301 for guides to giving a talk.)

153 **Use simple language.** The clearest and most forceful language is usually simple and direct. The use of many long, pretentious, and unfamiliar words interferes with easy communication and often creates the impression of insincerity.

FOR PRACTICE AND APPLICATION

A. Read the following paragraphs aloud. Which communicates better what the author is trying to say? Pick out in the one samples of extravagant or unfamiliar words; in the other, simple, forceful, expressive language.

Miss Valentine is a mixed bouquet of orchids, primroses, and buttercups. She is the sophistication of well-guided, obediently-learned technique, and the naïveté of youth at its first party. She is the headiness of a luxurious perfume, and the stamina of a glass of milk. She is the blush of dawn's sun on a hilltop field, and she is the glow of a sparkling gem in a Cartier case. She is Elizabeth Ann Valentine, whom the leading musicians of the country have welcomed into their sacrosanct realm with brilliant praise and prophecies. She is Betty Valentine, modern as the "Samba," ancient as music, and as far into the pathway of tomorrow as the volume of her luscious voice, singing on and on into the stars.*

* Adapted from the *New Yorker* (August 4, 1945, p. 51). Reprinted by permission of the Lewiston, Idaho, *Morning Tribune.*

All three children carried themselves rather better than the common run of "green" pupils that were brought to Miss Nixon. But the figure that challenged attention to the group was the tall, straight father, with his earnest face and fine forehead, nervous hands eloquent in gesture and a voice full of feeling. This foreigner, who brought his children to school as if it were an act of consecration, who regarded the teacher of the primer class with reverence, who spoke of visions, like a man inspired, in a common schoolroom, was not like other aliens, who brought their children in dull obedience to the law; was not like the native fathers, who brought their unmanageable boys, glad to be relieved of their care. I think Miss Nixon guessed what my father's best English could not convey. I think she divined that by the simple act of delivering our school certificates to her he took possession of America.*

B. Which sentences in the following pairs do you prefer? Give the reasons for your preferences.

1a. Will the designated speakers please indicate their identity by rising?

1b. Will the speakers please rise as I call their names?

2a. We can confidently say that our city owes its greatness to the wise and courageous leadership within our own Republocratic party.

2b. I say to you, without fear of successful contradiction, that this great metropolis owes its pre-eminence to the foresight, the courage, and the integrity of the illustrious leaders of our own glorious Republocratic Party.

3a. By what criterion can the younger generation determine what is the desirable course to follow?

3b. How shall the young man direct his way?

154 **Use exact and concrete language.** You should always choose words that represent most closely and accurately the ideas you have in mind. In most cases, *specific* words should outnumber *abstract* words.

When you review a book or a motion picture, tell as specifically as you can how you felt about it. If you say that the book is "interesting," one gets a general idea that you liked it, but he does not know why or in what way. Was it *exciting, suspenseful, thrilling, moving, unique, original, absorbing, imaginative, rich in new information,* or just *diverting, amusing, stimulating, thought-provoking,* or *soothing*?

Instead of saying, "The book has a rural setting," explain that the story is set against the background of "the flat prairie lands of central Illinois," or whatever the actual locale may have been. Treat the characters and the basic ideas in the same way, searching always for the words that will make the reader see in his own mind the things that you see.

---

* From *The Promised Land* by Mary Antin. Reprinted by permission of the publishers, Houghton Mifflin Company.

FOR PRACTICE AND APPLICATION

A. Find more specific expressions for each of the following phrases. Use actual or figurative comparisons if you wish.

1) A bad boy
2) A kind man
3) A fine day
4) Doing nicely
5) A good mother
6) A lovely scene
7) An interesting movie
8) Working hard
9) Hurrying home
10) Feeling unhappy
11) An ugly picture
12) A poor student
13) A pleasant holiday
14) An exciting mystery program

B. Express the intended meanings in the following sentences more precisely by substituting other expressions for those italicized.

Example

VAGUE: She is an *interesting* woman.
BETTER: She is a *captivating* (*witty, talented, alluring*) woman.

1. He had been ill *for some time*.
2. Mary entered the room, wearing *a greenish dress*.
3. One of his characteristics was that he was always *nicely dressed*.
4. The *sound* of the radio disturbed the air.
5. Barbara thinks that Bob is a *very nice* boy.
6. My relationship with Mr. Brown has been *important* to me.
7. Susan was *very happy* at receiving the scholarship.
8. The man was *very thin*.
9. The home was filled with *old-fashioned* furniture.

C. Carry out several of the following assignments; then compare work in class or in your small groups. You may wish to file some of the lists in your notebooks for later use.

1. Explain the difference between a *view*, a *sight*, a *vision*, a *show*, a *spectacle*.
2. List as many kinds of medical specialists as you know.
3. List as many kinds of scientists as you know.
4. List words describing people whom you know.
5. List words describing moods and feelings.
6. List words describing errors, weaknesses, offenses, crimes, and faults.

CORRELATING ENGLISH WITH YOUR OTHER CLASSES

Take a paper that you have prepared for another class. Try to improve the expression of your ideas by the use of more exact words. Exchange papers with someone else so that you may study each other's papers from the standpoint of exact diction.

155 **Use a helpful context to make meaning clear.** If your instructor placed on the blackboard the word *run*, what picture would come into your mind? The illustrations suggest some of the mental images which might be aroused by this word.

You may think of other uses of the word *run*, as in "a *run* of salmon," "the *run* from New York to Chicago," "*running* a business," "*running* a blockade," "a *run* of good luck." The word *run* has no meaning by itself; you can get its meaning only from its *context;* that is, from the words used with it.

Since, as the semanticists point out, the same words mean different things to different people, it is nearly impossible for one to convey to another the identical image seen in one's own mind. Using a helpful context is one of the best ways for a writer or speaker to convey to his audience as clear and accurate a reproduction as possible of the image that he himself has.

Examples

1. Consider the word *organize*. In one connection it may mean arranging into a logical whole the various ideas and facts of a long term paper. It may mean getting together in a union, or bringing others together in a union. It may mean creating a work unit out of a scattered group of people, as business executives might use the term. The general meaning of the word, "to make a working tool or instrument out of a group of ideas, things, or people," is of very little help without a context.

2. A newspaper story reports, "Pennywell lost all his money in the stock market crash." What does "all" mean? Can Pennywell still buy a five-cent newspaper? Is he on relief? Or did he merely have to sell his estates and yachts and move into a modest apartment? The story continues, "He has purchased a small variety store on State Street and hopes eventually to recover some of his losses." Now the reader has a more accurate notion of what is meant by "all."

FOR PRACTICE AND APPLICATION

Directions: Do as many of the following activities as time will permit. All of them are interesting exercises in semantics. All of them show the importance of choosing the right word. In many cases, you will want to carry out these activities orally.

A. Notice the different uses of the same words and phrases in the following groups of sentences. Tell the differences in meaning as indicated by the various contexts.

1a. Shortly after midnight Maizie's sleep was *disturbed* by the pounding at the door.
1b. The doctor was *disturbed* by the symptoms he observed in the patient.
1c. At first we thought a burglar had been there, but the books and papers had not been *disturbed*.
2a. The President *met* great opposition from Congress in carrying out his program.
2b. Lincoln *met* the emergency that confronted him, but at great cost to himself.
2c. Mr. Dalrymple, I wonder whether you have *met* the new secretary.
2d. We have *met* the enemy, and they are ours.
3a. The batter *missed* the next pitch.
3b. We shall meet, but we shall *miss* him.
3c. We must hurry, or we shall *miss* the only train that will get us there in time.
3d. Three officers and ten privates were *missing* after the encounter.
4a. The vessel *put out* to sea.
4b. The sailors *put out* the light.
4c. Junior *put out* the cat before going to bed.
4d. The wounded animal was *put out of its misery*.
4e. I was *put out* at his carelessness.
5a. As we walked along the railroad tracks, my foot caught in a *frog*.
5b. I've had a *frog* in my throat all day.
5c. One of the *frogs* on his jacket had been torn off.
5d. A nail had pierced the *frog* of the horse's left forefoot.
5e. The *frogs* have been croaking all night.
6a. He is a man of *honor*.
6b. He is an *honor* to his nation.
6c. Will you *honor* this draft?
6d. John was graduated with *honors*.
6e. Will you do the *honors*?

B. Each of the following expressions has at least four different meanings. Give oral sentences in which the context helps to indicate these meanings. The dictionary offers help. Here are the expressions: *show up, run out, go over, do up, get in.*

C. Find three different meanings for the phrase "make up" in these lines:

MAKE-UP ARTISTS *

Women, one finds,
Make up their minds,
Quarrels, and faces
In public places.

What other meanings for the phrase can you suggest? There are many.

D. The Declaration of Independence asserts that all men are created equal. The signers did not mean that all men are created equal in height, weight, complexion, wealth, or intelligence. Write a brief paragraph in which the context indicates clearly what they probably meant by the word *equal*. (See Chapter 8 for help in writing a good paragraph.)

E. In a letter to some public official or to your local newspaper express your opinion on some important issue in which you are interested. Some members of the class may wish to discuss their views with the group before writing the letter. Before sending it, study each important word or phrase to be sure that the meaning is made entirely clear by the context. If you are in doubt about any word, try it out on the class first to see whether there is uncertainty about your meaning. (Check the form of your letter by page 331.)

F. To show that words have different meanings for different people, try an experiment with a group of friends or fellow students. Ask each person to list the following words and phrases:

All	Some	Average amount
Most	None	The greater amount
Many	Few	A very few
Almost all	Very few	Rare exceptions

Now let everyone write a number, from 0 to 100, opposite each word in the list, choosing in each case a number that seems to express most accurately the meaning of the word. For instance, if "all" is 100, and "none" is 0, what would "most" be? When everyone has supplied numbers for all of the words, collect the papers and list the highest and lowest number given for each word.†

The *intended* meaning of such words as those listed above should always be made as clear as possible in the context.

G. Change or amplify the following statements so that the meaning of the italicized words may be clearer.

1. The school board allocated *most* of its funds to elementary education.
2. I *usually* listen to a mystery program in the evening.

---

* Permission of the *New Yorker*. Copyright 1945, by the F–R Publishing Company. Poem by Richard Armour.

† This experiment was made with a group of high school and college students by Ray H. Simpson, formerly of the University of Alabama, and reported in the *Quarterly Journal of Speech,* October 1945 (XXXI, No. 3, p. 327). He found a wide range of responses, particularly on some of the words near the middle of the list.

3. This book was written primarily for *young* girls.
4. The philanthropist made *substantial* contributions to the university.
5. The new mayor ordered *drastic* changes in the police department.
6. A check should be cashed within a *reasonable* period.
7. From Lydia's appearance, one might conclude that she was *an old maid*.
8. Father was a very *conservative* lawyer.
9. Although Sally makes change for hundreds of customers every day, she *seldom* is guilty of a mistake.
10. Frank and Audrey are a well-matched couple; they *never* quarrel.

H. How many meanings do you know for each of the following words: *magazine, face, body, fly, fast, strike, cabinet, book?* Write a sentence expressing each of the meanings, or offer such sentences orally.

I. Avoiding broad generalizations is one way to make meaning clear. Note this sentence: "The Spartans were a warlike people." Were all Spartans warlike? Which Spartans? When was Sparta warlike? Give examples of broad generalizations that people tend to make today.

156 **Use summarizing expressions.** To help fix a thought in the reader's mind, a writer may use an expression that summarizes or interprets the ideas expressed in a sentence.

Examples
1. On the table we saw such foods as Swedish Christmas pudding, German mandel bretzel, Czechoslovakian coffee cake, and Italian meatballs and spaghetti, each representing one of the nationalities included in the class.
2. Suzanne bought a notebook, a slide rule, a compass, a protractor, graph paper, and a manual of tables—equipment required for her math course.
3. Included in the watchman's tasks for the night were checking lights and doors, testing fire alarm signals, seeing that fire extinguishers were on hand, keeping a lookout for prowlers, and punching the time clock at intervals—enough work to keep him awake at all times.
4. Signs of last night's assault lay all about him—a broken pitcher, some playing cards, upturned furniture, scattered books and magazines, and several battered hats, all covered with particles of plaster.

FOR PRACTICE AND APPLICATION

A. In the preceding examples, find the summarizing expressions and show how they add to sentence meaning.

B. Find other examples of summarizing expressions in other textbooks that you are using or in books and magazines that you are reading.

C. Write three sentences of your own in which you use summarizing expressions. Discuss your sentences in class.

Proofreading What You Write

CHAPTER 6

When you write the first rough draft of a composition, your chief concern is the clear and forceful expression of ideas. Before preparing a final draft, however, you should carefully proofread your work to attain as nearly perfect mechanical form as possible. You will need to watch especially such matters as punctuation, capitalization, and spelling.

In writing the final draft, the writer assumes the point of view of the reader. The copy should be pleasing to the eye, with material legibly written and attractively arranged on the sheet. The final copy should again be checked for mechanical accuracy and for the possible omission of words.

WHAT TO LOOK FOR IN PROOFREADING

1. Are all sentences correctly punctuated?
2. Are abbreviations written correctly?
3. Is capitalization accurate?
4. Are words spelled correctly?
5. Are there adequate margins?
6. Have proper notations been used for any outline material or numbered series?
7. Are all bibliographical entries or footnotes correctly marked, and are they properly arranged?

1. Punctuation

READ AND DISCUSS

Correct punctuation is essential to the accurate expression of meaning. Notice the change in meaning given by the punctuation in the following:

> Ferguson said Father was ill at the time.
> "Ferguson," said Father, "was ill at the time."

How would you punctuate this rhyme to give it a sensible meaning?

> Every lady in our land
> Has twenty nails on each hand
> Five and twenty on hands and feet
> And this is true without deceit.

The trend today is toward using punctuation marks only when they will help to make meaning clear. A good test of effective punctuation is to read material aloud. If the correct meaning can be recognized quickly and easily without rereading, no further punctuation is likely to be required.

Read the following sentence aloud. Where would a comma aid in ready understanding of the sentence?

> When it was time to close the discussion became suddenly more animated.

Study the following definite rules for punctuation until you really understand how to apply them.

Punctuation marks may be divided into four classes. (1) The *externals* are those marks used chiefly to end sentences: the *period*, the *question mark*, and the *exclamation mark*. (2) The *internals* are those marks occurring within sentences: the *comma*, the *semicolon*, and the *colon*. (3) The *pairs* are those marks that receive this classification because they are used in pairs: *quotation marks, parentheses, brackets,* and *dashes*. (Dashes may also be used singly.) (4) The *special marks* are those that occur within a word: the *apostrophe* and the *hyphen*.

EXTERNAL PUNCTUATION MARKS

THE PERIOD

157a Use a period to close a declarative sentence.

> These statesmen are not of an age, but for all time.

157b Use a period to close an imperative sentence.

> Stay on the sidewalk.   Listen to him carefully.

157c Use a period after a simple request that is placed in question form for courtesy.

> Will the meeting please come to order.

157d Use a period after an indirect question.

> I wonder what he meant.

157e When a parenthesis forms the end of a declarative sentence, place the period *outside* the parenthesis.

> He was not at that address (617 Ridge Road).

157f When a complete sentence occurs within parentheses, place the period *inside* the closing parenthesis mark.

> He was a man with uncanny foresight. (I know, because I worked with him for many years.)

157g When a sentence ends with a quotation, always place the period within the quotation marks.

> Remember his words: "When in perplexity, read on."

157h A period is used at the end of an abbreviation. This use is treated on pages 154–55.

157i Use periods after initials.

> Write to C. M. (Charles Mason) Lucas.

157j Use the period as a decimal point.

> The dress cost $17.50.   The thermometer registered 87.6 degrees.

157k Use the period to indicate ellipses (omission of words).

> The delay . . . is having serious consequences.

Use three periods to indicate ellipses. If an ellipsis comes after a complete sentence, be sure to use the sentence period as well as the ellipses marks.

157l Place a period after each numeral or letter notation in an outline except for those numerals or letters enclosed in parentheses.

>   I. Note the alignment.
>   A. Note . . .
>   B. Note . . .
>   1. Note . . .
>   2. Note . . .
>   a. Note . . .
>   b. Note . . .
>   (1) Note . . .
>   (2) Note . . .
>   (a) Note . . .
>   (b) Note . . .
>   II. Note . . .

157m Use no period after a Roman numeral that is part of a name.

> Philip II   Louis XIV   John Sims Carroll III

FOR PRACTICE AND APPLICATION

Copy the following sentences, supplying periods where they are needed. Exchange papers for checking.

1. The horse stood still
2. I wonder why only one student raised his hand
3. Listen carefully to the signals
4. Report to the captain He expects you
5. Will you please close the window
6. The decision was of no interest to me (for he was no longer my friend)
7. (He had told me the story long ago)
8. He replied, "I shall do my best"
9. The entire repair bill, which included [*words omitted*] cost him one hundred dollars
10. Lincoln said, "[*words omitted*] that that government of the people might live"
11. The abbreviation COD means "collect on delivery"
12. For how many years did Henry V rule England?

THE QUESTION MARK AND THE EXCLAMATION POINT

158a **Use a question mark** (interrogation point) **after every direct question.**

Is it true that you are resigning?

158b **Use question marks after elliptical** (incomplete) **questions in a series.**

Where are your gloves? your glasses? your galoshes?

158c **Use the question mark in parentheses to express a doubt.**

He became a citizen on February 26 (?), 1945.

158d **Place the question mark inside quotation marks or parentheses only if it is part of the quoted or parenthetical material.**

He asked, "What are the new uses of atomic energy?"
This man (her uncle?) is the key figure in the mystery.
What is meant by "the strong arm of the law"?
What can you tell me about Hermosillo (the capital)?

159a **Use an exclamation mark after words, phrases, or longer expressions that show strong emotion. Many exclamations begin with** *how* **or** *what*.

Edna screamed, "Quick! Call the police!"
What a surprise his visit was!

159b **Rule 158d applies also to the location of the exclamation mark.**

Bill shouted, "Look out below!"
The change in plans (thank goodness!) does not affect us.
How I laughed when I read Leacock's "My Financial Career"!
What a time we had in Hermosillo (the capital)!

FOR PRACTICE AND APPLICATION

A. Copy the following sentences. Supply question marks where they are needed. Exchange papers for checking.
1. Have you seen our new car
2. The principal asked, "When did you return"
3. What is meant by the term "rhetorical question"
4. When can you meet me? tomorrow next Friday the day after
5. "Must you go" she queried plaintively. (Is she always plaintive)
6. John inquired, "When are you leaving, if it's not too personal a question"
7. We were met by a cheering crowd (incredible, is it) and taken home.

B. Copy the following sentences. Supply exclamation marks where they are needed. Check your work as sentences are put on the board.
1. How could you do such a dreadful thing
2. I am overjoyed
3. How astounding The footprints are a yard long
4. Help me My coat caught fire
5. Jack continued to yell, "Man the pumps"
6. How I thrilled to the strains of "Pomp and Circumstance"

C. Justify the use and location of the question marks and exclamation points in the following sentences. Make this an oral activity.
1. "This man (a perfect stranger!) called me by my first name," announced Nancy. "What a surprise that was!"
2. "O Captain! My Captain!" expresses Whitman's grief over the death of Lincoln.
3. He concluded by singing "Who Is Sylvia?"
4. Don't call me "Sukey"! (I've told you that over and over!)
5. He was born in 1920 (?) in Los Angeles, I believe.
6. What shall we do? see a movie? play canasta? go bowling?

D. Write sentences to illustrate rules 158b and 158d. Put sentences on the board for class criticism.

INTERNAL PUNCTUATION MARKS

THE COMMA

"Comma" comes from a Greek word meaning "to cut off." By doing just that, the comma helps to keep the sense of the various sections of a sentence clear. In oral reading it indicates a pause for the same purpose: to avoid blurring the sense of a sentence.

In general, commas are used (1) *to set off* elements within a sentence and (2) *to separate* elements within a sentence.

COMMAS USED TO SET OFF ELEMENTS WITHIN A SENTENCE

The term "set off by commas" means, depending upon the particular sentence, that a given sentence element is followed by a comma, preceded by a comma, or both preceded and followed by a comma.

160a **Use a comma or commas to set off words or phrases of direct address** (nominatives of address); **and the abbreviations** *Jr., Sr.,* **and** *Esq.*

> Bob, please open the window.
> What can I do for you, young man?
> Did Carl Ferris, Sr., send you here?

160b **Use a comma after the various parts of an address.** (House number and street form *one* part, as do city and zone number.)

> Mary's new address is Rural Route 4, Pekin, Illinois.
> Jane said that a letter addressed to her at 1454 Briar Lane, Cleveland 15, Ohio, would reach her.

160c **Use commas after the various parts of a date.** (The month and the day form a single part.)

> On Monday, January 31, 1953, our house burned to the ground.
> They were married in June, 1948, on her parents' anniversary.

160d **Use commas to set off contrasted expressions.**

> His brother, not his uncle, is the man to see.

160e **Use commas to set off parenthetical** (transitional or interrupting) **expressions. The term** *parenthetical* **is most frequently applied to such expressions as** *however, of course, on the other hand, in fact, for example, that is, by the way, after all, perhaps, indeed, also, too, nevertheless.*

> Lucille, on the other hand, is the domestic type.
> Your idea, nevertheless, may have merit.
> I might suggest my brother, for example, as a logical choice.

When any of the expressions in the preceding list are used purely as modifiers, not as parenthetical elements, they are not set off.

> I know perhaps six persons here.
> He is the owner in fact as well as in name.

160f **Use a comma or commas to separate the exact words of a speaker from the rest of the sentence, except when the sense of the sentence requires some other mark.** In the quoted words, the comma always goes inside the quotation marks.

> "I believe," he replied, "that you know the facts."
> She called after him, "Don't forget the appointment."
> "Come with me," pleaded Harriet.
> "Wait for me!" she shouted. (Sentence sense calls for an exclamation mark.)

160g **Use the comma after the salutation and the close of a friendly or social letter, and after the close of a business letter.**

> Dear Mary,   Lovingly yours,   Very truly yours,

138

160h **Use a comma or commas to set off an appositive that is not closely tied to the word that it explains or identifies.**

Tom Evans, my close *friend*, will address the meeting.

Dick Hamilton, a *lieutenant* who was captured behind enemy lines, was found in a prison camp.

My *cousin Irene* came to see me. (Appositive closely tied to the word explained)

160i **Use commas to set off nonrestrictive clauses and phrases.** They are "loose" modifiers and may be omitted from the sentence without changing the intended message of the main clause.

Our car, which has seen hard use, is in the repair shop. (*nonrestrictive clause*)

A car that has seen hard use often needs repairs. (*restrictive clause*)

[The restrictive clause is needed to convey the meaning intended in the sentence.]

Our new car, delivered last week, is a pleasure to drive. (*nonrestrictive phrase*)

A car bearing a Texas license was standing at the curb. (*restrictive phrase*)

160j **Use a comma or commas to set off words, phrases, or other modifiers that are transposed** (out of their natural order) **in the sentence.**

His face, *stern* and *set*, should have warned me. (*transposed adjectives*)

This man, *without question*, is too young. (*transposed phrase*)

Dad, *although he likes golf*, seldom plays. (*transposed clause*)

160k **Use a comma to set off a short clause that changes a statement into a question.**

He was here early this morning, wasn't he?

FOR PRACTICE AND APPLICATION

A. Copy the following sentences. Insert all missing punctuation marks. Not all sentences below need added punctuation. When you go over the sentences, give the reason for each comma inserted.

1. When you return Jeremy we'll examine your drawings.
2. I do not however anticipate a defeat.
3. Perhaps Mary did not know that you were coming.
4. "This constant rain" complained Don "is depressing."
5. Our track team conference champion for the last two years is again strong this year.
6. Harry you plan to come home for dinner don't you?
7. All the athletes eager to be in their best form retired early.
8. John Stone who ranks near the top of his class scholastically was elected president of the student council.

139

9. Any student who ranks near the top of his class scholastically has a good chance of being elected.
10. Usually the team playing the most consistent baseball wins the pennant.
11. The St. Louis Cardinals playing the most consistent baseball in their league won the pennant.
12. That corner building in spite of its age is still in good condition.
13. The tennis team elected Bruce winner of the conference singles title its captain.
14. In May 1948 we moved to our new home on Rural Route 2 Bluefield Kansas.
15. "Don I don't understand you" remarked his mother; "in fact neither does your father."
16. Arthur annoyed at my question frowned and said "You are of course aware that you are being very personal."
17. Farm life although it entails much hard work is gratifying.
18. Is 3246 Elm Street Toledo 12 Ohio the right address?
19. Seniors who reported for practice on Thursday night will not be expected to report tonight will they?
20. Do not gentlemen misinterpret my motives.

B. If any rule is particularly difficult for you, write original sentences to illustrate that rule. Use your sentences for class drill.

FOLLOW-UP

Proofread carefully all papers that you write for English and for other classes. Be sure that you have used punctuation marks correctly to help the reader understand your meaning.

COMMAS USED TO SEPARATE ELEMENTS WITHIN A SENTENCE

160l Use a comma to separate introductory words, such as mild interjections and the words *yes* and *no,* from the sentence that follows them.

> Oh, I hadn't heard that explanation.
> Yes, the Hollywood influence is noticeable here.

160m Commas are used to separate items in a series. These items may be words, phrases, short clauses, or numbers.

> Baseball, tennis, golf, and swimming are active sports. (*words*)
> When driving, keep a sharp lookout to the front, to the sides, and to the rear. (*phrases*)
> The orchestra began the overture, the lights dimmed, and the curtain rose. (*clauses*)
> He called the numbers 2, 3, 56, and 105.

140

160n Use a comma to separate co-ordinate modifiers. Consider modifiers co-ordinate if *and* sounds correct when placed between them.

> The warm, sunny day made the boy lazy. (*warm and sunny*)
> Jane was wearing a dashing red suit. (not *dashing and red*)

160o Use a comma between the clauses of a compound sentence joined by the co-ordinate conjunctions *and, but, or, nor,* or *for.* (Very short clauses joined by *and* may omit the comma.)

The teams are evenly matched, but we have the advantage of playing at home.

160p When a semicolon separates the clauses of a compound sentence, use a comma in the second clause to indicate an omitted verb.

> This box contains labels; that one, paper clips. (The comma replaces *contains.*)

160q Use a comma wherever necessary to prevent misreading.

> Although a real diamond, mine is a very small one.

160r Use a comma after any of these word groups when they are used in an introductory way: (1) *adverbial clauses,* (2) *phrases containing verbals* (infinitives, participles, or gerunds), (3) *long prepositional phrases,* or (4) *two or more consecutive prepositional phrases.*

> (1) As I was saying, we are pleased with your work.
> (2) To reach Tulsa by noon, we should leave here at once.
> (2) Having lost our way, we stopped to ask directions.
> (3) During those long-ago childhood days, time seemed to pass very slowly.
> (4) At the entrance to the cave, the explorers held a council.

FOR PRACTICE AND APPLICATION

A. Copy the following sentences. Supply missing punctuation marks and list the number of the rule for each mark that you insert.

1. No I have not read that story but I do enjoy historical novels.
2. Walter D. Edmonds Kenneth Roberts and Sir Walter Scott give me many hours of enjoyment.
3. Although many people say that Scott is outdated I find novels like *Ivanhoe* and *Quentin Durward* highly interesting.
4. Both Barton and Bill like sports and yet they do not have much in common.
5. Barton likes tennis and badminton; Bill hunting and fishing.
6. A hot dry climate pleases Barton for he likes a daily turn on the courts.
7. Bill doesn't care what the weather is but he does like to be in the woods on a river or a lake or simply out in the fields.
8. Gertrude first sold advertising space then reported news next wrote editorials and finally became editor in chief.

9. The most interesting fascinating part of newspaper work is meeting different types of people.
10. After all different people have different points of view and learning these has a tendency to jar one out of a rut.
11. Well to be frank with you I never did like that little black hat.
12. Considered from every angle your plan seems worth trying.
13. Yes I have spent many happy hours in New York City Cleveland Philadelphia and Baltimore.

B. If any rules in this lesson are new to you, write sentences to illustrate those rules. Use the sentences for class practice.

C. Copy the following sentences. They cover all uses of the comma that you have studied. Supply commas where they are needed. Exchange papers for checking. As you go over them, give the reason for each comma inserted.

1. Each man woman and child in the group was asked to contribute.
2. He spoke of a government "of the people by the people and for the people."
3. This message by the way arrived at noon did it not?
4. The temperature was below freezing but he went out without a hat.
5. The stage lighting was brilliant and the colors were vivid.
6. The warm green earth exuded a fragrance of spring.
7. "I doubt" he replied gravely "that there is sufficient evidence."
8. Waiter may I have the check?
9. Before curtain time however we reviewed the plot.
10. To tell the truth I'd forgotten the date.
11. Chicago Illinois has been called the meat-packing center of the world.
12. Mary's address is 951 Fairview Road Denver 7 Colorado.
13. Marie and Ray were married on April 24 1953 at four o'clock.
14. Mr. Williams the foreman will examine the broken machinery.
15. The bills receipts and canceled checks are in that drawer; the invoices in this one.
16. The first tulip which we hope will be red has pushed its way through the ground.
17. Bryant's "Thanatopsis" written when the poet was seventeen was widely acclaimed.
18. Mr. Chairman before we discuss the motion I should like to have it restated.
19. "We should perhaps" Elaine suggested "wait shouldn't we?"
20. Long after leaving the land of his birth he remembered the seaside with nostalgia a deep intense but unreasonable longing.

D. Choose three uses of the comma which you frequently neglect in your writing. Write sentences illustrating these uses. Submit your sentences to the class or to a classmate for approval.

E. In magazines or books, find and bring to class examples to illustrate the comma usages that you have studied. If you find sentences that are not punctuated according to the rules, decide whether the insertion of commas would make for easier reading.

CORRELATING ENGLISH WITH YOUR OTHER CLASSES

Proofread carefully any paper you are now writing for any class, or a paper you have recently written. Have you used commas correctly to help present your ideas? Bring questionable uses to class for discussion.

THE SEMICOLON

The semicolon indicates a greater degree of separation than is indicated by the comma. In general, the semicolon is indicative of a compound sentence, although it may be used in long sentences to separate phrases or clauses containing internal punctuation.

161a **Use a semicolon between the two clauses of a compound sentence when they are not joined by a co-ordinate conjunction.**

>There was a moment's silence; everyone was stunned by the news.

161b **Use a semicolon between the two clauses of a compound sentence joined by a co-ordinate conjunction if there are other commas in the sentence.** (If there is no possible chance of confusion in meaning, a comma may be used in place of the semicolon.)

>Although circumstantial evidence weighs heavily against him, I believe Tom's story; and I believe you do, too.

161c **Use a semicolon before a conjunctive adverb that introduces a clause in a compound sentence.** Common conjunctive adverbs are *therefore, nevertheless, moreover, consequently, furthermore, besides, then, thus, instead, accordingly, otherwise, so, yet, still, hence, however.*

>His principles have never been clear to me; therefore I cannot vote for him.
>You trust him implicitly; nevertheless, I should like to hear his story.
>(NOTE: When the conjunctive adverb is a loose modifier, use a comma after it, as in the preceding example.)

Explanatory expressions (*for example, namely, on the contrary, in fact, that is, on the other hand*) **are used in the same manner as the conjunctive adverb. If they join two independent clauses of a compound sentence, they must be preceded by a semicolon and followed by a comma.**

>Mary is an excellent student; on the other hand, she does not participate in any extracurricular activities.

161d **In general, use the semicolon to separate phrases or clauses of equal rank which contain internal punctuation** (commas). The use of the semicolon in such sentences serves as an aid to the reader and achieves clarity of meaning.

>We have lived in Bay City, Texas; Lakeland, Florida; Frankfort, Kentucky; and Monroe, Louisiana.

FOR PRACTICE AND APPLICATION

A. Copy the following sentences. Supply semicolons and commas where they are needed. Exchange papers for checking.
1. Betty has not been absent one day in three years she deserves special recognition.
2. Although he possesses all the other requisites for the job, he is not dependable I am afraid that we must discard his application.
3. Bob did not want to go in fact he flatly refused.
4. Jim expects to leave next Monday on the other hand he may be delayed for two or three weeks.
5. Harold sings tenor Fred baritone.
6. Paul has traveled widely for example he has visited Santiago Chile Helsinki Finland Sydney Australia and Barcelona Spain.
7. I have not heard the radio programs you mention therefore I cannot criticize them.
8. Although I prefer mathematics and science to English, I realize that all three subjects are required consequently I shall do my best to master them.
9. He searched unceasingly for the man who possessed the secret document: through the resorts and villas of the Mediterranean where the independently wealthy may indulge in idleness and leisure in the jungles of Africa where the torrid breath of disease and pestilence brought him close to the door of death and in the frozen wastes of the Arctic where no man had been known to survive.
10. The poem is written in iambic meter that is a short (unaccented) syllable is followed by a long (accented) syllable.

B. Write three original sentences for each rule governing the use of the semicolon. Omit the punctuation in your sentences and use them for class practice.

THE COLON

162a Use a colon after a formal salutation in a business letter.
      Gentlemen**:**   Dear Sir**:**   My dear Mrs. Callaway**:**

162b Use a colon before listed items that are introduced by such words as *the following, as follows, thus,* **and** *these;* **by a number; or by any other "pointing-out" expression.**
      I should like a conference with the following**:** Sue, Fred, and Mark.
      He has played three positions**:** guard, tackle, and end.

Use no colon before a list of predicate nominatives or direct objects.
      The three chairmen are Alvin, Estelle, and Leonard.
      We shall need you, Lorena, and Wilbur.

162c **Use a colon to separate two complete sentences when the second sentence explains, amplifies, or illustrates the first.**

> Louis has a good idea: he wants to call in an expert.

162d **Use a colon to introduce a long or formal quotation.**

> I am reminded of the words of Emerson: The true test of civilization is not the census, nor the size of cities, nor the crops—no, but the kind of man the country turns out.

162e **Use a colon to show hours and minutes numerically.**

> I shall take the 10:45 A.M. train.

162f **Use a colon to separate chapter and verse referring to a specific Bible selection.**

> I shall use as my text Job 5:7.

FOR PRACTICE AND APPLICATION

Copy the following sentences, supplying colons where they are needed. Exchange papers for checking.

1. The four types of poetic meter may be classified as follows iambic, trochaic, anapestic, and dactylic.
2. The chest has three dimensions length, width, and breadth.
3. The letter to his firm began as follows "Gentlemen We received your last shipment of goods on January 18."
4. She should report at 745 A.M.
5. He outlined his plans he would save his money; he would buy a car; and then he would tour the country.
6. Article 1, Section 1 of the Constitution of the United States reads as follows "All legislative powers herein granted shall be vested in a Congress of the United States, which shall consist of a Senate and a House of Representatives."
7. I am worried about Elmer he spends too much time alone; he is not eating enough; and he falls asleep at work.
8. One of the Bible verses most quoted is Micah 68.

QUOTATION MARKS

Quotation marks indicate that credit is being given to the original speaker or writer of the expression enclosed within the quotation marks, and that the exact words are being reproduced. Direct quotations are always enclosed by double quotation marks: the first set marks the beginning of the quoted material, and the second set marks the end.

163a Enclose a direct quotation in quotation marks.

The direct quotation may be unbroken by explanatory words.

"I'd like to try," said Alice.

James said timidly, "I think I have the answer."

He laughed. "The joke's on me."

The direct quotation may be broken by explanatory words. Then an extra set of quotation marks must be used.

"Why," he asked, "didn't you tell me?"

"We've caught five fish already!" he shouted exultantly. "By five o'clock we'll have our quota!"

(NOTE: In the first sentence *didn't* begins with a small letter because the entire quotation is one sentence, "Why didn't you tell me?" In the second sentence *By* begins with a capital letter because the quoted words are two sentences, (1) "We've caught five fish already." (2) "By five o'clock we'll have our quota.")

163b If a direct quotation consists of more than one paragraph, place quotation marks before each paragraph but at the end of the last only.

"The real beginnings of modern scientific agriculture can be dated from the passage of the Morrill Act of 1862. This law gave to the states 30,000 acres of the public domain for each congressman that they sent to Congress, the proceeds from which were to be used by the states for the establishment of agricultural and industrial schools.

"The result of this measure was the establishment of agricultural colleges, independently or in connection with the state universities, in almost every state of the Union. Such institutions as the universities of Illinois, Wisconsin, Minnesota, Nebraska, and California, and the Michigan, Iowa, Kansas, Oregon, and Texas agricultural colleges grew out of this general land grant.

"Twenty-five years later, in 1887, Congress passed the important Hatch Act, appropriating federal funds for the establishment and maintenance of agricultural experiment stations in every state in the Union. These stations have, through their research work and their educational activities, contributed incalculably to the improvement of agriculture." *

163c Enclose in single quotation marks a quotation within a quotation.

He said, "I heard Joe shout, 'Put down that knife!'"

163d In conversation, begin a paragraph for each change of speaker.

"I'm sorry to be late!" exclaimed Doris. "Have you been here long?"

"Oh, no," replied Cary, "only about an hour. Sometimes you keep me waiting much longer."

"Cary, you're just exaggerating. I'm not always late!"

---

* From *Our Nation* by Eugene C. Barker and Henry Steele Commager. Reprinted by permission of the publishers, Row, Peterson and Company.

163e Show by quotation marks, words or expressions used in a special sense. Such words may be (1) technical, (2) ironical, or (3) coined.

(1) A "tip-in" is a separately printed leaf pasted into a book.
(2) You show us how. You are the "expert."
(3) The big wheels went round with a noisy "ka-lunk! ka-lunk!"

163f Use quotation marks to enclose the titles of chapters; short stories; articles; art works; short poems, plays, and musical compositions; and radio and television programs.

This chapter is entitled "Through the Wilderness."
Have you watched that television program called "Finders Are Keepers"?

163g Do not use quotation marks around indirect quotations.

He said that he was ready to leave.

163h In quoting, always place the closing quotation marks outside a period or a comma, and inside a colon or a semicolon. If a question mark or an exclamation point is part of the quotation, put the quotation marks outside; otherwise, inside.

"I'll take over now," he said. "You rest."
He read lines from Frost's poem "Mending Wall."
I have just read "Miniver Cheevy"; are you familiar with it?
You remind me of that line from "A Psalm of Life":
 "Let us, then, be up and doing."
She queried, "When are you going?"
[The question mark belongs only to the quoted words.]
What did Shakespeare mean by "the milk of human kindness"?
[The question mark belongs to the whole sentence.]
The sergeant bellowed, "Stop!"
[The exclamation point belongs only to the quoted matter.]
Protect us from his "kindness"!
[The exclamation point belongs to the whole sentence.]

FOR PRACTICE AND APPLICATION

Copy the following sentences. Supply quotation marks where they are needed, being careful to apply Rule 163g. Exchange papers for checking.

1. Silas said that the meeting was well attended.
2. If you wish, said the mechanic, I'll grind the valves.
3. I should like to become a psychologist, Betty announced.
4. When I talked with him, said Bill, his exact words were, I declined the nomination.
5. What is meant by the quotation, The pen is mightier than the sword?
6. She mentioned her little dress; as a matter of fact, it was a creation by a famous Parisian designer.

7. The title of Thackeray's novel *Vanity Fair* was probably suggested by the chapter Vanity Fair in John Bunyan's *Pilgrim's Progress*.
8. Francis Scott Key wrote the words for our national anthem, The Star-Spangled Banner.
9. My favorite Sandburg poem is Fog; do you know it?
10. This painting, Square Sunlight, has won several awards.
11. Did he use the phrase in all my born days?
12. James asked petulantly, When can we finally get started?
13. After several days of deliberation, Al appeared before the committee and said simply, I cannot do it, and, after a moment, added, because I haven't the ability.
14. Don't read it that way, Sarah pleaded. You misinterpret the whole passage. You should pause just before honor!
15. The crowd chanted, Hold that line! and then let out a long sigh as the opponents scored another touchdown.
16. Janet wanted to read Vachel Lindsay's poem The Congo, but the instructor insisted that she read Amy Lowell's Patterns.
17. When I'm tired, announced Bert, I rest. That's the sensible thing to do.

PARENTHESES, DASHES, AND BRACKETS

164a **Use parentheses to mark numbered or lettered divisions within sentences or paragraphs.**

Your itinerary will be as follows: (1) Springfield, (2) Peoria, (3) Rockford, (4) Elgin.

164b **Use parentheses to enclose explanatory or purely incidental matter.**

Dean Ellis (you remember him) was married last week.

165a **Use a dash to show a break in thought or sentence structure.**

This man pretended to be—but you're not even listening!

165b **Use dashes to emphasize parenthetical matter.**

Tomorrow—how I dread it!—I must balance my account.

NOTE: If the parenthetical matter is a question or an exclamation (as above), punctuate it to indicate that fact.

165c **Use a dash to indicate a summarizing clause.**

Kitchen, living room, bedroom—they were just as I had left them.

165d **Use dashes to show hesitation.**

I—I—I don't know just how to tell you this.

165e **Use a dash to emphasize appositives or other explanatory matter.**

I want you to meet Ron Clark—the best friend I've ever had!

165f **Use dashes to set off a series of appositives.**

Everything—house, furniture, jewelry—must be sold.

It should be pointed out that parentheses set off *unimportant* matter; dashes, *emphatic*. Both should be used sparingly; in fact, only when they really help to make meaning clearer than it would otherwise be.

166a **Use brackets to enclose comments, criticisms, or corrections inserted by someone other than the original writer or speaker.**

>Everyone who knew him [Dr. Brown] respected his integrity.

166b **Use a bracketed** *sic* **[meaning "thus in the original"] to show that an error in quoted material is not an error in quoting, but one that occurs in the original text.**

>According to the note, the monie [*sic*] was buried in the garage.
>(The *sic* after "monie" indicates that the misspelling occurs in the original note.)

166c **Within a sentence, place a needed comma or other mark after the second parenthesis mark or bracket, and not before the first one.**

>Although he had had insufficient experience (according to the official records), he far surpassed the so-called "experts."

If an independent sentence is placed in parentheses or brackets, place the end punctuation inside the second parenthesis or bracket.

>A. E. Housman's "Epilogue" tells how a king prepared himself for the bitterness that he found in the world. (Robinson's "Cliff Klingenhagen," by the way, discusses the same subject.)

FOR PRACTICE AND APPLICATION

Copy these sentences, supplying parentheses, brackets, or dashes where they are needed. Go over the sentences in class, explaining why you used the marks.

1. Today has been but why bore you with my troubles!
2. Parentheses are used to set aside explanatory elements within a sentence. Usually it is better to use commas, however.
3. The note read, "This morning i *sic* found the safe open."
4. This game what a thriller it was! is one I'll not forget.
5. The name on the license read Eleanor Brontevitch stage name, Lee Brown.
6. The garage repaired the damage, replaced the fuse, greased the car, and washed it all in two hours.
7. When you revise your paper, be sure that the following items have been checked: 1 punctuation; 2 capitalization; 3 footnotes; 4 margins; and 5 outline notations.
8. Ladies and gentlemen, here he is the Great Gaffrey, in person!
9. Still another possibility these possibilities seemed endless! was suggested by the head of the science department.
10. There are a few individuals including myself, incidentally who resent the implication of that statement.

SPECIAL MARKS OF PUNCTUATION

THE APOSTROPHE

167a Use an apostrophe to show the possessive case of nouns. *

(*Singular nouns*) **To form the possessive case of a singular noun, first write the noun. Do not add any letters; do not drop any. Then add an apostrophe and** *s* **('*s*).**

      man   the man's hat
      Mr. Gross   Mr. Gross's store

Some authorities favor adding only an apostrophe if the noun itself ends in *s*. Following that rule works well enough in written material; in spoken language, however, unless the *s* is added, one cannot always be sure what the name is.

      Mr. Fred Byrne   Mr. Byrne's hat
      Mr. John Byrnes   Mr. Byrnes' hat

If you read those two possessives aloud, you will see that they sound exactly alike. To make clear that the name is "Byrnes," you must say "Mr. Byrnes's hat."

(*Plural nouns*) **To form the possessive case of a plural noun, first write the plural noun. Do not add any letters; do not drop any. If the plural form ends in** *s*, **add only an apostrophe. If the plural form does not end in** *s*, **add an apostrophe and** *s* **('*s*).**

Singular	*Plural*	*Plural Possessive*
Burns	the Burnses	the Burnses' car
woman	women	the women's purses

(*Compound nouns* and *else*) **To form the possessive of a compound noun or of a word followed by** *else*, **add** '*s* **to the last word only.**

      my sister-in-law's party
      someone else's book

(*Joint ownership*) **To show joint ownership, make the last noun a possessive. To show separate ownership, make each noun a possessive.**

      Ruth and Betty's brothers   Ruth's and Betty's brothers

(*Pronouns*) **Use no apostrophe in personal, interrogative, or relative pronoun possessives; but add** '*s* **to indefinite pronouns to show possession.**

      Is this book **yours**? Well, **whose** is it? It must be someone's.

(*Inanimate objects*) **As a rule, use the** *of* **phrase to show possession by (or connection with) inanimate objects:** *the edge of the lawn* [not *the lawn's edge*].

Exceptions include such expressions as *an hour's walk, a week's work, a dollar's worth.*

---

* Sometimes both an apostrophe and a phrase may be needed; for example, "I heard it from a friend *of my uncle's*."

167b **Use apostrophes to show omitted letters in contractions of words.** Contractions containing verbs are the most common kind, but other words may be contracted. As a rule, avoid contractions in formal writing.

> I haven't seen him since five o'clock.

167c **Use apostrophes to indicate missing figures in a date or missing letters in a word, as in colloquial or dialectal speech.**

> He lost his fortune in the crash of '29.
> I'm runnin' this place. I want no help from him 'r anyone else.
> You must've seen him when he drove past.

167d **Use apostrophes to form the plurals of letters, numbers, signs, or words referred to as words.**

> Do you spell your name with two *d*'s?
> Those *8*'s look like *3*'s to me.
> Count the total number of +'s.
> You use too many *well*'s.

FOR PRACTICE AND APPLICATION

A. Copy the following sentences, (1) using the possessive form of each word in parentheses and (2) supplying apostrophes wherever else they are needed. Exchange papers for checking.

1. Because (Lewis) mother was ill, the club postponed its meeting.
2. I asked (John) permission to attend the (Jones) open house.
3. Its important to dot your *is*.
4. The beginning wont matter, but the end is important.
5. Both listeners attention wandered.
6. They dont seem to understand its importance.
7. Theres an old saying, "If *ifs* and *ands* were pots and pans, thered be no need for tinkers."
8. (Sally) first money was earned by running errands for her neighbors.
9. She quoted the old bromide, "Alls well that ends well."
10. The report, which represented a weeks work, has disappeared.
11. (Harry and Bill) eyes are exactly the same color.
12. Baseballs are made of (horse) hides.
13. (Everyone else) tomatoes froze; we saved ours by covering them.
14. (Baker and Weeks) store has a sale on ladies dresses.
15. (James) coat was torn by the bulls horns.
16. Benny (Bass) first professional appearance was a failure.
17. The Holmeses have a new car. The (Lacey) car is old.

B. Have several students put sentences on the board to illustrate the following: (1) the possessive of *Phyllis;* (2) joint ownership of a canoe by Harry and Walter; (3) the plural of *why*. Let other students check the sentences and explain why they are or are not correct.

THE HYPHEN

168a Use a hyphen in the syllabication of words overrunning the line. (See "Syllabication," page 169.)

168b Use hyphens in the following types of compound words:

(1) Compound cardinal and ordinal numbers: fifty-five, two hundred twenty-five,* sixty-first
(2) Fractions used as adjectives: one-fourth cup of milk
(3) Compound direct adjectives (including coined ones): an I-dare-you-to-touch-me sneer, a better-than-ever price
(4) Compounds of a noun and a prepositional phrase: man-of-war
(5) Compounds ending in a proper noun: un-Christian
(6) Compound titles containing *vice, ex,* or *elect:* vice-consul, ex-captain, secretary-elect
(7) Compounds beginning with the prefix *self:* self-reliant, self-centered
(8) Special compounds, such as *tie-up, drive-in, jump-off*

If two or more compound words have the same base, hyphenate thus:

    the first- and second-place winners

(9) Compounds in which mispronunciation might result otherwise

    pre-existence   de-energize   anti-immune

168c Use a hyphen to show the omission of a connecting word.

    the Franco-Prussian War (*and* omitted)   chapters 1-6 (*through* omitted)

FOR PRACTICE AND APPLICATION

A. Supply hyphens where they are needed in the following exercises. Identify each type of compound word included.

1. What were the terms of the Clayton Bulwer Treaty?
2. Although Elliott won first place, Harold was runner up.
3. The chairman was elected by a two thirds majority.
4. She insisted that there were thirty two boxes in storage.
5. His so what attitude exasperated all his friends.
6. Although he is antiimperialist, antiFascist, and antiCommunist, Bill says that he is not procapitalist.
7. Her brother in law came to her aid.
8. He is the President elect.
9. More than one ex governor has become President.

B. Look through stories in popular magazines to find good use of original compound adjectives. In class, tell what you think the writer is trying to suggest. You may enjoy seeing whether you can coin similar expressions.

---

*Note that no *and* is used. In mathematical terminology, *and* between *hundred* and *twenty-five* would mean the presence of a decimal point.

152

ITALICS AND UNDERLINING

Matter that is italicized in print is underlined in typewritten or longhand work.

> PRINTED: Roget's *Thesaurus*, a book of synonyms and antonyms, is invaluable to any writer.
>
> TYPEWRITTEN: Roget's <u>Thesaurus</u>, a book of synonyms and antonyms, is invaluable to any writer.

169a Italicize foreign words not yet accepted as part of our language.

> This fashion is the *dernier cri*.

169b Italicize titles of books; of long plays, poems, motion pictures, or musical compositions; of newspapers and magazines; of ships, trains, and aircraft.

> I have enjoyed reading *The Sea around Us*.
> The next dramatic production will be *The Barretts of Wimpole Street*.
> A reporter on the *Baltimore Sun*, he also writes for the *Atlantic Monthly*.
> We traveled to California on the *City of Los Angeles*.

[NOTE: In titles of books, the introductory articles (*a, an, the*) are capitalized and italicized; but in periodicals, an introductory *the* is not, as a rule, capitalized or italicized.]

169c Italicize figures, letters, signs, and words referred to as words.

> How many *s*'s are there in your name?
> I'm tired of all your *if*'s.

169d Italicize words used emphatically, but do not overdo this usage.

> I do *not* agree at all!

FOR PRACTICE AND APPLICATION

Copy the following sentences, underlining all words that should be italicized. Exchange papers for checking.

1. I am reading Scott's The Heart of Midlothian.
2. I looked through two magazines—Newsweek and Life—and in two daily papers—the Chicago Daily News and the New York Times—but I could not find an account of the new discovery.
3. James likes to use the word stalwart.
4. Yvonne always uses the French expression tout à fait.
5. Her oral report was spoiled by the use of well-a.
6. Be sure that you have crossed each t.
7. Have you seen the motion picture The Best Years of Our Lives?
8. The senior class presented Gilbert and Sullivan's The Pirates of Penzance.
9. I find that Holiday is an interesting magazine.
10. If you don't dot your i's, the word Mississippi will be illegible.

ABBREVIATIONS AND NUMBERS

As a general rule, do not use abbreviations in any type of formal writing. The few exceptions to this general rule which are considered acceptable may be learned quickly.

170a Use these abbreviations of titles preceding names: *Mr., Messrs., Mrs., Dr.,* and *St.* (Saint). Spell out other titles unless first names or initials precede the last name. Use no period after *Miss;* it is not an abbreviation.

> Call **Mr.** Jones, **Dr.** Wells, **Mrs.** Laird, and **Miss** Quigley.
> The officer in charge is **Colonel** Adams. [not **Col.** Adams]
> **Supt. A. H.** Lewis will speak at the luncheon meeting.

170b Use these abbreviations following names: *Esq., Jr., Sr.* If *Esq.* follows a name, be sure that no title is used before the name. Abbreviate also names of academic and religious degrees.

> The sign bore these words: E. T. Beggs, **D.D.S.**
> Address the letter thus: Lee Hill, **Esq.** [not **Mr.** Lee Hill, **Esq.**]

170c Use the following special abbreviations:

(1) **A.M.** and **P.M.** with numbers to show time: 7:10 **P.M.**, 4:15 **A.M.** [*O'clock* is superfluous with **A.M.** or **P.M.**]

(2) **A.D.** and **B.C.** with numbers representing years. **A.D.** precedes and **B.C.** follows the date.

> The monument was erected **A.D.** 1715.
> Julius Caesar died in 44 **B.C.**

(3) **No.** (Number) when followed by a numeral, except at the beginning of a sentence: Who has **No.** 617? **Number** 617 is the missing ticket.

(4) Latin terms such as *i.e.* (that is), *e.g.* (for example), *viz.* (namely), *vs.* (versus)

(5) Such terms as *P.S., N.B., C.O.D., f.o.b.*

170d As a rule, use periods after abbreviations of names of associations, fraternal groups, or other organizations: **Y.M.C.A., U.N., I.O.O.F.** (Follow the style that the organization itself uses.)

170e Use periods after initials of radio and television networks, but omit periods (1) after initial letters of names of government agencies and of radio or television stations and (2) in the terms *IOU* and *SOS*.

> The **FCC** has issued its report.   This **IOU** is worthless.
> Is **WBBM** a **C.B.S.** station?

170f Spell out *Christmas;* that is, do not write *Xmas.*

170g Avoid abbreviating the following, except in footnotes, tabular matter, technical writings, and other special cases: (1) names of business firms; (2) weights and measures; (3) the parts of addresses and dates; (4) parts of geographical names, such as *Mount, Port, Fort,* except for *St.* [Saint], which is always abbreviated: St. Louis, Missouri.

171a Use figures in mathematical or statistical material. Spell out any number that begins a sentence; within a sentence, spell out any number of fewer than three digits.

>**Two hundred ten** men were called; **112** were accepted.
>This book has **thirty-five** illustrations in color.

171b Spell out round numbers; i.e., *hundreds, thousands,* **and so on.**

>He has sold **twenty-five hundred** acres. [*not* two thousand five hundred]
>The population has grown to over **thirty million.**

171c Use figures for dates, house numbers, and pages or parts of a book; for decimals and percentages; for hours and minutes with **A.M.** and **P.M.**; but (except where brevity is highly essential) **spell out street names.** Be sure also to spell out *per cent*.

>The new offices at **96 Twelfth Street** opened on **March 1, 1953.**
>Call again at **4:00** P.M. We shall be ready at **four o'clock.**
>According to the notice on **page 8,** we can get a **65 per cent** discount.

171d In writing dates, do not add any letters to the figures.

>Wrong: July **4th,** 1776   Right: July **4,** 1776
>Wrong: May **21st,** 1953   Right: May **21,** 1953
>Wrong: April **3rd,** 1865   Right: April **3,** 1865

171e Treat alike all numbers in connected groups. If the largest number has three digits, use figures throughout.

>The schools have, respectively, **9, 35, 87,** and **102** teachers.

171f In expressing sums of money, use *ciphers* (00) only with sums under $100 or with other numbers in a series containing dollars *and* cents.

>I owe you **$10.00.** I can pay only **$6.50** now.
>This television set sells for **$295.**
>I collected donations of **$68.75, $35.90,** and **$110.00.**

FOR PRACTICE AND APPLICATION

A. Copy the following sentences, correcting all the errors in the use of abbreviations and numbers. Exchange papers for checking.

1. The house will cost him eight thousand seven hundred fifty dollars after the two mortgages have been paid.
2. Miss Eva Long lives at fifty Beech Ave. with her grandfather, Dr. Todd.
3. The two boys hope to visit Mt. Wilson.
4. We called on Prof. Brown, who lives over on 3rd Street.
5. The letters were mailed on Mon., Feb. 10th.
6. Chas. and Wm. were in an automobile accident on Rush St.
7. 50 boys earned enough to pay ninety % of their expenses.
8. Station K.D.K.A. was a radio pioneer.
9. The mts. in the East are covered with vegetation.

10. Our Xmas holidays will begin on Dec. 20.
11. He is William Harvey, Junior, of Saint Paul, Minnesota.

B. Newspaper style sometimes does not follow all the rules in this lesson. Bring to class any such instances that you can find. What reasons can you suggest for the variation?

2. Capitalization

172a **Always capitalize proper nouns and proper adjectives formed from them.** A proper noun names a particular person, place, or thing, as distinguished from a common noun, which refers to any of a class of persons, places, or things. **Capitalize common nouns only if they form part of a proper noun, as shown in (1), (3), (5), (6), (7), (9) on this page and the next.**

(1) **Persons**

    Patrick MacGill*   Mrs. Dennis   Governor White   Dan O'Neill*

(2) **Days of the week, months of the year** (but not the seasons)

    We moved last winter, on the last Friday in February.

(3) **Religions, creeds, and denominations; names applied to the Bible and its parts; other sacred books; nouns and personal pronouns referring to the Deity. Do not capitalize references to pagan deities or relative pronouns that refer to the Deity.**

    Christianity   Judaism   Holy Scriptures   God the Father
    Protestants   Lutherans   Koran   Holy Spirit

(4) **Countries, nationalities, races, and languages, and adjectives derived from them.** In a few instances, adjectives derived from proper nouns have, by common usage, dropped the capital letter: *china* plates, *morocco* leather, *turkish* towel. Consult the dictionary if in doubt.

    France   Swedes   Negroes   Latin   English landscape
    French   Finns   Indians   Greek   Japanese customs

(5) **Geographic and place names**

    Hudson Bay   Mount Hood   Michigan Avenue   Fort Worth

(6) **Special organizations** (business, school, professional, social, . . .)

    Metropolitan Opera   Izaak Walton League   Audubon Society
    Burlington Railroad   Dallas Symphony Orchestra   Lincoln High School
    University of Michigan   Better Business Bureau   Sahara Coal Company

---

* Names beginning with *O'* (meaning "a descendant of") or *Mac, Mc* (meaning "son of") usually need two capital letters, depending upon the bearer's own wish.

(7) Special buildings and other man-made structures, ships, airplanes, and trains

    Fine Arts Building   Wrigley Field   the *Flying Cloud*
    the White House   Eiffel Tower   the *Sunset Limited*

(8) **Brand or trade names**

    Anchor work shirts   Choosy chocolates   Treadwell tires

(9) **Holidays, special or famous events, historical periods or eras, famous documents**

    Labor Day   Homecoming Day   the Dark Ages   Christian Era
    Senior Prom   Battle of the Bulge   the Crusades   Wagner Act

172b Capitalize titles of honor or respect that precede a proper name or that are used alone in place of the name of a specific individual.

    Is Colonel Molloy here? When did he become a colonel?
    Tell me, Colonel, where were you stationed in 1950?

172c Capitalize epithets used with or in place of proper nouns.

    the Iron Duke   the Lone-Star State   the Swedish Nightingale

172d Capitalize initials; abbreviations of titles preceding proper names; the abbreviations *Jr., Sr.,* and *Esq.* following names; the abbreviations of academic degrees, and the abbreviations *A.M., P.M., B.C.,* and *A.D.*

    A.D. 1492   Capt. R. L. Bannister   B. F. Wood, Jr.
    10:15 A.M.   Walter G. Maddock, M.D.   C. Dean Ray, Esq.

172e Capitalize words denoting family relationship only when they are used as a person's name or as a part of it.

    My mother was named for her Aunt Celia.
    Is Grandma coming for Christmas, Mother?
    Your grandmother is Dick's aunt, isn't she?

172f Capitalize the names of school subjects that are languages or that have a specific course number. Capitalize the proper adjective but not the noun in such course names as *American history.*

I am studying French, journalism, Geometry II, and United States history.

172g Capitalize the official names of governmental bodies, offices, and officers. In referring to the President of the United States, always capitalize President, even if no specific person is named. Capitalize the names of other officers when used in place of the names of specific individuals.

    He works in the State Department. He was a county judge.
    No, Judge, I have never been a congressman.
    Mr. Speaker, I yield to the Senator from North Carolina.

172h Capitalize points of the compass when they refer to definite geographical parts of the country or of the world, but do not capitalize them when they are used merely to indicate direction.

    I should like to visit the Far East someday.
    We live six miles east of town.

172i Capitalize the titles of books, newspapers, magazines, and all other kinds of literary works, whether or not published; of works of art; and of musical compositions. In such titles, do not capitalize the articles *a, an,* or *the,* prepositions, or conjunctions unless they come first or last.

> We have been reading Frost's "The Death of the Hired Man."
> Have you read *A Dog at His Heels?*
> This story appeared first in the *New Orleans Times-Picayune.*
> I call my painting "The Dawn Will Come, But—."

172j Do not capitalize a common noun used with a proper noun unless that common noun actually is a part of the specific name.

> Wayne High School is located between Elm and Cedar streets. [*Streets* is not part of either name; the names are *Elm Street* and *Cedar Street.*]
> Our high school is on Elm Street near Tenth Avenue.

172k Capitalize personifications.

> Knowing that Nature never did betray
> The heart that loved her.
> —Wordsworth

172l Capitalize the first word of a sentence and of a line of verse. Capitalize the first word of a quotation unless you use ellipses to indicate that the beginning has been omitted. (In quoting, always copy the exact capitalization used by the author.)

> I shall remember while the light lives yet.
> And in the night-time I shall not forget.
> —Swinburne
>
> Don asked, "When shall I see you again?"
> I heard only a few words: ". . . best for everyone."

172m Always capitalize the pronoun *I* and the vocative *O.*

> "What can I give thee, O my dearest?"

172n Capitalize the first word and any nouns in the salutation of a letter, but capitalize only the first word of the complimentary close.

> Dear Mother,   My dear Son and Daughter,   Your old friend,

FOR PRACTICE AND APPLICATION

A. Copy the following sentences. Supply capital letters where they are needed. Exchange papers for checking. Be ready to justify your use of capitals.

1. the clerk told me that the h. c. miller company sells more write-well pens than any other make.
2. the president of the united states chooses the members of his cabinet, but the senate must confirm his choices.
3. although this traveler quotes extensively from the talmud and the koran, he seems to have little knowledge of the bible.

4. the judges selected the girl dressed as the greek goddess diana.
5. the cape of good hope received its name from king john of portugal. It was first named "cape of storms" by bartolomeu dias, the first european to sail around it.
6. the exhibit included paintings by several mexican artists.
7. the university of maryland terrapins played the oklahoma sooners in the 1953 orange bowl contest.
8. "the holy trinity" means the father, the son, and the holy ghost.
9. manufacturing developed in the north faster than in the south.
10. because columbus day is a school holiday, several classes from lincoln school plan to visit the brookfield zoo.
11. the ohio river, a tributary of the mississippi river, overflowed its banks this spring. We were living in crown city at the time.
12. sam's father is a worker in the republican party.
13. betty is a senior at lake forest academy. she will attend college later.
14. the queen's coronation took place in westminster abbey.
15. chinese and japanese customs are referred to as oriental customs.
16. the greeley high school, which is in the block between sixth and seventh streets, was named in honor of horace greeley.
17. the international harvester company specializes in farm implements.
18. the lincoln memorial in washington, d.c., is an inspiring sight, especially when seen at night.
19. the first signature on the declaration of independence is that of john hancock.
20. they will be married in the first methodist church of glendale.
21. columbus planned to sail west in order to reach the east.
22. bob asked me whether i'd like to read the book or the magazine, *a tale of two cities* or the *national geographic*.
23. paul edwards, jr., won first place in the speech contest with his oration "the price of peace."
24. the duchess of york, sister-in-law of the king, was informed of the death of her husband, the duke.
25. the summer school catalogue lists courses in greek, psychology, english, mathematics, and science.

B. Here is further practice in capitalization. Treat as in *A*.
1. tonight dad said that uncle tim and my cousin had bought a cabin cruiser and had named it the *sea spray*.
2. homer brown, d.d.s., was graduated from new york university before he attended dental school.
3. the letter began, "my dear clare," and closed with the words, "your sincere friend."
4. "i forget, dad," said elmer, "whether i told you that i've been elected to the national honor society."
5. joe louis, known as "the brown bomber," was at all times a credit to boxing and to the negro race.

6. "and now, o lovely lady, i take my leave."
7. as if it had been a christian soul,
   we hailed it in god's name.
   —Coleridge
8. this is a recording of Beethoven's *ninth symphony,* played by the n.b.c. symphony orchestra with arturo toscanini conducting.
9. the employees of the enwood oil company held a dinner in the sunset room of the ashley hotel, honoring their retiring president, a. basil briggs.
10. the second baseman kept shouting, "don't let them score!"
11. the clinch river in tennessee is part of the tennessee valley authority project.
12. the snake river, one of the most interesting rivers in the united states, forms part of the boundary between idaho and oregon.
13. cliff and i have often wondered why some hollywood producer does not make a movie of sir walter scott's *the lady of the lake.*
14. my young brother and his friends built a shack of old boards on panther creek and organized a club which they called secret six.
15. last thanksgiving all our relatives came to our house, even old grandfather poindexter.
16. the street on the north side of school is elmwood avenue.
17. the high school on route 45 is called the monee consolidated high school.
18. ordinarily i do not like history, but history II was interesting.
19. of all the seasons, susan likes fall the best.
20. our school won the lafayette county championship this spring.
21. the *grumman wildcat* was a united states navy plane used in world war II.
22. a famous american playwright, eugene o'neill, who died in november, 1953, won the pulitzer prize three times: in 1920 (*beyond the horizon*), in 1922 (*anna christie*), and in 1928 (*strange interlude*).
23. the lord's prayer begins thus: "our father, which art in heaven."

C. For each capitalization error that you made in *A* and *B* write two original sentences to illustrate the rule that applies. Exchange papers with a classmate who will check your work by the rules.

CORRELATING ENGLISH WITH YOUR OTHER CLASSES

Bring to English class a paper that you are now preparing for some other class, or one that you wrote recently. Check the paper carefully for capitalization problems. Make any needed changes.

FOLLOW-UP

From now on, proofread for capitalization all letters that you write, as well as all papers that you prepare for any of your classes. Make such checking a habit.

Review practice

REVIEW

PUNCTUATION AND CAPITALIZATION

In the following exercises copy the sentences and supply the correct capital letters and punctuation marks. Also make necessary corrections in abbreviations and numbers. Exchange papers for checking.

Exercise A

1. for how long has hc larson been president of the rotary club
2. keats tells i think i'm right that he occasionally spent a little time adonizing
3. my father was fond of quoting from old dr johnson, especially these words that all who are happy, are equally happy is not true [*omitted words*] a small drinking glass and a large one [*omitted words*] may be equally full but the large one holds more than the small one
4. the greek gods often left mount olympus to mingle in human affairs
5. jupiter once assumed the disguise of a bull and in this form wooed a beautiful young maiden named europa
6. lou phil and arnold all are to be here at 830 am arent they
7. mr jones a highly superstitious man would not accept the reservation in the hotel because the room reserved for him was numbered thirteen
8. since miss graham entertained no numerical prejudices she was amused by mr joness superstition
9. your im never wrong attitude said frank annoys father therefore i suggest that you cultivate a little humility
10. only ten % of the $565.00 collected will be needed for expenses

Exercise B

1. we spent a glorious week at sylvan lake in the black hills of south dakota
2. my theme is entitled happy go lucky me
3. When supt james brill who is my brother in law lived in the south he taught school in st george a small town in south carolina near the edisto river
4. its the mens turn not the womens to plan the office picnic
5. having changed my mind i went to a movie wake now for me however I should have saved my 50 cents
6. the shedd aquarium located on chicagos lake front has many interesting tropical specimens in its balanced aquariums
7. who said that inspiration is 90% hard work
8. her grandmother by the way has the habit of prefacing every conversation with these words now when I was your age
9. a new years gift to the world said the frost,
   rich lace curtains which nothing cost
   —LELAND
10. she asked when is the plane due i must be in dow city by ten o'clock pm

Exercise C

1. the queen mary docked yesterday
2. people were permitted to inspect the cruiser uss chicago
3. it seems incredible but he could not tell me what bc means
4. mabel was it on may 4th that you moved to 2715 north 5 street
5. the king james version of the bible was begun by the authorization of king james I
6. the lord is my shepherd i shall not want is the 1st line of the 23rd psalm
7. it would be erroneous to conclude from the name the 30 years war that there was continuous fighting on the battlefield for 30 years
8. the city of saint augustine the oldest one in the united states was founded by the spanish in the year 1565
9. dr kevin o'brien esq owns a large estate 6 miles north of town
10. one of my favorite songs from gilbert and sullivans the mikado is ive got a little list

Exercise D

1. nbc has studios located in the merchandise mart in chicago but cbs has its radio studios in the wrigley building
2. is san francisco bay called the golden gate
3. saint louis missouri is located on the mississippi river
4. we drove through pasadena on our way to san diego
5. youre to arrive at 10 am on tuesday not at six pm on monday
6. a two thirds vote is required for election to our club north high thespians
7. but but he stammered i dont understand
8. smiling sadly the little old man admitted no i havent had a steady job since the winter of 39
9. saroyan a modest self styled genius wrote the book the daring young man on the flying trapeze
10. amenhotep III king of egypt reigned for about 36 years

Exercise E

jack is a shy boy but he doesnt know it or does he right now hes leaving the library with dale carnegies book how to win friends and influence people under his arm if you should ask him why he has chosen that book he would tell you that the title aroused his curiosity in his place wouldnt you say the same thing when you were seventeen were you ever seventeen and aware of being seventeen were you puzzled if or when the girl you were almost in love with made you feel that you were the remotest thing on her horizon jack knows such a girl last week he had a coke with her and they sat for about fifteen minutes and talked about this and that but not about anything in particular it was a lighthearted conversation he wants to take her to the senior prom she has sometimes been friendlier since that coke and yet part of the time she gives him that less than the dirt under her feet feeling why do girls have to act that way

3. Spelling

Whatever praises may justifiably be sung for the English language, few can be sung for its spelling. A study of the language reveals that its ancestry is a mixture of Anglo-Saxon, Roman, Norman-French, and later, Latin and Greek.

Until the advent of printing, writers were free to spell words as they pleased. As in punctuation, so in spelling, the printer has helped to give words their fixed forms.

Many attempts have been made, and are still being made, to simplify spelling. Among the persons interested have been men of such varied activities and professions as Henry Holt, Mark Twain, Andrew Carnegie, and Theodore Roosevelt. The results of these attempts so far have been negligible; whether a definite system of simplified spelling will ever be adopted is a question.

Certainly it is true that businessmen complain bitterly that typists, stenographers, and even clients continually violate accepted spelling usage. Their cry is, "They cannot spell and do not know that they cannot spell." Be sure that this criticism does not apply to you.

The following suggestions are helpful in learning to spell new words as you meet them in reading or listening.

HOW TO LEARN TO SPELL

1. Become acquainted with the spoken and the written form of the word at the same time. Frequently misspelling is caused by mispronunciation. When you consult the dictionary, check first for pronunciation. Pronounce the word accurately several times, and then spell it orally an equal number of times to fix it in your mind. After that, write it correctly until you feel that the correct spelling has become automatic. In this way, by hearing it correctly, seeing it correctly, and writing it correctly, you will spell it correctly the next time that you use the word. [Note: Although many words in our language are not spelled the way that they are pronounced, the process of sounding the word accurately with the correct spelling in mind should prove helpful.]

2. Study new words as you find them in your reading.

3. Practice writing them at frequent intervals. Spelling tends to become mechanical; that is, you form spelling habits.

RULES FOR SPELLING

Mastering and applying the following rules can help you to eliminate gross errors in spelling. Most of the rules you have met before; therefore this list should not be difficult for you.

173a Most nouns form their plurals by adding *s* to the singular.

        hat, hats   boy, boys   messenger, messengers

173b Nouns ending in *s, sh, ch* (except with the *k* sound), *x,* or *z* form their plurals by adding *es* to the singular.

        kis**s**, kis**ses**   mat**ch**, mat**ches**,   bu**sh**, bu**shes**   bo**x**, bo**xes**

173c Nouns ending in *o* preceded by a vowel generally add *s* to form the plural; if a consonant precedes the *o*, they add *es*. Exceptions include musical terms and certain other nouns. Always check with the dictionary.

        came**o**, came**os**   rati**o**, rati**os**   her**o**, her**oes**   vet**o**, vet**oes**
      [*Exceptions:* auto**s**, banjo**s**, piano**s**, solo**s**, . . .]

173d Nouns ending in *f* or *fe* change *f* or *fe* to *v* and add *es*.

        kni**fe**, kni**ves**   thie**f**, thie**ves**   hal**f**, hal**ves**
      [*Exceptions:* chief**s**, roof**s**, belief**s**, . . .]

173e Compound words generally add *s* to the main word. A few words make both parts of a compound noun plural.

        commander in chief   master sergeant
        commander**s** in chief   master sergeant**s**

        son-in-law   manservant
        son**s**-in-law   **men**servant**s**

173f Some words form their plurals irregularly.

        man   child   woman   foot   goose
        m**en**   child**ren**   wom**en**   f**ee**t   g**ee**se

173g Letters of the alphabet, signs, numbers, and words referred to as words form their plurals by adding an apostrophe and *s* ('s).

        3's   *i*'s   *a*'s   &'s   and's

173h Nouns ending in *y* preceded by a consonant change the *y* to *i* and add *es*; if the *y* is preceded by a vowel, they keep the *y* and simply add *s*.

        dais**y**, dais**ies**   part**y**, part**ies**   monke**y**, monke**ys**

173i Some words retain their foreign plurals.

        alumn**us** (*masc.*)   alumn**a** (*fem.*)   memorand**um**
        alumn**i**   alumn**ae**   memorand**a**
        parenthes**is**   phenomen**on**   cris**is**
        parenthes**es**   phenomen**a**   cris**es**

173j Established usage decrees that certain collective nouns shall be used in the singular, while others are used in the plural.

            Singular: news, mathematics, civics, economics, molasses
            Plural: trousers, thanks, oats, ashes

173k Proper nouns do not change internally when they are made plural. If the plural adds a syllable, they add *es;* if the plural does not add a syllable, they simply add *s.*

> Henry has red hair. Both Henry**s**, my uncle and my cousin, have red hair.
> Mr. Murphy, Mrs. Murphy, and all the little Murphy**s** came.
> I get Ed Jones confused with two other Jon**eses**.

173l Proper names preceded by titles may form their plurals in two ways.

> Mr. Fitzgerald—the Mr. Fitzgerald**s** *or* the **Messrs.** Fitzgerald
> Miss Ross—the Miss Ross**es** or the Miss**es** Ross
> Sergeant Brown—the Sergeant Brown**s** or the Sergeant**s** Brown

173m Some nouns may be used either in the singular or the plural sense without changing their form. Examples are such words as *sheep, gross, hose, series, deer, swine.*

173n Words ending in silent *e* usually drop the final *e* before the addition of suffixes beginning with a vowel.

> use, us**ing**   wave, wav**y**   move, mov**able**   base, bas**al**

173o Words ending in silent *e* keep the final *e* before the addition of suffixes beginning with a consonant.

> use, use**ful**   pale, pal**eness**   brave, brave**ly**   excite, excite**ment**

173p If a word ends in a consonant and *y,* the *y* changes to *i* before the addition of a suffix. (Proper nouns are an exception. See Rule 173k.)

> p**i**ty, p**i**tiful   hap**p**y, hap**p**iness   merry, merr**ily**

173q If a word ends in a vowel and *y,* the *y* does not change to *i* when a suffix is added.

> obe**y**, obe**ying**   pla**y**, pla**yful**   destro**y**, destro**yed**

173r One syllable words (monosyllables) or words accented on the last syllable, ending in a single consonant preceded by a single vowel, double the final consonant when adding a suffix beginning with a vowel.

> plan, pla**nned**   infer, infer**ring**   tan, tan**ning**   big, big**gest**

173s The letter *u* always follows the letter *q*.

    quart   bouquet   quinine   quiver   quip
    quota   croquet   quintet   squeal   quiz

173t The prefix *full* usually has a hyphen separating it from the other part of a compound; *ful* is a suffix.

    full-length   full-grown   tearful   spoonful   eyeful

173u In distinguishing between the *ie* and *ei* combinations when the sound is long *e*, note that *e* usually precedes *i* after soft *c*; in most other cases, *i* comes first. (Perhaps remembering the name *Alice* will help you. The *e* follows the *c*; after other letters, *i* appears first.)

    AFTER *c*: receive, deceive, perceive, receipt, conceit
    AFTER OTHER LETTERS: priest, field, piece, chief, relief
    [*Exceptions:* either, neither, leisure, weird, seize, species]
    [NOTE: When the sound is not that of long *e* (for example, long *a* as in *weigh*), use the combination *ei*, as in *eight, their, neighbor, vein, veil*.]

FOR PRACTICE AND APPLICATION

Directions: Work upon activities A–D in pairs or in your small groups. Pronounce the words and have both oral and written practice in spelling them.

A. Write the plural form of the following singular nouns:

1. alumna	11. woman	21. echo
2. alumnus	12. guest	22. great-grandmother
3. crisis	13. valley	23. Frenchman
4. parenthesis	14. knife	24. tooth
5. soprano	15. leaf	25. father-in-law
6. ally	16. mouse	26. deer
7. memento	17. box	27. sky
8. boy	18. foot	28. *x* (the letter)
9. child	19. Mr. Anderson	29. 9 (the number)
10. man	20. Miss Twohey	30. * (the sign)

B. Complete the spelling of these words by inserting *ie* or *ei*:

1. th--r	6. l--sure	11. n--ce
2. n--ghbor	7. f--ld	12. gr--ve
3. dec--t	8. w--ght	13. rec--ve
4. rel--ve	9. s--ze	14. c--ling
5. n--ther	10. w--rd	15. fr--ght

C. In the following list of words, add the suffixes as indicated. Make the necessary changes in the letters of the words to assure correct spelling.

1. arrange	plus –ment	6. happy	plus –ly
2. mercy	plus –less	7. admit	plus –ing
3. hearty	plus –ly	8. concur	plus –ed
4. study	plus –ed	9. like	plus –able
5. beauty	plus –ful	10. like	plus –ly

D. Students may find it helpful to make a careful study of the following list of common words frequently misspelled. Follow directions for study given at the beginning of this section.

1. absence	31. disappointment	61. necessary
2. accept	32. exaggerate	62. occur, occurred
3. accidentally	33. except	63. organize
4. accommodate	34. existence	64. physician
5. advice (*noun*)	35. familiar	65. practice
6. advise (*verb*)	36. foreign	66. prejudice
7. all ready	37. forfeit	67. preparation
8. already	38. formally	68. principal
9. although	39. formerly	69. principle
10. analyze, analyse	40. fulfill, fulfil	70. receipt
11. athlete	41. gauge, gage	71. receive
12. believe	42. grammar	72. recipe
13. benefited	43. huge	73. recipient
14. capital (*city*)	44. hygiene	74. rhyme, rime
15. capitol (*building*)	45. imaginary	75. schedule
16. changeable	46. incidentally	76. separate
17. chieftain	47. incredible	77. separation
18. column	48. indispensable	78. sieve
19. committee	49. irrelevant	79. similar
20. complement (*of a verb*)	50. irresistible	80. stationary
21. compliment (*praise*)	51. irreverent	81. stationery
22. conceive	52. khaki	82. statue
23. council	53. laboratory	83. statute
24. counsel	54. liable	84. symbol
25. deceive	55. librarian	85. thorough
26. describe	56. loose	86. though
27. description	57. lose	87. vacuum
28. desert	58. moral	88. vengeance
29. dessert	59. morale	89. warrior
30. disappearance	60. mischievous	90. weird

E. The following theme contains fifty-eight different misspelled words. They are actual misspellings taken from student papers. Probably not one of you would misspell all the words misspelled in this theme, but every one of them was found in student writing.

Copy the theme, correcting each misspelled word that you find. Use the dictionary to check each word that you think may be wrong. Exchange papers for checking. Have each misspelled word written correctly on the board as a guide. List in your notebook any of the words that give you trouble.

Representatives of a survey company were given promission to interupt our rehersal today to ask some signifigent and some humorus questions about our hobbies, schoolwork, enviramant, and interests. Our repsonses, when sumerized, are suposed to provide a reflexion of our peraperation for the future. The summaries show wheather our ackquired abilities, temperments, and charactirs jibe adiquetly with our interests.

As for my-self, my favorite past-times are rollar skating, paddeling a canoe, riding my bycicle, and collecting souveniers. My favorite subject is lititure, which this year has been predominently about Great Britian. One story I liked was a portrait of the cornation of a tyrranical and dictorial emperor. In the story the anonymouse auther discribed a preaty herione who, in a luxerious setting, exibited a rebelous and rathful heart in seeking vengance.

I also like Spainish and mathamatics, and I like chemistry since our laboratory was remodled. Machanical drawing dosen't intrest me, nor does our history, labled "Primative Man." I want to be a secratry, but ironicly, grammer, which would be most benificial, is my poorest subject. What can I hope to acomplish? Members of our class agreed unamiously that the best part of school is dismissle for the hollidays.

"THEY'RE NOT SPELLED RIGHT YET, BUT YOU'RE GETTING WARMER!"

FOLLOW-UP

Improvement of spelling is an individual matter. The best list of words for you is one compiled from your own errors. This list will have the virtue of truly reflecting your own needs and present interests.

If a misspelled word is called to your attention, add that word to your personal list. Then consult the dictionary. The dictionary is the authority not only on meanings but on accepted usage in spelling, pronunciation, and syllabication.

Arrange your list alphabetically so that you can use it for quick reference. Once you are sure of a word, cross that word off.

Keep the list in your notebook where it will be readily available—and then make using it a habit.

4. Syllabication

Division of words at the end of lines should be avoided whenever possible. If you must divide a word, consult a good dictionary if you are in doubt about how it should be divided. In addition, be guided by these rules.

174 The general rule is this: Divide a word only between syllables. A syllable is a part of a word pronounced by a single impulse of the voice.

174a Do not divide monosyllables (words of one syllable) or proper nouns.

    length, *not* leng-th   freight, *not* fre-ight
    walked, *not* walk-ed   William, *not* Wil-liam

174b Do not carry over a group of letters containing only a silent vowel.

    trouble, *not* trou-ble   flex-ible, *not* flexi-ble
    handle, *not* han-dle   vis-ible, *not* visi-ble
    muscle, *not* mus-cle   rustle, *not* rus-tle

174c Do not make one-letter divisions.

    enough, again, among (*not:* e-nough, a-gain, a-mong)

174d Avoid carrying over fewer than three letters. The following show correct division.

    per-former   in-com-pletely   re-ad-justed

174e Do not make divisions that may cause pronunciation difficulties.

    raging, *not* rag-ing   ref-eree, *not* re-feree

174f When a suffix is pronounced as a separate syllable, divide just before it, except in words covered by rules 174d and 174e.

    ring-ing   wait-ers   por-ous   self-ish

174g If a word contains a double consonant as the result of adding a suffix, divide as follows: *drop, drop-ping; excel, excel-ling; dip, dip-per.* Do not divide other double letters preceding suffixes: *call-ing, guess-ing, dress-ers.*

FOR PRACTICE AND APPLICATION

(1) Draw vertical lines to indicate where the following words may be divided at the end of a line. (2) Circle words that should not be divided. Exchange papers for checking.

1. abandon
2. ablaze
3. comparable
4. hidden
5. Franklin
6. shining
7. humming
8. instep
9. government
10. dimmer
11. little
12. manuscript
13. strictly
14. avoidable
15. liking
16. running
17. mystery
18. mysterious
19. Raleigh
20. deductible
21. explanation
22. equal
23. night
24. consul
25. picketed
26. picked
27. carry
28. dressed

CORRELATING ENGLISH WITH YOUR OTHER CLASSES

Go over papers that you have written for various classes. Make a list of all words that you divided at the end of the line, showing where you divided them. Have these put on the board for class consideration and criticism.

5. Manuscript Form

The following guides indicate points to remember in preparing class assignments or any other manuscripts. Special instructions for longhand and typewritten work follow the guides.

GUIDES FOR CORRECT MANUSCRIPT FORM

1. Use white paper 8½ x 11 inches in size. Do not use a transparent paper.
2. Leave a margin of one and one-half inches on the left, and a margin of one inch on the right; leave a margin of one and one-half inches at the top, and one inch at the bottom.
3. Center the title on the first line. Skip a line below the title. Unless the title is a quotation, a question, or an exclamation, end punctuation is usually unnecessary.
4. Write on one side of the paper only.
5. Number the pages of the manuscript; use Arabic numerals (1, 2, 3).
6. Fold your manuscript lengthwise unless your instructor gives other directions. Place your name, the title of the theme, the date due, and the course name and number on the outside page.

HANDWRITTEN COPY

If you write your paper in longhand, remember that the only purpose of writing is communication: your paper should be legible. Note these points:

1. Use black or blue-black ink.
2. Maintain uniformity in the slant of your letters and an even alignment of height in letters.

"IF YOU'D BE MORE CAREFUL, YOU WOULDN'T HAVE TO ERASE."

3. Use care in letter formation. For example, make distinct loops of the tops of such letters as *l* and *h;* do not make the top of a *t* a loop; close the tops of letters that should be closed, such as *a;* keep the top of the *u* open.

4. Do not crowd your writing. Make each letter distinct from its neighbor.

5. Maintain enough space between words so that all words are definitely separated.

6. Be sure that the letters of each word are connected, except in words in which an apostrophe is used.

7. Dot your *i*'s and *j*'s, and cross your *t*'s; but do not let the crossbar extend to adjacent letters.

TYPEWRITTEN COPY

1. Keep the type clean and the ribbon in good condition at all times.

2. The standard keyboard has no symbol for the figure *one*. Use the small *l* (not *I*). For a dash, use two hyphens spaced away from the words on each side.

3. Strikeovers are hard to read. A few mistakes can be corrected, but if there are many, the page should be retyped. Transposed letters should be erased and retyped.

4. Use double spacing for regular manuscript.

5. In typewritten copy (and in longhand copy also) underline words and passages that would be italicized in print.

6. Corrections and Insertions

Never erase indicated errors or the critical comments that an instructor puts on a manuscript.

If errors are relatively minor, your instructor probably will allow you to make corrections in the original copy. Draw a neat line through words that you change. To indicate a substitution or an addition, use a caret ($\wedge$).

With apparent ~~thought~~ ^thoughtfulness, the boys placed their hands in ^the correct position.

A manuscript that needs many corrections should be rewritten, and both the original and the rewritten copy should be handed in.

CORRECTION SYMBOLS

Marks	Meaning
1. cap	(1) capital letter needed or (2) capital unnecessarily used
2. sp	mistake in spelling
3. p	mistake in punctuation
4. ¶	new paragraph needed
5. no ¶	new paragraph not needed
6. mar	faulty margin
7. head	heading incorrectly placed or incomplete
8. ill	illegible handwriting
9. syl	syllabication (word incorrectly or poorly divided)
10. F	fragment (not a complete sentence)
11. RO	run-on sentence
12. voc	vocabulary (poor word choice)
13. abb	(1) incorrect abbreviation or (2) no abbreviation permissible
14. K	clumsy or awkward construction
15. ?	not clear
16. #	more space needed between words
17. $\wedge$	something omitted
18. agr	agreement (pronoun with antecedent, verb with subject)
19. u	faulty usage (illiterate expression, slang)
20. gr	faulty grammar
21. t	wrong tense of verb

These markings are usually written in the left-hand margin, beside the lines in which errors appear. When any such mark appears in the margin, you must read the line or sentence, find the error, and make the correction.

SECTION II

Using Language to Communicate

CHAPTER 7 *Exploring the Magic of Words*

CHAPTER 8 *Writing Good Paragraphs*

CHAPTER 9 *Gaining Skill in Creative Expression*

CHAPTER 10 *Gaining Skill in Research*

CHAPTER 11 *Speaking Effectively*

CHAPTER 12 *Reading, Looking, and Listening*

CHAPTER 13 *Using English in Business*

Exploring the Magic of Words

CHAPTER 7

1. English—A World Language

When Columbus discovered America, English was the language of a little handful of people on an island off the coast of the European mainland. In the short time, historically speaking, since that date, English has become the language, native or acquired, of nearly five hundred million people! No other country in the world has spread its language over the world as England has done.

Think of it: English is spoken by nearly two hundred million people in the Western Hemisphere; by thirty million people in Asia; by more than one hundred million people in Europe; by more than five million people in Africa; and by twenty million people in Oceania.

True, the people in different parts of the world speak English in somewhat different ways. Even those in England and in the United States do not use the same words for all purposes. Some differences are noted in the following list:

American	*British*	*American*	*British*
streetcar	tram	flashlight	torch
hood	bonnet	stand in line	queue up
gasoline	petrol	movies	cinema
truck	lorry	drugstore	chemist's
suspenders	braces	sidewalk	pavement
radio	wireless	mail	post

Pronunciation and spelling of words sometimes differ in the United States and Britain. Americans say "clerk," the English say "clark"; Americans say "lyootenant," the English say "leftenant"; Americans say "necessary," the English say "necess'ry." Americans write "labor," the English write "labour"; Americans write "judgment," the English write "judgement"; Americans write "defense," the English write "defence." American slang and English slang are very different. Nevertheless, Americans, Englishmen, Australians, New Zealanders, Canadians, and people from many other parts of the far-spread English-speaking world have little or no difficulty in understanding one another.

So too, within the United States itself, people in different parts of the country express themselves in different ways. Inhabitants of Alabama and Mississippi differ in their speech from those of New England; Texans differ from Oregonians in their pronunciation and their choice of words. Sometimes one may even note differences in language customs among people who live on "different sides of the tracks" in the same town. The English language is interesting because it varies so much from place to place, and because it is a living, ever-changing language.

"SO THAT'S WHAT AN UNABRIDGED DICTIONARY LOOKS LIKE!"

FOR YOU TO TALK ABOUT

A. What expressions in English do you know that are characteristic of the region in which you live?

B. How do you account for differences in the English language as noted in England, the United States, Canada, Australia?

C. How can American English influence the language of people in Great Britain?

D. What effect may radio and television have upon differences in speech within the United States?

E. Why has English come into such widespread use throughout the world?

F. What effect does this widespread use of English have upon the language?

G. French and English are used more or less equally in certain parts of Canada. How did this situation come about?

H. Many efforts have been made to devise a single world language. English has been mentioned as one possible language for world use. What would be the value of a world language? What would be the advantages and disadvantages of English as that world language?

2. English—A Changing Language

A living language is one that changes with the life of the people. All languages that are used widely change continually. Latin, which was used by the ancient Romans, changed into what are known today as the Romance languages Italian, French, and Spanish. English now is a very different tongue from that used by Chaucer. Note, for instance, these examples of English words that have changed in meaning down through the years.

1. *Girl* once was used to refer to a child of either sex.
2. *Nice* once meant "ignorant."
3. *Marshal* once meant "stable boy" (a boy who looked after mares).
4. *Shrewd* once meant "wicked."
5. *Smart* once meant "causing pain."
6. *Nimble* once meant "good at taking things."
7. *Barn* once meant "barley-place."
8. *Awful, terrible* once meant "fear-inspiring."
9. *Meat* once meant "food."
10. *Starve* once meant "to die."
11. *Villain* once meant "farm worker."
12. *Silly* once meant "fortunate."

ETYMOLOGY

Etymology is the study of the history of words. It is interesting to trace the original meaning, or *derivation,* of a word. Thus "hypocrite" originally meant "actor," then "pretender." "Doom" originally meant "any legal judgment." "Hussy" originally meant "housewife." The story of English words may be found in many reference works, some of which are probably in your school or public library. The *Webster's New International Dictionary,* the Funk and Wagnalls *New Standard Dictionary,* and Craigie's *Dictionary of American English* will be helpful. If you have access to W. W. Skeat's *Etymological Dictionary of the English Language* or Ernest Weekley's *Etymological Dictionary of Modern English,* by all means use them. If you wish to carry on more advanced study of words, look up Greenough and Kittredge's *Words and Their Ways in English Speech,* G. H. McKnight's *English Words and Their Background,* or Hixson and Colodny's *Word Ways: A Study of Our Living Language.* A great many more fine books have been written about the English language. Perhaps your teacher can secure copies of the leaflet *Word Study* from G. and C. Merriam, Springfield, Massachusetts, publishers of the *Webster's New International Dictionary.*

The study of the forms, history, and relationships of words is known as *linguistics,* literally the "study of tongues." Another word for this study is *philology,* the "love of words," which is especially concerned with the meaning of words that are found in written records. Perhaps some of you will wish to study this fascinating science in college.

FOR PRACTICE AND APPLICATION

A. With the aid of one of the preceding reference books, find the derivations of the following words. Go over them in class.

gossip	hero	June	glamour	geometry	barbarism
Tuesday	panic	January	vaccinate	pantaloon	vandal
journal	cereal	logic	virtue	carnival	vaunt

B. Trace the history of the twelve words listed on page 177 to see how they came to have changed meanings. Compare your findings in class or in your small groups.

C. Proper names have played an interesting part in the development of the English language. The following words, derived from the names of persons, have become common nouns. Find their meaning and history.

babbitt	boycott	dahlia	epicure	sandwich
guillotine	ampere	derby	lynch	zinnia
bloomers	burbank	derrick	fuchsia	chesterfield

D. The words in *C* have, through frequent use as descriptions of kinds of people, things, and actions, become common nouns. Other proper names have come to be applied generally to persons who exhibit some of the qualities of the famous persons who bore those names. To call a man a "Scrooge," for example, is to label him as a hard, miserly sort.

What, then, is implied of a person who is called a *Micawber, a Judas, a Croesus, a Hotspur, a Falstaff, a Rockefeller, a Lothario, a Romeo?* Do a little research on the names that are new to you; then compare your findings with those of your classmates.

E. The following words are derived from the names of places. Find their meaning and history. If you write this activity, exchange papers in class or in your small groups for checking.

| jersey | bedlam | Rugby | madeira |
| cologne | champagne | damask | milliner |

Add to this list as many additional words as you can that are derived from names of places.

FAMILY NAMES

Family names are often formed from the names of occupations. Smith, Mason, Carpenter, Brewer, and Fisher are examples. List other names taken from occupations. The name of the author of this book, "De Boer," is a Dutch word meaning *farmer.* Do you know anyone named *Farmer?*

Some family names are built on given names. The following family names are derived from William:

Williams	Wilkes	Wilson	Wilcox	Willis
Williamson	Wilkins	Woollcott	Wooley	Woolsey
Wilkinson	Wills	Wilcoxson	Willy	Wiley

Most of these names are *patronymics* (made by additions to the name of the father). Others are *diminutives* (derivations, often affectionate, denoting something small or young). *Wilkins,* for example, probably meant "little Will."

FOR YOU TO TALK ABOUT

A. What names have been formed from *John, Robert, Thomas?* What other "base" names can you suggest?

B. What languages use the suffixes *sen* or *son, vich, ski,* or *sky* to mean *son of?* What does *Fitz* before a name mean? *O'? de? von? Mac* or *Mc?*

English is a rich language. It has inherited its words from many sources. Many foreign languages have made their contributions to English. The full story of the English language is too long to tell here, since it is the product of the history of the English people. The languages of the Angles and the Saxons, who were Teutonic invaders, provided the base for the development of modern English. Anglo-Saxon later became enriched with Norman-French, after the invasion of William the Conqueror in 1066. You will find in *Ivanhoe* the story of the early rivalry between Anglo-Saxon and Norman-French. Chaucer (1340–1400) was one of the first English writers to demonstrate the beauty of the new combined language.

Directly and indirectly, English has borrowed words from many languages, including Greek, Latin, French, German, Italian, Dutch, Danish, Indian, and even the languages of the Orient (perhaps as a result of the Crusades). The word *assassin,* for example, comes from the Arabic word *hashshashin,* an eater of *hashish,* a drug that hired killers were thought to have used when committing their crimes.

Since a very large number of English words have been derived from Greek and Latin, you can help to build your vocabulary by learning the more common prefixes, suffixes, and roots in those languages.

COMMON LATIN ELEMENTS

(The abbreviation in parentheses indicates whether an element is a *prefix,* a *root,* or a *suffix.*)

1. **uni** (*p.*)—one
2. **escent** (*s.*)—becoming, growing
3. **bi** (*p.*)—two
4. **tri** (*p.*)—three
5. **quadr** (*p.*)—four
6. **cent** (*p.*)—hundred
7. **mill** (*p.*)—thousand
8. **ped** (*r.*)—foot
9. **super** (*p.*)—above
10. **fy** (*s.*)—make
11. **trans** (*p.*)—across
12. **per** (*p.*)—through
13. **ary** (*s.*)—pertaining to
14. **grav** (*r.*)—heavy
15. **ity** (*s.*)—condition, quality
16. **contra, contro** (*p.*)—against
17. **aqua** (*r.*)—water
18. **terr** (*r.*)—earth
19. **ocul** (*r.*)—eye
20. **ora** (*r.*)—mouth
21. **ous** (*s.*)—full of, like
22. **pater, patr** (*r.*)—father
23. **flor** (*r.*)—flower
24. **frater, fratr** (*r.*)—brother
25. **al** (*s.*)—pertaining to, suited to
26. **corpor** (*r.*)—body
27. **sub** (*p.*)—under
28. **pend** (*r.*)—hang
29. **ad** (*p.*)—to, toward
30. **mit** (*r.*)—send
31. **vid, vis** (*r.*)—see
32. **flect, flex** (*r.*)—bend

If you have studied Latin, you will recognize other Latin elements contained in English words.

COMMON GREEK ELEMENTS

(The abbreviation in parentheses indicates whether an element is a *prefix,* a *root,* or a *suffix.*)

1. **mono** (*p.*)—one
2. **tetra** (*p.*)—four
3. **penta** (*p.*)—five
4. **hexa** (*p.*)—six
5. **phon** (*r.*)—sound
6. **tele** (*p.*)—far, distant
7. **graph, gram** (*r.*)—write
8. **ophthalm** (*r.*)—eye
9. **theo** (*r.*)—god
10. **iso** (*p.*)—equal
11. **cracy, crat** (*s.*)—rule, government
12. **poly** (*p.*)—many
13. **phil** (*r.*)—love
14. **soph** (*r.*)—wisdom
15. **mania** (*s.*)—madness for
16. **chron** (*r.*)—time
17. **geo** (*r.*)—earth
18. **bio** (*r.*)—life
19. **homo** (*p.*)—same
20. **gam** (*r.*)—marriage
21. **therm** (*r.*)—heat
22. **astr, aster** (*r.*)—star
23. **cardi** (*r.*)—heart
24. **pneum** (*r.*)—air, wind, breath
25. **chloro** (*r.*)—green
26. **hemi** (*p.*)—half
27. **micro** (*p.*)—small
28. **neur** (*r.*)—nerve
29. **phos, phot** (*r.*)—light
30. **log** (*r.*)—word, science
31. **phobia** (*s.*)—fear of
32. **hydr** (*r.*)—water

"IT'S ALL ENGLISH TO ME."

FOR PRACTICE AND APPLICATION

A. Name one or more English words containing each of the Latin and the Greek elements in the preceding lists. Make this an oral activity.

B. In an unabridged dictionary, find the derivations of the following words. Explain the words in class.

beauty	alleviate	credit	manuscript
interjection	opera	conductor	incorrigible
preclude	operate	colloquial	pedagogue
elapse	autonomy	fervent	bibliophile
transpire	debonair	regenerate	lavender
courtesy	motto	hospital	colonel

C. In Lincoln's "Gettysburg Address" or in a passage of the King James Bible, find five nouns or verbs that are of Anglo-Saxon origin; find others that are of Norman-French or Latin origin.

D. Use the dictionary or other source books to help you answer the following questions. Compare your findings in class or in your small groups.

1. Which of the sciences use many Latin words? Which use many Greek words?
2. What is the history of the following words: *radical, congress, sermon, knight?* How does the present meaning differ from the older meaning?
3. How many meanings do you know for the word *romantic?* How many words do you know which have been formed from the word *Rome?* How is *Rome* related to *romance?*
4. What connection is there between *infant* and *infantry?*
5. From what language has the word *blitzkrieg* been borrowed? *caballero? chauffeur?*

NEOLOGISMS

The word *neologism* comes from two Greek words meaning *new* and *word*. A neologism is a new word added to the language. When the "horseless carriage" was first invented, a name had to be found for the new vehicle. It came to be called "automobile," from two words meaning "self" and "moving." It was soon known simply as *auto*. Later it came to be called *motor car,* or just *car. Automobile, auto, motor car, car*—these are neologisms. Science and invention have added, and continue to add, many new words to the language.

New words also come into the language as they are needed by the changing life of the people. Events and practices in government, sports, war, advertising, various occupations, school life, and every field of human activity constantly add to the stock of words. When the conditions change, the new words often disappear.

"EGAD——YOU'VE INVENTED A NEW WORD!"

FOR PRACTICE AND APPLICATION

A. For each question in this activity, have two or more members of the class volunteer to find the answers and then to report their findings.

1. What are some scientific words that did not exist twenty-five years ago? Ask your science teacher to help you to make a list.
2. What are several recent inventions (in the last twenty years) that are in common use today?
3. What are some well-known medical products recently discovered? (If you consult the *Readers' Guide*, articles listed under *medicine* may help you.)
4. What new terms has aviation brought into the language?
5. Look through recent editions of the daily newspaper. What terms relating to atomic energy can you find?

B. Use the questions in this activity for class discussion. Probably you will want to supplement the discussion by doing some research.

1. Many expressions have come from the history of the West. *Earmarked, pan out, strike it rich, pull up stakes, get the drop on,* and *jump a claim* are examples. What do these terms mean? What other Western expressions can you think of?
2. Expressions from politics are interesting. What is meant by *logrolling? throwing one's hat into the ring? mugwump? a me-tooer?* What others can you find?

3. What fields of activity created each of the following expressions: *cold war, ceiling zero, point of no return, go haywire, do a tailspin, hitting on all fours, this is where I came in, AWOL, on the beam, boondoggle, foxhole, black market, GI, baby-sitter?* What other expressions of similar origin can you give?
4. Some manufactured products come to be called by a single brand name, even when manufactured by competitors who cannot legally use the name. An example is the word *kodak*. What others can you name?
5. What modern development resulted in the use of the word *kitchenette? roomette?* Examine your local newspaper for similar words.
6. New words are sometimes made by variations of old words. "Marathon" suggested *walkathon* and *talkathon*. "Hamburger" suggested *cheeseburger* and *steakburger*. Can you think of similar neologisms?
7. Where did the expressions *veep* and *jeep* come from?
8. What type of dance music created the word *hepcat?* You may find it amusing to compile a vocabulary of terms used in modern popular music.

SLANG

One of the most interesting topics in language study is *slang*. People who constantly depend upon slang expressions generally leave the impression that they are not well educated. Slang must be distinguished, however, from vulgar and uncouth language. On occasion, a highly educated person may use a slang expression if it fits his purpose, though he will do so only rarely in public speeches or on formal occasions.

Much slang appears in the language for a while and then is lost. Some slang expressions, however, continue to be used and eventually form part of the language. *Lynch* and *blackmail* are examples; once slang terms, they are today standard English. It is important to know when a slang expression has become acceptable, and when it should be reserved for the playground or the "jam session." Remember—slang, if used, should be used sparingly or humorously.

FOR PRACTICE AND APPLICATION

A. Many occupations have their own vocabulary of slang. The busy lunch-counter attendant uses such expressions as these: *B.T.* (for a bacon and tomato sandwich); *clean up the kitchen* (for *hamburger* or *hash*); *draw one* (for *coffee*); *burn one* (for *steak*). List other such expressions that you have heard at one time or another in restaurants.

B. Give examples of the slang vocabularies of sailors, policemen, salesmen, teen-agers, actors, baseball players, newspapermen.

C. Give standard English words for the following slang terms: *big wheel, goon, What gives? Pipe down! Do you dig me? real gone.* Have any of them lost their popularity? If so, which?

D. What expressions, formerly slang, can you find that have become a part of the language? (The reference books listed on page 258 will help you.)

E. Many slang expressions have gone out of use. "Sparking" and "to rubber" are examples. What are some others?

F. Give some slang expressions for "money," for "the human head," for "making mistakes," for "a pretty girl," for "a killjoy."

G. Discuss these questions.
1. Would slang be appropriate in the framing of laws? Explain.
2. Why is the origin of slang words hard to trace?
3. How is slang spread?

3. THE USES OF THE DICTIONARY

You have already discovered the value of the dictionary in finding the derivations of words. In dictionaries you also find a guide to usage, a vocabulary that enables you to enlarge your supply of words, and a great quantity of other useful information. Therefore a good dictionary should be at the disposal of anyone who is interested in improving his diction.

In all circumstances the best dictionary to use is an unabridged dictionary, found in most libraries. An unabridged dictionary contains all the words of the language and labels the standing of each word as *slang, obsolete, technical, idiomatic* . . . Good unabridged dictionaries are *Webster's New International Dictionary,* Funk and Wagnalls *New Standard Dictionary,* the *Oxford English Dictionary.*

Because an unabridged dictionary contains all these words, it is cumbersome and too expensive for students to buy. Therefore a good abridged dictionary, which eliminates some of the words and sections included in the large dictionary but which is complete enough for most student needs, is recommended. The *Webster's Collegiate Dictionary, Fifth Edition;* the *Random House American College Dictionary;* the *Funk and Wagnalls College Standard Dictionary;* and the *Winston Dictionary, College Edition,* are a few examples.

handout   375   **harangue**

hand'out' (hănd'out'), n. *Slang, U.S.* Food or clothing given to a beggar at a house door. See HOBO, *Illust.*
hand'rail' (-rāl'), n. A rail to be grasped by the hand as a support; a railing serving as a guard.
hand'saw' (-sô), n. A saw used with one hand.
hand'sel (hănd'sĕl; hăn'-), **han'sel** (hăn'sĕl), n. [ON. *handsal*, the closing of a bargain by shaking hands, fr. *hand* + *sal* sale, bargain.] A gift as a token of good luck, esp. in an enterprise or experience; as: **a** A first gift at the new year. **b** A gift at the hand + *sal* sale, bargain.] -- *v. t.;* -SELED (-sĕld) or -SELLED; -SELING or -SEL·LING. **1.** To give a handsel to. **2.** To inaugurate with some token of pleasure. **3.** To use or do for the first time.
hand'set' (hănd'sĕt'), n. A combined telephone transmitter and receiver mounted on a handle. See TELEPHONE, *Illust.*
hand'some (hăn'sŭm), *adj.* [*hand* + *-some.*] **1.** *Dial. & Colloq.* Suitable; becoming; appropriate. **4.** Gracious; liberal; gen-

hand'y (hăn'dĭ), *adj.;* HAND'I·ER (-dĭ·ẽr); HAND'I·EST. **1.** *Obs.* Performed by the hand. **2.** Ready to the hand; conveniently near; also, convenient or suited for use; as, a *handy* tool. **3.** Skillful in using the hand; dexterous. **4.** *Naut.* Easily managed or handled; esp., obedient to the helm; -- said of a vessel.
handy man. A man serviceable for odd jobs.
hang (hăng), *v. t.;* HUNG (hŭng) or HANGED (hăngd); HANG'ING. With reference to the death penalty *hanged* is preferred to *hung*. [AS. *hangian, v. i., hōn, v. t.* (pret. *hēng,* past part. *hongen*).] **1.** To fasten to some elevated point without support from below; suspend. **2.** To put to death by suspending from a cross, gibbet, or gallows; specif., to suspend by the neck until life is extinct; -- also used in mild oaths; as, *hang* it. **3.** To fasten so as to allow free motion upon the point of suspension; as, to *hang* a pendulum, a swing, a door, etc. **4.** To cover, decorate, or furnish by hanging pictures, trophies, drapery, etc.; also, to fasten or adjust (drapery, a skirt, etc.) so as to fall gracefully or evenly. **5.** To hold or bear in a suspended or inclined manner or position; to droop. **6.** To fit or fix in position, as at a proper angle (a part of an implement

— *v. i.* Manner in which a thing hangs; as, the *hang* of a scythe; the *hang* of a gown. **2.** Meaning; plan; as, to get the *hang* of an argument; also, method of use; knack; as, to get the *hang* of handling a boat. **3.** A hesitancy, pause, or slackening, as in motion; as, *hang* of an oar in the air before entry into the water. **4.** The least bit; -- used in mild oaths; as, to care not a *hang*.

— **hang'a·ble,** *adj.*

hang'out' (-out'), n. A place where one "hangs out"; a rendezvous.
hang'o·ver (-ō'vẽr), n. **1.** Something that remains from what is past, as a surviving custom. **2.** *Slang.* The aftereffect of dissipation, esp. of overindulgence in intoxicating liquor.
hank (hăngk), n. [Of Scand. origin.] **1.** A coil or loop; specif., a coil or skein of yarn. A hank of cotton yarn contains 840 yd.; of worsted 560 yd. **2.** *Naut.* A ring of wood, iron, or, rarely, rope attached to the edge of a jib or staysail and running on a stay.
han'ker (hăng'kẽr), *v. i.* To long (*for*); -- usually with *for* or *after*.

— Syn. See LONG. — **han'ker·er,** n.

han'ky-pan'ky (hăng'kĭ-păng'kĭ), n. *Colloq.* Hocus-pocus; hence, jugglery; trickery.
Han·o·ve'ri·an (hăn'ō·vēr'ĭ·ăn), *adj.* Of, pert. to, or supporting, the former ducal house of Hanover, founded about 1125, to which belonged the four Georges and William IV, of England, and, by birth, Queen Victoria and her descendants. — **Han·o·ve'ri·an,** n.
Han'sard (hăn'sẽrd), n. An official report of proceedings in the British

Ha'nuk·kah, Ha'nuk·ka (hä'nŏŏ·kä; *Heb.* kä'), n. [Heb. *ḥanukkāh* dedication.] See JEWISH HOLIDAYS.
hap (hăp), n. [ON. *happ* good luck.] Chance; happening; luck. — *v. i.;* HAPPED (hăpt); HAP'PING. [ME. *happen.* See HAP Chance.] To happen; befall.
hap (hăp; ăp), *v. t.* *Dial.* Any covering, as a cloak. — n. *Dial.* To cover up; wrap.
hap'ax le·go'me·non (hăp'ăks lē·gŏm'ė·nŏn), [Gr.] Said or used but once; a term, word, or phrase, evidenced by a single citation.
hap'haz'ard (hăp'hăz'ẽrd), n. [*hap* + *hazard*.] Chance; accident; random. — (hăp'hăz'ẽrd; 2), *adj.* Random; determined by chance. — (hăp'hăz'ẽrd; 2), *adv.* In a haphazard manner. — Syn. See RANDOM. — **hap'haz'ard·ly,** *adv.*
haph'ta·rah' (hä·f'tä·rä'), **haf·to'ra**), n.; *pl.* -TAROTH (-rōth'), [Heb. *haphṭārāh* conclusion.] One of the lessons from the Nebiim (or Prophets) read in the Jewish synagogue after the parashoth. See PARASHAH.
hap'less (hăp'lĕs; -lĭs), *adj.* Without hap; unlucky. — **hap'less·ly,** *adv.* — **hap'less·ness,** n.
hap'lo- (hăp'lō-), **hapl-** [Gr. *haploos.*] A combining form meaning

Syn. Happen, chance, occur, transpire mean to come about. Happen may imply obvious causation or seeming accident in both personal and impersonal uses; chance differs from *happen* in uniformly implying lack of design; occur always implies a presentation to sight, to mind, etc. (as, the accident *happened* [or *occurred*] Friday; the word rarely *occurs* [never *happens*] in print); transpire, often used in this sense, is acceptable only when its primary implication is a leaking out or becoming known (as, what the chief said has never *transpired*).

By permission. From *Webster's New Collegiate Dictionary*, copyright 1949, 1951, 1953, by G. & C. Merriam Co.

WHAT THE DICTIONARY TELLS ABOUT WORDS

(The numbers here correspond to those on the excerpt from the dictionary on the facing page.)

1. Variant spellings and pronunciations
2. Division into syllables
3. Accent marks. The heavy mark shows the primary accent.
4. Hyphenation
5. Pronunciation
6. Part of speech
7. Irregular plural forms
8. Principal parts of irregular verbs
9. Comparison of irregular adjectives
10. Derivation
11. Numbered meanings
12. Synonyms and antonyms. Sometimes, as in the sample, the synonyms are discriminated; that is, the shades of their meanings are explained.
13. Proper nouns and adjectives
14. Specialized meanings
15. Foreign words. (Some dictionaries put these into a separate section.)
16. Prefixes and suffixes
17. Usage labels. These labels show the present standing of the words so marked.
18. Cross references. These indicate where to find more information.
19. Geographical labels. These indicate that the usage is current in a certain part of the world.

Most dictionaries contain special sections of useful information: abbreviations used in writing and printing; arbitrary signs and symbols; a vocabulary of rhymes; rules for punctuation, compounds, and capitals; a pronouncing biographical dictionary; a pronouncing gazetteer; and rules for preparing copy for the press.

Sometimes a word will be given a special label to indicate its standing in the language. The labels "Colloquial" and "Illiterate" are explained on page 5. You have also met them frequently if you have studied the usage sections in chapters 2 and 3. Here are some other dictionary labels.

1. *Dialectal.* Dialectal words, sometimes known also as *localisms* or *provincialisms,* are words or phrases current only in a particular section of the country. They should be avoided in writing except when used to give local color. "Reckon" for "think" and "poke" for "bag" or "sack" are examples.

2. *Obsolete.* If certain words or certain meanings for words have passed completely out of use, the dictionary labels those words or meanings as *obsolete.* "Ingeny," defined as "genius, mental ability," is an obsolete word; "kneel" is an obsolete meaning for "sit."

3. *Obsolescent.* This label refers to words or meanings that are gradually becoming obsolete.

"WELL, IT'S NOT ENTIRELY ORIGINAL — SOME OF THE WORDS WERE TAKEN FROM THE DICTIONARY."

4. *Archaic.* This label signifies that a word or a meaning is obsolete except in special usage, such as Biblical, legal, or poetic language. "Ween" for "think" and "close" to mean "fill up" are examples.

5. *Poetic.* This label signifies that a word is peculiar to poetry or to poetic prose. "Oft" for "often" and "morn" for "morning" are examples. Such expressions should, as a rule, be avoided.

FOR PRACTICE AND APPLICATION

A. Use dictionaries to help you carry out these assignments. Exchange papers and put work on the board for checking.

1. Indicate the number of syllables in each of the following words by dividing them correctly into syllables.

luster	macabre	election
irony	pedicure	disappear
paucity	sword	reactionary

2. Look up the pronunciation of these words:

senile	bourgeois	athlete
stifle	acclimate	presentation
puerile	municipal	perspiration

3. Should these words be written as one word or as two words, or should they be linked by a hyphen?

study hall	street car	drug store
news stand	next door	pocket knife
thirty three	stop over	out of date
court martial	piece work	commander in chief
loud speaker	bill fold	barber shop

4. Give the past tense and the past participle of each of the following verbs. Some of the verbs have more than one form.

swim	hang	drink	lie	burst
break	drop	drown	lay	overflow

188

5. The word *paper* may be used as three parts of speech: (1) as a noun, "The *paper* was neatly folded"; (2) as an adjective, "The *paper* lining was torn"; and (3) as a transitive verb, "We shall *paper* this room in yellow." Find five other words that may be used in at least three different ways. Write a sentence illustrating each use. Discuss your sentences in class.

6. Who were the following persons and when did they live?
    Robespierre   Keats   Garibaldi   Wagner
    Molière   Plato   Guy Fawkes   Leif Ericson

7. What is the meaning of the following foreign expressions? How are they pronounced?
    hoi polloi   ipse dixit   sauve qui peut
    dolce far niente   comme il faut   modus operandi

8. What and where is each of the following?
    Yap   Woolwich   Tahoe   Trapani   Quito

9. What do the following abbreviations mean?
    mer.   I.C.C.   L.P.S.   cwt.   U.S.C.G.
    std.   at. wt.   D.D.S.   J.P.   Sp.

B. Use the dictionary to learn the standing of the following words. Give a synonym for each word. Exchange papers for checking.
    quoth   bedight   shoon   dost
    enow   prithee   eke (*also*)   gramercy
    wight   eyne   kine   o'er

C. What obsolete meanings can you find for the following words? Compare your findings in class.
    girl   clear (*v.*)   drink (*v.*)   libel (*n.*)
    pen   rate (*n.*)   mount (*n.*)   hit (*v.*)

4. FIGURATIVE LANGUAGE

Often the vividness and color of language can be heightened by the use of figures of speech in expressions that suggest their meanings by comparisons, pictures, or surprise elements. Many words in common use are in reality figures of speech. In the preceding sentence, for example, the word *heightened*, which means "made higher," is used to suggest the idea "increased." There are many types of figures of speech, most of them with names of Greek origin. Here are some of the commoner ones.

GUIDES TO RECOGNIZING FIGURES OF SPEECH

1. A *simile* makes an actual comparison, usually with *like* or *as*.
    He is as unwelcome *as a woman's first gray hair*.
    Those memories are *like gold coins* to me.
2. A *metaphor* merely suggests or implies a comparison.
    Cheap magazines made up his daily reading *diet*.
    The fresh air proved a *tonic* for the weary traveler.
 When you use a metaphor, keep the comparison consistent.
 Consistent Metaphor: If we *sow* the wind, we shall *reap* the whirlwind. (Both metaphors deal with the raising of a crop.)
 Mixed Metaphor: He found himself in a sea of troubles, but he marched bravely through them. (One does not *march* in a sea.)

 To be effective, figures of speech should be original. Trite, hackneyed (worn-out) expressions are known as *clichés*. "Busy as a bee," "down life's pathway," "hungry as a bear" are examples.

3. An *allegory* is an extended metaphor. *Pilgrim's Progress* is an example.
4. *Personification* is a type of metaphor that gives human qualities to places, things, or ideas.
    At last the *wind sighed* itself to sleep.
5. *Apostrophe* is a form of personification in which the writer speaks directly to ideas or to inanimate objects.
    O wild West Wind, thou breath of Autumn's being.
    —Shelley
6. *Metonymy* is the use of one word for another that it suggests.
    We are studying *Shakespeare* [for *Shakespeare's writings*].
    Chicago [for *The Chicago team*] led by three runs in the eighth inning.
7. *Synecdoche* substitutes a part for the whole, or vice versa.[*]
    We hired fifty new *hands* [for *workers*] today.
8. *Litotes* is an understatement to give increased effect or a special shade of meaning.
    He is a person of *no small talent.* (*He has great talent.*)
    I am *not unhappy* here. (The speaker is *reasonably happy.*)
9. *Irony* is a type of light or humorous sarcasm in which the meaning is clearly opposite to what the words say. For example, an ironical "You're a big help!" means "You're no help at all!"
10. *Hyperbole* is extravagant exaggeration.
    I have *millions of things* to do today.

---

[*] Webster says that the distinction between *synecdoche* and *metonymy* is now little noted, the term *metonymy* serving for both.

It is not necessary to remember the names of all figures of speech given here or to be able to identify them. You should, however, be able to recognize a *simile* or a *metaphor* at any time.

FOR PRACTICE AND APPLICATION

A. In the following sentences, find and identify the figures of speech. Most of them are similes or metaphors. Some of the sentences have more than one figure of speech. Exchange papers for checking.

1. When Raz came out, only a handful of players was left in the locker room.
2. The events of the past week paraded before his eyes.
3. The tourists stood still, feasting their eyes on the view.
4. Phoebe's hair was like burnished copper.
5. The sun smiled on the crowds as the big game began.
6. Whitman loved the "tall masts of Manhattan."
7. Death lays his icy hand on kings.—JAMES SHIRLEY
8. Help me with this suitcase. It weighs a ton!
9. Sunlight sifted through the trees.
10. Kings are like stars—they rise and set, they have
    The worship of the world, but no repose.
    —SHELLEY
11. This flower has a not unpleasant scent.
12. Why hurry? We have oceans of time!
13. The grim visage of Danger stared him in the eyes.
14. Lakeview High slaughtered Central.
15. I gave my son a palace
    And a kingdom to control:
    The palace of his body,
    The kingdom of his soul.
    —JULIA WARD HOWE
16. Education should be as gradual as the moonrise, perceptible not in progress but in result.
    —GEORGE JOHN WHYTE-MELVILLE
17. That was a cruel thing to do. You must be proud of yourself!
18. Many loyal hearts followed him into exile.

19. Love is the lord and the slave of all.
—George Macdonald
20. Shelved round us lie
The mummied authors.
—Bayard Taylor
21. The day goes by like a shadow o'er the heart.
—Stephen Foster
22. Life is mostly froth and bubble.
—A. L. Gordon
23. What small potatoes we all are, compared with what we might be!
—Charles Dudley Warner
24. I resolved to take Fate by the throat and shake a living out of her.
—Louisa May Alcott
25. The surest way to hit a woman's heart is to take aim kneeling.
—Douglas Jerrold

B. In the following sentences, find examples of mixed metaphors. Which are consistent figures of speech? Make this an oral activity.
1. If we fail to uproot the menace of juvenile delinquency, we shall be shipwrecked on the rocks of our own complacency.
2. The coach thought that he was courting trouble when he challenged the state university team.
3. The speaker cut through a maze of superstition.
4. Shall we take arms against a sea of troubles?
5. Sally never fully recovered from this blow at her natural pride.

C. Substitute more original expressions for the italicized trite figures and phrases used in the following sentences. Make this a small-group activity; then go over your choices in class.
1. As Wolfe walked along this street of *imposing edifices,* he could not help recalling his home in the village *nestling in the hills* of Vermont.
2. Jim felt *fit as a fiddle,* though he had worked into the *wee, small hours.*
3. Silas emerged from the gruesome experience a *sadder but wiser* man.
4. We returned home *none the worse for wear.*
5. Lincoln first *saw the light of day* on February 12, 1809.
6. In all the excitement, Hannah remained *cool as a cucumber.*
7. If we pursue this policy, we shall *unleash the dogs of war.*
8. Finally the *festive company* approached the *groaning board.*
9. Frances *quaked in her boots* as she looked at the *sea of faces.*

D. In your literature book or from stories in magazines, find three examples of each of these: *simile, metaphor, personification.* Copy these examples. In your small groups, read and comment on their effectiveness.

E. Sports pages in newspapers use many figures of speech. Read several articles. Point out to the class comparisons that you think are good and some that you think are trite. Be alert to find any mixed metaphors.

5. Word Sounds

Good writing takes into account the sounds as well as the meanings of words. The selection and arrangement of words to produce a smooth, melodious effect is known as *euphony.*

Alliteration, or the repetition of the same consonant sound at the beginning of a number of accented syllables in succeeding words, is a useful poetic device if wisely used. In everyday prose, however, alliteration is likely to be awkward and irritating. Good writing avoids disagreeable combinations of sounds—known as *cacophony*—because they are likely to distract the reader's attention. Bad also is the unintentional use of words that rhyme or, in most cases, the use in a sentence of two words that are homonyms. Reading aloud is a good method of detecting sounds that are not euphonious.

Onomatopoeia, sometimes considered a figure of speech, is a device by which the sense of a word is suggested by its sound. *Crash, boom,* and *murmur* are examples.

FOR PRACTICE AND APPLICATION

A. Rewrite the following sentences, making them more euphonious. Compare your work in class.

1. Terry tried to tie the tail of the terrier into a knot.
2. He ran to the train in the rain.
3. That balmy breeze blowing in from the bay blew me to sleep.
4. Jane does not care if you cut your hair.
5. Having no more to say, I went on my way on the following day.
6. Each screech seemed to reach into the center of my brain.
7. Would you go through the wood?
8. Henry hopes to hire a helper who can do the heavy hauling.
9. Betty searched the seaside for shells.
10. Bob found the bill in the till.

B. What onomatopoeic words would you use to describe the sound of these: *a car motor, the wind, a motorboat, the waves, water boiling, the purring of a cat, the barking of a dog, the wail of a train whistle, the creaking of a door?* Make this an oral activity.

C. Decide which of the following words are onomatopoeic. What do they suggest to you? Make this a written activity, but compare work in class.

zoom	whir	buzz	fall	squeak
sail	spin	creak	swish	laugh
sniff	caw	sink	snicker	puff

6. Careful Word Usage

The effectiveness of your speaking and writing is determined in a large measure by the words at your disposal. Therefore the study of *diction*—the choice of words for expressing ideas—is important to everyone.

"Choice of words" implies many words from which to choose. How do these words differ? What standards can you use to help you in your choice of the best word to use in a given context? Although many factors must be considered in any discussion of diction, keeping in mind the characteristics of good thinking should aid you in your choice of words. These characteristics are *correctness, clarity,* and *effectiveness.*

DENOTATION AND CONNOTATION

The *denotation* of a word is its dictionary definition. The *connotation* is the cluster of ideas and emotions that the word arouses. This difference can be understood easily by making a list of words which have the same denotation as the word *woman,* but which display widely different connotations. Thus each of the terms *female, wife, mother, matron, spinster, maiden, bachelor girl,* and *dowager* denotes the creature known as "woman." But the associations and attitudes suggested by such extremes as *dowager* and *maiden,* for example, are very different.

The seriousness of the error in choosing the correct word may vary from the extreme of giving a wrong meaning to the other extreme of merely arousing amusement in the reader. Because the meaning of a word, particularly its connotations, is constantly shifting, the utmost attention and skill are called for in choosing the precisely appropriate word for any given situation. Some examples of the use of words that have the wrong denotation follow.

> WRONG DENOTATION: Your story is wholly *incredulous.*
> RIGHT: Your story is wholly *incredible.*
> WRONG DENOTATION: She played golf *continuously* that summer.
> RIGHT: She played golf *continually* that summer.

The following are examples of the use of words that have the wrong connotation.

> WRONG CONNOTATION: He rounded up the large *bunch* of cattle.
> BETTER: He rounded up the large *herd* of cattle.
> WRONG CONNOTATION: The hobos *resided* in huts by the tracks.
> BETTER: The hobos *camped* in huts by the tracks.

Consult the dictionary if you cannot understand why the words labeled *wrong* are misused in the preceding sentences.

Some words are symbols that stand for facts alone: "This kindergarten class includes ten boys and nine girls." Some words report not only facts but also the attitude that the speaker or writer takes toward the facts: "This kindergarten class includes ten *rowdy* little boys and nine *lovely* little girls." In the first sentence the *denotations* of the words stand out; in the second, the *connotations*. In speaking, writing, reading, and listening, it is important to know whether you are dealing with facts alone or with the speaker's or writer's reaction to the facts. A special field of study, known as *semantics,* deals with the varying connotations that words have for different people and with their significance in influencing reactions to what is heard or read. Science tends to use denotative language; poetry, connotative.

FOR PRACTICE AND APPLICATION

A. The italicized words in the following sentences have the wrong denotation. Rewrite the sentences. With the aid of a dictionary, substitute the correct word or words for the faulty expressions. In class or in your small groups, go over the corrected sentences orally.

1. He *aggravated* me with his uninteresting chatter.
2. We plan to spend the *balance* of the summer here.
3. I *expect* that he is wrong in his conclusions.
4. He invented a highly *ingenuous* machine.
5. The fresh air proved very *enervating* after our conference in that smoke-filled room.
6. The book and the flowers are for Jimmy and Sue *respectfully*.
7. Dr. Bradford was an *imminent* man in our community.
8. Mary *inferred* by what she said that you will be invited.
9. For three hours he lay in the *luxurious* grass.
10. The *affect* of the setting sun was an *allusion* of grandeur.

B. The italicized words in the following sentences have the wrong connotation. Rewrite the sentences. With the aid of a dictionary, substitute better expressions. Compare papers in class.

1. We took a *vessel* to Bedloe's Island.
2. The sharp salt *zephyrs* of the sea had roughened his skin.
3. His *cranium* was protected by an enormous pith helmet.
4. The West Wind is the *supervisor* of the destinies of ships.
5. After the *severe* snowstorm, many buses were found stranded.
6. He is *disgustingly* clever.
7. The Church and the State were always *boon* companions.
8. The brilliant cloak that *enshrouded* her evening dress was the sensation of the dance.

C. Tell which of the following sentences may be called denotational and which, connotational. Make this an oral activity.
1. The diameter of the moon is one fourth that of the earth.
2. Bellamy, who had long been in frail health, contracted tuberculosis while writing *Equality*.
3. Mark Twain was born in 1835.
4. I was brought up in a small town.
5. Jackson had many fine qualities, and he served his country well.
6. "Your words are arrows to my heart."
7. He is the stubbornest man alive!
8. Many of the acres in this area cannot be used for wheat growing.

FAULTY OR CONFUSED EXPRESSIONS

The words covered in the following list fall into several classes: (1) words confused as to spelling; (2) words confused as to meaning; (3) expressions that are not standard English and that have not been covered in the usage lessons in Chapter 2 and Chapter 3. (All usage items are listed in the Index.)

Accept, except. *Accept,* a verb, means *receive; except,* a verb or a preposition, has to do with *omitting* or *leaving out.*
> RIGHT: I cannot *accept* this present.   WRONG: I *except* with thanks.
> RIGHT: Everyone *except* Jim plays ball.
> RIGHT: Since you are ill, we shall *except* your name from the list.

Ad. Colloquial for *advertisement.*

Affect, effect. To *affect* means to *influence.* To *effect* means to *bring about* or to *accomplish. Effect,* the noun, means *result.*
> RIGHT: The new rules did not *affect* the old players.
> RIGHT: Will this plan *effect* any improvement?
> RIGHT: The *effect* of the new gasoline was to increase speed.

Aggravate, annoy. To *aggravate* means to *make worse,* to *intensify;* to *annoy* means to *disturb,* to *irritate.*
> RIGHT: Her second fall *aggravated* her lameness.
> RIGHT: The cold weather *annoyed* her.

All ready, already. *All ready* means *completely* or *entirely ready; already* means *by this time* or *beforehand.*
> RIGHT: I shall be *all ready* soon.
> RIGHT: It is *already* three o'clock.

All together, altogether. *All together* means *collectively* or *in a group; altogether* means *wholly* or *entirely.*
> RIGHT: They sang the song *all together.*
> RIGHT: That report was *altogether* wrong.

Allusion, illusion, delusion. An *allusion* is an *indirect reference;* an *illusion* is a *deceptive appearance* or a *false impression;* a *delusion* is a *false belief.*
    RIGHT: He made an *allusion* to Hamlet.
    RIGHT: A mirage is only an *illusion.*
    RIGHT: He has the *delusion* that he is Napoleon.

Alright. Incorrect for *all right.*

Alumni, alumnae. *Alumni* are men graduates of a school, or a group of men and women graduates. *Alumnae* are women graduates.

Annoy. See *Aggravate, annoy.*

Anxious, eager. Used loosely as synonyms. In a strict sense, "anxious" implies a state of *worry* or *fearfulness;* "eager," of *keen desire.*
    I am *anxious* for his safety.   I am *eager* to see you.

Apt. See *Likely, liable, apt.*

Attackted. Illiterate for *attacked.*

Avocation, vocation. An *avocation* is a *hobby; vocation, customary employment.* Although he was a successful banker, Fitz was widely known for his *avocation* of photography.

Balance. Colloquial when used in the sense of *the rest, the others,* or *the remainder.* Standard English in the sense of *remainder* only when referring to the difference between two amounts.
    COLLOQUIAL: The *balance* of the week was spent indoors.
    STANDARD: The *balance* came to $4.40.
    STANDARD: The *rest* of the group stayed behind.

Blowed. Illiterate for *blew* or *blown.*

Bound, determined. *Bound* is colloquial for *determined.*
    COLLOQUIAL: He is *bound* to have his own way.
    STANDARD: I am *determined* to do it.

Brang, brung. Illiterate for *brought.*

Busted. Dialectal for *burst* or *broken.*

Censor, censure. To *censor* means to *examine in order to forbid if objectionable.* To *censure* means to *condemn* or to *reprimand.*
    RIGHT: All his army letters were *censored.*
    RIGHT: What have I done that you *censure* me?

Clumb. Illiterate for *climbed.*

Complected. Dialectal for *complexioned.*

Compliment, complement. A *compliment* is an expression of *praise* or *admiration.* A *complement* supplies a lack; it *completes.*
    RIGHT: He paid her a *compliment.*
    RIGHT: Angle A *complements* Angle B.
    RIGHT: Susan and Jane are different, but they *complement* each other.

Comprise, compose. To *comprise* means to *include*. To *compose* means to *form*, to *make up*.
> RIGHT: His possessions *comprise* an oil well and a copper mine.
> RIGHT: Mystery stories *compose* his reading activities.

Condition. See *Shape, condition*.

Contemptible, contemptuous. *Contemptible* means *base, worthless, despicable*. *Contemptuous* means *expressing contempt* or *disdain*.
> RIGHT: Your behavior is *contemptible*. You should be ashamed.
> RIGHT: He gave me a *contemptuous* smile.

Continually, continuously. *Continually* implies that an action takes place *at closely recurrent intervals*. *Continuously* implies that the action takes place *without pause or break*.
> RIGHT: He *continually* asks for more money.
> RIGHT: The bell rang *continuously* for an hour.

Credible, creditable, credulous. *Credible* means *believable; creditable* means *deserving credit or honor; credulous* means *ready to believe anything*.
> RIGHT: That is hardly a *credible* story.
> RIGHT: His deed was a *creditable* one.
> RIGHT: John is a *credulous* person.

Cunning. Means *crafty, sly*. The word *cunning* is colloquial when used for *prettily interesting*.

Cute. Colloquial for *clever, shrewd;* trite for *attractive*. Avoid using it in formal writing; and avoid overusing it colloquially.

Data. The plural of *datum*.
> NOTE: "The data *is*" may be heard more frequently today than formerly. When the term refers to a mass of material, the use of a singular verb is justifiable. Otherwise say, "The data *are*."

Delusion. See *Allusion, illusion, delusion*.

Disinterested, uninterested. *Disinterested* means *impartial* or *not influenced by self-interest*. *Uninterested* means *not interested*.
> RIGHT: The umpire should be *disinterested*.
> RIGHT: He was *uninterested* in the book.

Drawed. Illiterate for *drew* or *drawn*.

Drownded. Illiterate for *drowned*.

Drug. Dialectal and illiterate for *dragged*.

Effect. See *Affect, effect*.

Eligible, illegible. *Eligible* means *qualified to be chosen; illegible* means *unable to be read*.
> RIGHT: He is *eligible* for the position.
> RIGHT: His writing is *illegible*.

Emigrate, immigrate. To *emigrate* means to *leave one country to settle in another;* to *immigrate* means to *enter a country to settle there.*
  RIGHT: She *emigrated* from Europe.
  RIGHT: She is ninety years old. When she *immigrated* here, she was a child.

Eminent, imminent. *Eminent* means *noted* or *renowned; imminent* means *impending,* especially of something evil.
  RIGHT: He was *eminent* in the community.
  RIGHT: A storm was *imminent;* therefore we hurried to shelter.

Enervating, invigorating. *Enervating* means *weakening. Invigorating* means *stimulating.*
  RIGHT: She found the hot climate *enervating.*
  RIGHT: The cool nights were *invigorating.*

Et. Dialectal for *ate* or *eaten.*

Except. See *Accept, except.*

Exceptional, exceptionable. *Exceptional* means *out of the ordinary. Exceptionable* means *objectionable.*
  RIGHT: Her piano playing was *exceptional.*
  RIGHT: His *exceptionable* actions caused his dismissal.

Famous. See *Notorious, famous.*

Farther, further. In careful expression, *farther* is used to express distance in space; *further,* for distance in time, quality, or degree.
  She walked one block *farther.*   Do not speak *further* on this topic.

Folks. Colloquial for *family, parents, relatives.*

Formally, formerly. *Formally* means *in a formal manner; formerly* means *in the past:* Are you dressing *formally?* I *formerly* wore slacks.

Gent. Vulgar or humorous for *gentleman.*

Grand. Colloquial when used for *admirable, excellent, very fine.*

Growed. Illiterate and dialectal for *grew* or *grown.*

Guy. Colloquial for *man.* Avoid its use.

Healthy, healthful, wholesome. *Healthy* means *possessing health; healthful* means *conducive to health; wholesome* means *healthful* as applied to food or climate.
  RIGHT: Those are *healthy* children.
  RIGHT: Exercise in moderation is *healthful.*
  RIGHT: Citrus fruits are *wholesome.*

Idioms. (See pages 204–5.)

Illegible. See *Eligible, illegible.*

Illusion. See *Allusion, illusion, delusion.*

Immigrate. See *Emigrate, immigrate.*

Imminent. See *Eminent, imminent.*

Ingenious, ingenuous. *Ingenious* means *clever* or *resourceful; ingenuous* means *innocently frank or candid.*
RIGHT: That is an *ingenious* invention.
RIGHT: The child gave me an *ingenuous* answer.

Instance, instant, incident. An *instance* is an *example;* an *instant* is a *moment of time;* an *incident* is an *event* or an *occurrence.*
RIGHT: Her actions are an *instance* of what I was saying.
RIGHT: This will take only an *instant.*
RIGHT: That is an *incident* I shall never forget.

Invigorating. See *Enervating, invigorating.*

Irregardless. Erroneous or humorous for *regardless.*

Knowed. Illiterate for *knew* or *known.*

Later, latter. *Later* means *after the usual time. Latter* is used to designate the second of two things mentioned.

Likely, liable, apt. Loosely, these are used synonymously. Standard English calls for these distinctions: *likely* implies a favorable *probability; liable* means *legally responsible* (followed by *to* with an infinitive, *liable* means exposed to a risk or an evil consequence); *apt* implies a *natural fitness or tendency.*
RIGHT: The sun is *likely* to come out.
RIGHT: He is *liable* for the damage.
RIGHT: Chauncey works so hard that he is *liable* to collapse.
RIGHT: Edith is an *apt* pupil.

Locate. Colloquial for *to settle. To locate* means *to establish in a particular spot, to find, to place.*
COLLOQUIAL: We *located* in New York in 1920.
STANDARD: We *settled* in New York in 1920.
STANDARD: They *located* the fire quickly.

Lose, loose. *Lose* is a verb; *loose* is an adjective.
How did you *lose* it?   The chain is *loose.*

Luxuriant, luxurious. *Luxuriant* refers to *abundant growth; luxurious* pertains to *luxury.*
RIGHT: Her *luxuriant* hair fell to her shoulders.
RIGHT: The *luxurious* apartment awed her.

May be, maybe. *May be* is a verb; *maybe* is an adverb meaning *perhaps.*
You *may be* right.   *Maybe* you are right.

Nice. Colloquial for *pleasant* or *agreeable.* This is a much overworked word.

Notorious, famous. *Notorious* means *widely but unfavorably known; famous* means *well-known, remarkable.*
He is a *notorious* gangster.   She is a *famous* singer.

Oral. See *Verbal, oral.*

Party. Not to be used indiscriminately for *person*.
   Poor: Will the *party* who left a parcel here please call me?
   Better: Will the *person* who left a parcel here please call me?

Persecute, prosecute. To *persecute* means to *afflict* or *harass;* to *prosecute* means to *pursue until finished* or to *bring legal action against a defendant*.
   Right: They were *persecuted* because of their religious beliefs.
   Right: Mr. Arnold *prosecuted* the search for the missing heir.

Plenty. Colloquial when used as an adverb, as in *plenty good enough*.

Plumb. Colloquial for *absolutely, completely*.

Practical, practicable. *Practical* means *related or adapted to actual conditions, opposed to theoretical; practicable* means *capable of being accomplished*.
        He has a *practical* mind.   This is a *practicable* design.

Principal, principle. Think of *principal,* the noun, as meaning *leader, chief; principal,* the adjective, as meaning *main; principle* as meaning a *rule* or *truth*.
   Right: Mr. James is an efficient *principal*.
   Right: His *principal* reason was a personal one.
   Right: I shall always follow this *principle*.

Quiet, quite. *Quiet* means *in a state of calm* or *free from noise. Quite* means *completely, wholly;* it is colloquial for *to a considerable degree*.
   Colloquial: He was *quite* ill after the operation.
   Standard: I *quite* agree with you.
   Standard: The librarian said to be *quiet*.

Recommend. Colloquial for *recommendation*.

Respectively, respectfully. *Respectively* means *severally* or *each in the order given; respectfully* means *in a respectful manner*.
   Right: John and James are my son and nephew, *respectively*.
   Right: He spoke *respectfully* to his old aunt.

Reverend. Use only as part of a complete title.
        He is *the Reverend John Luke*.

Said. *Said* and *same* should not be used as modifiers except in legal language.
   Poor: We received *said* book and will ship *same* today.
   Better: We received *the* book and will ship *it* today.

Shape, condition. *Shape,* meaning *condition of being,* is colloquial; formally it means *form*.
   Colloquial: The patient is in bad *shape*.
   Standard: The patient is in a critical *condition*.
   Standard: This object has a strange *shape*.

Show up. Colloquial for *arrive, attend, appear, expose*.

Size up. Slang for *evaluate, understand*.

Snuck. Dialectal for *sneaked*.

So. Do not use *so* for *so that*. Do not use *so* for *exceedingly, really, very,* . . .
  Poor: He lowered the seat *so* he could reach the pedals.
  Better: He lowered the seat *so that* he could reach the pedals.
  Weak: He was *so* enthusiastic about that trip.
  Better: He was *exceedingly* enthusiastic about that trip.

Specie, species. *Specie* means *coin,* usually gold or silver; *species* means a *kind* or *variety.*
  Right: The country needed a new form of *specie.*
  Right: That *species* of melon does not appeal to me.

Stoled. Illiterate for *stole* or *stolen.*

Stop, stay. *Stop* should not be used as a synonym for *stay* in the sense of *remaining for a time.*
  Poor: We *stopped* at the Regis Hotel for a week.
  Better: We *stayed* at the Regis Hotel for a week.

Till, until. Should not be used for *when.*
  Wrong: Mary had scarcely begun *until* they told her to stop.
  Right: Mary had scarcely begun *when* they told her to stop.

Throwed. Dialectal for *threw* or *thrown.*

Verbal, oral. *Verbal* applies to that which is communicated in *words,* spoken or written; *oral* applies only to that which is *spoken.*

Vocation. See *Avocation, vocation.*

Writ. Archaic and dialectal for *wrote* or *written.*

FOR PRACTICE AND APPLICATION

   A. The following sentences contain erroneously or inappropriately used words. Rewrite the sentences, improving the choice of words, or read the sentences correctly aloud, as your instructor directs. Some sentences need more than one change.
   1. I am writing in reply to your ad in the morning paper.
   2. The girls were bound to make up for that omission.
   3. Your words seem to have no affect on him.
   4. This window has already been busted three times.
   5. The enemy attackted twice that day.
   6. Is it alright to fish in this stream? We are anxious to do so.
   7. He argues with me continually. I'm plumb disgusted.
   8. I am plenty credible by nature.
   9. Light-complected persons often sunburn easily.
   10. Dick says that he is illegible for the job.
   11. This table is an instant of shabby workmanship.
   12. He was formally a major in the army.
   13. This ingenuous device automatically turns on the radio at any time set.

14. His principle reason for buying that car was its price.
15. An imminent lawyer gave the main address.
16. The luxuriant dwelling seemed odd in that particular setting.
17. The orchestra is notorious for its fine performances.
18. This specie of plum is unknown to me.
19. After his operation, the pitcher was again in good shape.
20. I feel much better in this enervating climate.
21. He was afraid that he might loose the address.
22. George made an exceptionable record, one to be proud of.
23. I had a grand time at the party.
24. I'm glad oranges are healthy. I really like them.
25. Call me latter in the day; then we can talk farther.
26. He plans to locate in Arizona.
27. The children, awed by the storm, became quite.
28. You maybe right in refusing to give him a recommend.
29. What a practicable person he is!
30. Fold the material so it will fit into this box.
31. We stopped for a week at Valleyview Inn.
32. The play had hardly begun till a fire broke out.
33. Helen read the balance of that book in one hour.
34. They were severely censored for having disobeyed orders.
35. Everyone missed the error accept Hortense.
36. I had to report that the drawing was all together wrong.
37. The speaker made an illusion to the recent police investigation.
38. That army was comprised entirely of malcontents.
39. What is the compliment of the verb in this sentence?

B. In the following little story, find and identify all colloquial, overworked, or incorrect forms. If your teacher wishes, rewrite the story, supplying good substitutes for these expressions.

Last night we et early, because my folks wanted to go bowling. They are liable to bowl almost any evening, incidentally. Irregardless of the fact that I had homework to do, I went with them. As usual, Dad brung his own bowling ball; and I drug along behind, carrying Mom's.

Dad was aggravated when he saw that all the alleys were busy, but he was bound to bowl; so we stayed.

After a while a big, dark-complected guy who was bowling alone in the third alley began to get angry at himself. Most of the time he was sending the ball down the gutters, and the balance of his throws knocked down hardly any pins. I sized him up as a party who could be a good bowler if he would only get himself in shape. Finally he growed disgusted and left.

Dad managed to get that alley, because the man who had reserved it for seven o'clock did not show up. We bowled three lines. Both Mom and Dad made nice scores, but I was so anxious to impress a cute blonde in the next alley that I was a disgrace to my family.

IDIOMATIC USAGE

An idiomatic expression is one that comes naturally to native speakers of a language. Often there is no logical guide to idiomatic English—one simply accepts the prevailing practice. The following list of phrases illustrates idiomatic usage, especially in the selection of prepositions following verbs:

Unidiomatic (Avoid these.)	*Idiomatic* (Use these.)
abhorrence to	abhorrence of
accord to	accord with
acquiesce to	acquiesce in
aim at proving	aim to prove
angry at (a person)	angry with
as regards to	in regard to, regarding
burden by	burden with
capable to	capable of
comply to	comply with
confidence about	confidence in
conform in	conform to, with
convince to	convince that
correspond with (a thing)	correspond to
craving of	craving for
desire of	desire to
desirous to	desirous of
die with (a disease)	die of
dissent with	dissent from
distaste of	distaste for
enamored with	enamored of
envious toward	envious of
fearful for *or* about	fearful of
frightened of	frightened by, at
graduated (school)	graduated from
heedless for	heedless of
hint toward	hint at
in accordance to	in accordance with
independent from	independent of
in search for	in search of
interest for *or* toward	interest in
listen at	listen to
mania of	mania for
monopoly for, on	monopoly of
negligent for *or* about	negligent of
object at	object to
out loud	aloud
prior than	prior to
proficient at	proficient in
superior than	superior to

Unidiomatic	Idiomatic
(Avoid these.)	(Use these.)
treat on (a subject)	treat of
unequal for	unequal to
unmindful about	unmindful of
vie against	vie with

Certain words require different prepositions to express different meanings. Here are examples:

agree **to** a proposal; **on** a plan; **with** a person

aim **at** the barn; **to** please

compare **to** to represent as similar; **with** to discover likenesses or differences

differ **from** something else; **about, over** a question; **with** someone

good **at** singing; **for** him

impatient **with** someone else; **of** restraint; **at** someone's conduct

overrun **by** an army; **with** mice

FOR PRACTICE AND APPLICATION

A. In class, go over the preceding lists to be sure that they are clear to everyone; then take turns using the idiomatic expressions in oral sentences.

B. Improve the wording of the following sentences so that each conforms to current English idiom. Exchange papers for checking.

1. Jefferson differed from Hamilton in his opinions.
2. The superintendent finally acquiesced to Peter's plan for selling tickets.
3. The Fourth of July speaker announced that he aimed at proving the superiority of democracy over Fascism.
4. The minister reminded the squire that one should not be too much enamored with material things.
5. After working in the sun for an hour, Jimmy had a strong desire of resting awhile.
6. What do you call the tendency to be frightened at loud noises?
7. Forrest secured a monopoly on the wheat supply.
8. It was almost impossible to vie against the greater efficiency of the automatic machines.
9. Heedless for our safety, Llewellyn increased his speed.
10. This compartment is independent from the rest of the ship.
11. More than one man lost his life in search for the rumored treasure.
12. With practice anyone can become proficient at the art.
13. In this work one must not become negligent about his appearance.

TRITE EXPRESSIONS

Triteness is the use of hackneyed, outworn phrases or figures of speech. The expressions may once have been concrete and vivid, but they have been used so often that they have grown stale. These tired expressions, known as *clichés,* are so numerous that it is possible to list only a few of them. Although they come to mind easily because of their very familiarity, you should make a conscious effort to replace such expressions with fresh and timely phrases in your speech and writing.

HACKNEYED EXPRESSIONS

sadder but wiser	easier said than done
hard as a rock	beat a hasty retreat
hungry as wolves	brave as a lion
irony of fate	teeth like pearls
last but not least	wee, small hours
red as a rose	busy as a bee
green with envy	pretty as a picture
at one fell swoop	sharp as a razor
beautiful but dumb	brown as a berry
happy as a lark	white as snow
good as gold	neck like a swan
cool as a cucumber	silly as a goose
quick as a flash	sings like a bird
straight as an arrow	wild as an Indian
trip the light fantastic	silence reigned supreme
honest as the day is long	tall, dark, and handsome
conspicuous by its absence	beyond the shadow of a doubt
to no avail	cross as a bear

OUTWORN QUOTATIONS AND PROVERBS

All the world's a stage.
All that glitters is not gold.
Variety is the spice of life.
Where ignorance is bliss . . .
To err is human; to forgive, divine.
A little learning is a dangerous thing.
All's well that ends well.
When the cat's away, the mice will play.
It's not the heat; it's the humidity.
Money is the root of all evil.
In the spring a young man's fancy . . .
Time and tide wait for no man.
There is method in his madness.
Where there's a will, there's a way.

FOR PRACTICE AND APPLICATION

A. Revise the following sentences by substituting clear, simple words or phrases for all trite expressions.
1. The budding genius favored us with a piano selection.
2. Words cannot describe what he suffered.
3. Please get down to brass tacks and give it to us cold turkey; we can take it.
4. From that day forth, he was a sadder but wiser man.
5. We offer you our heartfelt thanks for your noteworthy achievement in bringing order out of chaos.
6. He had expected Betty to look like love's young dream, but he was doomed to disappointment.
7. John was conspicuous by his absence when the family spokesman invited us to partake of refreshments.
8. The tree in all its glory stood like a sentinel clothed in a white mantle of snow.
9. By the irony of fate, the city, which once had flowed with milk and honey, was now desolate as a wasteland.
10. The happy pair were wreathed in smiles as they took the holy vows of wedlock.

B. Make a list of hackneyed expressions and outworn quotations commonly used in your school or community. Discuss appropriate substitutes. Go over your lists in class.

C. In the following passage a newspaper columnist ridicules certain trite expressions. He indicates them by means of capital letters. Go over the article in class. Make a list of the trite phrases that the author has included.

ALL'S TRITE WITH THE WORLD [*]

My friend, whom we will call Sandy, because that is not his name, works for a newspaper in a Midwestern city that shall also be anonymous. Sandy is employed as a feature writer, and his editors are (I assume) quite proud of his literary abilities.

Sandy specializes in Poignant stories. He can be Sad at a moment's notice. He particularly likes to write about little girls who have lost their dogs and the old ladies wandering alone in the big city. Touching.

The readers go for Sandy's vibrant prose, because he is never at a loss for a word or a phrase. He puts things so beautifully and so simply that even a sixth-grader can understand him and marvel at his verbal powers.

For instance, when someone's child dies, Sandy knows it leaves an Aching Void in the parents' lives. They also face Blank Despair at this tragedy that struck them like a Bolt from the Blue. Life, as Sandy loves to repeat, is no Bed of Roses.

[*] By special permission of Sydney J. Harris and the *Chicago Daily News*.

Oh, Sandy is a whiz with words. He knows all about the things that are put to the Acid Test and the men who see these things through to the Bitter End. He also knows that every man has his Achilles' Heel, even Captains of Industry, Gay Lotharios, Good Samaritans, and Social Butterflies.

Sometimes the editors set Sandy loose on a juicy crime, and then how vividly he tells of the Blunt Instrument, the bandits Armed to the Teeth, the police Spreading a Dragnet, and later the convict whose Doom is Sealed. Sometimes the convict walks the Last Mile Sneering at the Grim Reaper.

Why, you could go right through Sandy's stories and pick out these little gems of expression in every paragraph. Take the Battle Royal, the Crack of Doom, the Fly in the Ointment, the Eternal Triangle, the Errand of Mercy, the Wry Jest, the Dog's Life, the Gala Event, and lots more just as good.

In Sandy's world, people are never merely ignorant; they are Blissfully Ignorant. They are not in earnest, but in Deadly Earnest. Sometimes they are Conspicuous by Their Absence, while others Beat around the Bush, and Disaster Overtakes Them at One Fell Swoop. Last but Not Least, that is.

You can see why Sandy is such a valuable man. His appeal is universal; it reaches down into the Nethermost Depths of Humanity. Even a moron can understand him.

—SYDNEY J. HARRIS

FOLLOW-UP

From the trite and hackneyed expressions that you have been studying, make a list of clichés that you yourself may have a tendency to use. Put the list into your notebook and then use it as a check when you write a theme.

WORDINESS

Effective diction is as economical as possible. Unnecessary repetitions, roundabout expressions, unimportant details, or general wordiness—these obscure the thought of the sentence. The terms that follow are closely related types of wordiness.

Tautology or *redundance* is the unnecessary repetition of the same idea in different words. Notice these examples:

few in number	join together	repeat over
square in shape	descend down	joint partnership
visible to the sight	continue to remain	return back

Circumlocution is talking around the point, as in this example: "The man to whom he looked for instruction in the advanced study of the manipulation of numbers was Mr. Roberts." That sentence is merely a wordy way of saying, "Mr. Roberts was his mathematics instructor."

Prolixity is emphasis on unimportant details. "Mary took her new bonnet, with its pink velvet ribbons, its pink veiling, and its white flowers to New York with her."

Verbosity is excessive wordiness. "It is often the case that pretty girls marry young," could be better stated, "Pretty girls often marry young."

FOR PRACTICE AND APPLICATION

Rewrite the following sentences, eliminating the wordiness. Discuss your sentences in class.

1. Mary would not give her consent to doing anything that most people considered improper.
2. Collect together the damaged machines.
3. Did you ever in your life meet up with such a man before?
4. A strange sound was audible to my ears.
5. He was frequently thirsty at numerous intervals.
6. She was universally admired by everyone.
7. Don't be hard on him; he is just a youthful adolescent.
8. As a young woman, she performed many household duties and made a success of them.
9. A governing official of the city gave vent to a discourse on taxation.
10. Be sure to endorse this check on the back.

CORRELATING ENGLISH WITH YOUR OTHER CLASSES

Bring to your English class a paper that you are now preparing for another class. Check it carefully for wordiness. Discuss constructions in class to see whether you can effect greater economy in diction.

General review of diction

REVIEW

Rewrite the following sentences, eliminating slang, trite or wordy expressions, and other faulty diction.

1. I am anxious to see you wear that cute new dress.
2. His pals are not apt to show up.
3. He is notorious for having won two Pulitzer prizes.
4. These people have been prosecuted for their religious beliefs.
5. Please be quite or the speaker will be angry.

6. His alibi for fouling up the deal was that he couldn't dope out the instructions. That alibi sounds all together too weak.
7. Where did you loose your purse? I'll go in search for it.
8. It's easy to spot her for she's very dark complected.
9. You should be independent from him.
10. After sizing up the situation, he decided that she was plumb crazy.
11. The teacher advised them to adopt and take over the more efficient way of doing the exercise.
12. He was whilom a brilliant orator.
13. Seize the bit in your teeth and go on to the bitter end.
14. Finally, in conclusion, let us glance briefly at the consequences that followed the taking of this stand.
15. Our finances are in bad shape.
16. Why don't you except the nomination?
17. He told her that words could not describe what he had suffered.
18. Each country has its own particular customs, traditions, and habits which characterize it.
19. The clock ticked continually.
20. It is liable to rain today.
21. She sank blissfully down in the umbrage of the old apple tree.
22. One district may border on the edge of another, and consequently the customs of each may become intermingled with the other.
23. Why don't you ask the Reverend what to do?
24. He was plenty angry when he heard the news.
25. I have no desire of seeing him.
26. Her brother, y-clept Jonathan, was but a child.
27. When he told her that her golden tresses, pearly teeth, and form divine thrilled him, it was the last straw.
28. Dick and I left, but the balance of the group stayed.
29. Neatness is a necessary essential of all people who wish to be hired for these jobs.
30. It was with great difficulty that he managed to pass the examination.
31. She was told not to sign up with that organization.
32. All her habits, mannerisms, and gestures served to indicate the fact that she was ill at ease in those surroundings.
33. The gridiron heroes were given a feast fit for a king.
34. As luck would have it, at this moment he was at a loss for words.
35. John evidently has not succeeded in that most difficult of all feats, the winning of the universal respect and admiration of his fellow men.
36. Sitting in her room alone by herself, she repeated the lesson over again.
37. Your illusion to that play is a clever one.
38. The nature of the required reading in the philosophy course serves to keep students away.
39. All in all, she regretted not keeping abreast of the times.
40. The drastic action plunged him into the depths of despair.

Writing Good Paragraphs

CHAPTER 8

You probably began to write in paragraphs when you were in the third grade. Most of the time you will paragraph almost instinctively. But there is a very definite skill to paragraphing.

First of all, what is a paragraph? Webster defines it as a "distinct section or subdivision of a discourse, chapter, or writing, whether of one or many sentences, that forms a rhetorical unit as dealing with a particular point of the subject, or as comprising the words of a distinct speaker, etc." In other words, it consists of a sentence or sentences developing a single thought.

When you are in doubt about a paragraph, ask yourself these questions: (1) Does it adequately develop a central idea? (2) Do all the sentences relate to that idea? (3) Do the sentences follow in natural, logical order?

A well written paragraph will have the basic elements of good writing: unity, coherence, and emphasis. When all the sentences in a paragraph relate to a central idea, the paragraph has *unity*. When the sentences follow each other in natural, logical order, it has *coherence*. When the sentences are arranged to create the strongest effect, it has *force,* or *emphasis.*

However, you must remember that no sentence, no paragraph, no theme, no letter can be clear, interesting, or persuasive unless the writer first has a thought that is clear, interesting, and important. Be sure, therefore, that you have clarified in your own mind the things that you wish to say before putting pen to paper.

The Topic Sentence

The central thought, or idea, of a paragraph is often expressed in a *topic sentence*. The first sentence may be the topic sentence, as it is in this one:

> The Englishmen felt that their trip had been successful. They certainly had not been treated as vassals, but with the greatest honor and courtesy; they had been immensely interested in all that they saw; the artists had made drawings everywhere they went and a long book was written by one of the secretaries; letters had been exchanged by the rulers of the two nations. Had they opened the way for friendly trade and intercourse? What answer had the Emperor sent to their requests?*

Sometimes the topic of a paragraph is expressed in the middle. In the following paragraph, the second sentence expresses the central thought.

> As we look at real glaciers among the mountains, we cannot see them move. But scientists have proved that they do and even have measured their speed. Small glaciers in the Rockies travel eight to fifteen inches per day, but big ones among mountains of Alaska move four to twelve feet. The speediest glacier of all is one that moves down the rocky coast of Greenland at a rate of fifty to seventy feet in a day. That is as far as "ice streams" of the Rockies go in a whole month! †

In the following paragraph the last sentence states the central thought.

> Who first discovered the principle of gravity? Not Newton, for Galileo, who died the year that Newton was born, had measured its force in the descent of falling bodies. Who invented Lavoisierian chemistry? The English say Dr. Black, by the preparatory discovery of latent heat. Who invented the steamboat? Was it Gerbert, the Marquis of Worcester, Newcomen, Savary, Papin, Fitch, Fulton? The fact is that one new idea leads to another, that to a third, and so on through a course of time until someone, with whom no one of these ideas was original, combines them all into what is justly called a new invention. ‡

This paragraph has no topic sentence. What is the central idea?

> Are we in an inter-glacial epoch? Are we in a new period of geologic history? Who can say? We who read will never know. Much as we may wish to push aside the curtain, we have not the knowledge. The old makes a story fascinating in its unreality. The new, containing perhaps the explanation of the past, may be as intensely interesting. §

---

* From Elizabeth Seeger, *The Pageant of Chinese History*, p. 322. New York: Longmans, Green and Co., 1944.

† From *Mountains*, by Carroll Lane Fenton and Mildred Adams Fenton. Copyright 1942 by Doubleday and Company, Inc.

‡ From *Thomas Jefferson, Selections from His Writings*, edited by Phillip S. Foner. Reprinted by permission of International Publishers.

§ From *The Earth Changes* by Jannette May Lucas and Helene Carter. Reprinted by permission of J. B. Lippincott Company.

Read the following review of the book *Flush—A Biography* by Virginia Woolf. In what way does the organization of the paragraphs help to make the student's ideas clear to the reader?

In a rather indirect but highly individualistic manner, Virginia Woolf in her *Flush—A Biography* gives the reader an entertaining, if slightly cloudy, life story of Elizabeth Barrett Browning through the eyes of her beloved cocker spaniel, Flush. From the beginning of this unusual but steadfast friendship between the young dog and the frail, bedridden Miss Barrett, from the early days at 50 Wimpole Street, "the most respectable street in London, indeed, in all the world," to the last days of Flush, spent with Miss Barrett, then Mrs. Browning, in Italy, Miss Woolf acquaints the reader with a good many foibles and experiences of both dog and poet.

It is certain that beast and human being were never closer in mutual respect than were these two in the first five years of their acquaintance. These years, as Miss Woolf informs us, were spent by Miss Barrett in the bed of her back bedroom; and Flush, with only occasional airings in the prim British parks, lay at Miss Barrett's feet while she wrote and read and very often addressed him as though he were a person. With the frequent letters and finally the visits of a strange man wearing yellow gloves, whom Miss Barrett called Mr. Browning in a tone of voice that she had never used with Flush, this poet-and-dog relationship gradually shifted to poet and man and—dog. As Miss Woolf leads us to believe, all this man business was infuriating, and Flush really loathed this Mr. Browning quite as much as he loved Miss Barrett. Here was a country-born and country-bred dog who had given up a world of running rabbits in the bright sunshine for a back bedroom and the compensating devotion of his dear friend, but Flush shared the leftovers of Miss Barrett's devotion now with this Mr. Browning, and it did not suit him in the least. Miss Barrett, to make matters worse, sensed Flush's dislike for her Mr. Browning, and her suspicions were confirmed when her cocker thoroughly bit his enemy, as he was leaving 50 Wimpole Street after one of his frequent visits. After this incident, surprisingly enough, things began to improve for everyone in general. Flush saw that it would do him no good to dislike this man who took so much of Miss Barrett's time; hence he resolved in his canine mind to like Mr. Browning. By this time Miss Barrett too had made up her mind to like him—so much, in fact, that the courageous little poet and her Mr. Browning secretly married and sailed off to Italy taking Flush with them.

These days in Italy as they grew into weeks and then years were the happiest that both Flush and Mrs. Browning had ever known. Flush was getting used to Mr. Browning and was even beginning to feel real affection for this gentle, friendly man. He also grew to love the baby, born in Italy in a few years after the arrival of the Brownings. In short, the aging dog was enjoying life.

Flush died in Italy at the feet of his beloved mistress, who lived to write the beautiful moving poetry that holds meaning for all people who have ever loved anyone or anything; and Flush has been immortalized in many of Elizabeth Barrett Browning's poems—a tribute to make even a thoroughbred British cocker spaniel feel that even rabbits are not everything in life.

Miss Woolf did tell the story of Flush rather than that of Elizabeth Barrett Browning, but what was thus lost in clear fact was gained in delightful fancy that makes *Flush—A Biography* a book doubly worth reading because it gives the picture of a truly famous person through the eyes of her truly remarkable dog.

USING SHORT PARAGRAPHS

The writer of the foregoing review might have written the entire composition as one paragraph. Essay writers of a hundred years ago would have done so. In this streamlined age, however, ideas are presented in smaller units. The new way has the advantage of making each idea stand out by means of a separate paragraph devoted to it.

In conversation, whenever the speaker changes, a new paragraph is used. Reference to almost any short story will illustrate this fact.

FOR PRACTICE AND APPLICATION

A. Write ten topic sentences based on ideas about your school. Read them in class or in your small groups.

B. Choose one of the topic sentences and write a paragraph developing the idea. Use exactly one hundred words. Underline the topic sentence.

C. Reduce to fifty words or less the paragraph that you wrote for *B*. In your small groups, read first your long paragraph and then your short one. Decide among yourselves which of the two is the better. Then choose the best paragraphs from each group and read them aloud before the class. Perhaps some of the best paragraphs might be printed in your school paper.

D. Explain the Webster definition (page 211) in your own words. Assume that you are writing for someone who does not know what a paragraph is. Underline your topic sentence. Compare your paragraphs in class.

E. Write a short paragraph in which you develop one of your topic sentences through the conversation of two people. Compare them in your small groups and read to the class the best one from each group.

Development of Paragraphs

There are as many different kinds of paragraphs as there are writers and purposes for writing. Many good paragraphs, however, follow a fairly definite kind of development. Here and on pages 216–17 are examples of paragraphs developed (1) by examples, (2) by details, (3) by explanation of cause, (4) by contrast, (5) by comparison, (6) by repetition, and (7) by definition.

By examples

Several ghost stories center around the mansion. It is said that whenever August has two full moons, on the night of the first moon Governor Dummer rides his white horse up the broad staircase as he did on the night of the grand housewarming in 1715. Another story concerns the smiling ghost of a child who peeped through the kitchen doorway. Not until her bones were discovered in a moldering box in the cellar and given proper burial, did the little apparition vanish. It is also averred that the ghost of an English officer who was killed in a duel on the lawn occasionally reappears in full-dress uniform, with powdered wig, embroidered cloak, and sword.*

By supporting details

In prewar days, half the people on earth subsisted on less than 2250 calories a day. These people lived, for the most part, in Asia—although there are some substandard countries in the Western Hemisphere, such as Mexico, Colombia, and Costa Rica. People in these areas present much the same picture—small farms, poor land, primitive agriculture. To each family head the problem is the same: how to scratch enough nourishment from his land to feed his family. Contrast this with the U.S. where the average farmer feeds his own family and four others.†

By explanation of cause

I left the woods for as good a reason as I went there. Perhaps it seemed to me that I had several more lives to live, and could not spare any more time for that one. It is remarkable how easily and insensibly we fall into a particular route, and make a beaten track for ourselves. I had not lived there a week before my feet wore a path from my door to the pondside; and though it is five or six years since I trod it, it is still quite distinct. It is true, I fear, that others may have fallen into it, and so helped

---

* From *U.S. One, Maine to Florida.* Federal Writers Project, WPA. Modern Age Books, Inc.
† From "The World's Food" by J. D. Ratcliff, in '47, (July, 1947, p. 97). Published by Associated Magazine Contributors, Inc.

to keep it open. The surface of the earth is soft and impressible by the feet of men; and so with the paths which the mind travels. How worn and dusty, then, must be the highways of the world—how deep the ruts of tradition and conformity! I did not wish to take a cabin passage, but rather to go before the mast and on the deck of the world, for there I could best see the moonlight amid the mountains. I do not wish to go below now.

—THOREAU

By contrast

Talent repeats; Genius creates. Talent is a cistern; Genius, a fountain. Talent deals with the actual, with discovered and realized truths, analyzing, arranging, combining, applying positive knowledge, and in action looking to precedents. Genius deals with the possible, creates new combinations, discovers new laws, and acts from an insight into principles. Talent jogs to conclusions to which Genius takes giant leaps. Talent accumulates knowledge, and has it packed up in the memory; Genius assimilates it with its own substance, grows with every new accession, and converts knowledge into *power*. Talent, in difficult situations, strives to untie knots, which Genius instantly cuts, with one swift decision. Talent is full of thoughts; Genius, of thought: one has definite acquisitions; the other, indefinite power.

—WHIPPLE

By comparison

The same winds bring heat and cold to the United States and Canada, and the same currents of air flow across the border in circles, to keep us geographically one. The winters are colder in some parts of civilized Canada, but the summers are much like our own, though mostly shorter. And the Great Lakes belong as much to one shore as another, so that the United States, to Canadians, is something down beyond. It's all in the way you happen to be facing.*

By repetition

When I look upon the tombs of the great, every emotion of envy dies within me; when I read the epitaphs of the beautiful, every inordinate desire dies out; when I meet with the grief of parents upon a tombstone, I consider the vanity of grieving for those whom we must quickly follow. When I see kings lying by those who deposed them, . . . I reflect with sorrow and astonishment on the little competitions, factions, and debates of mankind. When I read the dates on the tombs of some that died yesterday, and some six hundred years ago, I consider that great day when we shall all of us be contemporaries, and make our appearance together.

—ADDISON

* From *Here's to Canada* by Dorothy Duncan. Reprinted by permission of the publishers, Harper & Brothers.

By definition

Education is a device for helping a man to grow to his full stature. It enables him to realize his nature both mentally and spiritually and in that realization to become all that he has it in him to be. It is to the child what perfect gardening is to the tree, a help so to grow that it may develop its own personality. A good gardener helps each plant to put forth that essential quality of its own that differentiates it from all other plants and makes it a thing of use and beauty in the world. The good educator performs a similar office for the human being.*

Most paragraphs that you read today in books and magazines are not developed by any single method. Usually they represent a mixture of several types. The preceding examples merely show that paragraphs *can* have regular patterns, especially in exposition.

FOR PRACTICE AND APPLICATION

A. Tell what type of development is illustrated by each of the following paragraphs.

1. My uneasiness, however, prevented me from sleeping, and about midnight I went upon deck. As I placed my foot upon the upper step of the companion-ladder, I was startled by a loud humming noise, like that occasioned by the rapid revolution of a millwheel, and before I could ascertain its meaning, I found the ship quivering to its centre. In the next instant, a wilderness of foam hurled us upon our beam ends, and, rushing over us fore and aft, swept the entire deck from stem to stern.

—POE

2. The cold, however, played some grotesque pranks with us. My beard, moustache, cap, and fur collar were soon one undivided lump of ice. Our eyelashes became snow-white and heavy with frost, and it required constant motion to keep them from freezing together. We saw everything through visors barred with ivory. Our eyebrows and hair were as hoary as those of an octogenarian, and our cheeks a mixture of crimson and orange, so that we were scarcely recognizable by each other. Every one we met had snow-white locks, no matter how youthful the face, and whatever was the color of our horses at starting, we always drove milk-white steeds at the close of the post. The irritation of our nostrils occasioned the greatest inconvenience, and as the handkerchiefs froze instantly, it soon became a matter of pain and difficulty to use them. You might as well attempt to blow your nose with a poplar chip.

TAYLOR

---

* From *About Education* by C. E. M. Joad. Reprinted by permission of Faber and Faber, Ltd.

3. And that was last Thursday. Tonight is Tuesday. Tonight is Tuesday and my homework's done, and I darned some stockings that didn't really need it, and I worked a crossword puzzle and I listened to the radio, and now I'm just sitting. I'm just sitting because I can't think of anything else to do. I can't think of anything, anything but snowflakes and ice skates and yellow moons and Thursday night. The telephone is sitting on the corner table with its old black face turned to the wall so I can't see its leer. I don't even jump when it rings any more. My heart still prays, but my mind just laughs. Outside the night is still, so still I think I'll go crazy, and the white snow's all dirtied and smoked into grayness and the wind is blowing the arc light so it throws weird, waving shadows from the trees onto the lawn—like thin, starved arms begging for I don't know what. And so I'm just sitting here and I'm not feeling anything; I'm not even sad, because all of a sudden I know. All of a sudden I know. I can sit here now forever and laugh and laugh while the tears run salty in the corners of my mouth. For all of a sudden I know what the stars knew all the time—he'll never, never call—never.*

4. Mr. Fox had a captivating *earnestness* of tone and manner; Mr. Pitt was more *dignified* than earnest. The action of Mr. Fox was easy and graceful; Mr. Pitt's cannot be praised. It was an observation of the reporters in the gallery, that it required great exertion to follow Mr. Fox while he was speaking; none, to remember what he had said; that it was easy and delightful to follow Mr. Pitt; not so easy to recollect what had delighted them. It may be added, that, in all Mr. Fox's speeches, even when he was most violent, there was an unquestionable indication of good humour, which attracted every heart.

—Butler

5. What is a minority? The chosen heroes of this earth have been in the minority. There is not a social, political, or religious privilege that you enjoy today that was not bought for you by the blood and tears and patient sufferings of the minority. It is the minority that have vindicated humanity in every struggle. . . . It is the minority that have stood in the van of every moral conflict, and achieved all that is noble in the history of the world. You will find that each generation has been always busy in gathering up the scattered ashes of the martyred heroes of the past, to deposit them in the golden urn of a nation's history.

—John B. Gough

B. In your small groups, go over a paper that you are writing or have written for a social studies or science class, and ask your fellow students to identify the type of organization that you have used in each paragraph.

C. Revise a paper that you are writing or have written for this class or for some other class. Secure variety by using different types of paragraph development.

---

* Reprinted from "Sixteen" by Maureen Daly; copyright 1938, by Scholastic Corporation, all rights reserved.

D. Write three paragraphs on the life of an author, an historical figure, or a character from literature. Use a different type of development in writing each paragraph. Indicate which type each is. Underline your topic sentences. (If a paragraph has no topic sentence, state its central idea.) Read them in your small groups or with a partner to see whether you have been successful in using the types that you chose.

RELATIONS WITHIN AND BETWEEN PARAGRAPHS

When you were studying the *sentence,* you learned that the word order should be natural, and the relation of its parts clear. The same principle holds for the structure of the *paragraph.*

One paragraph may be linked to another, and one sentence *within* a paragraph may be linked to another, with the aid of pronouns, transitional words and phrases, demonstrative adjectives, and adverbs. When the continuity of thought in a paragraph is unbroken, the paragraph is said to have *coherence* (literally, its parts *stick together*).

Try "lifting" a paragraph out of a well-written editorial or essay. You will find that almost any paragraph except the first is difficult to separate from the rest because it is tied to the preceding by a pronoun or other linking or transitional expression. You will get the idea when you read the opening sentences of a series of paragraphs from a magazine article.

Note these opening sentences taken from an article called "Putting the Wind to Work" with the order numbers of their paragraphs:

Paragraph 10. "*The two boys* and their father bought an old tower . . ." (You need to read paragraphs 1-9 to know who "the two boys" are.)

Paragraph 11. "From *that test* a new industry swiftly grew." ("That test" refers to a passage in paragraph 10.)

Paragraph 12. "*These batteries* are expensive but are necessary to supply power when there is no wind. . . ." ("These batteries" refers to paragraph 11.)

However, moreover, further, nevertheless, also, by the same token, in the same way, and, but, on the other hand are examples of transitional words and phrases that bind paragraphs and sentences together.

TRANSITIONAL PARAGRAPHS

Some paragraphs are written for the specific purpose of bridging the thought expressed in one paragraph and that in the succeeding one. They are called *transitional paragraphs*.

The paragraph that follows is an example.

> We have seen that the new biography, as practiced by Strachey, Maurois, and Ludwig, is extraordinarily uniform in conception, in structure, in philosophy, and even in literary style. How can we account for such singular similarities? How explain the practically simultaneous emergence in the three great languages of Europe of an identical literary form? *

Here is a short selection showing various transitional words.

> To the visitor to South America, many things are strange. He is not only on another continent but in another hemisphere.
>
> *However*, he soon finds that any fears he may have had are groundless. The people are friendly and full of fun. The American who speaks only English is likely to find that his attempts to communicate bring on bursts of good-natured laughter in which he will be moved to join.
>
> *On the other hand*, if he has even a few words of Spanish, the South Americans will make valiant attempts to understand him and will do their best to fill in the words that they think he is using.
>
> *Almost without exception*, the Latin Americans are courteous and helpful. Indeed, I have found many of them unusually kind to strangers.
>
> One day, *for example*, I was riding in a bus in Rio. The ocean air coming through the open window was a bit brisk. I put up my hand to tuck in my hair and pull down my veil. Instantly the man next to me lowered the glass. I was glad I could say, "Gracias, Señor."

FOR PRACTICE AND APPLICATION

A. Look through a newspaper editorial or an article in your class magazine or in a periodical in your home, and find out which paragraphs could be quoted separately without further explanation, and which are bound to the preceding paragraphs. In the latter, what transitional devices are used?

B. Write a letter consisting of at least three paragraphs, in which you tell a friend the story of a recent, exciting basketball game, an interesting social event, or a book you have read. Show how you created a smooth transition from one paragraph to the next.

---

* From "The New Biography: Ludwig, Maurois, and Strachey" by George A. Johnston. Reprinted by permission of the *Atlantic Monthly*, March, 1929.

Concluding the Paragraph

Pay particular attention to the concluding sentence of a paragraph. Does it "let the reader down" after great expectations have been aroused, or does it bring the thought to a climax? Does it "clinch" the argument? Does it skillfully summarize the facts? Does it leave the reader satisfied?

FOR PRACTICE AND APPLICATION

In each of the following paragraphs, notice the final sentence. In what way does each lend force to the paragraph?

1. So far then as the nineteenth century remade American education, Pestalozzi deserves most credit; and what he did likewise best prepared us for the twentieth century. As the years come and go, it will, however, be the great loving heart of Pestalozzi that will most stand out. He did love his children and they did respond to his love. Men saw this and heeded. School children have been happier ever since; and besides that, they have learned better. This is the debt we owe to Pestalozzi.*

2. Great honor is due to those officers who remained true, despite the example of their treacherous associates; but the greatest honor, and most important fact of all, is the unanimous firmness of the common soldiers and the common sailors. To the last man, so far as is known, they have successfully resisted the traitorous efforts of those whose commands, but an hour before, they obeyed as absolute law. This is the patriotic instinct of the plain people. They understand, without an argument, that the destroying of the government which was made by Washington means no good to them. †

3. Together this man and this woman stood before the gods of their fields. The woman watched the ends of the incense redden and turn gray. When the ash grew heavy, she leaned over and with her forefinger she pushed the head of ash away. Then as though fearful of what she had done, she looked quickly at Wang Lung, her eyes dumb. But there was something he liked in her movement. It was as though she felt the incense belonged to them both; it was a moment of marriage. They stood there in complete silence, side by side, while the incense smouldered into ashes; and then because the sun was sinking, Wang Lung shouldered the box and they went home. ‡

---

* From "What American Education Owes to Pestalozzi" by William Heard Kilpatrick. Reprinted by permission of the *Journal of the NEA*.
† From "Lincoln's Message to Congress in Special Session, July 4, 1861." *Selected Writing and Speeches of Abraham Lincoln,* edited by T. H. Williams. Reprinted by permission of Packard and Company, Publishers.
‡ From *The Good Earth* by Pearl Buck. Reprinted by author's permission.

Single-Sentence Paragraphs

When a paragraph consists of a single sentence, it becomes especially desirable for that one sentence to carry a heavy content of fact, insight, or feeling. The following paragraph from the concluding passages of Sinclair Lewis's *Arrowsmith* deals with two beloved characters who played important parts in the story. Can you see why it lends power to the final scene, even though you may not know the setting that makes it dramatic?

> That evening, the hot breeze languished along the palm-waving ridge where the ashes of Gustaf Sondelius were lost among cinders, and a depression in a garden marked the grave of Leora.*

Do Your Paragraphs Really Communicate?

Remember that no rules or formulas can guarantee that you will write a good paragraph. Each writer has freedom to develop it according to his needs. The important principle to remember is that a paragraph must be an efficient instrument in the communication of an idea. It must be a unit; it must "hang together"; it must proceed logically and smoothly; it must be vivid and forceful. In other words, it must possess the classic qualities of *unity, coherence,* and *emphasis.*

FOR PRACTICE AND APPLICATION

You will write your best paragraphs on topics that arise out of your own interests and experiences. If, however, you are lacking just now in a suitable topic for development into a paragraph, try one or more of these for practice.

1. Too much of college life these days consists of frivolous activities.
2. Franklin's statement, "We must all hang together, or we shall all assuredly hang separately," certainly applies today to the great nations of the world.
3. The Federal Communications Commission should limit radio "commercials" to not more than 10 per cent of program time.
4. The UN differs in important respects from the old League of Nations.
5. The voting age should be reduced to eighteen.
6. I like humor in detective stories.
7. Quiz programs vary widely in quality and originality.

---

* From *Arrowsmith* by Sinclair Lewis. Reprinted by permission of Harcourt, Brace and Company, Inc.

Gaining Skill in Creative Expression

CHAPTER 9

Creative writing is writing in which you express your own ideas in your own words. It is writing that has some literary quality, some "style." It must express your ideas with clearness, exactness, and force. It is to achieve that style that you should study, as on pages 211–22, the correct and effective organization of sentences and paragraphs.

All writers, professional as well as amateur, must answer the question that may be bothering you: "What shall I write about?"

1. What Shall I Write About?

The world is so suspenseful and exciting that it is hard to understand how anyone can say, "I don't have anything to write about."

Look at today's newspaper. You can afford to skip the murder stories and the scandal. What new developments in the manufacture of labor-saving devices; in the control of disease; in aviation, radio, and television can you read about? What is happening in Congress or in your state legislature? What stories do you find about ways in which America is cooperating with other nations? about ways in which Americans of different nationalities, races, and religions are working together? What do you find about the need for better safety measures, more education, better medical care? Are any new roads, bridges, factories being built in your community?

"THE TEACHER SAID TO BRING TO SCHOOL AN IDEA FOR A THEME."

Look about you in your school. What can you and your schoolmates do to make it a more stimulating place in which young people may live and work together? Do you know any interesting new people among students or faculty? What new educational programs are being planned? What auditorium activities are in prospect?

Have you heard any fine radio programs lately, or seen any motion pictures of high quality? Have you ever thought of writing a letter of appreciation to the author of a recent book that you have enjoyed? Have you taken any trips, played any games, or visited any places that you could describe vividly for others?

Telling a story, making an explanation, expressing a mood or feeling, announcing a forthcoming event, or expressing an opinion—all present different problems of expression. Each type of writing or speaking provides unlimited opportunity for display of your skill in conveying thought.

Telling simply, with humor and with sympathy, about an incident at breakfast or on the bus may be more effective than describing the autumn woods in language picked up in some book. If you do try to picture the changing colors of leaves in the fall, stay close to the facts in naming the colors and shapes and the feelings that they arouse in you. And remember, the most rewarding subjects of all are the human beings whom you know— what they look like, what they do and say, what they want to be.

A teacher's magazine recently published a list of one thousand topics for composition.* To give you an idea of the great variety of subjects open to you, selected topics from this list are reproduced here.

* From "A Thousand Topics for Composition" in the *Illinois English Bulletin,* December, 1951. The topics listed have been taken from this list, by permission. The original list was compiled by Marjorie E. Fox.

PERSONAL REMINISCENCES

My First Date
My First Job
My Most Important Decision
My Most Embarrassing Moment
Musical Memories
Meet the Family
An Inexpensive Good Time

My Narrowest Escape
How I Learned to Drive a Car
Moving into a Strange Town
Things I Have Lost
When I Was Your Age
Blind Date
The Best Class Period This Semester

PERSONAL REACTIONS

Why I Like a Small Town
Why I Prefer Jazz to Classical Music (or vice versa)
My Idea of a Dull Evening
My Idea of a Perfect School
How I Feel in a Dentist's Chair
My Favorite Hero in Fiction

If I Had But Three Days to Live
What I'd Do to Prevent World War III
My Hobby and Why I Like It
My Favorite Writer
My Favorite Magazine
Being Lonesome
Things I Could Get Along Without

DESCRIPTION

The Most Beautiful Spot I Know
Snowfall
Full Moon
Night Shift
School Sounds
The Main Street of My Home Town
Sounds at Night
Farm Sale
A Lonesome Road

A Meal at a Quick-Lunch Counter
Classroom Atmosphere
A Typical Railway Station
Getting a Meal in a Crowded Restaurant
An Old Shop
A Favorite Haunt
Sunday Dinner
My Room
Nightly Bus Passengers

CHARACTER SKETCHES

Daydreamer
Jukebox Addict
Master of Ceremonies
Student Waiter
That Tired Waitress
Bleacher Athlete
The Local Policeman
Little Old Lady
The Great Lover

A Person I Have Almost Forgotten
A Person I Can't Bear
My Favorite Teacher (Relative, ...)
My Best Friend
What I Learned from Dad
Meet the Dean
Grandfather
The Most Abused Public Servant
Brothers under the Skin

225

FAMILIAR ESSAYS

Pet Peeves
Bargain Shopping
Crushes and Hero-Worship
The Girl (Boy) I Marry
Advice to Entering Freshmen
Why Girls Wear Make-up
Table Manners
Mental Cruelty
What a Home Ought to Be

Never Take a Girl to a Football Game
Worrying Is Good for You
Unnatural Characters in Literature
New Brooms Raise a Great Dust
Soap Operas
Radio Commercials
Today's Slang
The Values of Sleep
Baby-tending, a Harrowing Job

MISCELLANEOUS

How to Take Good Snapshots
How to Enjoy Exam Week
How to Keep Friends
How to Get Along with a Brother (or Sister)
How to Be Nonchalant When Embarrassed
How to Approach Dad
Large School *versus* Small School
Television *versus* Radio as Entertainment
A Dog's Life—and Mine
Winter Sports
Gambling in Professional Sports
An Exciting Moment in a Game
The Housing Problem
A Modern Invention
House of Tomorrow

How I Would Change Present Traffic Laws
There Ought to Be a Law
Roadside Advertising
Suggestions for the Improvement of English Courses
One Argument against War
Early Marriage Is Desirable
Comics Serve a Purpose
Students Are Smarter Than Teachers Believe
Is Our Grading System Fair?
Simplified Spelling
Scientific Farming
Religion and Life
Social Prestige in High School
The Right to Strike
Schools Try to Do Too Much
Some Advantages of a Teacher's Life

2. Being a Good Observer

For all creative, imaginative writing, you must become a good observer. To do so, you must know what to look for. You can train yourself to find in the commonplace experiences of everyday life the extraordinary qualities that give life meaning and beauty. A well-known writer once wrote for the

Chicago Daily News a series of brief articles entitled *A Thousand and One Afternoons in Chicago.* In these stories he drew sketches—"vignettes," as they are sometimes called—of humble characters whom he observed along Halsted Street: a bootblack, a vendor of shoelaces, a pawnbroker . . . He knew how to tell a story about ordinary people and places; but most of all, he had a genius for observation, and he reported in detail what he observed.

Detail! This is the secret of all effective imaginative writing. The idea is to portray, to *reproduce* a scene, rather than to make statements *about* it. Thus, it is less effective to say, "Susan is in a cheerful mood," than to say, "Susan is singing as she washes the dishes."

Sometimes a flat statement such as "Susan is in a cheerful mood" may be followed by illustrative details. However, it is usually better to state the details, paint the picture, and let the reader form his own impressions. It should ordinarily not be necessary to "spell out" the meaning of a scene or an incident for the reader. Let the details speak for themselves. The reader is not moved when you say, "What a wonderful view it is!" Help him to *see* the view so that *he* will say, "How wonderful!"

Here are specific ways to help the reader become aware of your ideas.

1. Use words that are vivid and specific.

2. Appeal to the reader's senses.

3. Suggest an idea instead of putting it into a flat statement.

4. Use simple rather than involved language.

FOR PRACTICE AND APPLICATION

A. Divide the class into four small groups. Let each group write on one of these four topics. Read your paragraphs aloud in your group and revise them according to the suggestions of the other members. Have the best ones from each group read aloud to the class.

1. Write a description, using only words that appeal to the sense of smell.
2. Write a description, using only words that appeal to the senses of hearing and touch.
3. Write a short description in which you use vivid nouns and verbs but no adverbs or descriptive adjectives.
4. Choose a topic from the list on pages 225–26 and write a short paragraph (50–75 words) using few or no words of more than two syllables.

B. Let each person in the class expand to twenty-five words this sentence: "Men succeed." Read your papers in your small groups and select the best ones to be read to the entire class.

3. Creative Personal Letters

Next best to a personal visit with a friend is a letter from him. Well written, such a letter is a real substitute for a person-to-person chat. As a matter of fact, a good friendly letter is lively conversation set down on paper. In conversation, you tell of your experiences; you comment on the events of the day; you inquire about the activities of the one to whom you are writing. You should do those same things in letters.

WHAT TO WRITE ABOUT

What you write about in a personal letter depends upon the occasion, the purpose, and your relationship with the reader. You may wish to express your pleasure about some happy incident in the life of your friend—a new job, graduation, a trip, a scholarship. You may wish to express sympathy about an unhappy experience. You may wish to extend an informal invitation to a hike, a party, or a visit in your home. You may wish to cheer up a friend who is ill, or to inquire about the activities of a friend who is away from home. If you have been in the habit of talking about political or social questions, you may wish to offer your opinions about some current event.

However, keep in mind that your friend wants primarily to know about you—where you have been; what you have seen or done; and, if you are a girl writing to a girl, even what you wore. The topics with which a friendly letter may deal are almost limitless. It may develop a single idea in a systematic way, or it may ramble on like easy conversation. It is the freest kind of writing in the world.

FOR PRACTICE AND APPLICATION

A. In class write a friendly letter to a relative or friend whom you have not seen for some time. Perhaps you would like to write a rough draft first, thinking only about what might interest your reader. Then rewrite, if necessary. In any case, proofread your letter, paying careful attention to spelling, vocabulary, sentence structure, and handwriting.

B. (1) Write the first paragraph of a letter to someone your own age whom you know very well. (2) Write the first paragraph of a letter to someone your own age whom you have just met but whom you would like to know better. In your small groups discuss the differences between the two paragraphs.

C. Let everyone in the class, including the teacher, write a letter of at least three paragraphs that will explain what he hopes to accomplish in English during the current school year. Take time to read these letters aloud. When you have finished, you should know one another better.

4. Writing Letters of Opinion

Letter writing is one of the ways by which the people in a democracy make their views and wishes known. Every year the various government agencies in Washington receive thousands of letters. When important legislation is being considered in Congress, members of the House and Senate are flooded with mail from "the folks back home." State and local authorities likewise hear from citizens through correspondence. These letters receive careful consideration, but it is only natural to assume that the most effective letters will get the most attention.

People also express their opinions in letters to the editors of newspapers or magazines; to radio and television stations or performers; to screen players, athletes, and other public figures; to authors of articles or books. Some of these letters are mere fan letters; others offer criticisms. All are read, for public opinion is important to those who deal in mass media.

GUIDES TO WRITING LETTERS OF OPINION

1. Keep the letter as brief as possible.

2. State your subject clearly at the outset.

3. Explain your stand on the question that you are discussing.

4. Advance in an orderly fashion the arguments supporting your opinion.

5. Avoid abusive terms or violent language. Keep the general tone good-tempered. Be forceful but not tactless.

6. Avoid writing from a prejudiced viewpoint; do your best to be fair.

7. Be as ready to write letters of praise as of criticism or condemnation.

8. Hold a letter of criticism or disagreement a day or so before mailing it. Once you have "cooled off," you may wish to destroy the letter or at least to change it.

"FOR HOMEWORK, I HAVE TO WRITE A THEME OF AT LEAST 500 PUFFS."

FOR PRACTICE AND APPLICATION

A. Examine recent issues of a newspaper for letters from readers. Read and discuss the letters. What kinds of subjects do they deal with? Is the correspondence section an interesting forum on significant topics? Are the letters thoughtful, tactful, interesting? Do they deal with matters worth writing about? Give reasons for your answers.

B. Compare the letters in daily newspapers with those in magazines. Talk them over in class. What are the differences in the topics with which they deal? in their average length? in style?

C. If you disagree with any of the letters, write a reply to the editor. Discuss your letters in your small groups. Before mailing, proofread and revise to make sure that your letters are technically perfect.

D. Do one or more of the following letter-writing assignments. Proofread your own letters to catch careless mistakes. Then meet in your small groups to criticize and make further improvements.

1. If you have enjoyed a book written by a living author, write a letter of appreciation, telling the author what pleased you most about the book. If you address it in care of the publisher, the letter will be forwarded to the author.
2. If you have read a magazine article with which you disagree, write a letter to the editor, explaining your reasons for disagreement.
3. Write a letter to the President of the United States or to your senator or representative, expressing your views about some public issue. *Webster's New International Dictionary* has a section that tells how to address public figures when writing to them.
4. Write a letter to a radio or television commentator with whom you strongly disagree. Be courteous. Check your information carefully before you express your ideas.

E. Have each member of the class, speaking for the class, write a letter to some newspaper columnist about an opinion expressed by him with which the class strongly agrees. Check all the letters in your small groups, and from the best ones of each group, choose one letter to send. Make it clear that the letter expresses the opinion of the group rather than that of an individual.

5. Evaluating What Others Have Written

When you analyze the writing of other people, whether they are professionals or your fellow students, you should keep in mind the principles of good writing that you have studied in chapters 2–9. Asking yourself the questions in the following guides will help you to be a good critic.

GUIDES FOR EVALUATING WRITING

1. Is the subject one that the writer seems to know something about?
2. Is the author's purpose clear?
3. Is the writing sincere; that is, does it seem to reflect the true feeling or belief of the writer, or does he use "stock" phrases and ideas?
4. Is the narrative or argument convincing; that is, does it correspond to truth and fact as you see them?
5. Is the writing imaginative and original?
6. Is the theme well-planned? Is the sequence of ideas or events clear and logical? Does it have unity, coherence, and emphasis?
7. Does the writing show keen observation?
8. Does it arouse the interest of the reader?
9. Are specific, colorful, forceful words and phrases used? Do they arouse vivid images?
10. Is there variety in the kinds of sentences used?
11. Are spelling, grammar, punctuation, and sentence structure correct?
12. Is the division into paragraphs helpful and effective?

FOR PRACTICE AND APPLICATION

The following themes include good, fair, and poor examples of compositions.* Among the first four themes, watch for various kinds of errors, especially in spelling, punctuation, and sentence structure. Study and discuss the themes in class. Base your discussion on the preceding list of questions. In each case be ready to justify your conclusions by specific references to the compositions.

THEME 1: A SOLUTION FOR WORLD PEACE

During a period of less than thirty years, the United States has participated in two major wars. The First World War involved most of the nations of the North Atlantic. The Second World War affected all great nations.

One would think that, as a result of the terrible costs and distress of the First World War, man would not want to pass through this experience again. War has always been one of the greatest sources of suffering and misery for the human race.

Let us look at some of the causes of war. Commercial rivalries of great powers have been 'the basis of war. The desire of dictators to increase their power and prestige is also a cause of war. Disputes over trade problems, territories, and national boundaries have been the causes of war.

After the First World War, organizations for peace did not prove strong enough to avert the Second World War. After this War, the United Nations was established. It was a plan for world government, which supposedly was to be effective in bringing about world peace. It seeks to recognize individual rights throughout all nations, and among all peoples, regardless of race, sex, language, or religion.

We must establish a government of justice in the world which will make extensive military training and the manufacture of war equipment unnecessary. Lasting peace is not an idle dream. Just because we haven't had it is no sign that it can't be obtained. Of course, as long as independent nations exist, there will be disputes, but they could be settled by means other than war. Today, if we as individuals have many disputes, we expect to settle them by peaceful means. This is what will have to be done in international affairs if the world is to usher in an era of permanent peace.

Today, with the atomic bomb and other mighty weapons, we should be convinced that further war is dangerous. This is why we should strive so earnestly for world peace. Modern society cannot afford war as a means of settling disputes. All men know this, and yet they have been unable to find the way to peace.

---

* Themes 1–4 quoted by permission from the April, 1953, *Illinois English Bulletin,* a publication of the Illinois Association of Teachers of English.

Since the Second World War, the United Nations has become a disputing and turbulent organization. Its members have many different viewpoints and are unable to give the world what it is craving for—lasting peace.

What *can* we, as a great nation, turn to in this age of turmoil? The answer is in a universal need of man, which can be met only by realizing the existence of something wiser and more powerful than man. If the nations of the world would but turn to Him for guidance, we would have a lasting world peace.

THEME 2: ORGANIZED CONFUSION

I awoke that morning to the hum and the honk of traffic beneath my window. I dressed and ate as I had every morning for the last year. Stumbling down the dark stairs I swung the door open to greet another day. The soft morning sunshine caused me to blink as I walked down the busy street toward the towering black "El" station. Dodging a pigeon, I climbed up the stairs carpeted with cigarette butts and broken whiskey bottles. Immediately I ducked outside to escape the screams of angry children and the booming of the loud speaker. I stood there with people brushing past me and trains whizzing by. Finally my train came snaking down the track and with a screeching of brakes, it halted before me. It yawned and I stepped aboard.

I swayed back into the car and threw myself into a dusty green seat. Suddenly a bell rang, and off we jerked. I sat there watching the back porches and trash littered lots whiz by. Even the sun didn't seem to reach these forbidden places. Often it halted at stations and swallowed more people. Soon we burrowed underground into musty blackness. Lights flashed on and hand-holds sway in rythm. The roar of the train drowned out all other noises. Suddenly the train squeeled and scraped to a stop and vomited its load. I rushed off the train but halted in my tracks to gaze down at the poor begger. How ugly and cruel the city seemed. I forlornly scaled the stairs and stepped into the light and air. Beautiful sky scrapers ice-berged heavenward, illuminated by bright sun-shine. I then realized that there is real beauty in a big city.

THEME 3: RIVERS

Did you ever stop to think what a river was? A river is used for many things such as a home for the beaver and fish. They supply us with natural beauty like the Mississippi River as illustrated by the colorful writer Mark Twain. They are used as a source of transportation and of course in the days gone by the river boat.

There are rivers other than the Mississippi, such as the Wabash, the Missouri, the Red river, the Rio-Grande, the Arkansas, the Ohio, and the Kishwakee.

THEME 4: "THE ROCKIES"

Almost everyone has five senses. These five senses are: seeing, hearing, smelling, feeling, and tasting. In general, these five senses are used most when the person is closest to nature. Maybe this is because most people are used to being around things made by man, like the cities. In all my travel, the heart of the Rockies, near Denver, is what I consider closest to nature.

Have you ever been in the Rocky Mountains or in any kind of big mountains? Well, if you haven't, I can say very truthfully that you have missed something. Upon arriving at the Rockies, the first sense affected is sight. Your eye sight is very deceiving here because of the vastness of the mountains. For instance, maybe you look at a large mountain and say that it might be five miles away when really it is twenty, or maybe you start out to hike to the top of a small one and later find out it would have been a day's walk.

Since the Rockies are so tall and up-standing, the echo can be heard almost anywhere. The echo of a car horn can be heard for miles. The roar of the wind through the pine trees and the roar of a mountain stream in a canyon are sounds I will never forget. Also the smell of the pine and fir trees, with the thin and pure air is something very worth while. At night, it freezes, thus making the air feel so cool and pure in the early morning. Sometimes the fog is so thick that the visibility is zero. When it gets near noon time the fog leaves and the sun shines very freely. Never have I tasted such delicious fried chicken in my life as that which I ate in the Rockies.

THEME 5: CASE NO. I

"Strangers, beware of dog." Jim stared for a moment at the sign, the first words of which seemed especially prominent, and tried unsuccessfully to compose himself. He was scared, plenty scared. This ominous sign and the gloomy appearance of the house, which reminded him of something out of a story by Hawthorne, added nothing to his self-assurance.

For most of the men on the force, this would have been little more than a routine assignment. Jim, however, was new—a tenderfoot in every sense of the word. He had, of course, gone through a rigid period of training, but this was his first real assignment. Naturally, Jim had expected something easy to start with. But the Riegal case was, at least in his eyes, far from easy. Evasion, though these agents are skillfully trained in the matter, can be a serious and touchy business, particularly when it involves a highly *respectable* citizen.

In a brief moment Jim saw many things in retrospect. He remembered the ambitions he had had since boyhood for adventure—real adventure. This work was the most natural outgrowth of that ambition. He always liked to think of it as a battle between the two conflicting forces—a battle between men's minds. Yes, this, unquestionably, was what he had always wanted. Now, however, with the big moment upon him, Jim began seriously to doubt that he had the courage to carry through on it.

For another instant Jim's thoughts turned to some of his famous and fabled predecessors. He chuckled, though it seemed out of keeping, as he tried to picture himself with the glib tongue and analytic mind which, according to the novels, is standard equipment for all in this profession.

Well, delay was getting him nowhere. Reassuring himself that the vast power of the law was behind him, Jim marched with as much conviction as he could muster through the gate and up to the porch. He rang the bell and waited. Now, the first words must be polite but very firm. Ah, at last.

"Good afternoon, madam. I'm an agent for the Fowler Brush Company. We have here a bill for one dollar and sixty-two cents . . ."

THEME 6: THE LIFE AND HARD TIMES OF MY CELLO

My cello is truly a work of art in instrument making. She is one hundred and fifty years old, yet is in better condition than most of us are when we reach forty. There is no gray in her strings, and she has retained her hourglass figure. Her wood is not wrinkled, and every year it seems to glow more and more. She certainly doesn't show her age.

You may wonder why I use a feminine pronoun when I speak of my cello. The truth of the matter is that I consider her a beautiful woman. She has the temperament of one, and she definitely likes compliments. In fact, if she ever reads this theme, she will be no good for a month.

Since she fell into my hands as a reward for being a good boy when I had my tonsils removed, things have been popping, or rather cracking, for her. She has not only been injured, but she has suffered through many embarrassing situations. Her first serious injury occurred when I fell on her. It was my habit when I went for my lesson to rest her on the handlebars of my bike. One day, coming into the home stretch, late as usual, I hit a patch of ice. Out went my bicycle from under me—but not my cello. Bam! Whack! I landed flat on top of her. When I picked her up, her beautiful curved neck was broken, her shapely body bruised, and her beautiful blue dress ruined. I ran to the doctor, crying, "Save my loved one!" and he did.

She has had other accidents. Once in junior high she fell downstairs and broke her neck again; another time she was trampled on in a bus. This accident resulted in a caved-in side. However, in spite of all her accidents, she remains beautiful and aloof.

The most recent mishap occurred in the bus depot, where I accidentally deserted her. I hopped off the departing bus just in time to see her eloping in the arms of a friend of mine. I won her back, though; and we shall live happily ever after, I hope.

THEME 7: THE HALL OF FAME

Father had always hoped for a boy, and the fact that I was not one came as a blow to him. It is not that he dislikes girls, but he was hoping for a second Ty Cobb in the family. I don't mean to brag, but that famous slugger was Father's third cousin twice removed, and nothing would have pleased my pop more than to have me follow in my celebrated relative's footsteps. Therefore he proceeded to mold me into a junior Babe Didrikson.

At the age of four, I was torn away from my precious dolls for batting practice. I regret to report that as a slugger I was a flop! Every night after supper Dad and I would spend an hour in the back yard amidst mosquitoes galore while I fanned the air with force never yet equaled. When the batting proved futile, I pitched. My throws never came anywhere near the bat.

My failure at baseball led Father to believe that maybe bowling was my forte. Mother objected, arguing that I couldn't even lift the ball. She proved to be right, and I switched to swimming.

The lifeguard at the neighborhood pool was employed to teach me to swim. Father was preparing for my first trip across the English Channel when the doctor announced that I had sinus trouble and couldn't possibly go near anything deeper than a bathtub. I have always wondered why the lifeguard slipped Doc that ten-dollar bill.

My last sport was horseback riding. Father, still undefeated, bought me a beautiful five-year-old Arabian horse, and Mother purchased three very smart riding habits for me. But their efforts were to no avail. The horse, appropriately named Unlucky, and I just didn't get along. He went his way and I went mine. I landed in the hospital with a broken collar bone, two broken arms, and three fractured ribs. Unlucky was luckily sent to a dude ranch in Arizona, along with two perfectly new riding habits.

As for me, I do believe that Father has conceded. I'm just not the athletic type. I get my exercise on the dance floor or in a hammock on a summer day. Ty Cobb will probably remain the last of our family in the Hall of Fame.

6. Other Types of Original Writing

On the next few pages you will find guides for writing various literary types. Much of this material should already be familiar to you, since you have been doing this kind of writing for many years. However, review is always valuable.

WRITING DESCRIPTION

1. Be able to see clearly in your own mind the pictures that you want your readers to see.
2. Give only a few graphic details. Avoid the catalogue method.
3. Appeal to the reader's five senses: sight, smell, taste, touch, and hearing.
4. Make effective use of both actual and figurative comparisons.
5. Choose words wisely. Do not use just any word; find the one that is just right for your purpose.

WRITING EXPOSITION

1. Tell your readers exactly what you are going to explain.
2. Be sure that you completely understand the topic that you are explaining.
3. Organize carefully; develop the idea logically, using the step-by-step method.
4. Include all necessary details, but omit any that do not help the reader to understand.
5. Use simple words as far as possible. Define terms wherever you think that your reader may be in doubt. Whenever a word has several interpretations, make clear which meaning you are using.
6. As a further aid to communication, use tables, graphs, charts, and illustrations.
7. In concluding, sum up all the points that you hope you have made.

WRITING ESSAYS

1. Keep in mind the original meaning of *essay*—a *try* or an *attempt*. In an essay you try to tell readers what you feel or think.
2. Always remember that the essay is *you;* it should reflect your personality, your tastes, and your attitudes.
3. Treat your subject formally or informally, depending upon your purpose in writing.
   Be sure that you have a central idea. You may, especially in the informal essay, digress—literally, "step away"—from your original topic; but you must always come back to it.

If you are writing lightly or humorously, apply these suggestions:
   a) Do not label your humor as such. Let the reader discover it.
   b) Appear to be perfectly serious.
   c) Be able to laugh at yourself.
   d) Keep the humor kindly. Never let it develop a barb.
   e) Make use of incongruity and hyperbole.
4. Be clear yourself about the kind of essay that you are writing. Though they may have elements of more than one type, essays fall generally into one of these classes:
   a) Informative or instructive
   b) Persuasive or argumentative
   c) Critical or analytical
   d) Historical
   e) Personal
   f) Descriptive
   g) Entertaining or humorous
   h) Biographical

"THE SALESMAN SAID IT'S A NEW GADGET FOR WRITING SHORT STORIES."

WRITING SHORT STORIES

1. Begin by deciding on a central idea—the idea that makes the plot. Most stories have one of the following as the basic theme:

a) Courage	*d*) Greed	*g*) Honesty
b) Jealousy or hatred	*e*) Rivalry	*h*) Misunderstanding
c) Loyalty	*f*) Fear	*i*) Love

2. Be sure that there is a real conflict between (a) persons, (b) people and ideas, (c) people and circumstances, or (d) a man and himself. This struggle may be mental, moral, or physical—or all three.

3. Construct the plot carefully. *Note these four steps:
   a) The setting up of a situation
   b) The introduction of complications
   c) The coming of the crisis
   d) The reaching of the climax. (This should come near or at the end.)

4. Make your characters believable. They should be consistent in what they do and say, and they should leave the reader feeling that their lives will go on after the story ends. The kind of person that a character is may be shown in various ways:
   a) By what the character says
   b) By what other characters say about him
   c) By the way that he acts
   d) By the thoughts that are indicated as passing through his mind
   e) By the way that other characters treat him
   f) By what the author says directly: "Joe was a coward." (Skilled authors rarely make much use of this method.)

5. Give your story a definite setting, actual or imaginary. Describe it in detail, or merely hint at it.

6. Work for natural dialogue. Note these hints:
   a) Suit the language to the character.
   b) Use contractions to give naturalness.
   c) Whenever you can, omit such explanatory words as "Jane said."
   d) Read conversations aloud to check their naturalness.

7. Begin in a way that will set the tone and mood of the story.

8. Choose an interest-provoking title, one that will not give away the ending.

WRITING ARGUMENTATION

1. Remember that argumentation is literally writing "to make clear." It should be an intellectual, not an emotional, presentation.

2. Organize your argument with great care. Use an outline.

3. Present your points both logically and emphatically. Use strong words with definite connotations.

---

*The term "short story" often is applied loosely to narrative sketches that do not follow a real plot. Such sketches are really a cross between essays and short stories, having something of the nature of each.

4. Define or explain words that you think might not mean to your readers what they mean to you. Suit your language to the audience for which you intend it.

5. Anticipate and answer any objections or opposing arguments that you think might occur to your readers.

6. Keep one point of view throughout.

7. Be courteous and fair.

"I'M TRYING MY HAND AT POETRY."

WRITING POETRY *

1. Remember that poetry is written to be read aloud. Learn to hear it in your mind even when you are where you must read it silently.

2. Use rhyme if you like, but remember that poetry need not rhyme.

3. Use a rhythm that fits your theme or mood. For example, do not use a marching rhythm if you are writing a serious love poem.

4. Be economical in your use of words. Poetry is more concise than prose; it suggests far more than it actually says.

5. Avoid false "poetic language." Many words characteristic in the poetry of bygone days have dropped out of use. "Dost" for "do" is an example.

6. If you really want to write good poetry, read much of it, especially the work of the great poets.

7. Suggest ideas and moods oftener than you present them literally. Figurative language, sense words, onomatopoeic words, and alliteration are devices that can help you to do so. (See the glossary on pages 242–44 for definitions of the preceding terms.)

8. Rewrite, polish, discard—and begin all over again.

* The books preceding this one in "The New Building Better English" series discuss many technical aspects of poetry and cover study of various fixed forms. Students will find such material also in encyclopedias or in books on writing poetry that may be in the school library. One of the best is Clement Wood's *Rhyming Dictionary*.

FOR PRACTICE AND APPLICATION

A. In class or in your small groups, decide which of the topics on pages 225–26 can be developed best through description; which through exposition; which through argumentation.

B. Choose a topic from one of the six groups and write a three-paragraph composition about it. Exchange papers for evaluation.

C. Write a short story, developing its plot by means of dialogue. Make the dialogue sound natural. Review the rules for punctuating conversation, page 146. You may wish to read the stories aloud for class or group criticism.

D. As a class activity, write a short poem. Choose a subject and decide on the rhythm and the rhyme scheme. Ask your teacher or a classmate to write the poem on the board as the lines are suggested.

E. Make a copy of the poem written by the class. Work on it individually to see how much you can improve it. Read the revised poems aloud in class. Decide what makes them better than the original poem. If several classes are writing poems at the same time, it is interesting to keep all the poems on the board so that they may be read by all the classes.

F. Choose a topic about which you feel strongly. Write an argument in which you try to convert someone to your opinion. Determine beforehand the person to whom your arguments will be addressed and decide what you want him to do about your idea. Discuss the papers in your small groups. If they are sound and well written, you might like to make these arguments into letters to be sent to your daily newspaper.

G. Write an essay. Make this the crowning achievement of your writing experience. Choose a subject that actually means something to you. Write with every bit of personality that you have. Review the suggestions for writing sentences and paragraphs, for getting variety, for choosing words wisely. Check through the glossary on pages 242–44 for helpful hints.

Then proofread and revise. Read the essays aloud in class.

FOLLOW-UP

To secure for your creative writing a wider audience than that of your classroom, use one or more of the following methods.

1. Plan to compile a book made up of the best selections written by members of the class. Circulate it in other classrooms or in the library.
2. Submit good work to your school newspaper.
3. If you can, arrange with your town or community newspaper to print selections that the editor thinks merit publication.
4. Use the bulletin board to display good work, especially poems and brief prose selections.

Glossary of Terms Used in Creative Writing

This glossary contains most of the terms used by writers. In many cases, reference is made to pages in this book where a topic is discussed more fully.

Action in a narrative means the progress of the story; that is, the development of the plot.

Allegories are narratives in which the characters are not living human beings but are types of personifications carrying out symbolic actions. Spenser's *Faerie Queene* is an example.

Alliteration is the repetition of the same consonant sound at the beginning of several accented syllables that occur near one another. Example: But the man remembered his mighty power.

Argumentation is writing in which the author seeks to convince the reader of some idea.

An **autobiography** is literally a "writing about one's own life." It is a nonfiction narrative in which the author tells his own story.

A **biography** is literally a "writing about life." It is a nonfiction narrative in which the author tells the story of someone else's life.

Characterization is the process of depicting character and personality in a narrative so that the characters seem real. (See page 239.)

Clarity is literally "clearness." A basic idea and its development must be clear to the reader. Clarity is achieved through use of unity, coherence, and emphasis. (See page 211.)

The **climax** is the spot at which a narrative reaches its highest point. All action builds toward it. In short stories the climax usually comes close to the end. What happens after the climax is often *anticlimax*.

Coherence is literally "a sticking together." It results from arranging ideas logically and is helped by the correct use of *connectives*. (See page 219.) Used with emphasis and unity, it helps to achieve a well-rounded composition.

Conflict in a narrative is the problem or struggle on which a story is based.

The **crisis** in a narrative is the turning point in the plot; it leads to the climax.

Criticism comes from the word that means "to be able to discuss, to judge, discern." Webster says it is "the art of judging or evaluating ... the beauties and faults of works of art or literature."

Description is writing that makes the reader see or become aware of details. It may be accomplished through appealing to any or all of the five *senses*. (See page 237; see also *Point of view*.)

Dialogue is conversation. Used to show character or to develop plot, it helps to make writing come alive. (See page 239.)

Didactic writing is the kind that teaches a lesson or points a moral. An example is *Aesop's Fables.*

An **editorial** is the formal expression of an editor's opinions, appearing usually in magazines and newspapers.

Emphasis is literally "force of expression." It results from arranging ideas so that the important ones stand out. (See page 211.)

An **essay** is a literary composition that sets forth the opinions or feelings that a writer has on any subject. (See pages 237–38.)

Exposition is literally "a setting forth." It is writing that explains or informs.

Fiction is literally "made up" writing, developed not through fact but through the imagination, although it may be about real people or events and have some historical truth.

Figures of speech are literary devices used to suggest ideas, pictures, or moods. Among the most useful are *metaphor, simile, personification, hyperbole.* (See page 190.)

A **flashback** is a literary device in which the author interrupts a narrative to give scenes from the past lives of the characters.

Imagery is figurative language that presents pictures in words.

Local color is the descriptive details with which an author creates a strong impression of the locale of a story. It helps the reader to sense atmosphere and background.

A **metaphor** is a figure of speech giving an implied comparison of two unlike things that have one thing in common. (See page 190.)

Mood is the basic feeling in a piece of writing. The mood of a story, for example, may be one of *gloom, fear, happiness, despair, suspense,* . . .

Narration is any writing that tells a story.

Nonfiction is literally "not made up." It is writing based on fact rather than on the imagination.

A **novel** is a book-length work of fiction.

Personification is a figure of speech in which inanimate objects or ideas are given life and considered as persons. (See page 190.)

Plagiarism is the act of stealing and passing off as one's own the exact words of another—literally "kidnaping." Always use quotation marks to indicate the exact words of another.

The **plot** is the plan, scheme, or basic idea of a literary composition, the "story." Sources of plots are (1) personal experiences, (2) observation and conversation, and (3) reading.

Poetry is writing that has a consistent pattern or rhythm; it may have rhyme. All poetry is written to be read aloud. (See page 240.)

Point of view is the relative position or angle from which an author writes. In a description the point of view must not change unless the observer changes his position; for example, if the author says, "From his seat at the window, James could see ... ," he must describe nothing but what can actually be seen from that spot.

Proportion is the arrangement of ideas in writing so that the most important ones get the most space.

Prose is writing that is not intentionally rhythmical. It is the ordinary language of speaking or writing, any writing that is not poetry.

Sense appeals are those made to the five senses—*sight, smell, taste, touch,* and *hearing*—to give the reader vivid impressions.

Sentimentality is an overdose of emotion in a piece of writing.

Setting is the place and time in which a narrative is laid. It may be real or imaginary, but all stories must take place somewhere at some time.

A **short story** is a short narrative having a single crisis that usually is resolved at the climax. (See pages 238–39.)

A **simile** is a figure of speech that states an actual comparison between two things of different kinds or qualities. (See page 190.)

Style is the indefinable quality that makes one author's writing different from anyone else's.

Suspense is literally a "hanging from." It is that quality in a story which makes the reader "hang on" to find out what is going to happen.

A **transition** is literally "a going across." It is a term applied to any device used by a writer to get a reader from one idea to the next. (See page 220.)

Unity is literally "oneness," the quality that makes a piece of writing a single unit. It is achieved by including all necessary information and ideas and by excluding all ideas that do not belong. (See page 211.)

Variety results from using different writing devices to avoid monotony.

Gaining Skill in Research

CHAPTER 10

READ AND DISCUSS

In your play, in your work, in your conversations, in your studies, you constantly raise questions about which you do not have sufficient information. Sometimes you may talk as though you do know the answers to the questions, and you may debate heatedly with others who are just as lacking in precise information as you are. At other times, if you are wise, you say, "I do not know, but I can find out, and I will."

The thoughtful student is one who insists upon accurate facts before he draws conclusions. He knows how to find the facts that are available. He knows also how to report to others the facts that he has found.

The following illustrations will show some of the kinds of questions for which people seek answers. How would you proceed in trying to find the answers to each of them?

1. A businessman thinks that his telephone rates are too high. He wants to know what businessmen in other towns must pay.
2. There is a spot on the living-room rug. Mother wants to find out how to remove it safely.
3. A telephone quiz program asks for the title of the literary work containing the following quotation: "Neither a borrower nor a lender be."
4. The members of the class are discussing education in Japan today. They want to know what kinds of schoolbooks are being used there.
5. Two students disagree as to whether Thomas Jefferson could have met Napoleon. They want to investigate whether the paths of these men ever crossed.

6. A high school senior is considering aviation as a career. He wants to know the advantages and the disadvantages of an occupation in this field.
7. A young man has just finished reading Kenneth Roberts's *Oliver Wiswell*. He wants to find out whether the author's interpretation of the Revolutionary War is historically accurate.
8. A girl is intrigued by a passage in her history book describing the heroism of pioneer women in the Westward Movement. She wants to know more about the kind of life that some of these women led.
9. Several members of an English class have just seen a play by Shaw, Ibsen, Chekhov, Barrie, or some other dramatist of an earlier period. They want to know something about other plays the author has written and about the social conditions that formed the background of the play.
10. A newspaper story tells of a boy who attempted suicide because of a facial deformity. Several young people become interested in the subject of plastic surgery and the developments in the field during World War II.

Notice that in the preceding list of examples some of the problems are fairly simple, while others are rather complex. Some of them can be answered by a telephone call, an interview, or a glance at the encyclopedia. Others call for careful and prolonged investigation and study in many sources, most of them in the library. In each instance, however, the basic steps are the same.

MAJOR STEPS IN RESEARCH

Step 1. Selecting and defining the problem
Step 2. Finding the facts
Step 3. Organizing the facts
Step 4. Reporting the facts

FOR PRACTICE AND APPLICATION

When the question is a simple one, steps 1 and 3 require little thought. Steps 2 and 4 may offer more difficulty. Select one of the following questions, or supply one of your own, and find the answer in your school or public library. Report your findings to the class orally or in writing, as your teacher may direct, indicating the source or sources that you used.

If there are any questions with which you have difficulty, return to those questions after you have finished studying this chapter.
1. What was the name of the pilot of the *Santa Maria,* Columbus's flagship?
2. In what field did George Washington Carver distinguish himself?
3. Where is the birthplace of Carl Sandburg?
4. What is the meaning of *photosynthesis?*
5. When was the first commercial airline established in the United States?
6. What are the chief national festivals of Mexico?
7. Who said, "Barkis is willin' "?
8. What is meant by "surrealism" in art?
9. What is the total population of the world today?
10. How many students were enrolled in colleges and universities in this country last year?
11. What form of government does Norway have?
12. When were the Olympic Games revived in modern times?
13. Where can you find the poem "The Highwayman"?
14. Who was the man referred to in Browning's poem "The Lost Leader"?
15. How much money was spent for education in your community last year?
16. How is the board of directors of your public library chosen?
17. How much wheat was produced in the U.S. last year as compared with the year before?
18. What is the most common cause of fatal accidents in American homes?
19. What diseases are caused by vitamin deficiency?

Step 1 . Selecting the Subject

The best way to become familiar with the methods of investigation is to choose an interesting topic and prepare a report on it. Perhaps you already have a question in your mind on which you desire information. If not, take time to think about a good topic. Remember that much of the success of your study depends on a wise choice of subject.

Observe the following rules in making your selection:
1. Choose a subject in which you are keenly interested. Your investigation should be a pleasant adventure, not a chore.
    a) It may be related to an occupation that appeals to you.
    b) It may be suggested by a hobby that you have developed or by some experience that you have had.
    c) Your reading in school textbooks or of favorite stories may arouse your interest in a subject for further investigation.
    d) A class discussion or a conversation at the dinner table at home may stimulate your curiosity.

2. Choose a subject that you can treat satisfactorily in the time at your disposal.
   a) Avoid subjects that call for extensive and detailed study. You are not expected to write a book or to make a startlingly original contribution to human knowledge. The purpose of this paper is simply to satisfy your curiosity about an interesting subject and to give you experience in using the tools and techniques of finding, organizing, and reporting information.
   b) Limit your subject to a specific phase of a question that you can conveniently study in a relatively short time.
3. Choose a subject that is not too difficult. "Modern Surgery," for example, would be both too broad and too technical, except as a discussion of the training and qualifications required for the profession of surgery. Choose a subject on which material is available in popular and semipopular magazines. Such magazines as the *Journal of the American Medical Association* or the *Journal of Applied Psychology* are too technical to be of much help to most high school students.
4. Choose a subject that has some importance to most people. Even for purposes of practice in research, it seems wasteful to spend a considerable part of a semester on "Fashions in Shakespeare's Day" or "The Manufacture of Perfume," for example. Subjects should appeal to the average reader as in some way significant or interesting.

    Students who have difficulty in finding a suitable topic may want to use one of the following:

1. New Uses for Plastics
2. Peacetime Uses for Atomic Energy
3. Who Supports the Symphony Orchestras?
4. Changing Public Taste in Novels
5. The Rise of the Picture Magazines
6. The Vocation of Journalism, Yesterday and Today
7. New Kinds of Documentary Films
8. New Methods of Crime Detection
9. Devices in Horror Stories, from Poe to Ellery Queen
10. The Conservation of Wildlife
11. The Fight against Cancer
12. Safety on the Turnpike
13. The History of Our Town
14. The Early History of Our Town
15. Different Types of Travel Guides
16. The Conquest of Polio (*or some other disease*)
17. Aviation (*or anything else*) as a Career
18. Recreation in Our Town
19. Juvenile Delinquency in Our Town
20. The Growth of Private Flying
21. Machines That "Think" (Automatic Scoring and Classifying Devices)
22. Talking Books

23. The Use of Microfilm
24. The Magic of Electronics
25. The Uses of Soybeans
26. Skyscrapers
27. The Library of Congress and Its Services
28. Heroes of the Telephone Lines
29. Great Fires of History
30. Peacetime Sea Disasters
31. International Student Exchanges
32. High Points in the Olympic Games
33. Great Subways of the World
34. Life in the Coal Mines
35. Dangerous Occupations
36. Changing Designs in Automobiles
37. The Early History of Baseball (*or* Football)
38. Public Opinion Polls

DEFINING THE PROBLEM

When you have chosen the general subject of your investigation, you should formulate clearly the general question that you want to ask about it. This step is important, because your basic question determines what *kind* of information to look for. You are not simply gathering all the facts that happen to fall under a general heading. You must decide exactly what you want to know.

If your general subject is "The Prohibition Movement Today," for example, you may wish to define your problem as follows: "To what extent is prohibition returning to America, as indicated by state and local laws and by public opinion?" If your general subject is "Changing Designs in Automobiles," your problem practically defines itself: "What are the latest trends in the body designs of automobiles?" Do not confuse the *problem* of the paper with the *title,* which should be short and striking.

THE PRELIMINARY OUTLINE

For convenience in gathering information, the basic question of your study should be subdivided at once into a group of more specific questions. These questions together may serve as your preliminary outline, although they will later on be further subdivided as you become more familiar with your problem in the course of your research. You will then be ready to draft a *working outline.* Right now a short list of questions without subheads will be sufficient.

By way of illustration, take another look at the problem, "What are the latest trends in the body designs of automobiles?" Just what do you want to know about these trends? Before studying the subject, you may wish to ask yourself these questions:

1. What principles do modern designers employ in planning new designs?
2. How do today's cars differ from those manufactured before World War II?
3. How have new materials affected body design?
4. How has the airplane affected body design?
5. What will the car of tomorrow probably look like?

After reading on the subject, you may wish to change these questions, drop some, and add others.

FOR PRACTICE AND APPLICATION

On a sheet of paper, write your name, the general subject of your investigation, the basic problem of the study, and the major questions into which you have subdivided your problem. Be ready to hand in this sheet on the date designated by your instructor. When you have done so, you will have completed Step 1 in the preparation of your report.

Step 2. Finding the Facts

Armed with your basic problem and your preliminary outline, you are now ready to search for the facts. You should begin with an inventory of information that you may already have in your mind. Since your own supply of information is likely to be limited, however, you look for other sources. There are at least four types of sources: (1) personal observation or experience; (2) the personal interview; (3) current documents or reports, such as you may obtain for yourself; and (4) books, pamphlets, magazines, newspapers, and pictures, available to you in the library. Films and phonograph records may in some instances also be useful. All these sources have both advantages and disadvantages. You may wish to use some or all of them, depending on the nature of your problem.

PERSONAL OBSERVATION OR EXPERIENCE

If you can speak about your subject from personal observation or experience, your report is likely to be more vivid and interesting than one written entirely from books. If you are writing about our national parks, an anecdote about a visit that you made to one of them will be effective. If you are writing about housing conditions in your neighborhood, a personal inspection of different kinds of homes, at least from the outside, will be essential.

Personal observation is valuable, but by itself it is not a reliable source. Individual impressions are often misleading, especially those which have to do with people. Lawyers know that two witnesses of the same incident often give widely differing reports of what they have seen. For this reason you should not depend upon personal observations exclusively.

"THIS IS NOT MY OWN CONCLUSION— I'M QUOTING SOMEONE WHO KNOWS WHAT HE'S TALKING ABOUT!"

PERSONAL INTERVIEWS

All around you are people who have had interesting experiences and who have interesting ideas. Members of your own family, your neighbors, the fireman, the librarian, the football coach, the minister, businessmen, the school superintendent or principal, the chemistry or history teacher—these, and many other people whom you know, can often supply you with just the information or background material that you need. To ignore the help that such persons can give you would be a wasteful procedure.

Methods of getting facts in interviews require almost as much thought as those involved in library work. The following suggestions are only a few of the ideas that must be kept in mind.

GUIDES FOR INTERVIEWING

1. *Courtesy is the first rule of the interview.* Making an appointment with the person to be interviewed is the first important step. Ask (*a*) whether the individual concerned can give you time, and (*b*) what will be the most convenient hour and place for the interview. Most people will be delighted to co-operate, but it is necessary to be tactful in requesting co-operation.
2. *Prepare carefully for the interview.*
   a) Know just how you will introduce yourself and how you will introduce the subject of the interview.
   b) Be sure that what you want to know is clear in your own mind.
   c) Be ready with thoughtful questions. Sometimes a few remarks and a single question from you will be sufficient to launch the interviewee on his reminiscences. At other times you may need to insert a tactful question or comment to bring him back to the subject. In other instances you will need to make specific requests for explanation.
   d) Plan in advance how you will conclude.
3. *You must make careful notes of the interview.* In some cases it will be possible to take notes in the course of the interview, as newspaper reporters frequently do. At other times it is better to conduct an informal conversation and to record your notes immediately afterward. The nature of the subject and the attitude of the person interviewed should determine your method of taking notes.

The interview is a valuable source because it contributes the human interest element to your study and because it often affords explanations that are difficult or impossible to obtain in print. On the other hand, because it offers just one man's opinion or recollection (unless you conduct a series of interviews), it should not be used to the exclusion of other sources.

CURRENT DOCUMENTS AND REPORTS

In your everyday affairs you probably often fail to make use of valuable sources of information available to all. You may hold mistaken opinions or lack exact proofs for your statements because you do not use the facts and ideas that you could have for the asking. A three-cent stamp will bring to your home many kinds of materials that will help to answer your questions or to solve your problems.

For your research study, you should find out whether there is any agency that can supply information or arguments bearing on your problem. The following list includes only a few of the agencies that can supply facts and ideas on various subjects. Examine the list and select those which are likely to have materials on your subject. When you write to these agencies for such materials, be sure to state your problem clearly.

A word of caution: Some of the sources listed are more reliable than others. The most reliable sources of information in this list are the official government agencies and established scientific or educational organizations. Some of the other agencies are propaganda organizations. Propaganda may prove helpful, but you must know the source and its purposes. You must compare the various sources of propaganda.

READ AND DISCUSS

In the following list, which sources are likely to distribute intentional propaganda? Is propaganda always false and dangerous? May it be used in a worthy cause?

Sources of Information (Non-Library)

Agencies of the U.S. Government
   U.S. Department of Agriculture
   Bureau of Standards
   Census Bureau
   U.S. Office of Education
   Bureau of Labor Statistics
   U.S. Department of Agriculture
   Federal Bureau of Investigation
   Library of Congress
Junior Red Cross
National Association of Manufacturers
U.S. Chamber of Commerce
Educational Department, C.I.O.
American Federation of Labor
Travel agencies
Intercultural relations groups
New York Public Library
Meat Institute
Iron and Steel Institute
The National Education Association
The American Federation of Teachers
American Medical Association
Pure Food and Drugs Administration
National Association of Broadcasters

THE RESOURCES OF THE LIBRARY

A recent study of the work of college students revealed that those who scored high on the entrance test dealing with library skills were the most successful in their later college work. Library skills proved even more important than high scores on the psychological or English tests. But whether they go on to college or enter the business world, students should know how libraries are organized so that they can make good use of the information available therein.

FINDING THE RIGHT BOOK

Library resources are of many kinds, but chief among them are the books. In order to make the most effective use of the books, you must know how they are classified.

THE CARD CATALOGUE

The books in a library are listed in the card catalogue. The cards are filed alphabetically according to the first important word (disregarding *a, an,* and *the*).

Most card catalogues contain three cards for each book:

1. *Author card.* The author's surname, followed by his given name, appears as the first line.
2. *Title card.* The book title appears as the first line.
3. *Subject card.* A word or phrase indicating the subject of the book appears as the first line.

Following are author, title, and subject cards for the book *Sport Tales and Anecdotes* by Frank Grant Menke. Notice that the three cards are the same except for the first line; the title and subject cards have typed at the top of the card either the title or the subject.

Author Card

796
M23s **Menke, Frank Grant,** 1885–

　　　Sport tales and anecdotes; more than 250 highlights and highspots of human interest from the recorded annals of more than a dozen sports. New York, A. S. Barnes [1953]

　　308 p. 24 cm.

　　　1. Sports stories.　　I. Title.

　　GV191.M4　　　　　796　　　　　　53–8305 ‡

　　Library of Congress　　[20]

Title Card

```
796      Sport tales and anecdotes
M23s  Menke, Frank Grant, 1885–
            Sport tales and anecdotes; more than 250 highlights and
         highspots of human interest from the recorded annals of
         more than a dozen sports.  New York, A. S. Barnes [1953]
            308 p.  24 cm.
```

Subject Card

```
796      Sports stories
M23s  Menke, Frank Grant, 1885–
            Sport tales and anecdotes; more than 250 highlights and
         highspots of human interest from the recorded annals of
         more than a dozen sports.  New York, A. S. Barnes [1953]
            308 p.  24 cm.
```

GUIDES FOR OBTAINING LIBRARY BOOKS

1. *Reference books.* If the call number on the catalogue card is preceded by the Symbol "R," the book is shelved in the reading room or reference room. Reference books, which do not circulate, must be used at the library.

2. *Books located in "closed stacks."* The bulk of the volumes in a library are stored in the stacks. Some libraries do not permit their patrons to enter the stacks. Instead, it is necessary to fill out a "call slip," a form on which the borrower records the call number of the desired book, the author's name, the title (all taken from the card catalogue), and the borrower's name. The call slip is handed to the librarian, who obtains the book from the stacks.

3. *Books located in "open stacks."* If you are permitted to obtain books yourself from the stacks, you can quickly find the book on the shelves if you have some knowledge of the system of arranging books in your school or town library.

ARRANGEMENT OF BOOKS IN THE STACKS OF A LIBRARY

Books are arranged according to one of several systems, the most common of which are the *Dewey Decimal System* and the *Library of Congress* classification. In each of these systems, the book is classified on the basis of its subject matter and is given a call number. The call number is printed on the backbone of the book and also appears, as you know, on the catalogue card. In the stacks, books are shelved in order of their call numbers.

THE DEWEY DECIMAL SYSTEM

The Dewey Decimal System classifies books under the following ten major headings:

000–099 General Works	500–599 Pure Science
100–199 Philosophy	600–699 Useful Arts
200–299 Religion	700–799 Fine Arts
300–399 Social Science	800–899 Literature
400–499 Philology	900–999 History

These general headings are divided into smaller classifications, as shown in the following illustration:

800–899 Literature

800 General Works	850 Italian Literature
810 American Literature	860 Spanish Literature
820 English Literature	870 Latin Literature
830 German Literature	880 Greek Literature
840 French Literature	890 Literature of Other Languages

Each of these classifications is again subdivided; for example:

820 English Literature

821 Poetry	825 Oratory
822 Drama	826 Letters
823 Fiction	827 Satire and Humor
824 Essays	828 Miscellany

By using decimals, these headings are further subdivided; for example:

822 English Drama
822.1 Early English Drama (1066–1400)
    822.11 Chester Plays
    822.12 Coventry Plays
    822.13 Townley Plays

THE LIBRARY OF CONGRESS CLASSIFICATION

The Library of Congress system classifies books as follows:

A General Works	M Music
B Philosophy, Religion	N Fine Arts
C History	P Language and Literature
D Foreign History	Q Science
E, F American History	R Medicine
G Geography, Anthropology	S Agriculture
H Social Sciences	T Technology
J Political Science	U Military Science
K Law	V Naval Science
L Education	Z Library Science, Bibliography

You should familiarize yourself with the general divisions of the systems of library classification: if the stacks of a library are open to you, you can save much time by going directly to the shelves that contain books dealing with your subject.

FOR PRACTICE AND APPLICATION

Discuss the following questions:
1. What system of classification does your school library use?
2. Under what number is your favorite school subject to be found?
3. Is there any difference between the system that your community public library uses and that which your school uses?
4. Are there any specialized libraries in your city?
5. Does your school library have any special collections? your community library? If so, describe briefly.

REFERENCE BOOKS

The most commonly used of the books catalogued as "Reference" books are encyclopedias, dictionaries, books of facts, reference works in special fields, guidebooks, bibliographies, and guides to periodicals.

ENCYCLOPEDIAS

Articles in encyclopedias are among the first sources a student consults in the course of his research, because they usually provide a general overview of the subject and a bibliography (list of books and articles) for further investigation. Some of the best-known encyclopedias are the following:

Encyclopedia Americana. This work is especially valuable for topics connected with government, industry, business, and science.

Encyclopaedia Britannica. This set of books contains information on almost every topic of general interest. The Index volume makes the *Britannica* easy to use.

Collier's Encyclopedia. This set of books is particularly useful for senior high school and college students.

Columbia Encyclopedia. This is a one-volume encyclopedia having concise articles and no illustrations. It is most useful for quick reference.

Lincoln Library of Essential Information. This is a serviceable one-volume encyclopedia.

Encyclopedias are kept up to date by supplements issued each year, such as *Americana Annual* and *Britannica Book of the Year.*

UNABRIDGED DICTIONARIES

Dictionaries are also valuable reference works. Among the best-known dictionaries are the following:

Funk and Wagnalls *New Standard Dictionary of the English Language*

New Century Dictionary (2 vols.)

Oxford English Dictionary. This 13-volume dictionary traces the history of words and their meanings.

Webster's New International Dictionary, Second Edition

OTHER DICTIONARIES

Allen, F. Sturges. *Allen's Synonyms and Antonyms*

Crabb, George. *English Synonyms*

Fernald, J. C. *Standard Handbook of Synonyms, Antonyms, and Prepositions*

Fowler, H. W. *A Dictionary of Modern English Usage*

Roget, P. M. *Thesaurus of English Words and Phrases*

BOOKS OF FACTS

The following are miscellaneous reference books:

Century Cyclopedia of Names. This book is in part out of date, but still useful.

United States Government Publications: Monthly Catalogue. This gives a complete list of government publications for the month.

Rand McNally Commercial Atlas and Marketing Guide. This contains maps, statistics on population and manufacturing, information about transportation, and so on.

World Almanac and Book of Facts. This contains valuable miscellaneous information, such as social, political, and commercial statistics, recent laws, and lists of important events.

Information Please Almanac. This is a comprehensive reference book of world facts and a record and review of the year.

SPECIAL REFERENCE WORKS

Information in general reference works, such as those just described, is necessarily concise, and their bibliographies are usually limited. Hence, if you wish more detailed information, you must go to special reference works. Here is a list of special reference books in various fields of knowledge. Most of them provide bibliographies as well as information about the subjects treated.

ART

Reinach, Salomon. *Apollo; an Illustrated Manual of the History of Art throughout the Ages.*

BIOGRAPHY

Current Biography. This is a monthly publication, but each year's issues are bound into one volume. There is a cumulative index.

Dictionary of American Biography. 1928–1937. This contains no biographies of *living* Americans.

Dictionary of National Biography. 1885–1937. British. This contains no biographies of *living* Englishmen.

International Who's Who. This volume contains brief sketches of prominent personalities throughout the world.

Webster's Biographical Dictionary

Who's Who. This is a valuable reference on living Englishmen.

Who's Who in America. This reference book, published every two years, is valuable for sketches of living Americans.

HISTORY

Cambridge Ancient History.
Cambridge Medieval History.
Cambridge Modern History.
Richard B. Morris. *Encyclopedia of American History*

LITERATURE AND QUOTATIONS

Bartlett, John. *Familiar Quotations*
Stevenson, Burton. *The Home Book of Quotations*
Cambridge History of American Literature
Cambridge History of English Literature. The bibliographies contained in this work are now out of date; the student should consult the *Cambridge Bibliography of English Literature.*
Kunitz, Stanley J., and Haycraft, Howard. *Twentieth Century Authors*
Millett, Fred B. *Contemporary British Literature* (rev.)

MUSIC

Thompson, Oscar. *The International Cyclopedia of Music and Musicians*

RELIGION

Catholic Encyclopedia
Hastings, James, (ed.). *Encyclopaedia of Religion and Ethics*
Universal Jewish Encyclopedia

SCIENCE

Cattell, Jacques. *American Men of Science* (1949)
Van Nostrand's Scientific Encyclopedia (1947)

SOCIAL SCIENCES

Encyclopaedia of the Social Sciences

GUIDEBOOKS AND BIBLIOGRAPHIES

If your topic is not treated fully enough in any of the reference works listed above, look in a guidebook or a bibliography. The following are among the most useful references:

Hutchins, Margaret; Johnson, Alice S.; and Williams, Margaret S. *Guide to the Use of Libraries*

Winchell, Constance M. *Guide to Reference Books*. This work does not supply information on a subject, but lists and describes reference books where information can be found on a great many subjects. It is the successor to Isadore G. Mudge's publication of the same name.

United States Catalog. This lists books that were in print in English in 1928. Listings are arranged alphabetically by subject, author, and title.

Cumulative Book Index. This is a continuation of the *United States Catalog*, listing books published in English throughout the world from 1928 to the present. Monthly supplements (except in August) keep it up to date. To use this work, begin with the most recent issue and work backward through the bound volumes.

THE READERS' GUIDE

Some of the most interesting and up-to-date material on your subject will be found in magazines. In order to locate such material, you should use one of the guides to periodical literature found on the reference shelf.

Best known and most useful of these library aids is the *Readers' Guide to Periodical Literature*. It is published semimonthly from September to June, and monthly in July and August. Begin with the current issue and continue with the bound volumes for recent years until you have found the information that you want.

Articles in the *Readers' Guide* are arranged alphabetically by author and by subject. When you have found the subject related to your research problem, run down the list of titles until you find those which seem most likely to answer the questions in your mind. Copy these titles and publication facts and add them to your working bibliography (see page 263).

Entries in the *Readers' Guide* contain numerous abbreviations. A key to the names of the magazines and to the abbreviations used may be found at the front of each volume of the guide. A sample entry follows:

Answers for armchair pilots. H. Wilson. diags.
Flying 49:34 + Jl '51

This entry means that an article with diagrams entitled "Answers for Armchair Pilots," written by H. Wilson, appeared in the magazine *Flying*, volume 49, page 34 and following, the July, 1951, number.

OTHER GUIDES TO PERIODICALS

Other useful guides to periodicals are the following:

Education Index. This is an author and subject index to books and periodicals about education.

Industrial Arts Index. This indexes (by subject only) books, pamphlets, and periodicals dealing with engineering, trade, and business.

FOR PRACTICE AND APPLICATION

A. From the list found on pages 248–49, select six topics and find three articles on each of them in the *Readers' Guide.* Find three additional references on each of the six topics in some source other than the *Readers' Guide.*

B. Consult the Index volume of the *Encyclopaedia Britannica* for references on five of the topics listed on pages 248–49. Ask the librarian of your school or public library to show you other special indexes and reference books in such special fields as architecture, fashions, music, geology, . . .

C. Using the references on pages 257–60, find answers to these questions.
1. What is the Twentieth Century Fund? Name two or more reports done for this organization.
2. Name three people who have written a "Life" of Lincoln. Who wrote the first authorized sketch of his life?
3. According to the 1950 census, what was the educational attainment of the population of the United States?
4. Who won the Pulitzer prize for distinguished editorial writing in the year 1948? for the best cartoon of 1945? for the most distinguished novel in 1952? for history in 1940? for poetry in 1944? for music in 1950? How many times has Robert Frost won the poetry award?
5. When did Handel compose *The Messiah?* When and where was it first performed?
6. Who wrote the following lines?
>But there's nothing half so sweet in life
>As love's young dream.
7. When was the first Rose Bowl football game played? What teams played, and who won?
8. For what is Sir Alexander Fleming most famous?
9. Who were the "Pre-Raphaelites"?
10. For what kind of poetry is Edward Lear known best?

D. Make one or more of the following brief oral reports.
1. Give a report on four notable libraries in the United States.
2. Give a brief report on two museums that you would like to visit if you had the opportunity.

3. Give a report on how to detect counterfeit money.
4. From the following titles, choose one. Report on the cause which led to the writing of the work mentioned. Answer the following questions:
   a) Was the cause a personal one or a social circumstance?
   b) Could a similar selection be written today for similar reasons?
   English Writers
       "The Cloud"—Percy Bysshe Shelley
       "Lycidas"—John Milton
       "The Shortest Way with Dissenters"—Daniel Defoe
       "A Modest Proposal"—Jonathan Swift
   American Writers
       "When Lilacs Last in the Dooryard Bloomed"—Walt Whitman
       Spoon River Anthology—Edgar Lee Masters
       "Mending Wall"—Robert Frost
       "Lincoln and Douglas Debates"—Carl Sandburg

E. Report in detail (beyond encyclopedia article) on one of these topics.
1. What was the purpose of Admiral Byrd's expedition to Antarctica?
2. What was Alexander Graham Bell's original purpose in performing the research which eventually led to the invention of the telephone?
3. What led to the discovery of the X-ray?

COMPILING A WORKING BIBLIOGRAPHY

You have just reviewed the four *general* sources of information from which you may obtain material for your research paper: (1) personal observation or experience; (2) personal interviews; (3) pamphlets obtained from various sources; and (4) library material. You are now ready to make a list of *specific* sources from which you will later write the notes for your paper. This list of specific sources is called a *working bibliography*. Some of the items in the working bibliography may be derived from the first three general sources of information, but most of them will probably consist of books and articles from the library.

The working bibliography is compiled on bibliography cards, which are ruled cards, usually 3 x 5 inches in size. Note the following pointers.

1. Make a separate bibliography card for each book, periodical article, pamphlet, or personal interview.
2. Keep your cards in alphabetical order in a special fiber envelope or in a small file large enough to hold the note cards which you add.
3. To save time, you should see that the information on the bibliography cards follows the same form that you will use later for the final bibliography (see pages 276–77). The form for a bibliography card varies for a book, a magazine article, or a part of a book.

BIBLIOGRAPHY CARD FOR A BOOK

A bibliography card for a book contains the following data:
1. The author's name (surname first)
2. The title of the book (underscored)
3. The edition (if other than the first)
4. The place of publication
5. The name of the publisher
6. The date of the publication

In addition, it is helpful to write on the bibliography card the following information:
7. A brief statement as to the nature or contents of the book
8. The call number of the book. Having the number will make it unnecessary for you to go to the card catalogue when you are ready to use the book. The lower left-hand corner of the card is a good place for writing this information.
9. The name of the library where the book is located. This is a time-saver if you are using several libraries. The name of the library (or an abbreviation which will be clear to you) may be placed in the lower left-hand corner after the call number.

Example of a Bibliography Card for a Book

```
Scott, Sir Harold
    Scotland Yard. New York: Random House, 1955.




364.1
S 74 s
School Library
```

BIBLIOGRAPHY CARD FOR AN ARTICLE

Bibliography cards for articles follow the same general rules about form as do bibliography cards for books. In addition, several special rules are observed:
1. The title of the article is put in quotation marks and is not underscored.
2. The title of the periodical is underscored.

3. The volume number and year are given.
4. The page or pages on which the article occurs are given. (Sometimes in bound volumes the pages for the entire year will be numbered consecutively; then the page numbers will refer not to the issue in which the article appeared, but to the bound volume.)

Example of a Bibliography Card for an Article

> Cannon, Grant
>   "Nitrogen Will Feed Us." <u>Atlantic Monthly</u>, CXCII (September, 1953), 50-53.

BIBLIOGRAPHY CARD FOR A PART OF A BOOK

Bibliography cards for parts of books are similar to those for magazine articles:

1. The title of the section referred to is put in quotation marks and is not underscored.
2. The title of the book is underscored.
3. The page or pages of the section referred to are given.

Example of a Bibliography Card for a Part of a Book

> Teale, Edwin Way
>   "Ant Lore." <u>Grassroot Jungle</u>. 147-53.
> New York: Dodd, Mead & Company, 1937.
>
>
> 393.7
> T 769
> Public Library

265

PROCEDURE IN COMPILING A BIBLIOGRAPHY

The procedure in compiling a bibliography varies somewhat with the nature of the subject, but in most cases you can save time and energy by taking the following steps in approximately the order indicated.

GUIDES FOR COMPILING A BIBLIOGRAPHY

1. Look up your subject in general reference books, such as encyclopedias (see pages 257–58). If your topic is not listed, look under related topics. If your topic is a very narrow one, look under a broader topic that includes it. For instance, if you are writing on the Black Hawk War, you may find your topic discussed under Indian Wars. Read carefully the articles that you find, to get a general acquaintance with the subject. Write on bibliography cards the titles of all books and articles recommended by the reference work. Also make out a bibliography card for the reference work itself.

2. Look for your topic in special reference works (see pages 259–60) to obtain additional bibliographical references. If the special reference work itself contains a discussion of your topic, make out a bibliography card for the reference work so that you can return to it later and make notes.

3. If your topic is not listed, or is not treated fully, in the works referred to in points 1 and 2, turn to a guidebook or bibliography (see page 261) to learn where you can find references on the subject. Then look in these sources for information and bibliography.

4. Obtain additional references from the *Readers' Guide* (see page 261) and, if necessary, from other guides to periodicals.

5. Consult the card catalogues of libraries. If you do not find your topic listed, look under related topics. You will probably find the titles of several books for which you already have bibliography cards; if so, this is a good time to put the call numbers on the cards.

6. Send for pamphlets and other published material for which you have bibliography cards. (Often these cannot be obtained from the library.) Order promptly so that the material will arrive in time to be used for your paper. Make out a bibliography card for each piece of material.

7. Arrange for interviews if you expect to make use of this source of information. (In practice, this step can be taken much earlier; the time must be determined by your own convenience and that of the person interviewed.) Write out a bibliography card for each interview, giving the date, the name of the person interviewed, and the reason for considering him an authority on your subject.

FOR PRACTICE AND APPLICATION

Assemble on bibliography cards the following information about books and articles. Follow carefully the form used in the examples on pages 264–65.
1. A book by Byrd Douglas called The Science of Baseball. It was published in Chicago by T. E. Wilson and Company in 1922.
2. An article in Coronet magazine for June, 1953, page 133, called Baseball in Reverse. The author is G. Drake. This is volume 34 of the magazine.
3. Alfred Henry Spink's The National Game. The National Game Publishing Company first published it in St. Louis, Missouri, in 1910.
4. William Jacobellis's Sports Photo Album, a book published in 1951 by David McKay Company, New York.
5. The Official Encyclopedia of Baseball, a book written by Hy. Turkin and S. C. Thompson. It was published in 1951 by A. S. Barnes and Company, New York.
6. They Can All Be Pitched To, an article, page 22, Saturday Evening Post. It was written by Frank Frisch and edited by H. T. Paxton. It appeared in the 225 volume of the May 23, 1953, issue.
7. H. S. Commager's article called Play Ball!, which appeared on page 8 of the September 30, 1946, issue of the Scholastic magazine, the 49 volume.
8. Baseball; Official Major and Minor League Records is published each year in Chicago by the Office of the Commissioner.
9. In 1922, C. Scribner's Sons of New York published William Jones Clarke's book called Baseball, Individual Play and Team Play.
10. Volume 193 of Harper's Magazine, pages 371–6, the October, 1946, issue, carried an article called West Coast Baseball: Too Big for Its Britches, written by D. Endsley.

STEP 3. ORGANIZING THE FACTS

In gathering information on your topic, you must be sure to classify it carefully as you proceed so that you may put it to effective use when you have reached the stage at which you are ready to write your paper.

When you have made your working bibliography with the aid of the reference tools discussed in the preceding section, you will consult the titles in order to discover what they have to offer. Many will deal with the topic as a whole; others will deal with special phases of the topic. Your job is to bring together in one place in your notes all the material that deals with a single phase of the topic. This process is known as the *classification* of the material. The *plan* of classification is called the *working outline*.

THE WORKING OUTLINE

As you begin your study, you will probably have a very general outline in mind. This may be your preliminary outline (see pages 249–50), or it may be a revision of your preliminary outline suggested by ideas that you had while making your bibliography cards. For example, if you are studying the topic "Atomic Energy," you might naturally think of such subdivisions as "Peacetime Uses of Atomic Energy," "Wartime Uses of Atomic Energy," "International Control of Atomic Energy." As you read further on the subject, you may wish to rearrange your topics, to eliminate some, to add others. The working outline is always tentative and flexible; never think of it as a final form.

TAKING NOTES AS YOU READ

You should now look at each of the sources listed on your bibliography cards. To save time when consulting a book, first check the table of contents and the index to find the parts of the text that bear on your subject. Turn to these parts without wasting time on other sections. Learn to scan, or skim, books and articles before reading them carefully. (See page 312.) After a little practice, you can tell very quickly whether a source contains anything of value to you. If your first examination of the source shows that it is unsuitable, eliminate that item from your bibliography and proceed to the next one. Continue this scanning process until you have left only cards that you feel will be of real value to you in preparing your paper.

When a source contains useful information, you will wish to take detailed notes. These reading notes are of two kinds: (1) direct quotations and (2) paraphrases. *Direct quotations* are any material copied word for word from the source. *Paraphrases* are restatements in your own words of the material that you are consulting.

GUIDES FOR TAKING NOTES

1. Use ruled index cards, 3 x 5 inches or 4 x 6 inches. Many persons prefer to use the larger size so that the note cards can be easily distinguished from the 3 x 5-inch bibliography cards.

2. As a rule, use direct quotations only if the material is very concisely expressed or very skillfully written. *Place quotation marks around every quotation.* If you wish to omit part of a quotation, indicate the omission by using ellipses. (See Rule 157k, page 135.)

3. In paraphrasing, express ideas as briefly as possible. Use disjointed phrases rather than complete sentences. If you know shorthand or have developed a system of shorthand of your own, you can save time by using such a short cut in making paraphrases. Of course, you will expand this material into smooth, correct English when you write your paper. Use no quotation marks for paraphrased material.

4. Write the subject of each note at the top of the card. This method permits you to file your notes according to topic. Later, when you arrange the materials for your paper, you can easily arrange your notes in the proper order for use.

5. Write on the card the exact source of each note so that you can give proper credit for ideas that you use.
    a) If the note is based on a book, give (1) author and title (if the title is long, give just enough of it so that you can identify it from the bibliography card) and (2) the page from which you took the material.
    b) If the note is based on an article, give (1) author and title of the article; (2) name and volume number of the periodical; (3) page from which the material is taken.

Note Card—Direct Quotation

Birth rate in Spain
"The birth rate ... has been more steady in Spain than in the other large countries of Europe. It oscillated from 1878 to 1908 between 33.2 and 37.1, and from 1909 to 1930 between 27.7 and 32.9."

—Kuczynski, *The Balance of Births and Deaths*, Vol. II, *page* 57.

Note Card—Paraphrase

```
Requirements of a test for color-blindness

   Chief requirement: efficiency in picking
men unfit for military service. Apparatus
must be simple, inexpensive, compact, easily
transportable. Results must be simple, so
average applicant can understand purpose and
meaning of test. Test should demand nearly
the same type of response as will the pro-
fessional duties of applicant.


--Haupt, ''Tests for Color-Blindness,''
Journal of General Psychology III (1934),
223.
```

THE FINAL OUTLINE

The outline is a great help to the writer of a research paper, because it helps to keep him on the subject and to remind him of the important points to be made in the paper.

You will recall that, after you selected your subject, you made a working outline, consisting of a series of questions to which you hoped to find the answers. As you begin to gather material on note cards, your outline begins to change and grow: you discard some questions and add others. As you continue to read and take notes, you come to see that your material falls into certain main divisions. This is the time to begin the final outline. The principal divisions of your subject will be the main heads of the outline. The subdivisions will be subheads and sub-subheads. You may wish to add an introduction and a conclusion. For these sections you may have found material in your reading, or you may prefer to write them from your general knowledge of the subject. In either case, if you write an introduction and a conclusion, those parts should appear in the outline.

To complete the outline as early as possible in the process of note-taking saves time, because to do so helps prevent the taking of notes that are not clearly related to your subject and which therefore would be discarded later. Keep your outline flexible, however; it should always be subject to change as your grasp of the problem becomes clearer and more complete. For example, you may find that a point assigned first to one part of your outline fits more logically or more dramatically into another part. In such a case, you can easily change the outline to suit the new arrangement.

KINDS OF OUTLINES

Your outline may be either a *sentence* outline or a *topic* outline. In a sentence outline, all heads and subheads are expressed in complete sentences; in a topic outline, they are merely brief phrases or single words. The sentence outline has the advantage of helping to clarify your thought on each point as you go along; it brings you one step nearer the writing of the paper. The topic outline has the advantage of conciseness; it shows clearly at a glance what the divisions and subdivisions of the subject are. Each writer must decide for himself which type of outline will be more practical for his particular subject. But he should stick to one type of outline: an outline should never be a mixture of topics and sentences. Further, a topic outline should use *parallel structure;* in the sample outline, for example, each point under the Roman numerals begins with a gerund.

Below are examples of parts of (1) a topic outline and (2) a sentence outline. After examining them carefully, decide which type you think will be more effective for your research paper.

Making Student Government Work
(*A Topic Outline*)

I. Introduction
   A. Pointing out the values of student government
   B. Explaining the importance of making student government work

II. Body
   A. Building on a good Constitution
      1. Selecting an able draft committee
      2. Discussing fully before adopting
      3. Following the rules faithfully
   B. Selecting the right officers and committees
      1. Choosing for ability, not popularity
      2. Considering both boys and girls
      3. Giving careful thought to selection
   C. Using parliamentary procedure effectively
      1. Knowing the important rules and procedures
      2. Using the rules skillfully
      3. Avoiding parliamentary "tangles"
   D. Maintaining good morale
      1. Respecting one another's opinions
      2. Giving support to the officers
      3. Assuming appropriate responsibilities

III. Conclusion
    A. Summing up the importance of co-operation
    B. Making general observations
        1. Using common sense in meeting problems
        2. Observing a spirit of fair play
        3. Putting the welfare of the school first

Making Student Government Work
(*A Sentence Outline*)

I. Introduction
    A. Student government can help to improve the life of the school.
    B. Student government, to be effective, calls for the co-operation of everyone.

II. Body
    A. It is important to build on a good Constitution.
        1. Care should be taken in choosing the committee that is to draft the Constitution.
        2. There should be full discussion by the student body before the provisions are adopted.
        3. Once adopted, the rules should be followed faithfully.
    B. Great care should be taken to select the right officers and appoint the right committees.
        1. Officers and committees should be chosen for their ability, not their popularity.
        2. Both boys and girls should be considered for positions.
        3. Officers and committees should not be chosen hastily.
    C. All students should learn how to use the method of parliamentary procedure effectively.
        1. Students should become acquainted with the main rules of parliamentary procedure.
        2. Students should learn how to make skillful use of the rules.
        3. Officers and members should strive to avoid parliamentary "tangles."
    D. Good morale is important to successful student government.
        1. Students should show respect for one another's opinions.
        2. Members should give support to their officers.
        3. Both officers and members should faithfully discharge their appropriate responsibilities.

III. Conclusion
    A. In summary, successful student government calls for the intelligent co-operation of everyone.
    B. Certain general observations remain to be made.
        1. Common sense, as well as rules, is needed in the solution of problems.
        2. In the operation of student government, everyone should observe the spirit of fair play.
        3. The welfare of the school should always be placed before selfish individual interests.

ARRANGING THE NOTE CARDS TO FIT THE OUTLINE

When you have completed the outline, mark each note card to show to what section and subsection of the outline it corresponds. The upper right-hand corner is a good place for this symbol.

Now arrange the note cards in the order indicated by the outline; each note will then automatically appear in its proper place when you need it for the writing of the paper. Numbering the cards will help to keep them in order.

Next, compare the outline with the note cards. The main headings of the outline will correspond to the chapters or sections of your paper, the subheadings with the subsections. Do you have too much material for some chapters or sections and not enough material for others, so that the paper is in danger of being poorly proportioned? If so, you should discard some notes from the former or look up additional references and add new notes to the latter. When you have just the right amount of material to cover each point adequately, you are ready to begin the writing of the paper.

Step 4. Reporting the Facts

THE FIRST DRAFT

For the first draft of your paper, write rapidly and freely, using your outline for a guide and your note cards for content. Concentrate on the ideas rather than on grammar, punctuation, and other matters of mechanics; these things can be attended to later. The important point at this stage is to get your thoughts down on paper in logical order. You will find that you need to write short connecting passages, or transitions, to link the material covered in various notes. (See page 220.) The notes, too (except for direct quotations), will be rephrased to suit your individual style.

QUOTATIONS AND PARAPHRASES

When you quote the precise words of another writer (direct quotation), all the words quoted should be placed in quotation marks, just as was done on your note cards. There is an exception to this rule in cases of quotations that are four lines or more in length. For such quotations, no quotation marks are used; instead, the quoted matter is indented a few spaces from each side margin and (in typing) is single spaced.

A paraphrase, since it is your own language and not the words of another, is not indented or set off by quotation marks.

FOOTNOTES

Since both the quotation and the paraphrase contain material taken from other writers, you must give proper credit to the authors. Employ footnotes for this purpose. The procedure is the same for quotations and for paraphrases. At the end of the quoted or paraphrased matter, place just above the line a small numeral, called a *superscript*. Footnotes are numbered consecutively in the order of their appearance on a single page, in a single chapter or section, or throughout the paper.

When you know that a certain literary expression has become part of the cultural heritage of the language, acknowledgment by footnotes or quotation marks is not necessary. For example:

All's well that ends well.
A land flowing with milk and honey.

However, if you have any doubts, always give credit to the source.

FORM OF FOOTNOTES

The form of a footnote depends on whether or not it is the first reference in your paper to a particular source. The first footnote referring to a *book* gives the author, title, place of publication, publisher, date of publication, and page reference, thus:[*]

[1] Ray Faulkner, Edwin Ziegfeld, and Gerald Hill, *Art Today* (New York: H. Holt and Co., 1941), pp. 87–95.
[2] "Drama," *Encyclopaedia Britannica* (1945 ed.), VII, 597.

The first footnote referring to a *magazine article* gives the author, the title of the article, the name of the periodical, the volume number, the year, and the page reference, thus:

[2] V. W. Peterson, "Citizen Failure Means Corrupt Government," *Ladies Home Journal*, LXX (June, 1953), 53.

The abbreviations *p.* for *page* or *pp.* for *pages* are not used following a Roman numeral which indicates the volume number of a magazine.

After the first reference to a source, subsequent references are indicated by the abbreviations *ibid.* and *op. cit.* Both should be underscored because they are from the Latin.

Ibid. means "in the same place." When a footnote refers to the same work as the previous footnote, *ibid.*, followed by the page reference, is used instead of repeating the full citation. Example:

[1] Grove Samuel Dow, *Society and Its Problems* (New York: Thomas Y. Crowell Co., 1922), p. 127.
[2] *Ibid.*, p. 305f.

---

[*] Different publishers follow different practices with regard to footnotes and bibliographies. The important thing to remember is that the form must be consistent throughout the paper.

When a footnote refers to the same work and the same page as the previous footnote, *ibid.* alone is used. Example:

> [3] Alta Gwinn Saunders, *Effective Business English* (New York: The Macmillan Co., 1933), p. 150.
> [4] *Ibid.*

Here both footnotes refer to page 150 of Saunders's book.

Op. cit. means "in the work cited." When a footnote refers to a work mentioned in a previous footnote, but not in the footnote immediately preceding, the author's surname, followed by *op. cit.,* and the new page number are used instead of a full citation. Example:

> [5] Lou Eastward Anderson, *Basketball for Women* (New York: The Macmillan Co., 1929), p. 24.
> [6] James Garfield Bliss, *Basketball* (Philadelphia: Lea and Febiger, 1929), p. 50.
> [7] Anderson, *op. cit.,* p. 110ff.

Other abbreviations often used in footnotes are these:

Art.—Article	*f.*—and the page following
Chap.—Chapter	*ff*—and the pages following
Chaps.—Chapters	*l.*—line
Vol.—Volume	*ll.*—lines
Vols.—Volumes	*p.*—page
ed.—edition	*pp.*—pages

Here are examples of quotations and a paraphrase, with their superscripts and corresponding footnotes:

A Short Quotation

Of the words "meagre," "barefoot," "wan," de Selincourt says: "A favorite collation of epithets producing a cadence which was suggested by Atherton."[13]

> [13] Ernest de Selincourt, ed., *The Poems of John Keats* (New York: Dodd, Mead & Co., 1921), p. 24.

A Long Quotation

> There was little vernacular writing before Greece won its independence from the Turks in 1823. Thereafter classical models had a strong influence on the form adopted. As a written language, modern Greek is therefore a product, and a highly artificial product, of the last century.[2]

> [2] Frederick Bodmer, *The Loom of Language* (New York: W. W. Norton and Co., 1944), p. 249.

A Paraphrase

Troilus is introduced to the reader as a young man who scorns love and has mocked lovers in general, saying that they worshipped Saint Idiot. However, as he walks with his friends through the festival, he sees Criseyde; he begins to notice her carefully. His heart begins to swell; he sighs softly lest his men should hear him.[11]

> [11] J.S.P. Tatlock and P. Mackaye, *The Complete Poetical Works of Geoffrey Chaucer* (New York: The Macmillan Co., 1932), pp. 381–85.

REVISING THE FIRST DRAFT

The first draft, once you have it down on paper, should be thoroughly revised. Since the purpose of a good research paper is to convey information rather than to entertain or convince, the most important quality to work for is *clearness*. Precise choice of words, logically constructed sentences, and well-proportioned paragraphs are necessary for a clear research paper. The style should be dignified but not bookish. Of course, you should keep in mind what you have learned about unity, coherence, and emphasis, as well as about the principles of grammar and punctuation.

THE BIBLIOGRAPHY

After the last page of your paper proper, and on a separate page or pages, place the bibliography. The bibliography consists of all the books and articles that you read and made use of in the writing of the paper. Besides the books noted in the footnotes, you will list those books from which you gleaned a general background for your topic.

To make the bibliography, separate your bibliography cards into two piles—those referring to books and those referring to periodicals. Arrange each pile alphabetically according to the author's name. (If a reference lacks the author's name, classify it alphabetically according to the title.)

Then make two alphabetical lists, one of books and the other of periodicals, copying the information that is written on the cards. If you have noted on the cards any comments about the books or articles, omit these comments in the bibliography.

The following is an example of a bibliography.

Bibliography
Books

Barzun, Jacques. *Teacher in America*. Boston: Little, Brown & Company, 1945.
Dewey, John. *Democracy and Education*. New York: Macmillan Co., 1924.
"Drama," *Encyclopaedia Britannica* (1945 ed.), VII, 597.
Fine, Benjamin. *Democratic Education. A Report on the Colleges*. New York: Crowell Publishing Company, 1945.
Havighurst, Robert J. *Human Development and Education*. New York: Longmans, Green & Co., 1953.
Meland, Bernard E. *Higher Education and the Human Spirit*. Chicago: University of Chicago Press, 1953.

Periodicals

Bagley, W. C. "A Demand for Higher Education Is Increasingly Impressive," *School and Society,* LXII (April 20, 1946), 277–78.

Berdie, Ralph F. "Why Don't They Go to College?" *Personnel and Guidance Journal,* XXXI (March, 1953), 352–56.

Kimpton, Lawrence A. "The Junior College in American Education," *Junior College Journal,* XXIII (February, 1953), 303–5.

Seyfert, Warren C. "Do You Recommend This Student for College?" *School Review,* LX (March, 1952), 129–33.

────── "Time to Take a Stand," *School Review,* LXI (March, 1953), 129–34.

[NOTE: The dotted line at the beginning of the last reference means that this article is written by the same author as the preceding article, Warren C. Seyfert.]

MAKING THE FINAL DRAFT

Now your paper is ready to be copied and handed in. Be guided by the following points as you prepare this final draft.

GUIDES FOR PREPARING THE FINAL DRAFT

1. Type your paper if possible, or write neatly in ink, using paper of good quality.
2. Write on one side of the page only.
3. In the center of the first line of the first page, write the title of the paper.
4. Skip a line between the title and the first line.
5. If you are typing the paper, use double spacing, except for quotations four lines or more in length, footnotes, and the bibliography, all of which are single spaced.
6. Leave a good margin at each side, and leave plenty of room at the bottom for your footnotes.
7. Number all the pages consecutively in the center, six spaces down from the top of the page.
8. Begin each chapter or section on a new page, placing the title three spaces below the page number.

SUPPLEMENTARY PAGES

THE TITLE PAGE

Prepare a separate page, called the *title page,* to be placed first. The title page will carry the title of your paper, written a little above the center of the page. Below the title will appear your name, and below that, the name of the course for which you are writing the paper. The date may be added if your instructor so directs.

THE TABLE OF CONTENTS

Prepare a *table of contents* to follow the title page. Show in the table of contents the title and page reference of each chapter or section, of the bibliography, and of the outline if it is to be included.

THE FINAL CHECK

When you have finished copying the paper, read it carefully to guard against errors of pen or typewriter; then clip or staple the pages together (be sure that they are in the right order), or fasten them into a folder with your name clearly inscribed on the outside. Your research paper is now finished and ready to be handed to your instructor.

ORIGINALITY IN RESEARCH PAPERS

The type of research paper described in this chapter makes use of information found in written and printed sources or secured directly by word of mouth. The originality of the paper will depend upon the skill with which the writer assembles, organizes, interprets, and presents his information. There is room for humor, climax, original figures of speech or turns of phrase; but the essential content is derived, or "secondary."

Other kinds of research papers may be the result of original research, of one's own experimentation, exploration, or theorizing. Such papers usually include also materials derived from other sources. Before attempting to write an original research paper, however, a person should ordinarily have had experience in writing the kind of paper described in this chapter.

With experience in writing, one can gradually dispense with some of the formal steps prescribed in the preceding pages. For beginners, it is best to follow them carefully.

Speaking Effectively

CHAPTER 11

1. Speech—A Learned Activity

As you think back over the speaking that you have done during the past week, it probably will not take you long to recall many times when you wish that you had been more effective—in class recitation when you "knew it but just couldn't say it," in applying for a job, in trying to turn your father to your opinion in an argument at home. You are constantly being made aware that your speech does not do for you what you wish it would.

Speech is a learned activity; you were not born knowing how to speak. All that you now know about speaking you have learned by conscious imitation or by subconscious assimilation. As a result you have a set of speech habits which probably are not the best ones that you could have. As you read this chapter, constantly check your speech patterns with the standards that are suggested. Where old habits appear either bad or unnecessary, begin to change those habits. Work for the best speech of which you are capable. Obviously you will not be able to make many permanent changes in your speech if you work only while studying this chapter. You will need to use the material presented here in your other classes, in your life outside school, and as a springboard into a lifelong program of speech improvement.

FOR YOU TO TALK ABOUT

A. What relationship do you see between speech and personality?

B. How would you go about breaking a bad habit and creating a better one? Explain how you would apply these suggestions to speech habits.

C. At the present time, what would you consider your greatest assets in speaking? How can you capitalize on these assets? What others would you like to develop?

D. As you listen to others, what are the commonest speech faults that you hear? Are you also guilty of them? Agree in class on two or three of the commoner faults. Suggest ways to help one another to overcome them.

2. Speech as a Means of Communication

Gracious speech is never out of place, just as a clean face, neatly combed hair, and trim nails are never out of place. Inevitably, by your way of speaking, you add to, or detract from, the impression that you make.

Speech is a part of getting along with people; it helps others to know you, and it helps you to know others. You will become a more alert audience as you become a better speaker. You will be better able to distinguish between the person who has a message and the person who merely wishes to perform.

Consider speech as a means of communication with others. Everything that you can see in someone's actions, everything that you can hear in his voice may be a sign or signal of his meaning and may thus be considered a form of speech. More than formal speech situations—debating, platform speaking, taking part in stage plays, radio and TV work—speech includes all forms of speech activities: conversation, interviewing, storytelling, formal and informal discussions.

To carry on this communication, you are provided with the necessary tools—body and voice.

THE BODY AS A TOOL OF COMMUNICATION

At first glance, it may appear that the body plays a small part in communication; but stop to think a bit. Have you ever remarked to a friend, before he had told you how he felt, that he looked glum, happy, bored, or sick? Without uttering a word, he had communicated to you; his body had told the story. In fact, whether or not you want it to, your body is constantly "talking." Take a look around the class right now; notice how much each member is telling you about himself even though he is not uttering a word.

Since the body does thus constantly communicate, your problem becomes clear: how to make it speak for you most effectively.

SYNCHRONIZING BODY AND VOICE

The first thing to remember as you begin to improve your habits of bodily communication is that both body and voice must convey the same idea. Never confuse your listeners by communicating one idea with your actions while communicating another with your words. The speaker who urges you with a strong voice but with a limp, lifeless body to "get in there and fight" is not very convincing. If a speaker tells you that there are five reasons for doing a thing and holds up three fingers to emphasize his point, you will not know which to believe, his action or his words. In every situation, you must learn to think first of what you are saying and then of what you are doing, and to make both body and voice communicate the total idea to your hearers.

AMOUNT OF BODILY RESPONSE

A second way in which the body can be made more effective as a communicator is in the use of proper amounts of bodily response. The amount of bodily activity that you should use depends upon four things: (1) you, (2) your audience, (3) your topic, and (4) the speaking occasion.

1. *You.* Not everyone is given to showing his feelings outwardly; some persons tend to cover them up. Others reflect in their actions how they feel in every situation. If you are the reserved type, you probably can increase your skill in communication by using more clear-cut movements. If, on the other hand, you are the overly active type, using fewer but stronger movements will probably make you more successful in centering attention on what you have to say.

2. *The Audience.* The amount of bodily response should be adapted to the size of the audience. If it is a small group, you will probably tend to use smaller and more frequent gestures. With a large audience, fewer and broader movements will help listeners to interpret your meaning.

3. *The Subject.* The amount of bodily movement also should be influenced by the subject. If you are describing a football game or a fire, your movements will almost automatically be different from those that you would use in reading a lyric poem.

4. *The Occasion.* The amount of movement that you use likewise should depend upon the occasion. Obviously you would feel free to use many large movements and gestures in addressing the student body at a pep rally than you would if you were making a committee report in a club meeting.

KINDS OF BODILY RESPONSE

The bodily activity that you use in speaking falls into three classes:

1. *Posture,* or bodily carriage, is important in all speaking situations, formal and informal. Good posture enables the vocal machine to function easily; it is the sign of an aware, vital, alive individual. One of the simplest and most effective ways for getting and maintaining good posture is to keep the ribs away from the hips. Try it. See how it straightens the whole body. Since it has as much health value as speech value, make a habit of this posture, not only when you speak but also when you are merely sitting, walking, or standing.

2. *Movement,* or change of bodily position, must, like posture, be developed. In informal situations, movement comes easily. In a more formal situation, however, when many pairs of eyes are focused upon you, moving in a natural manner may become a problem.

As you approach the place from which you are to speak, be alive, use your regular walking speed, and give the impression that you are eager to make the speech. While you are speaking, stand with the feet slightly apart and with one foot slightly ahead of the other. Move from one position to another purposefully, taking full steps. Avoid aimless shifting or swaying.

Bodily movement follows a thought or an idea; it precedes the speaking of that thought or idea. When you come to the end of an idea, you may take a step or two to another comfortable position. In this way your movements indicate a change of idea and at the same time help to release the nervous tension which may build up in you as you speak. This is a good plan to remember: first the thought, then the action, then the word.

3. *Gestures* are expressive movements of the hands, arms, head, and face. The face is by far the most communicative. Use it. Let it respond to your thought and feelings so that the audience can more easily interpret your meaning. Let your expression be alive. Establish eye contact with your listeners, glancing around the group as you speak. Your purpose should be to make each person feel that you are addressing him, that you want particularly to have him grasp your message. And never overlook the value of a smile.

Another way to get your audience with you is to arouse *empathy,* or imaginative bodily response. A dynamic speaker can make his listeners strain their muscles to help him lift a weight, lean against a strong gale with him, or wince with pain at the thought of his suffering. Theater and television audiences nearly always show an empathic response.

Use your head, hands, or arms whenever you think that a gesture will help to put over your point. Do not plan your gestures in advance; let them come spontaneously. Little nervous gestures or mannerisms get in the way of meaningful communication, and you will have to fight to eliminate them. Do not let your hands make vague movements, or you may find that your audience is fascinated by them and is missing your message. Keep your body under control until a movement would stress a point; then use a voluntary gesture.

FOR PRACTICE AND APPLICATION

A. Imagine that you are in a foreign country and cannot speak the language. Using only gestures and bodily movement, ask one of the citizens for some information.

B. Give a pantomime showing some strong emotion. Let the class guess what the feeling is.

C. Have your teacher and classmates analyze your movements during a formal speech. From their analysis, make a plan to eliminate your bad habits and to strengthen your good ones.

D. During your next speech assignment, establish eye contact with four different people and say at least two sentences to each of them. Choose persons in different locations so that you will have to move your glance around the classroom.

E. If possible, watch a group of television viewers during an exciting telecast. Report to the class on their empathic response and tell what they responded to.

FOLLOW-UP

During the next few days, take an inventory of your effectiveness in bodily communication. Are your posture, bodily movements, and gestures synchronized with the idea that you are expressing? How do they fit your personality, the audience, and the occasion?

THE VOICE AS A TOOL OF COMMUNICATION

The second tool of communication, the voice, is formed by a stream of air that issues as a tiny sound from the larynx and is enlarged and modified by the lips, the tongue, the teeth, and the resonance chambers. (See diagram, page 288.)

CONTROLLING THE BREATH

Your first concern with the utterance of vocal sounds is to make sure that you breathe correctly. Take these simple steps to correct breathing.

1. Inhale deeply, filling the lungs. Do not move the shoulders.
2. Exhale smoothly, letting your breath ride out through an open, relaxed throat. Relax your throat by feeling a yawn.
3. Control your breathing at the diaphragm.

FOR PRACTICE AND APPLICATION

A. At home lie flat on your back to discover the natural breathing pattern. Relax, and put a hand or a small book on your middle; you will find that you expand when you are inflated with air and contract when you are deflated.

B. While you are standing in an erect yet comfortable position, locate the middle section by panting (deep breathing in and out through the mouth) or by becoming aware of the spontaneous bodily action in hiccoughing or laughing. Put your hands flat on your torso above the waist. While you may notice most of the motion in the front, expansion and contraction are taking place all around, just above the belt line.

C. Practice for steadiness and adequacy of air. Do not keep going until you are entirely out of breath. Purse your lips as for a *wh* sound; draw a controlled breath, and use the abdominal muscles to blow a steady stream of air on the back of your hand. (Do this and all succeeding exercises while standing.)

D. Work for smoothness and for rhythm. Inhale. Exhale by saying the following until all breath is used up. Do not strain.

    1–2–3; 1–2–3; 1–2–3 . . .
    1–2–3–4–5; 1–2–3–4–5; 1–2–3–4–5 . . .
    Monday Tuesday Wednesday; Thursday Friday Saturday . . .

E. *Ascending force.* In the usual pattern of stress, the climax comes at the end, frequently in the last word. Just so, after expanding with an ample breath, count as follows: "1–2–3–4–5" giving increased force to each succeeding number. Repeat: "1–2–3–4–5"; "1–2–3–4–5"; "1–2–3–4–5." Force is attained by controlling the breath, not by yelling.

F. Work for volume. For these commands, you will use the entire breath in one sharp, sustained volley. Make the air come from the stomach. Your abdominal muscles should contract suddenly and firmly.

    Ho! Out! Halt! Stop! Go!
    Ho! March! [Pronounced "har (ch)" in the army]

VOICE AND MEANING

In Chapter Seven you learned the difference between the denotative and the connotative meanings of words. It is a simple process to communicate denotative (dictionary) meanings when your hearers understand the words that you are using, but it becomes an art to be able always to express the particular connotation (emotional implication) in your mind so that it is clear to the listener. If you say, "I'm going home," and want your listeners to know nothing but that fact, you need not worry about vocal expression—a dull, monotonous voice will convey the meaning. But if you wish to show your pleasure and excitement at going home or the love that you have for your home, you will need to do something vocally to indicate that feeling.

FOR PRACTICE AND APPLICATION

Try this experiment. Say the name "Fred" to indicate the following:
1. I'm so happy to see you again.
2. What a beautiful orchid! Thanks a million.
3. Keep out of the cookie jar, young man!
4. Stop! There's a car coming!
5. You want me to have a date with *him?*

Notice as you do this exercise that it is only as you change your tone of voice that you can convey the ideas suggested.

VOCAL FACTORS

The human voice has four factors: *quality, pitch, loudness,* and *rate.*

1. QUALITY

Quality is that indefinable something which makes one voice different from another so that you can recognize a person merely by hearing him speak. Since it remains relatively constant in most speaking situations, quality will not be discussed here. The other factors are combined in many ways to indicate connotation in the words that you choose.

2. PITCH

Pitch refers to the height of the tone on the musical scale. Each person has a pitch which, because of the construction of his vocal mechanism, is the best one for him to use for most of his speaking. Many other pitches both above and below it can be used to stress a word or to give it special connotative value.

Changes from habitual pitch can be made either within the word or between words. Say the word "hello." Notice how the voice slides from one pitch to another. Now say the words "Step down!" as you have heard them in courtroom scenes in films. Notice that the first word is on one pitch and the second is on a lower pitch, the change coming between the words. *Inflection*—that is, a variety of these vocal slides and vocal steps—makes a voice interesting to listen to. It is wise to check your own voice to make sure that it is not marked by monotony (lack of variety).

3. LOUDNESS

Loudness refers to the intensity of the auditory sensation as it is received by each individual listener. Too often persons try to judge the loudness of their own voices by trying to listen to themselves. It is better to check with a listener, asking him to judge whether or not the loudness is adequate. If your friends, parents, and teachers constantly ask you to repeat what you have said, you probably need to make a conscious effort to increase your loudness level. Adjusting the size of the tone to a certain room is called *projection,* which means literally a "throwing forward" of your voice.

It is not necessary to raise the pitch of your voice to secure more volume. Although it is true that tone is really formed in the larynx, it is the breath stream that provides the power of voice. Thus it will help you to think of the throat as a passive agent, concentrating your efforts at voice projection upon control of the breath stream.

Learn to speak without effort, and you will speak in a deeper, more pleasant tone. A yawn is valuable to teach your muscles how an open throat should feel.

4. RATE

Rate refers to the number of words spoken per minute. A good general rate of speaking is somewhere between 150–180 words per minute. *People rarely speak too slowly.* If you will read aloud a passage of factual prose in what is close to the speed with which you generally speak, you can get some idea of your typical reading rate.

Normal reading rate can be varied in two ways: (1) by changing the length of time that it takes to utter a word or (2) by changing the length of the pauses between words. The first method is often used to suggest emotional attitudes. Say "I hate you" at your normal rate, and then say it holding on to the vowel sounds in each word. Note the change in meaning. This lengthening of vowel sounds offers no exact measurement of the *degree* of hatred, but it does present a cue by which listeners can make some judgment of the feelings of the speaker. The second method of rate change —pausing between words—is used chiefly for clarity or for emphasis. Slowing down when ideas are hard to follow makes it easier for the audience to keep up with the meaning. A pause before a word makes it stand out by itself; in fact, this pause, this sudden cessation of sound, is often more emphatic than increased volume. For example, "I looked into the darkened room and saw—nothing."

Remember that separating words from each other is done for a specific effect. In general, you should read in word groups or thought phrases. You are trying to convey ideas, not words. In practicing a selection to be read aloud, it is sometimes helpful to mark the thought phrases; punctuation will often indicate places for pausing, but not always.

FOR PRACTICE AND APPLICATION

A. Stand in any easy yet erect position. Breathe with a measured rhythm, in through the nose, out through the mouth. Keep the same rhythm, and with the throat passively open, sing "hah" on each exhalation five times.

B. Do as above, but say in a relaxed, dreamy manner: "How are you?" "Higher, higher, higher!" "Hip, hip, hooray!"

C. Say "aha" like the villain foreclosing the heroine's mortgage. Then relax your throat, yawn, and say "aha" in this open-throat manner. Note the contrast in the feel of the muscles.

D. For each phrase (thought-unit), whether one line or less in length, use a separate breath, and mark these inhalations with a vertical line. Then start a yawn; but instead of finishing the yawn, use that open feeling to carry you more musically through the unit.

>Through the hushed air| the whitening shower descends,|
>At first thin-wavering,| till at last the flakes
>Fall broad,| and wide,| and fast,| dimming the day
>With a continual flow.|
>
>—Thomson

Do the following in like manner.

1. The sun is warm, the sky is clear,
   The waves are dancing fast and bright,
   Blue isles and snowy mountains wear
   The purple moon's transparent might.
   —Shelley

2. The time I've lost in wooing,
   In watching and pursuing
   The light that lies
   In woman's eyes
   Has been my heart's undoing.
   —Moore

3. Crime can only be truly hindered by letting no man grow up a criminal—by taking away the *will* to commit sin; not by mere punishment of its commission. Crime, small and great, can only be truly stayed by education—not the education of the intellect only, which is, on some men, wasted, and for others mischievous; but education of the heart, which is alike good and necessary for all.
   —Ruskin

VOICE IMPROVEMENT

On the preceding pages you have had an opportunity to learn what constitutes good breathing and what the vocal factors are that contribute to effective speech. It is now time to take stock of your own speech habits.

1. AN ANALYSIS OF VOICE

Analyze your voice. It is extremely difficult to hear yourself accurately. True, the same sound waves reach your ears as reach the ears of others. But what you hear when you listen to yourself is colored by the thought that your brain knows what you meant to say and by the reverberations of sound within your head. Besides, you are prejudiced: you like yourself and wish to think well of yourself; you even deceive yourself by occasional white lies. Today, however, is the time for honest listening. Resolve to make an effort to hear yourself as others hear you. Resolve also to believe what teachers and friends who have keen ears tell you about your speaking voice.

A sensitive recording instrument will be of immeasurable help to you. The chances are that you will not like what you hear, for the "average" of American speech is not so high as the "average" of American health and looks. If you speak no better than that, you do not speak well at all. Listen to the voices of such as these: students in the cafeteria, passengers on the bus, housewives in the grocery, couples in the theater lobby. Only recently have beauty contests begun to include on the rating scale charm and personality (both of which are reflected in the voice). Voices are one reason that so many otherwise attractive girls are working as waitresses instead of actresses in Hollywood. If, when you do not like what the recorder tells you, you decide to do something about the raucous tones or the indistinct words, you have taken a truly important step.

2. THE VOCAL MACHINE

Become acquainted with the vocal mechanism. Air from the lungs travels upward through the trachea and comes through the larynx (a small box at the top), vibrating the two folds of muscle that cover it. This vibration if properly controlled will become a sound. It is enlarged by the resonance chambers of the head: mouth, pharynx, and nasal and head cavities. It is then acted upon by tongue, teeth, and lips, emerging as words.

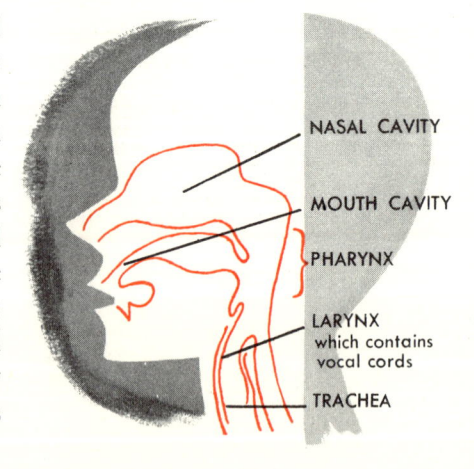

- NASAL CAVITY
- MOUTH CAVITY
- PHARYNX
- LARYNX which contains vocal cords
- TRACHEA

3. VOICE POTENTIAL

Recognize the possibilities that your voice has. Experiment with your voice and learn the great variety of which it is capable. Do not be satisfied until you can do more with it than you could last year or last week.

4. DESIRE TO COMMUNICATE

Have a strong desire to communicate your ideas to others. When you are really eager to speak, your voice responds automatically with greater aliveness and variety. No amount of analysis, awareness, and drill will be of value unless this desire to communicate is firmly fixed in your thinking. A real interest in what you are saying, coupled with an intense desire to share your ideas with others, will be the greatest single steppingstone to an improved voice.

5. PRONUNCIATION

Closely allied to the problems of voice production is that of *pronunciation*. Correct pronunciation involves five different elements, each of which you should check to make sure that you are saying words correctly.

1. Form the individual sounds correctly; say "this, that, these, those"; not "dis, dat, dese, dose."
2. Utter the sounds in the proper order; say "**pers**piration," not "**pres**piration."
3. Include all necessary sounds; say "li-**bra**-ry," not "li-**ba**-ry."
4. Omit unnecessary sounds; say "film," not "fil**lum**."
5. Accent the proper syllable; say "en-**tire**'," not "**en**'tire."

FOR PRACTICE AND APPLICATION

A. Tell the class a story in which three different characters speak. Differentiate the characters by vocal changes. List the different types of characters depicted by the class.

B. Listen to the voices of several good radio or TV performers. Compare these voices with those that you hear in the hall between classes. What are the most obvious differences between announcers and students? What specific suggestions could you make to the students for improving their voices?

C. After your next school play, discuss in class how each member of the cast used the four factors of voice in creating the character that he portrayed. Which voice was pleasantest to listen to? Why?

D. After an assembly program at which some stranger has spoken, discuss these points about the speaker: How would you describe the basic quality of his voice? What changes in rate, pitch, or volume did he use for variety?

E. If possible, make a tape recording of your own voice. Read a selection that you have prepared carefully beforehand. How much vocal variety do you have? How long would you enjoy listening to your voice on the radio?

F. Write a radio commercial and read it from a spot where the listeners cannot see you. Let the class comment on your performance.

G. Read to the class a short, carefully prepared poem. Choose one that has a very obvious mood (joy, grief, hope, despair, longing, ...). Try to express that mood vocally. After you have finished reading, ask the class to identify the mood.

H. Here is a list of words often mispronounced. Check with the dictionary to learn the proper pronunciation of each word. When two pronunciations are given, give both, in order; underline your preference.

abdomen	bureaucracy	finance	literature
accessories	college	forehead	margarine
acclimate	consul	garage	partner
address (*n. & v.*)	contrast (*n. & v.*)	gauge	precedence
advertisement	council	genuine	precedent (*n.*)
adult	coupé	handkerchief	research
airplane	coupon	hero	romance
alias	data	heroine	Roosevelt
amateur	decadence	hiccough	route
appreciation	desert (*n. & v.*)	illustrate	similar
arctic	dessert	inquiry	solder
athletic	diphthong	irrevocable	suggestion
automobile	economics	isolate	suit
bade	err	Italian	suite
bouquet	escape	larynx	theater
buoy	etiquette	learned (*adj.*)	tune

I. You have words in your reading (understanding) vocabulary that you do not have in your speaking (pronouncing and using) vocabulary. What words have you found recently that you did not "bother" to look up? Collect ten of these words and give them the same treatment as in *H*.

FOLLOW-UP

Keep on the board a weekly list of words that have been mispronounced by members of the class. Use the list for end-of-the-hour pronunciation drill.

3. Informal Speaking Activities

Conversation, telephoning, and interviewing are informal speaking activities that all of you have been carrying on throughout your lives, with varying degrees of success. A brief review of each should suffice to let you check those areas in which you still need to develop skill.

HOW TO BE A GOOD CONVERSATIONALIST

1. Read, listen, and observe so that you can have something to say that will be worth listening to.
2. Say clearly and economically what you have to say. Do not use words that have indefinite meanings or that are likely to mean something different to your listener from what they mean to you. Do not over-explain or overdescribe.
3. Be considerate in your choice of topics. Choose those that will be of most interest to the persons with whom you are conversing.
4. Learn to sense when a topic is boring or distasteful. The effective conversationalist knows how to discard a subject as well as how to initiate one.
5. Do not monopolize the conversation, even when the topic is one on which you may be an authority. Roughly divide the time by the number of people in the group, and you will not infringe upon the rights of others.
6. Listen with full attention to those with whom you converse. The ability to learn from listening will greatly increase your knowledge. Show your interest by responding to the other fellow's ideas. Remember, if you are interested in people, they will be interested in you.
7. Do not overuse bodily activity in conversation. Talk with your voice and your eyes rather than with your hands.
8. Control your voice. Do not go on a "national hookup" in public places. Adjust your voice to the size of the room and of the group.
9. Look at your listeners. Include in your glance all persons in the group so that each of them will feel that he "belongs."

WHAT TO REMEMBER IN TELEPHONING

1. Keep social conversations to a minimum both in time and in number, especially when you are on a party line.
2. Listen attentively, during social as well as business calls.
3. Speak distinctly. You must enunciate even more clearly than in a face-to-face situation, since your listener cannot aid his understanding by reading your lips.
4. In business calls, give and get all necessary information, briefly but courteously.
5. If you make a call, be the one to terminate the conversation. Do so politely but firmly, as soon as the purpose of the call has been achieved.

HOW TO CONDUCT AN INTERVIEW

1. As much as you can, plan your questions in advance. These will form a skeleton for the interview and will lead you into other questions as the talk develops. Be ready with your questions. Do not expect the guest to conduct the interview.
2. When you arrive, introduce yourself, remind the person being interviewed of your reason for being there, and ask a general question or two before getting down to the main part of the interview.
3. Listen carefully to the answers to your questions. Take notes of those that you wish to repeat. In such cases, ask, "May I quote you?"
4. Be conscious of the passing of time. If the person being interviewed answers your questions quickly and without elaboration, keep the interview moving rapidly. If he appears eager to talk, make use of this opportunity within reason.
5. Throughout the interview, be polite, interested, and friendly.
6. Terminate the conversation by thanking the person for the time and information that he has given you.

HOW TO MAKE A GOOD IMPRESSION IN A JOB INTERVIEW

1. Be neat in dress and appearance. Polished shoes, clean fingernails, and well-combed hair are often decisive factors.
2. Be punctual. Introduce yourself and remind the interviewer of your reason for being there.
3. Have information at hand so that you can answer questions quickly and accurately. Bring with you a list of all qualifications that you think fit you for the job. Before you go to the interview, think through the questions that might possibly be asked, and have your answers ready.
4. Listen carefully to all that is said. Some fact—for example, that you must begin work at a very early hour—may make you decide that you do not want the job even though it is offered to you.
5. Throughout the interview be courteous, pleasant, and attentive. Do not be afraid to ask questions if they will help you to understand what the employer wants.
6. If you are asked to fill out an application blank, take time to think out your answers; then write them neatly and accurately.
7. Let the interviewer terminate the meeting. When he does, thank him for his time and consideration; then leave at once.

WHAT TO REMEMBER IN APPEARING ON RADIO OR TELEVISION

1. Speak slowly and distinctly.
2. In appearing on radio, speak directly into the microphone. Keep the location that the director sets for you. Do not touch the microphone and do not rattle your manuscript. Both such actions send violent sounds over the air.
3. Know your material well enough so that you can speak in phrases with correct interpretation.
4. Wear dark, inconspicuous clothes when you appear on television.
5. Avoid excessive movements of the hands. Sit or stand quietly.
6. Attend carefully to what the other people on the program are doing. Be as interested as you would be if you were in the audience.
7. If you use a manuscript, keep the pages down so that they will not cover your face and muffle your words.

FOR PRACTICE AND APPLICATION

A. Carry out one or more of these activities in conversation.

1. Listen to the conversations that you hear in the halls, in the cafeteria, on the bus, and in other public places. Write and read to the class a short essay in which you make specific suggestions for improving a few of the poor speech habits that you have heard.
2. Tell the class about a really "good" conversation in which you have participated. What made it good?
3. Write and present before the class a skit showing the *do*'s and *don't*'s of conversation.
4. Have three or four members of the class study an up-to-date etiquette book and review for the class the rules of social introductions. Let some members of the class illustrate the correct procedures both for the actual introductions and for conversing after the introductions.

B. Find out what rules and services your telephone company has. Discuss them in class. Often a telephone company issues booklets which describe good telephone manners. Appoint someone to call the telephone company and request a copy for each member of the class. If you get the booklets, be sure to write a note of thanks. After you have discussed them in class, take the booklets home for future reference.

C. Do one or more of the following activities in interviewing.

1. Plan an interview with a local businessman. Report to the class on your planning and on the interview itself. How successful was it? How did the planning help?

2. Present a series of skits before the class showing good interviewing techniques. Work in pairs so that everyone in the class will have a chance either to interview or be interviewed. Discuss in class the ones which you thought were the best interviews and tell why.
3. Let pupils who have been interviewed for jobs tell of their experiences.

D. Carry out an imaginary radio or television program. Perhaps some of the interviews prepared in the second activity under *C* might be presented in this manner. A fake mike—or a real one—is helpful.

4. Discussion

The word *discussion* has several connotations. Usually it means any conversation in which there is an exchange of opinions. Technically, however, it has a much narrower, more specific meaning.

DISCUSSION DEFINED

Discussion as it is treated here is that form of speaking in which the speakers attempt, through co-operative exchange of ideas, to solve a problem or move toward its solution by a better understanding of it. Although they have some of the characteristics of conversation, discussions tend to be more definitely planned, more formal, and more carefully directed.

Discussion begins with a *question* rather than with a statement. At the time that the discussion opens, the answer to the question is not known, but during the discussion the discussants pool their information, air their views, and suggest possible answers.

In some cases, though not always, they arrive at a conclusion or reach a solution to the problem. Discussion is used both as a learning device and as a policy-making device. For example, in one of your social science classes, you might discuss the question, "Is democracy the best form of government?" Your purpose would be to uncover the facts in the case that would enable you to conclude the discussion with a "yes" or a "no" or an "under-some-conditions" answer. Or again, at one of its meetings, the student council might consider the question, "Should our high school have more dances?" In this discussion the purpose would be to establish a policy rather than merely to uncover facts.

Note the difference in the verbs used in stating these two questions. The discussion of facts centers around the verb "is"; the discussion of policy, around the verb "should."

THE DISCUSSION OUTLINE

Getting a group of people together and letting them "sound off" does not make a discussion. Most authorities on discussion techniques feel that a five-step discussion plan or outline is the most helpful one to use.

1. *Definition of terms.* Much time can be saved in formal discussion by having the meaning of all words in the question clearly understood at the outset by all members of the group. Sometimes very limited definitions will have to be imposed; in other cases, broader and more flexible meanings can be adopted.
2. *Analysis of the problem.* After terms have been defined, the problem must be analyzed: What caused it? What is its past history? What contributing factors make it what it is? How important is it? Answers to these and similar questions will aid the group in understanding the problem.
3. *Suggested solutions.* At this point each discussant contributes every solution that he can think of, not with the idea that any one of them is the best, but with the idea of presenting for consideration every possible solution.
4. *Choice of the best solution.* After shifting the *pros* and *cons* of each, the group now decide which solution has the most merit. The solution that they choose may be "best" because it is the most immediately feasible, because it is the most economical, because it benefits the largest group concerned, because it has the best long-range possibilities, or because of any other factor. Few solutions meet all these requirements.
5. *Plan for putting the solution into operation.* If they can do so, the discussion group should plan to put the solution into operation. The type of question will determine whether the plan will involve direct, concerted action or only passive acceptance.

TYPES OF DISCUSSION

Discussion may take several forms. The names given the forms are sometimes interchanged loosely, but in general the distinctions are those given here.

1. Round table:
    a) Has a leader who keeps the discussion moving.
    b) Includes everyone present.
    c) Is useful for committees.
    d) Follows discussion outline (modified to fit).
    e) Has its participants contribute informally.

"IT IS THE DUTY OF THE CHAIRMAN TO KEEP THE DISCUSSION UNDER CONTROL."

2. Panel
   a) Takes place before an audience.
   b) Has a leader.
   c) Follows an outline.
   d) Has four to six members seated at a table in front of the audience.
   e) Begins with prepared short talks on various phases of the question.
   f) Follows with informal discussion on the points raised.

3. Panel-Forum

   Like the panel, but audience may ask questions at the conclusion.

4. Symposium
   a) Like the panel except that the speeches prepared beforehand are longer and more formal.
   b) Presents a suggested solution to be acted upon by panel and audience.

5. Lecture-Forum
   a) Has a single speaker.
   b) Provides for audience participation.

6. Debate
   a) Has opposing teams, usually of two members.
   b) Follows a rigid pattern in the order of speaking.
   c) Has speakers coming to a speaker's stand to deliver their remarks.
   d) Has a chairman who merely states the question and introduces the speakers.
   e) Is a contest of skill, not an attempt to solve a problem.
   f) May have judges who decide which team has been the more convincing.
   g) Should discuss a question of *policy*, not of fact.

LEADING A DISCUSSION

If you are a leader in a discussion group, you must do the following:

1. Introduce the members of the group and state the question.
2. Keep the discussion moving forward. Have the discussion outline in mind and check panel members if they stray from the topic.
3. See that all members participate as equally as possible. Encourage the less communicative. Pleasantly but firmly discourage the person who talks too much.
4. Summarize the main points from time to time so that both participants and audience will know what has been agreed upon and what has been discarded.
5. Have a broad general knowledge of the whole question so that you may act as arbiter in case of an argument. Remember, however, that you are not to take over the job of participating as well as that of leading.
6. Present a final summary, restating the conclusions which have been reached; then close the discussion.

PARTICIPATING IN THE DISCUSSION

If you are a participant in a discussion, be careful to apply the following suggestions:

1. Prepare carefully in advance, even though you are not going to deliver a set speech. Get your points well in mind, decide on definitions, analyze the problem, and consider some possible solutions.
2. Be willing to compromise. Do not stick doggedly to your opinions, but accept others gracefully if they are shown to be better than yours.
3. Let the other members have their fair share of the time.
4. Listen carefully to what is said so that you may respond to it, and so that you will not repeat it unnecessarily at some later point.
5. Learn to recognize worth-while ideas and to reject those that are weak or false. Keep your thoughts properly "sorted" as the discussion progresses.
6. Avoid arguing. Even if you disagree strongly, speak courteously, avoiding such flat statements as "You're absolutely wrong!"
7. Remain open minded until the close of the discussion.
8. If a course of action must be settled upon, be willing to abide by the majority opinion.

FOR PRACTICE AND APPLICATION

A. In a society built upon democratic principles, what is the value of knowing good discussion techniques?

B. Describe situations in which you have been where a knowledge of good discussion techniques would have led to a better solution than was reached.

C. Divide the class into groups of five or six and let each group prepare a discussion suitable for presentation before another class, before a church or civic group, before the P.T.A., ... If possible, give the discussion before the group for whom it was prepared. Let one member of each group (1) report to the class on the success of the presentations and (2) give suggestions for improved discussion techniques.

D. List the types of discussion programs that members of the class listen to regularly on radio or television. Decide on the type of each one reported. Which do you think are most valuable to listeners? Why?

E. To show that you understand the difference between discussion questions of *fact* and those of *policy,* formulate five discussion questions of each type. Keep your list for possible use in the future.

5. MAKING A SPEECH

Through your previous instruction and experiences in speaking and writing, many of the processes used in the preparation of a speech are already familiar to you. Although speaking and writing differ in many ways, the collecting and organizing of ideas is the same.

This section will review for you the elements of preparation for such speeches as a report on a class subject, demonstrations in classes and clubs, reports to the student council, and special reports of all types.

TYPES OF SPEECHES

1. *Impromptu.* Here the speaker is given no time for preparation but is called upon to speak spontaneously.
2. *Extempore.* This type of speech is prepared for with great care and thoroughness, but the actual wording is left to the moment of speaking. It is in its way harder to give than any other, but it is likewise the most effective when done well.

"I JOTTED DOWN A FEW NOTES TO GUIDE ME IN TALKING TO YOU TODAY."

3. *Read from a manuscript*. This type is used principally by speakers with messages that must not be misquoted and with a strict time limit imposed. Good professional speakers are adept at reading from a manuscript in such a way that the speech sounds extemporaneous.
4. *Memorized*. This type is used now principally for contests. It requires great skill to make a memorized speech sound extemporaneous.

Speeches differ as much as the people who make them. There is no basic "recipe." There are, however, basic ingredients.

CHOOSING A SUBJECT

In choosing a subject, be guided by these points:

1. *Consider yourself*. Choose a topic about which you know a great deal or in which you feel a vital interest and a desire to know more.
2. *Consider your audience*. Choose a subject in which your listeners are interested or in which you are sure you can make them take an interest.
3. *Analyze the occasion*. Be sure that your subject is in good taste for the particular time and place. At a pep meeting, for example, you would not make a speech urging students to study hard for exams.

Any subject, then, is a good subject for a speech if the speaker is actively interested in it, if the potential audience is at least passively interested in it, and if it shows no lack of taste or judgment as regards the occasion.

LIMITING THE SUBJECT

After you have chosen a topic, select one phase of it to develop. Anyone can speak on a general topic, but only an authority can deal with a carefully limited subject. Forcing yourself to become an authority on some small phase of a broad area increases your confidence and at the same time enables you to offer new and unusual information to your listeners.

DECIDING ON A PURPOSE

There are three general purposes for speaking:
1. *To inform.* Here you give the *how* or the *what* of a topic, with the aim of getting your listeners to *believe* something.
2. *To persuade.* Here you give the *why,* with the aim of getting your listeners to *do* something.
3. *To entertain.* Here you merely try to give your listeners enjoyment.

Most speeches contain some element of all of these. However, it is wise to choose one of the purposes for your major emphasis.

COLLECTING MATERIAL

You can collect your information from four sources:
1. *Your own knowledge.* Use those points of which you are absolutely sure; check those on which your information is limited.
2. *Other people.* Consult authorities; ask them intelligent questions; make notes of their replies.
3. *Observation and experimentation.* Wherever possible, check your material by actual observation or experimentation.
4. *Reading.* Supplement the preceding sources by reading original source material, reference books, magazines, newspapers, reports, . . . (See pages 252–70 for information on sources and on taking notes.)

ORGANIZING MATERIAL

Organize your material into (1) *general statements* (those that must be explained, described, or proved) and (2) *supporting statements* (those which explain, describe, or prove the general statements). In general, use *many* supporting statements to prove a *few* general statements.

MAKING AN OUTLINE

Arrange the materials for your speech into an outline by making the general statements into the main points and the supporting statements into subheads. (See page 270.)

Your material may be arranged in various kinds of order:

1. Chronological order (according to the time that events happened)
2. Order of importance (from least to most)
3. Space order (from near to far or from far to near; from top to bottom; from outside to inside)
4. Logical order (any order that seems clear and easy to follow)

PLANNING THE INTRODUCTION AND THE CONCLUSION

After organizing the body of your speech by outlining it, you will need to plan carefully for the opening and closing parts. The importance of an interest-catching beginning can hardly be estimated. It has often been said that if the beginning and the ending really impress the audience, what goes between is of no great importance, comparatively speaking. Experienced speakers can sometimes retrieve an audience lost by a poor beginning, but once they have been lost, the average speaker never recovers his listeners. Prepare your opening sentence or sentences with extraordinary care; if you wish, memorize them. The ideas that you express in your closing sentences will, in most cases, be the ones that your listeners will take away. Make them live. Memorizing them will make it easier for you to conclude—sometimes a difficult task for the inexperienced speaker.

REHEARSING

When most of the preparation has been completed, begin to rehearse your speech. Make sure that you know *what* you want to say and *how* you want to say it. During these rehearsals, notice your word choice; if you hit upon an exceptionally good word, remember to use that word when you finally give the speech.

Some speakers find it helpful to practice before a mirror, using gestures in the delivery. However, a great deal of your preparation can be done mentally. Change any parts of the speech that you think can be improved. Above all, have a good time during your preparation; if you do, you probably will enjoy making the speech.

6. Introducing a Speaker

The person who introduces a speaker has it in his power to make the speaker's task either easy or difficult. An introduction is intended to tell the audience a few important facts about the speaker. It should be sincere; it should never be flippant or flowery. The introducer must remember that he is not the main speaker. At the conclusion of his brief remarks, he should say simply, "It is a pleasure to introduce . . ." or something equally simple. He should never say, "I give you . . ." As he concludes, he should turn toward the speaker and, by a nod, a smile, or a gesture, indicate that it is time for the speaker to come forward. The introducer should take a few steps away from the lectern (the speaker's stand) and indicate to the speaker to take his place. Not until the speaker has done so should the introducer return to his seat.

The speaker may acknowledge the introduction briefly and should then greet the audience, addressing them with "Ladies and gentlemen," or some other suitable phrase.

7. Evaluating a Speech

Part of the process of becoming a good speaker should include analysis of the speeches given in class. You must learn to recognize your own good points as well as those of your classmates. It is helpful to have the teacher and the other members of the class discuss with you those things that can be improved.

The following questions provide a good basis for analysis.

1. Was the subject well chosen and properly limited?
2. Did the first sentence of the introduction get the attention of the audience?
3. Was the purpose of the speech evident? What was it?
4. Were the general statements (main ideas) kept at a minimum so that they could be completely supported? How many were there?
5. Was there adequate support for each main idea?

6. Were the main ideas arranged in an order that was easy to follow? (You should be able to list them.)
7. Was the conclusion satisfactory? Why do you think so?
8. Did bodily activity aid or hinder the communication of the ideas that the voice was expressing? How? Did you feel empathic response?
9. Was the voice full of life, and did it have variety in pitch, rate, and loudness?
10. How would you rate this speech: excellent, good, fair?

FOR PRACTICE AND APPLICATION

Directions: Do *A,B,C* in order; then do one or more of *D,E,F,* and *G;* then do *H* and *I.* In all cases, evaluate each speaker, either in writing or in oral analysis.

A. Write and deliver opening sentences for three different speeches, one for each type of speech: informative, persuasive, entertaining.

B. Do the same for closing remarks.

C. Take turns at introducing a "speaker" to the class. If you wish, choose the name of some famous person in fact or in fiction and imagine that you are presenting him to an audience. Begin by saying "Ladies and gentlemen." The person introduced should acknowledge the introduction and should give a formal greeting. He may then make a short speech or may simply go on to introduce the next speaker. This activity should continue until every person in the class has carried out both parts.

D. Choose an editorial from a newspaper. Mark the thought phrases in the first ten lines; then read the whole editorial as if you were doing so over the radio.

E. Find and read an article in *Harper's Magazine,* the *Atlantic Monthly,* or the *Saturday Review.* Give a summary for the class; read aloud several paragraphs that illustrate your remarks.

F. Tell the class a humorous anecdote. Make it sound like good conversation.

G. Read or recite a carefully prepared poem. Be sure to speak in thought phrases. Check the effectiveness of your reading by asking a member of the class to tell you what the poem means. If no one can do so, probably the fault is yours.

H. Let each person in the class hand in five topics on specific subjects. The teacher or a chairman will choose among them and assign one to each person for a two-minute impromptu speech. Allow two minutes for preparation.

I. Prepare a formal speech in which you follow, step by step, the order of preparation given in pages 298–301. Allow a week or more in which to prepare.

CHAPTER 12

Reading, Looking, and Listening

LEARNING THROUGH READING

Learning takes place in many ways. You learn by talking with people, by doing things—such as baking a cake, writing a letter, or throwing a baseball—by traveling, by looking at motion pictures or television, by listening to the radio. All such experiences help you to learn. One of the most important ways of learning, however, is through reading. Success in school and in life depends in large part on your ability to read. Just how well *do* you read?

304

TAKING INVENTORY

People differ widely in their ability to read. They differ in the speed with which they read, in their ability to recognize new words, in their ability to organize the author's ideas in their minds, in their ability to get the author's meaning. But everyone, the poorest reader as well as the best reader, can improve his reading ability.

If you have already taken reading tests since coming to high school, your teacher may be willing to discuss your performance with you. These tests will reveal not only your general proficiency but also some of your specific strengths and weaknesses. In any case, you should ask yourself such questions as these: Do I enjoy reading in my leisure time? Do I have trouble in identifying new words from context? Do I remember the important details in what I read? You can answer these questions only in a very general way, but your answers will give you a clue as to whether you need to make special effort to improve your reading. The sections that follow offer you practical help for increasing your efficiency as a reader.

DEVELOPING GOOD READING HABITS

If you really want to improve your reading ability, you should make the following procedures habitual.

1. *Maintain a healthful routine.* To read at your best, you should be in good physical condition. Be sure to sleep eight hours every night. Get a moderate amount of fresh air and physical exercise. Eat well-balanced meals. Do not strain your eyes by reading in poor light or for excessively long periods. If you have not had an eye examination for some time, you should have one now. If you are abnormally and frequently tired, arrange to have a physical examination.

2. *Avoid unnecessary distractions.* Some people have trained themselves to read in noisy surroundings. Most persons, however, find it easier to read and study in an atmosphere of quiet, away from distracting sights and sounds. Quiet music on the radio usually will not interfere—it may even help—but most other programs are likely to reduce reading efficiency.

3. *Plan a time schedule.* For study-type reading, it is best to adhere to a regular schedule. Recreational reading can be fitted in at any time when there is a leisure moment or a vacant hour. Many students find it helpful to draw up a daily or weekly schedule that indicates the school program, time for recreation and meals, and time for reading and study.

4. *Have a clear purpose for reading.* When you turn to the printed page, you should have in mind a clear purpose for reading. Just saying the words silently while your mind is elsewhere, or when you have no goal for your reading, is a

waste of time. Ask questions of your author; reach out for the answers. Reading is an active process, not a passive one. When you read a story, you ask, "What will happen next? What will Susan do, now that Dick has left her?" When you read a description of a scene, read in order to visualize it in your mind, to fill in the missing details. Make the printed page your servant; do not let it be your master.

Your purpose in reading will determine *how* you read. Sometimes, as with an easy story, you will read rapidly, perhaps skipping passages that are not too important. At other times, as with a history textbook, you will read slowly, with careful attention to details.

5. *Get the habit of reading widely.* You can improve your reading only by reading abundantly. Get the habit of reading a great deal. You may wish to begin with easy material—with the daily newspaper, a popular magazine, or a book of easy short stories. As you develop fluency and pleasure in reading, try something harder. Read an article on a topic of interest in *Harper's* or the *Atlantic Monthly*. Choose an encyclopedia article dealing with a subject that really interests you—hunting or fishing, automobiles, airplanes, electronics, atomic energy, or some similar topic. Try a novel that calls for more than usual effort to read—Dickens's *Pickwick Papers*, Reade's *The Cloister and the Hearth*, Hardy's *Far from the Madding Crowd*, or some other that your teacher recommends. Have patience with the book; do not give up after the first few pages. Stay with it for several chapters until you know definitely whether or not you like it. Probably you will find yourself enjoying it.

Choosing good books is part of the job of reading widely. You will be helped by having at hand a good booklist. *Books for You: A Reading List for Teen-Agers*, published by the National Council of Teachers of English, is an excellent list. It probably is in your school library.

FOR PRACTICE AND APPLICATION

A. The following conversation* between a man and a book never took place. It might have taken place if a book could talk. After you have read this conversation, write in one sentence the central idea. Compare your ideas in class. Do you agree with the statement that no piece of writing says exactly the same thing to any two people? Explain.

BOOK: Won't you please ask me a question?
MAN: Why do you ask that?
BOOK: Because I can only ask you to ask me questions and can only answer the questions you ask.
MAN: Why don't you just tell me what you have to say?

* From *Creative Reading* by Helen Rand Miller and John J. De Boer, Seymour, Indiana: The Graessle-Mercer Co., 1950.

Book: I can't. I have nothing to tell you except answers to your questions.

Man: Haven't you the same thing to say to every reader, all put down in black and white?

Book: No! I never say the same thing twice. Black letters on white paper are nothing in themselves. You can only read meaning, and so much of that is in you. You never ask the same question twice because you are living, and that means changing all the time. Your experiences and your interests grow if you are alive.

Man: I'll read you from cover to cover; I'll read every word. I won't miss a thing. I'll pass an examination on you!

Book: Oh, vain, stupid, foolish little man to say that you will get out of me all that is in me. You can't. There is nothing in me except as you bring me to life in your living mind, imagination, and heart.

Man: So you don't live except as you live with living people?

Book: That's right. Nothing does. You don't yourself.

Man: But how can I ask you questions before I know what you have to say?

Book: Use your brain. Think what I might be able to tell you. I didn't say that you had to ask all your questions before you began to read. Let's have a little co-operation. Ask me one question at a time and look for my answer. Keep on asking questions as you read. Think ahead as you look ahead when you drive your car. What happens when you don't know where you are driving? It's your responsibility to ask the questions that will let me be at my best in answering you.

Man: I don't want to work always when I read. Sometimes I just want to enjoy my reading. I'd like to relax while you entertain me.

Book: And I want you to enjoy yourself whether you are working or just enjoying yourself. You'll have more fun if you are a bit companionable. It won't tire you to go along with a character and ask, "Does he love me? Will he come?"

Man: So I must play along with the characters in a story I'm reading for pleasure?

Book: Of course, if you are to share their pleasure. If you don't do your part, you let me down.

Man: And what if you don't answer the questions I want answered?

Book: Then I let you down. Don't waste your time and wear me out unless I have what you want.

Man: Don't I have to read you to find out whether you have what I want?

Book: No, not if you know how to have a good look at me.

Man: So I must learn to ask questions?

Book: Yes, Everything depends upon that.

B. In his autobiography Benjamin Franklin tells of his experience with the time schedule that he had set up for himself:

This article [his schedule] caused me so much painful attention, and my faults in it vexed me so much, and I made so little progress . . . and had such frequent relapses that I was almost ready to give up . . . like the man who, in buying an ax, . . . desired to have the whole of its surface as bright as the edge. The smith consented to grind it bright for him if he would turn the wheel . . . while the smith pressed the broad face of the ax hard and heavily on the stone, which made the turning of it very fatiguing. The man ... at length said that he would take the ax as it was ... "No," said the smith, "turn on, turn on; we shall have it bright by and by; as yet it is only speckled." "Yes," says the man, "but I think I like a speckled ax best." ...

In truth, I found myself incorrigible with respect to Order [that is, following his schedule]; and now I am grown old, and my memory bad, I feel very sensibly the want of it. But, on the whole, though I never arrived at the perfection I had been so ambitious of attaining, ... yet I was ... a better and happier man than I should have been without it.

Discuss the preceding quotation. Do you agree with Franklin that his schedule was of value to him even though he failed in his attempts to follow it exactly? Why or why not?

C. Draw up a time schedule for your school week; then do your best to follow it. Do not allow yourself to become discouraged: remember Franklin's experience.

D. Make a list of the various fields in which you read—fiction, travel, biography, science, sports, and so on. Go over your lists in class. How does the variety of your reading compare with that of your classmates? If you need wider reading interests, ask for suggestions. Compare notes also on the medium—books, magazines, newspapers—in which you do most of your leisure reading. If you now spend more time on the latter two than on books, your reading needs to be widened. Try to form the habit of having at least one book "under way" at all times.

RECOGNIZING NEW WORDS

An important factor in the improvement of reading is the ability to recognize new words. Every reader encounters words that he has not met before. Efficient readers know how to deal with such words. It is possible, of course, to look them up in the dictionary; and sometimes it is necessary and desirable to do so. However, if you were obliged to look up all new words, your reading would be very slow, and you would soon become discouraged. More commonly you will deal with new words in other ways.

USING CONTEXT CLUES

One of the most helpful ways of recognizing new words is through *context;* that is, by noting the connection in which they appear in the sentence. Several kinds of context clues help one to determine the approximate meaning of unfamiliar words.

1. One kind of context clue is the *synonym;* that is, a word that has approximately the same meaning as the unfamiliar word used in the sentence.

> A *stiletto,* or *dagger,* hung at his belt.

2. Another kind of context clue is the *antonym,* or a word with a meaning directly contrary to that of the unfamiliar word.

> Unlike his *excitable* wife, Jeeves had a *phlegmatic* disposition.

3. Sometimes a previous word or sentence will describe a mood or a situation that gives meaning to the new word.

> It was a silent and humiliated team that trudged into the locker room after the upset. Nor did the *lugubrious* expression on the coach's face serve to lift their spirits.

4. Sometimes the unfamiliar word is a summary word that can be understood from the illustrations.

> The new law provided for an extensive *conservation* program—new dams were to be built, reservoirs constructed, whole areas reforested, and crop rotation encouraged with subsidies.

5. Sometimes the meaning of a word can be *inferred* from the general context.

> The doctor prescribed a *sedative* to relieve the patient's suffering.

6. Sometimes the unfamiliar word is explained by an appositive.

> *Krilium,* a **chemical soil conditioner,** is derived from *acrylonitrile,* a **chemical obtained from natural gas.**

7. Sometimes the sentence following the one in which an unfamiliar word appears will give the explanation.

> *Stereophotography* has aroused great enthusiasm among hobbyists. Three-dimensional pictures, especially on color film, are not merely accurate images of the subject; they look like the real thing.

8. Sometimes the reading material supplies an outright definition of the new word.

> The defendant entered a plea of *nolo contendere.* This action means that the defendant, without pleading innocent or guilty, does not desire to contest the charge against him.

FOR PRACTICE AND APPLICATION

A. In the following sentences explain the meaning of the italicized words with the aid of synonyms, antonyms, or other related words found in the sentences. Make this an oral activity.

1. Roger felt a growing resentment toward the intrusive stranger, but he succeeded in concealing his *pique* until the interview was over.
2. The candidate never resorted to outright insult, but relied constantly upon sly *innuendo.*

3. Great literature deals with lasting, not *ephemeral,* themes.
4. These frontiersmen were armed with *musketoons,* or blunderbusses, and thus had the advantage over the natives, who possessed no firearms.
5. The new employer's *parsimony* became as unpopular as his predecessor's generosity had been popular.
6. The captain's *petulant,* peevish remarks made guests uncomfortable.
7. Impatient with *chicanery,* the President set new standards for fair dealing with all.
8. The caliph remained *obdurate* in the face of all the ambassador's entreaties.
9. Although he was very wealthy, Snodgrass dressed simply and avoided all forms of *ostentation.*
10. A lifelong champion of freedom of speech, Jefferson has become for us the symbol of the *untrammeled* mind.

B. Find and copy at least one other example of each of the eight context clues described on page 309. Underline the unfamiliar words. Use literature anthologies, history textbooks, or library books as sources for your illustrations. Exchange papers and use the various context clues to interpret the underlined words.

ANALYZING NEW WORDS

In some cases you can learn the meaning of an unfamiliar word by examining its parts. Sometimes a prefix or a suffix may help you to get at the meaning. Sometimes the root—the part that is left when any prefixes and suffixes are taken away—will give a clue. Being familiar with the Greek and Latin word elements found on pages 180–81 will help. Remember that the derivation of a word may not yield its exact meaning. Derivation is merely a clue.

FOR PRACTICE AND APPLICATION

With the aid of the Greek and Latin word elements on pages 180–81 and of others that you may know, give the meanings of the following words. Use a dictionary if necessary. Compare your work in class.

unilateral	audio-visual	tetrad
filial	oculist	cacophony
affiliation	aquatic	chlorophyll
circumlocution	premonition	theosophy
abduction	Anglomania	pentagon
contradiction	pneumatic	geopolitics
ophthalmologist	necrology	heterogeneous
fratricide	micrometer	decapitate
pendant	hexagonal	nonconformity

INCREASING READING SPEED

How rapidly do you read? People vary widely in their speed of reading. Some people manage only 150 words per minute; others read nearly 1,000 words per minute. Average speed probably is 350–400 words per minute. These rates assume, of course, that the reader understands what he reads. You should realize, too, that speed will vary with the type of material read. Mathematics or science problems should be read slowly and carefully, as a rule; most fiction can be read rapidly.

How can you increase your reading speed? Here are some suggestions.

1. LEARNING TO SEE WORD GROUPS

One important way to increase reading speed is to get the habit of seeing *word groups* or phrases instead of only one word at a time.

In the following passage, notice the difference in the effect that word-by-word reading gives compared with that of phrase-reading.

> Chicago, | chief | city | of | Illinois, | is | the | world's | greatest | railroad | center. | The | Chicago | area | switching | district | has | more | miles | of | track | than | the | entire | mileage | of | any | one | of | thirty-eight | states. |

> Chicago, | chief city | of Illinois, | is the world's | greatest | railroad center. | The Chicago area | switching district | has more miles | of track | than | the entire mileage | of any one | of thirty-eight | states. |

2. WIDENING THE EYE SPAN

When your eyes "fix" upon a point on the printed page, they see not only straight ahead, but to right and left as well. The extent to which you can see to right and left while stopping is known as the *eye span*.

If you are a slow reader, you might practice making better use of your eye span. For example, when your eyes return to the left margin, practice beginning the line a half inch or so away from the margin. Do not waste time beginning at the blank space in the margin. Also, try leaving the line a half inch or so before you reach the blank space in the right margin.

When you practice to increase your eye span, you will lose time at first, because your attention is taken away from the meaning. After you have established the habit, however, you will soon gain speed; and the new habit will save you much time. Newspapers, with their short lines, offer good practice material.

3. READING KEY WORDS

You can increase your speed also by finding the *key words;* that is, the important ones. Skip over the other words. If the key words make sense together, read on. If not, slow up and look for the connecting words.

Note the italicized key words in the following passage:

> All *persons born* or *naturalized* in the *United States,* and *subject* to the *jurisdiction* thereof, are *citizens* of the *United States* and of the *State* wherein they *reside. No State* shall *make* or *enforce* any *law* which shall *abridge* the *privileges* or *immunities* of *citizens* of the United States; *nor* shall any State *deprive* any *person* of *life, liberty,* or *property,* without *due process* of *law; nor deny* to any *person* within its *jurisdiction* the *equal protection* of the *laws.*
>
> —Amendment XIV, Section 1, of the Constitution of the United States.

Remember that the kind of material you read and the purpose for which you read will determine how rapidly you should read. Usually you will improve your understanding as you increase your speed.

You can train yourself, with practice, to "skim" what you read; that is, to move your eye rapidly down the lines to pick up the key words. You are really reading, not while your eyes are moving, but while they "fix" upon a word or group of words. In order to read rapidly, you must get as much meaning as possible from every "stop."

FOR PRACTICE AND APPLICATION

A. Here is a little exercise that will show you the importance of key words and the unimportance of other words in a sentence.

Copy the following sentences, putting a word into each blank space. (One sentence has only unimportant words in it; the other, only key words.) Read your sentences in class. Which sentences are alike or almost alike, the ones that you wrote for *1* or those that you wrote for *2?* What conclusion do you draw?

1. In the .... of the ...., ... were .... of ....
2. .... owner .... house next .... ours says .... sell .... first opportunity.

B. Test your ability to pick out key words. Copy a short paragraph (eight or ten lines) from a book or a magazine, omitting, however, all but key words, as in sentence 2 of the preceding activity. Leave a blank for each word that you omit. Exchange papers with a classmate and fill in the blanks as well as you can. Return the papers and check the work. If you did a good job of selecting key words, the person who filled the blanks probably will have come close to the original wording.

C. Clip magazine advertisements of two different automobiles, television sets, or refrigerators. Underline what seem to you the key words. How do these compare? What special devices are used (color, capital letters, italics, and so on) to make particular key words stand out? Discuss the effectiveness of these devices.

UNDERSTANDING WHAT YOU READ

How do you study your assignments? Do you approach the reading material in a systematic way? Do you aim at *understanding* what you read, or are you merely trying to remember the words from the textbook? The following suggestions can help you to become more efficient in studying assignments or in grasping other factual material in books and magazines.

GUIDES TO BETTER STUDYING

1. Adjust your speed of reading to the kind of material that you are trying to read. Mathematics problems or difficult passages in a history or science textbook should be read slowly and carefully.
2. Approach the printed page with an active mind. Ask questions of your author and search for the answers.
3. Ask yourself how the material that you are reading relates to what you knew before, or how it compares with what you thought before.
4. Make use of the various clues provided to suggest the main ideas. These include the table of contents, the chapter headings, center "heads," paragraph headings, topic sentences, words and phrases in italics or heavy type, and similar devices.
5. Repeat to yourself, in your own words, the main ideas that you have derived from your reading.
6. If you have trouble in recognizing or remembering the main ideas in the book, make an outline of the material. If you need help in outlining, see pages 270–72.
7. Supply illustrations and supporting details from the book or, if possible, from your own mind.
8. Put into your notebook any of the preceding guides that you personally need to apply; then check yourself systematically to see that you use them.

READING NEWSPAPERS AND MAGAZINES

You have been studying about the reading of books. Books contain treasures of knowledge, inspiration, and enjoyment from all the ages. But you will learn much also from other kinds of printed matter, especially newspapers and magazines.

It has been said that for every book reader in the United States there are two magazine readers. More than 6,000 magazines, with a total circulation of 240 million copies, are published in the United States. More than 21 million newspapers are sold every morning; more than 31 million, every evening; more than 46 million, every Sunday.

By means of newspapers and magazines, Americans are provided with news, fiction, political and philosophical discussions, scientific information; with suggestions for homemaking, family relations, child care, choice of schools or vacation spots; with material about gardening, hobbies, sports, and many other topics.

FOR YOU TO TALK ABOUT

1. How well do newspapers keep the people informed?
2. How can magazines make life pleasanter and more interesting?
3. What kinds of information would you like to get from newspapers?
4. What kinds of material do you like best in magazines?
5. What are your favorite magazines? Why?
6. What part of the newspaper do you read first?

EXPLORING THE WORLD OF MAGAZINES

Most of you are familiar with numerous magazines. Many girls read the *Ladies' Home Journal,* the *Woman's Home Companion,* or *Good Housekeeping.* Boys read *Popular Science* and *Popular Mechanics.* Both boys and girls read the *Saturday Evening Post, Coronet, Collier's, Life,* and *Time.* There are, however, many other magazines, not so well known, that have much to offer.

Girls interested in a nursing career may enjoy *Life and Health* or the *Journal of Public Health Nursing.* Boys interested in architecture may find pleasure in reading *Architectural Forum* or *Better Homes and Gardens;* those interested in outdoor sports will enjoy *Outdoor Life, Field and Stream, Sports Afield.* Anyone interested in travel will enjoy *National Geographic* and *Holiday.* Special magazines deal with nearly all the sports and hobbies that one can think of. Churches, business organizations, labor and farm groups, and social and political organizations publish periodicals representing many different points of view. Here indeed is a world worth exploring.

FOR PRACTICE AND APPLICATION

A. Carry out the following group activities.

1. In a visit to your school or public library, note how many different kinds of magazines it has. How many appeal especially to men? to women? to both? to young people? How many are for the general reader? How many are technical? How many are news magazines or journals of opinion? fiction magazines? fashion magazines? movie magazines? Make notes of any with which you would like to become acquainted.

2. If your teacher agrees, make a survey of the magazine reading habits of your class, school, or community. With the aid of charts and graphs, give reports of your findings.

3. Choose topics from the following list for class or small-group discussions:
    a) What are "pulp," "slick," and "quality" magazines? How do they differ?
    b) What magazines may help one to choose a vocation?
    c) Where can one find suggestions for books to buy or films to see?
    d) Is the reading of pulp or comic magazines harmful?
    e) What "digest" magazines do you know? What are their values? What are their shortcomings?
    f) How does your family choose its magazines?
    g) Do advertisers influence the content of magazines? If so, how?
    h) What standards would you set up for judging a magazine?
    i) To what extent do magazines *reflect* public opinion? To what extent do they *create* public opinion?

B. The following are individual projects. Try to do at least *1* and *2*.

1. Bring to class magazines that you read at home. Exchange them with your classmates. Spend a period or two in class examining magazines that you have not read before, or read them outside class. Be prepared to give a talk to the class about one or more stories or articles that have interested you. Plan your talk well. (See page 301.)
2. Write a letter to the editor of a magazine or to the author of an article or story, telling him what you liked or did not like about the magazine, article, or story. Unless you know his address, send a letter to an author in care of the magazine. Think carefully how you will express your approval graciously and your disapproval tactfully. If you wish, ask your teacher to let you read your letter to the class to get suggestions for improvement. Be sure to rewrite and proofread it before mailing. Follow proper letter form. (See page 331.)
3. Examine copies of such "quality" magazines as the *Atlantic Monthly, Harper's,* and the *Saturday Review.* What do you find in them of interest?
4. Make a chart of the subscription prices of magazines in which you are interested. Compare the annual rates with the prices of single copies.

FOLLOW-UP

A. On your classroom bulletin board, post announcements of outstanding articles or stories that you find in current magazines.

B. You may wish to make a magazine anthology. If so, have a magazine hour for the presentation of poems, stories, articles, or of quotations from them. From these, select the materials that the class wants to have included in the anthology. Perhaps someone in the class can design an attractive cover and section headings.

C. Organize a magazine club to meet weekly or monthly, perhaps during the activity period. In your meetings, discuss the contents of magazines that interest you. Recommend worth-while stories, articles, and special features.

EXPLORING THE WORLD OF NEWSPAPERS

In spite of the growth of radio and television, the reading of newspapers has not declined. How can you make the best use of this medium? What are some of the problems involved in newspaper reading?

How much can you believe of what you read in the newspapers? How impartial are papers in their reporting of news? How many newspapers—or people, for that matter—are completely unbiased? To get the most out of your newspaper reading, you should think about such questions as the preceding ones.

"I THINK THIS NEWS IS SLANTED."

Newspapers seldom make deliberate misstatements of facts. They distort news, however, when they emphasize certain items and "play down," "bury," or omit others entirely. Newspapers try to tell the truth, but they do not always tell the whole truth. Sometimes reporting is slipshod and inefficient, and as a result the facts may be garbled. The greatest danger for the reader occurs, however, when a newspaper "slants" its material; that is, when it selects and arranges the facts to harmonize with its bias. Likewise, the newspaper may be guilty of using emotion-arousing words that reflect its bias. Since certain biases are common to most newspapers and news magazines, especially on political and economic questions, one should read a variety of journals of opinion in order to get all sides.

Some readers of the newspaper fail to make full use of its services. They limit themselves to the comic page, the sports page, the fashion page, the financial page, or the advertisements. Of course, not all newspaper features are important or interesting to all readers, but many people leave valuable parts of the newspaper unused simply because they have never been introduced to them.

FOR PRACTICE AND APPLICATION

A. The following activities are designed as class or group projects. Carry out as many as you can. Try to do at least *1* and *7*.

1. Make a list of various departments and features to be found in your daily newspaper. If your library has daily newspapers from other cities, compare the variety to be found in your paper with the variety that is provided by these other papers.

2. Dr. Edgar Dale has suggested the following "canons" of journalism: responsibility, freedom of the press, independence, sincerity, truthfulness, accuracy, impartiality, fair play, decency. To what extent do the newspapers of your community observe these principles? By selecting specific articles from the papers, apply these tests as well as you are able. Discuss your findings in class or in your small groups.
3. Examine in the library recent issues of the *New York Times,* the *Christian Science Monitor,* the *St. Louis Post-Dispatch,* or other well-known newspapers. Compare their treatment of some topic of national interest. How does your local paper treat this topic? Compare the wording of the headlines and of the articles themselves. Note any "slanted" words. For example, "Labor Boss Defies Court Order" suggests an attitude far different from that which "Union Official Opposes Court Order" suggests.
4. Visit the editorial rooms and plant of a local newspaper.
5. Newspapers have a vocabulary of their own. Investigate and then discuss in class the items that follow.
    a) Make a list of "headline" words and give their meaning. What is meant in newspaper jargon by *probe? Meet* as a noun, and *near* as a verb are other examples of newspaper jargon.
    b) What is meant by the following terms: *rotogravure, news syndicate, AP, U.P., INS, tabloid, newspaper chain, yellow journalism, jingoism, facsimile newspaper?*
6. By means of almanacs, books about the press (ask your librarian to help you find them), and other sources, find out all you can about newspaper control. How many cities have only one newspaper? How many newspapers own their own radio stations? What dangers lie in these two situations? Talk over this question.
7. Conduct a class or panel discussion on one of the following topics:
    a) How do newspapers and radio stations differ in the way that they report and interpret the news?
    b) What influence do advertisers have on newspaper policy?
    c) To what extent should newspapers be permitted to criticize the actions of the government?
    d) Should newspapers publish the names of first offenders in criminal cases?
    e) How do headlines sometimes misrepresent the content of a news story? Can you find illustrations?
    f) Do most newspapers usually present a fair treatment of opposing political parties?
    g) What are the values of advertisements? How can advertisements be improved?
    h) Should paid advertisements contain political propaganda?
8. Make a survey of the comic strip interests of the class. What are some really good comic strips? Give reasons for your answer. What does *comic* mean?

B. By yourself, carry out one of the following activities. Then report to the class what you have found out.

1. It is generally believed that newspapers should present the news impartially and that they should confine their opinions to the editorial page. What examples can you find, if any, of "editorializing" in the news columns of your local newspaper?
2. Compare the viewpoints of several newspaper columnists on each of four or five timely questions. This project will require research in the library.
3. Try to secure an interview with a local newspaperman. Be prepared with suitable questions. (See page 292 for help in planning the interview.)
4. In your daily paper, compare the space devoted to crime with that given to announcements and reviews of new books.

C. Write a letter of opinion to your local paper. Perhaps you will want to disagree with a letter that you have read in the paper. Check your letter by the form on page 331.

Enjoying Radio and Television

Almost everybody in the United States has access to the radio. Almost everybody listens at some time or other; millions of people spend many hours per week in listening. Today an increasingly large number of people are spending time with television. Perhaps television audiences someday will exceed radio audiences.

Doing the activities that follow will give you some interesting data about the radio and television habits of your class.

FOR PRACTICE AND APPLICATION

A. Have a committee draw up a questionnaire about the radio and television interests of the class. The committee may use the following form as a guide.

1. Rate the following types of programs. Write *1* for your favorites; *2* for those that you like; *3* for those that you do not care much for; *4* for those that you dislike strongly.

    Type of program   *Rating*

    "Thriller" dramas
    Westerns
    Serious dramas
    Disc jockey programs
    Serious music (symphonic, opera, . . .)
    Sports programs
    Special events
    News broadcasts
    News commentaries
    Variety programs
    Comedy programs
    Public forums
    Panel shows
    Public addresses
    Quiz and "give-away" shows
    Amateur hours
    Religious programs
    Book reviews and literary discussions
    Informative broadcasts (science, travel, etc.)

2. Make a list of your present favorite radio and TV programs.
3. How much time do you spend with radio and TV per week?
4. What time of day do you listen to radio or view TV?
5. Do you listen while studying?
6. Who is your favorite news commentator?
7. Who is your favorite radio or TV performer?
8. If you have ever written to a station or a performer on radio or TV, what was your comment?

B. Appoint or elect a committee to summarize the entries on the questionnaires and to report to the class.

C. Discuss in class the results of the questionnaire. What do they show about the listening and viewing habits of your class?

PROBLEMS OF RADIO AND TV

Although everyone recognizes that radio and TV are wonderful inventions, many people have strong criticisms to make of the content of some programs. They point to the great amount of violence, horror, and crime portrayed. Some people believe that radio and TV contribute to nervousness, tension, delinquency, and criminal behavior. They call attention to the large proportion of "soap operas," "formula" plays, and superficial variety programs to which large numbers of people listen. They think that many radio and TV offerings cause a serious waste of time for both young people and adults.

Another problem that disturbs some people is the danger of one-sided propaganda on radio and TV. The very nature of these media makes it impossible for everybody to express his opinions on radio or TV. Many towns have only one station. How can you be sure that the news and commentary which you get will be balanced and unbiased?

FOR PRACTICE AND APPLICATION

Let the class choose some of the following questions for study and discussion. After having given them sufficient study and thought, choose a panel of students to discuss the questions. Permit the entire class to join the discussion after the panel has initiated it.

1. Do radio and TV programs influence opinion on public questions? Are radio and TV more or less influential than newspapers? Do people believe everything they hear on radio and TV?
2. Do crime and horror stories have any effect upon people's behavior?
3. What are the best types of radio and TV humor? the worst? What programs are noted for humor that is gay and warm? What programs depend on unkind characterizations of groups of people? What programs use cheap or silly jokes?
4. Should there be censorship of radio and TV programs? Ask your librarian to help you find information about the work of the Federal Communications Commission. Should the FCC be strengthened?
5. Who should be permitted to speak on the radio or TV?
6. Do producers, directors, advertising agencies, sponsors, or the audience have the most control over programs?
7. Who is likely to determine which radio commentators are to be kept on or off the air?
8. In what ways would you like to see radio and TV commercials improved?
9. Should there be more sustaining (unsponsored) programs? Are the present sustaining programs presented at desirable hours?
10. How can citizens help to improve the quality of radio and TV programs?

STANDARDS OF SELECTION

Some radio and TV programs are excellent; others are worthless and perhaps harmful. Some are of interest to one group of people; others have appeal for another group. In order to make proper selection among the programs, you need a set of standards, or *criteria*.

One class, for example, drew up the following criteria by which to measure the quality of a newscast:

1. Has the broadcast been carefully prepared?
2. Is the news presented in an interesting way?
3. Does the speaker have a pleasant voice?
4. Is the speaker's presentation calm or highly emotional?
5. Is the news timely? Is it significant?
6. Does the announcer pronounce words correctly?
7. Does the speaker seem to be fair in his presentation?
8. Does the news have balance and variety?
9. What are the announcer's politics or the politics of the station?
10. Who is the sponsor of the program?

FOR PRACTICE AND APPLICATION

A. In class draw up a list of criteria for some of the other types of radio and TV programs mentioned on page 320.

B. Use the criteria to check at least one program.

C. Report your findings to the class.

MAKING THE MOST OF RADIO AND TV

In spite of their weaknesses, radio and TV can make, and have made, enormous contributions to American life. By means of these media, one is exposed to some of the very best as well as to some of the very worst music. Through TV one can see events of public interest at first hand. One can listen to discussions of great books and observe the performance of great plays. What are some of the things you can do in class in order to get more benefit from radio and TV? The following activities offer help in answering that question.

FOR PRACTICE AND APPLICATION

A. The following twelve activities are designed for class use. Try to do at least *1, 3*, and *6*. Carry out any others that appeal to your class.

1. Keep a section of the bulletin board for announcements of good radio and TV programs. Each of you should keep on the alert for well-known plays, good record programs, symphony concerts, public addresses by important speakers, quality comedy programs, and other features, especially those—FM, for example—that may be less familiar. Include clippings of reviews of good radio and TV programs, news of the industry, announcements of new programs, and similar information. Be sure to keep the arrangement attractive.
2. Keep a class radio-and-TV log. By keeping a separate record of listening or viewing experiences for each month, it will be possible to determine any changes in program selection on the part of members of the class.
3. If you have a recording machine in your school, record interviews with students and others giving their comments about radio and TV. Let the class listen and discuss the interviews.
4. Plan and produce a short radio program for broadcast on a local station or the public address system of your school.
5. Present a panel discussion about radio and TV before a civic club or school assembly.
6. Make a list of "emotion" words often used on radio and TV that interfere with clear thinking.
7. Analyze the technique of a radio or TV drama. Ask such questions as these:
    a) What background is provided, and how?
    b) How is the setting provided for the opening scenes?
    c) What use is made of foreshadowing? of flashbacks?
    d) What use is made, if any, of comic relief?
    e) How valuable were the sound effects?
    f) In television, how effective were the camera angles?
8. Visit a radio station and interview members of the staff. Be sure to make proper arrangements beforehand.
9. Invite a guest speaker to your class to talk about radio or TV.
10. Evaluate the speech qualities of well-known broadcasters.
11. Organize a radio club.
12. "Monitor" a series of radio or TV programs for a week. Do the programs from the various stations, networks, commentators, and forums represent a balance of viewpoints?

B. The following eight activities are for you to do as individuals. Do at least *1* and *8*. Carry out any others that seem interesting or valuable.

1. Write letters of approval or criticism to radio or TV stations or performers after listening or viewing. Get your families to write, too. Check your letters by the form on page 331.
2. Interview friends and neighbors to get their views about radio and TV programs; then report your findings to the class.

3. Make a survey of the listening habits of the people in your neighborhood.
4. Make an analysis of a political speech or a news commentary, noting any propaganda devices that have been used.
5. Adapt a story or a play for radio presentation.
6. Write a review of a radio or TV program for the room or school newspaper.
7. Read magazine articles about radio and TV, and report to the class.
8. Prepare and present to the class a report on some topic from any of the following fields:
   a) Newscasting
   b) Radio and TV propaganda
   c) Radio and TV advertising
   d) Radio or TV music
   e) Radio or TV drama
   f) Radio or TV as an industry

Enjoying Motion Pictures

How do you choose motion pictures to see? How do you judge them?

America has several thousand motion-picture theaters, attended by many millions of people weekly. About one fifth of those attending are young people of high school age, who average one attendance per week.

Since motion pictures influence thinking and behavior, one needs to know how to choose films well. Many films give a false picture of life and encourage unworthy ideals. Others are enlightening and inspiring. Worthwhile pictures entertain, faithfully reflect real life, and are wholesome.

FOR PRACTICE AND APPLICATION

A. The following five activities are designed as class projects. Do as many as you can. Carry out at least *1*, *2*, and *3*.

1. Hold a class discussion. Talk about the following questions or about others concerned with motion pictures.
    a) What undesirable elements have you seen in films? (For example, a race or nationality may be caricatured or ridiculed.)
    b) What do you consider to be bad manners at the motion pictures?
    c) How adequate, fair, and well balanced are most newsreels?
    d) How is crime treated? Is it made to seem attractive and exciting? Is the criminal portrayed as an appealing or glamorous character?
    e) How do various magazine reviews of films compare with advertisements for the same films? Which are more reliable, do you think?
    f) How much are high school students influenced by their favorite stars? In what ways do they try to imitate these favorites?

2. Keep a corner of the bulletin board for announcements and descriptions of good films coming to town.

3. With the aid of the *Readers' Guide*, film magazines, and other sources, make a study of the motion-picture industry. Find out what the major companies are, who owns them, what the costs of production are, who owns the big picture houses, what is meant by Class A and Class B pictures, who censors the movies, what pressure groups influence the movies, and similar kinds of information. You may wish to organize small groups to work on these problems and to report their findings to the class in panel discussions.

4. If you have seen a film based on a well-known novel, compare the two. Are the differences justified by the difference in the medium? Give reasons for your answer.

5. Invite a guest speaker to discuss some aspect of the motion-picture industry.

B. The following five activities are for you to do individually. Carry out at least *1*, *3*, and *5*.

1. Before the class, give an oral criticism of a picture that you have seen recently. Cover such points as these:
    a) What type of picture is it?
    b) Describe the setting of the story.
    c) Tell who the main characters are.
    d) Summarize briefly the "problem" of the play and how it was solved.
    e) Did the solution seem plausible? Why or why not?
    f) Do you approve of the purposes of the characters? Do you approve of the film itself? Why or why not?
    g) What scene did you enjoy most?
    h) Did the acting seem natural and convincing? Why or why not?
    i) Were there any especially effective photographic shots? Describe them.

2. Rewrite the advertisements for a picture as you think they should be written from the point of view of accuracy. Choose a film that you have seen within the past two weeks.
3. Write a letter of commendation or criticism to the producer of a film that you have seen recently. Proofread your letter carefully and check it by the form on page 331.
4. Interview a local theater manager. Find out how he selects the films shown at his theater.
5. Choose one of the following topics for a talk about some phase of motion pictures.

   a) Educational value
   b) Sound photography
   c) American *vs.* foreign films
   d) Types of humor
   e) Censorship
   f) My movie scrapbook
   g) Film titles
   h) Three-dimensional films
   i) Film magazines
   j) My favorite movie
   k) My favorite star
   l) Animated cartoons
   m) Music in films
   n) Stereotyped characters
   o) Stereotyped plots
   p) Westerns and serials

The Art of Listening

Are you a good listener? Offhand, you probably would say *yes*. It seems so easy just to listen. Actually, intelligent listening requires as much skill as intelligent reading. In some ways, good listening is even harder than good reading. When you have missed something on the printed page, you can go back to reread. When you listen, except to recordings, you must comprehend everything the first time.

How many kinds of listening do you do inside and outside school? Of course you listen to the radio and television; and you listen at the movies, in church, in meetings of your club, and at concerts. But how well do you listen to a new name when someone is introduced to you? How carefully do you listen to instructions when the teacher makes an assignment or when the principal reads announcements in assembly periods? How do you listen to student reports or to the oral reading of a poem or story? Are you a good listener in conversation and on the telephone? Perhaps most important of all, how well do you listen in group discussion?

FOR PRACTICE AND APPLICATION

A. From the following class or group activities, choose any that interest you. Try to do at least *1* and *2*.
1. Discuss any of the following questions:
    a) In what ways does listening differ from reading?
    b) How does listening to a story differ from listening to directions or to an explanation, such as in science?
    c) How can you disagree courteously with the opinions expressed by someone else? Is it important to be able to do so? Why?
    d) How may a speaker try to influence an audience by the tone of his voice? For example, what different purposes may be in the mind of a speaker who says this sentence: "Of course, the mayor promises to improve the condition of our streets next year"? Illustrate by reading the sentence aloud in varying tones of voice.
2. Draw up a list of guides to good listening.
3. Plan a group discussion of one of the topics suggested on pages 248 or 249. During this discussion, whenever you express a disagreement with another member of the group, begin by saying something like this: "What I think Sally meant is . . . Am I right, Sally?" If she agrees, go on to explain how you differ.

B. Carry out individually as many as you can of the following activities. Try to do at least *1* and *2*.
1. Analyze your own listening as a member of a discussion group. How do you listen during a group discussion? Do you listen to find out what each speaker has to contribute to group understanding? Do you listen in order to find fault with what other members are saying? Do you weigh and consider what others are saying, or do you merely wait until you have your turn to speak? Decide what you must do to improve your listening habits—then do it!
2. From any of the lists of discussion topics given earlier in this chapter, choose a topic for a brief talk. Prepare a quiz to give the class at the end of your talk to find out how well the class remembered your main points.
3. Listen to a radio commentator tonight. Be ready to report to the class the main ideas that he tried to express.
4. Write a paragraph or more on the subject "Sounds I Enjoy Listening To."
5. Listen to a story or an explanation on a record or to one read by the teacher. Tell briefly what you remember of what you heard. Play the record over, or listen to the reading again, to check how accurate your report was.

CHAPTER 13

Using English in Business

Everybody is concerned with business. For some, business is an occupation. For others, it includes only the activities of personal and family economics—buying and selling, making agreements, renting, employing, borrowing, saving. For all, it requires the ability to speak and write clearly and persuasively. Young people leaving high school should know especially how to carry on effective interviews and to write successful letters. This chapter deals with those two activities.

A well-known writer has explained some of the reasons that it is important for young people who expect to be employees to speak and write well: *

> As an employee you work with and through other people. This means that your success as an employee—and I am talking of much more here than getting promoted—will depend on your ability to communicate with people and to present your own thoughts and ideas to them so they will both understand what you are driving at and be persuaded. The letter, the report or memorandum, the ten-minute spoken "presentation" to a committee are basic tools of the employee. . . .
>
> Of course, skill in expression is not enough by itself. You must have something to say in the first place. The popular picture of the engineer, for instance, is that of a man who works with a slide rule, T square, and compass. And engineering students reflect this picture in their attitude toward the written word as something quite irrelevant to their jobs. But the effectiveness of the engineer—and with it his usefulness—depends as much on his ability to make other people understand his work as it does on the quality of the work itself.

---

* Peter F. Drucker, "How to Be an Employee." Reprinted by special permission from the May 1952 issue of *Fortune* Magazine. Copyrighted 1952 by Time, Inc.

Expressing one's thoughts is one skill that the school can really teach, especially to people born without natural writing or speaking talent. Many other skills can be learned later—in this country there are literally thousands of places that offer training to adult people at work. But the foundations for skill in expression have to be laid early: an interest in and an ear for language; experience in organizing ideas and data, in brushing aside the irrelevant, in wedding outward form and inner content into one structure; and above all, the habit of verbal expression. If you do not lay these foundations during your school years, you may never have an opportunity again. . . .

I know very well that the typical employer does not understand this as yet, and that he may look with suspicion on a young college graduate who has majored, let us say, in short-story writing. But the same employer will complain—and with good reason—that the young men whom he hires when they get out of college do not know how to write a simple report, do not know how to tell a simple story, and are in fact virtually illiterate. And he will conclude—rightly—that the young men are not really effective, and certainly not employees who are likely to go very far.

WRITING BUSINESS LETTERS

The principles of good, clear English discussed throughout this book apply to all kinds of communication—personal, social, or business. There are, however, certain special problems involved in business communication, especially letter writing, which everyone encounters at some time.

PRETEST ON BUSINESS LETTER FORM

Before studying the section on the form of business letters, test your own skill by performing the following exercise. If you can do it correctly, take the mastery test on page 340. If you make no errors in the mastery test, you may omit the material on pages 330–40.

Write the following communication as a letter, using semiblock form and open punctuation. Divide into paragraphs if necessary. Supply transcriber's initials and other necessary symbols or punctuation. Address the envelope, and fold and insert the letter.

3894 State Street Drive, New Orleans 9, Louisiana, March 18, 19—. The Southern Clothing Co., 843 Canal Street, New Orleans 1, Louisiana, Attention Adjustment Bureau, Gentlemen: Two months ago I brought into your store a pair of nylon hose for repair. When I inquired about them at the store last week, the manager of the repair department informed me that they had been misplaced, but that a further search for them would be made. Since I have had no further communication about the results of the search, would you be good enough to investigate the matter for me and indicate whether an adjustment will be made? I am enclosing the claim check. Very sincerely yours, Miss Linda Hayworth. Enclosure.

GENERAL APPEARANCE OF LETTERS

The standard size sheet for business correspondence is 8½ x 11 inches. White, unruled paper of firm texture and finish is considered in good taste for most types of letters.

The business letterhead identifies the business. It is the introduction of the writer to the receiver. As such it should be in character; it should reflect dignity and integrity.

In the case of the business letter written on stationery that has no printed heading, it is not essential to use the standard business size. A businesslike, unfolded sheet of good quality is acceptable. In any case, the general appearance of the page should be clean, well balanced, and attractive.

STANDARD FORMS FOR LETTERS

Almost all business letters are written in either of two standard forms or layouts, the *semiblock* form or the *block* form. Occasionally the *indented* form is used, but that style is reserved mostly for social letters. The block and semiblock forms are preferred in business letters because of the ease with which they may be typed and because of the attractive, balanced appearance that they give to the page. A handwritten letter is preferably done in semiblock style and without additional space between paragraphs.

The only difference between the block and semiblock forms is that in the semiblock form the first line of each paragraph is set in from the left margin a uniform distance. In the indented form, not only are paragraphs indented, but each successive line in the heading, in the inside address, and in the signature is indented to the right of the line preceding it.

EXAMPLE OF SEMIBLOCK FORM

                                          722 Peach Street
                                          Albany 5, New York
                                          September 26, 19—

University College
19 South La Salle Street
Chicago 5, Illinois

Gentlemen:

  Will you please send me a copy of your fall catalogue? I am especially interested in the Great Books course which you are offering in the evening. If you have any literature on this course, please send it to me with the catalogue.

                                                Yours truly,

                                                Jean Stevens

                                                Jean Stevens

EXAMPLE OF BLOCK FORM

693 Newton Road
Sterling, Colorado
December 17, 19—

Adjustment Department
T. L. White and Sons
Denver 6, Colorado

Gentlemen:

On December third I ordered from your firm three books: <u>The Last Conquest</u> by J. Short, <u>Success in Business</u> by R. R. Brown, and <u>Your Home</u> by M. Johnson. I enclosed a check for $9.45 to cover the cost of the three books and the mailing charge.

Yesterday I received only two of the books (Short's and Brown's). However, no money was refunded to me, nor was any mention made of the book which was not sent. No doubt this omission has occurred through some oversight. I feel confident that it can and will be corrected.

Yours truly,

Dorothy Coleman

(Mrs. Robert Coleman)

OPEN AND CLOSED PUNCTUATION

Either open or closed punctuation may be used, although modern usage favors open punctuation. Note all variations as illustrated in the examples below.

Closed Punctuation

HEADING   1444 South Ashland Avenue,
               Chicago 7, Illinois,
               April 6, 19—.

INSIDE ADDRESS Mr. James Brown, Manager,
               The Modern Paint Company,
               336 Main Street,
               Topeka 5, Kansas.

Open Punctuation

<table>
<tr><td>Heading</td><td>1444 South Ashland Avenue
Chicago 7, Illinois
April 6, 19—</td></tr>
<tr><td>Inside Address</td><td>Mr. James Brown, Manager
The Modern Paint Company
336 Main Street
Topeka 5, Kansas</td></tr>
</table>

It is customary to use a colon after the salutation and a comma following the complimentary close.

PARTS OF THE LETTER

The letter is composed of six sections: *heading, inside address, salutation, body, complimentary close,* and *signature.*

1. THE HEADING OF A LETTER

The heading consists of the writer's address (street, city, zone number, and state) and the date line. However, when letterhead stationery is used, the date is all that is necessary. It is placed about two spaces below the letterhead.

If the letter is written on stationery without a printed heading, the written heading should begin at least half an inch from the top of the page. The placing of the heading will depend on the length of the letter. In the case of a short letter, the heading should begin lower than in the case of a long letter.

The end of the longest line in the heading usually determines the width of the right-hand margin. Always not less than half an inch should be allowed for the right-hand margin, and, if the letter is short, it should be wider. Some writers place the heading in the center, at the top of the page.

The date is typed in full: *October 26, 1955.* The month is spelled out, and the day and year are expressed in figures. It is incorrect to use a number for the month and to abbreviate the year (as 2/3/55). The day of the month should be given as a simple figure, without any letters.

In both the heading and the inside address, abbreviations should be avoided. Numerical names of streets should be written out unless they involve too many words:

    34 East Forty-first Street   79 West 111 Street
    New York 18, New York   Chicago 23, Illinois

2. THE INSIDE ADDRESS

The inside address consists of the name and complete address of the firm or individual to whom the letter is being written. The name of the company should be given in its exact form. Names of individuals should always be preceded by either their special title (*Dr., The Honorable, The Reverend*) or the ordinary courtesy form (*Mr., Mrs.,* or *Miss*).

> Dr. Theodore Van Lunt
> Director of the Reading Clinics
> The University of Rochester
> Rochester 6, New York

As is true in all parts of a business letter, abbreviations are to be used sparingly, if at all, in the inside address. State names may be abbreviated if the names of the city and state are long. If state names are abbreviated, every effort should be made to avoid confusion among names that look alike in abbreviations. *California,* for example, should be written *Calif.*

> Mr. Frederick H. Waters   Miss Sandra Trilbourne
> 39 Wabasha Drive   917 Cemetery Lane
> Old Greenwich, Connecticut   San Francisco 18, Calif.

Some firms prefer to have all mail addressed to the company, and to the attention of an individual. In such instances a special line is provided beneath the inside address or beneath the salutation. Note this example:

> Marshall Field & Company
> 111 North State Street
> Chicago 90, Illinois
>
> *Attention: Mr. Frank Smithers*
> Gentlemen:

3. THE SALUTATION

The salutation is placed flush with the left margin and is generally two spaces below the inside address. A colon is the customary punctuation.

> Dear Mr. Brown: Dear Mrs. Borden:
> Dear Sir: Dear Madam:
> Gentlemen: Dear Miss Brown:

Modern business firms prefer the more personal salutations (*Dear Mr. Brown, Dear Mrs. Borden*) to the more formal (*Dear Sir, Dear Madam, My dear Mr. Brown*). When two or more men are addressed, the title *Messrs.* (pronounced měs′erz) is used (*Messrs. La Salle and Van Buren*). When two or more married women are addressed, the title *Mmes.* (pronounced mā dảm′) is used (*Mmes. Garbo and Tucker*). When two or more unmarried women are addressed, the title *Misses* is used (*The Misses Ruth and Sarah Fenton*).

4. THE BODY OF A LETTER

The body, the part of the letter which contains the message, begins two spaces below the salutation.

In a business letter, as in every other type of letter, clarity and readability are of the greatest importance. Short paragraphs and concise sentences enable the writer to deliver his message clearly and quickly. The aims of all good writing—unity, coherence, and emphasis—apply to business letters as well. Therefore all principles of good writing should be followed in business writing.

Trite, stilted expressions should be avoided.

Trite	Natural
at hand, to hand	We have received your letter
our Mr. B.	our representative, Mr. B.
yours of the 4th	your letter of October 4
yours of the 4th inst.	your letter of October 4
contents carefully noted	We have read your letter carefully.
Hoping to hear from you	We (*or* I) hope to hear from you.
Thanking you again	Thank you again.
and oblige	(*Avoid this phrase.*)
We are not in a position	We are not able
by return mail	at once, promptly
at this writing	now
beg to advise	(*Avoid this phrase.*)
will send same	We will send it (*or* them)
as per instructions	following your instructions
Attached please find	A copy of my letter is attached.
Enclosed please find	A copy of my letter is enclosed.
We are enclosing herewith	We are enclosing
party	person or man
re. *or* in re.	concerning
the writer	I

"IT SAYS, 'YOUR MESSAGE OF THE 4TH INST. RECEIVED AND CONTENTS CAREFULLY NOTED.'"

If the body of the letter is too long to be completed on one page, a sufficient margin (at least half an inch) should be left at the bottom of the sheet, and the letter should be continued on a second page. Printed letterheads should not be used for second or later pages. Note this example of the first line on a second page:

    Mr. William Campbell, page 2   May 4, 19—

5. THE COMPLIMENTARY CLOSE

The complimentary close is placed two spaces below the last sentence of the body, to the right of the center of the sheet.

    Yours truly,
    Sincerely yours,

Only the first word of the complimentary close is capitalized. A practice which is now out of date is that of joining the body and the complimentary close by means of a participial phrase.

OUTMODED

    Thanking you for your interest in this matter, I am,
        Sincerely yours,

PREFERRED

    Thank you for your interest in this matter.
        Sincerely yours,

6. THE SIGNATURE

The signature of a letter written by an individual consists of the name of the writer (handwritten). If the letter is typed, the name should be typed beneath the written signature.

A letter written by a representative of a business firm, however, should contain four elements in the signature: the company name, the writer's name (handwritten), the writer's name (typed), and the writer's title:

    The Standard Paper Company
    John W. Brown
    John W. Brown
    Personnel Manager

In the case of a married woman, it is customary to sign her full legal name, followed by her married name in parentheses:

    Very truly yours,
    Margaret E. Crendall
    (Mrs. Harry M. Crendall)

It is not necessary for an unmarried woman to write *Miss* before her name in the signature unless her name is one which might be mistaken for that of a man. However, a safe practice is to use the *Miss*.

Initials of the dictator and the transcriber, separated by a dash, colon, or other mark, are conventionally typed flush with the left margin on the last line of the signature block or two spaces below it. The dictator's initials are given first. Often the dictator's initials are capitalized; the transcriber's, in small letters: JWP/er.

If any items are enclosed with the letter, the symbol *Enc.* (*2 Enc., 3 Enc., 4 Enc.*) should appear below the initials of the dictator and transcriber:

                  ABC:mb
                  2 Enc.

SUMMARY EXAMPLE OF LETTER FORM
(Block Form, Open Punctuation)

Heading

                                                  605 Rose Avenue
                                                  Ruston, Louisiana
                                                  February 15, 19—

Inside Address

    American Red Cross
    511 North Broad Street
    Philadelphia 23, Pennsylvania

    Attention of Mr. Samuel Everett

Salutation   Gentlemen:

Body

    I am informed that you are the publishers of a pamphlet describing music and games for use with children of different cultural backgrounds.

    I have been working with such a group of children and should like to receive a copy of this publication. A check for $1.25 to cover the cost is enclosed.

Complimentary Close

                                                  Very truly yours,

Signature

                                                 Roger B. Schoy

    RBS:hg
    Enc.

FOLDING THE LETTER

There are four separate steps involved in folding the standard-size letter so that it can be fitted into the standard envelope, known as a *No. 6 envelope* (3¾ x 6¾):

1. Place the letter on the desk, face up, bottom toward you.
2. Bring the lower edge up to within one-half inch of the top, and fold.
3. Fold from right to left one third the width of the sheet.
4. Fold the remaining portion from left to right.

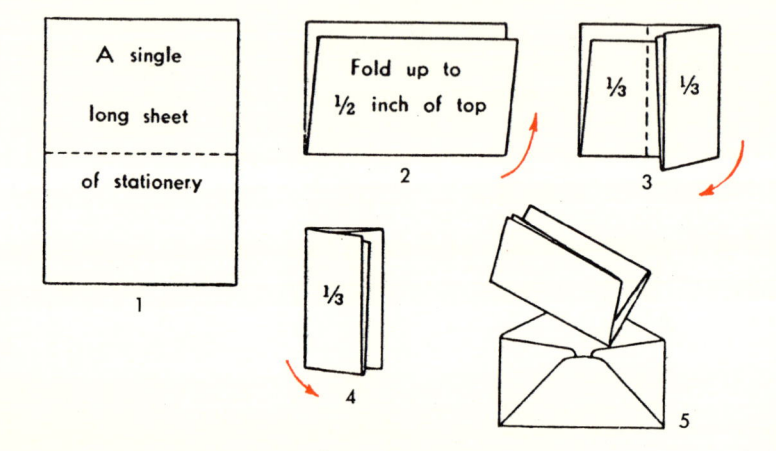

For the large *No. 10 envelope* (4 x 9½), proceed thus:

1. Fold the bottom upward one third the length of the sheet.
2. Fold the top down to within one quarter inch of the lower fold.

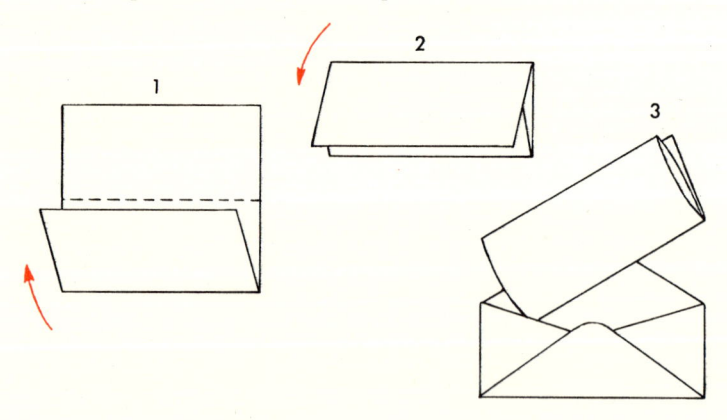

The letter should be inserted with the closed edge down and the flap against the front of the envelope, as is shown in the lower right-hand illustration at the bottom of this page.

ADDRESSING THE ENVELOPE

The sender's return address should always appear on the envelope, usually in the upper left corner. The addressee's name should be placed a little below the center of the envelope; and the address should be blocked or indented, and should use open or closed punctuation, in accordance with the form of the enclosed letter.

In the return address, the name of the city and the state may be placed on the same line, separated by a comma. In the address itself, always place the name of the state on a separate line. Use no abbreviations.

If the address is written in longhand, legibility is of prime importance. Every year thousands of letters fail to reach their destination and are sent to the Dead Letter Office in Washington simply because the handwriting on the envelope is impossible to decipher.

```
James L. Mordell
405 Bishop Street
Buffalo 5, New York




            Mr. Henry Smith
            10126 Avenue O
            Chicago 27
            Illinois
```

```
John H. Lourd
Asbury Heights
Portland 4, Oregon



            The J. M. Haynes Company
            2104 Madison Avenue
            New York 10
            New York

Attention: Mr. Herbert Maley
```

FOR PRACTICE AND APPLICATION

A. Write a letter to the credit manager of a department store asking how a charge account may be opened. Assume that you are the stenographer and that the letter was dictated by your employer.

B. Write a letter applying for admission to a college. Address the letter to the registrar.

C. Write a letter to an auto supply house asking that a new battery be shipped at once. Give the catalogue number of the battery and enclose a check.

D. You are the manager of a branch of a newspaper circulation department. Write to the circulation manager of the newspaper asking permission to employ an additional carrier.

E. You have initiated a service for parents of young children. You offer to supply reliable baby sitters on short notice. Write a form letter, individually addressed, explaining your service and stating the commission that you charge.

MASTERY TEST ON BUSINESS LETTER FORM

Copy the following communication as a letter, using semiblock form and open punctuation. Divide the letter into paragraphs if necessary. Supply whatever abbreviations and symbols are necessary. Address the envelope, and fold and insert the letter.

3365 Ocean View Ave., Seattle 6, Washington, February 6, 19—. Sully and Sully, 597 Avenue of the Americas, New York 17, New York. Attention of Personal Shopping Service. Gentlemen: Shortly before last Christmas I placed an order with you for a Federal electric clock-radio which was described in your catalogue, as indicated by the enclosed clipping. You then informed me that this article was out of stock, but that you would have a supply sometime in January. Since I have had no further word from you, I am writing to inquire whether I may expect soon to receive the clock-radio. I shall appreciate hearing from you. Sincerely yours, Susan Sheridan. Enclosure.

TYPES OF LETTERS

Business letters are classified according to their purpose. No matter what the purpose, a letter must deliver its message in the most effective manner. The types of letters which are described in this chapter are the letter of application, the letter of order, the letter of adjustment, the letter of payment, and the letter of inquiry or request.

THE LETTER OF APPLICATION

The letter of application, although a business letter, must necessarily be personal in nature. It is essentially a sales letter, and the product offered for sale is the writer's services. If the letter is a reply to an advertisement, it will usually have to compete with the other applications which the employer will receive. Of the hundred or more letters that may reach his desk, he will probably select the ten or fifteen which make the best impression at first glance.

How can you be sure your letter will be one of those chosen? There are certain steps to be followed in the writing of a successful letter of application, but the letter must, in its final form, reflect the character of the writer.

APPEARANCE

The first consideration of an applicant should be to make a favorable first impression by the faultless form of the letter. Typing, grammar, sentence structure, spelling, and punctuation are the mere mechanics of letter writing, but they must be perfect if the applicant is to have a good chance for further consideration.

Because an application is a business letter, white bond paper of good quality and standard (8½ x 11) size is the most satisfactory. Personal, hotel, fraternity, and other special types of stationery are to be avoided.

The message should make a pleasing appearance on the page. A margin of at least a half inch on each side, and slightly more at top and bottom, makes the message stand out clearly. Paragraph headings, such as *Education, Experience, References,* are useful in guiding the reader and in breaking up the text so that it is easier to read.

OPENING PARAGRAPH

The first few sentences should arouse the interest of the reader, reveal the purpose of the letter, and indicate where or how the applicant learned of the vacancy. The sentences should be direct and simply worded, but should avoid stereotyped phrases. Beginnings which are either colorless and worn (for example, "In reply to your advertisement in today's News, I wish to apply for the position") or too obviously straining to be "different" (for example, "Well, here I am!") are not likely to be effective.

An applicant who has learned of the position through a person known to the reader should mention this fact in his first sentence in order to ensure attention. Another device is to focus attention upon the applicant's most important qualification by mentioning it in the opening sentence.

STATEMENT OF QUALIFICATIONS

The opening sentences have gained the employer's attention. Now the applicant must state his qualifications for the position. Qualifications are of three general types: personal qualities, education or training, and experience. The applicant should write first and most fully about the qualification which is most important for this position. The advertisement may have given a hint about what the employer is most interested in. If he stressed education and indicated that experience is not necessary, then the applicant should state his educational qualifications first. Many factors will decide which qualifications should be stressed, and a little thought will usually indicate which ones they are.

In the section of the letter in which the applicant's education is described, there should be specific reference to his school or schools and the dates of attendance. Any honors which may have been attained, either scholastic or extracurricular, should also be mentioned. The points to be stressed are those which show what in his training has especially qualified him for the position he is seeking.

Experience should be presented in a logical fashion. The name of the firm, the kind of position, the duties connected with it, and the dates of employment should be stated. An applicant who is new in the field should mention any experience that he may have had in meeting and dealing with people, for such experience is an asset in any position.

Personal information is usually desired by an employer. He wants to know the applicant's age, nationality, health, marital status, and similar facts. The advertisement usually indicates the desired information, and much useless correspondence can be avoided if the first letter contains all the necessary facts.

Character traits, such as initiative, reliability, ambition, and loyalty, are important to an employer. Young people are wise to stress those qualities which they possess that may compensate for their lack of experience. A brief statement should be sufficient for this first letter; a long autobiography would be inappropriate.

REFERENCES

After describing his qualifications, the applicant must next offer proof that his statements are true. References should be chosen wisely; three are normally sufficient. One general character reference and two references from persons familiar with his work in the field (either employers or instructors) should be given if possible. It is important that the applicant inform the persons used as references that he is using their names. He must also be sure that they are willing to write a recommendation for him.

CLOSING PARAGRAPH

A brief explanation telling why the writer would like the position and why he feels qualified for it offers a personal note upon which to end the section on qualifications.

Mention of salary should be left for the interview. If the advertisement specifically asks for the "salary expected," a general statement is better than the naming of a specific figure.

Usually the purpose of the letter is to obtain an interview, and the letter should end with this request, phrased simply and naturally.

SUPPLEMENTARY DATA SHEET

Another type of letter of application is that which divides the letter into two parts: (1) an informal letter stressing only the most important facts and (2) a data sheet giving details of the applicant's qualifications.

The data sheet usually offers the information grouped under such headings as *Education, Experience, Personal Details,* and *References.* The material should be arranged so that it is easy to read.

An Example of a Letter of Application

> DENTIST'S ASSISTANT Requirements include ability to meet people with tact and courtesy; keep appointment calendar and monthly bills; answer telephone; learn simple laboratory routines; assist in dentist's operating room. Permanent position. Salary $175.00 per month to start. High school graduation but no experience required. Address L C 335, *Herald.*

```
                              245 Walton Place
                              Atlanta 2, Georgia
                              March 1, 19--

L C 335
Atlanta Herald
Atlanta 1, Georgia

Dear Sir:

You are looking for a young woman who can serve as
a dentist's receptionist, practical nurse, and
```

laboratory assistant. I am looking for just such a position. Would it be possible for us to meet to discuss the position and my fitness for it?

What I Have to Offer

Education

I have a high school diploma from Walker High School. My major was science, including courses in chemistry, botany, zoology, and physiology. I feel at home in the laboratory and believe I could learn to be efficient as an assistant in a dental laboratory.

I have also had some work in shorthand and typing, although I have not had a business course. I have attained sufficient speed in typing to do my school papers on the machine.

Experience

As president of the Senior Girls Club and member of several other student organizations, I had a great deal of experience in meeting people and in being tactful with them. In fact, the receptionist part of the position you describe lends it a special appeal for me.

Personal Data

I am nineteen years old, five feet two inches tall, and weigh 110 pounds. I have always given special attention to neatness of person.

References

You may secure further information about my qualifications from Mr. Arthur Lyons, principal of the Walker High School, and Miss Eleanor Shute, adviser to the senior class. Mr. Newton Lodge, general manager of Atlanta Frozen Foods Corporation, can also tell you about me. All of these have consented to respond to inquiries from you.

I should very much appreciate an interview.

Sincerely yours,

Madeline Rogers

Madeline Rogers

EMPLOYMENT APPLICATION BLANKS

Applicants for positions with the larger firms are asked to fill in forms calling for information about their background and training. Filling in these blanks should be a relatively simple task, but employers say that many applicants fail to fill them in correctly.

If the forms are filled in in longhand, the responses should be written in ink. Draw a line after any question that clearly does not apply to you. If blots or smudges are made, the applicant should request another copy of the application form, since an untidy appearance of a form may prejudice a prospective employer against the applicant. Correct spelling of all words used is likewise important.

If the application form is mailed to the employer, it should be accompanied by a covering letter calling attention to the enclosure, and possibly adding information not included in the application form.

FOR PRACTICE AND APPLICATION

A. Write a letter of application to a firm in your community for which you would like to work in your summer vacation.

B. Write a letter of application in response to a "blind" advertisement which appeared in your evening paper. Choose an advertisement calling for qualifications which you think you have. Use open punctuation and semiblock form. Attach the advertisement.

C. Write a letter applying for a position that a friend told you would be open in a month. Your friend now holds this position and will recommend you for the job.

D. Write a letter to a federal, state, or local employment service or to a private employment agency, setting forth your qualifications and inquiring about vacancies in positions for which you are fitted.

THE LETTER OF ORDER

A letter ordering goods or services should begin immediately with a description of the items ordered and should contain any special instructions necessary. If you are ordering from a mail-order house, fill in every space of the order forms which they provide. In ordering from a firm which does not provide blanks, the chief requirements are clearness and completeness. The size, color, quantity, and price of the articles desired should be stated. Directions for shipment must include the complete name and address of the person to whom the goods are to be sent, the date on which the shipment is to be made, and the manner of shipment—freight, express, or parcel post.

If a remittance accompanies the order, state in the letter the exact amount and the form in which it is sent—check, draft, or money order. If goods are to be charged to your account or sent C.O.D., the letter should so indicate.

When ordering from a department store, the customer, unless he is referring to a specific advertisement, frequently does not have complete data on the article desired. In such cases, a general description of the goods, plus size, color, and approximate price, is usually sufficient. Many of the larger stores have shopping services which handle requests of this kind.

An Example of a Letter of Order

```
                                    424 West Elm Street
                                    Wilmette, Illinois
                                    May 2, 19__

Carson Pirie Scott & Co.
One South State Street
Chicago 3, Illinois

Gentlemen:

Please send me, at once, the following items. I do
not wish to pay more than the prices I have
indicated.

    One pair of ladies' black doeskin
    gloves, four-button length, size 6 .......$5.00
    One ladies' white wool muffler, light weight.$3.50

These items are to be charged to my account.

                                    Yours truly,

                                    Roberta Smith

                                    (Mrs. James Smith)
```

FOR PRACTICE AND APPLICATION

A. Write a letter ordering a dress in the catalogue of a mail-order house.

B. Write a letter to a large department store asking their shopping service to pick out a sweater for a four-year-old child. You want them to send the sweater, wrapped as a gift, directly to the child. Be sure to give them the address. They are to charge the sweater to your account.

C. Write a letter to the U. S. Department of Commerce, Washington 6, D.C., ordering a copy of the summary volume of the most recent census report. Indicate that you are enclosing a money order to cover the cost.

D. Write a letter to the Pickemup Vacuum Cleaner Company ordering a hose for your vacuum cleaner. Be sure to indicate the model number of your machine.

E. Write a letter to the Scientific Book of the Year Club ordering a one-year membership.

F. Write a letter to a sporting goods house ordering a book on how to play softball.

THE LETTER OF ADJUSTMENT

Letters of adjustment are sent when some error has occurred in the course of a business transaction. The customer should assume that the firm did not make the mistake intentionally and that it will be glad to adjust the matter once it understands the circumstances. Therefore a first letter of complaint should be calm, courteous, and tactful. Reasonable letters will be more likely to win the quick co-operation of the reader than will a heated accusation.

What is to be adjusted should be the first item in the letter. If it was a purchase, tell what it was and when it was purchased. Next tell exactly what you want. If there is a defect in the goods, or if the wrong goods were shipped, tell how you want the adjustment made. If there is a mistake about money, explain what you think the error is. Above all, by assuming a reasonable attitude in your letter, imply that you expect to be treated fairly. See page 332 for an example of a letter of adjustment.

FOR PRACTICE AND APPLICATION

A. When you traveled by railroad from Chicago to Kansas City recently, the Pullman conductor informed you that your sleeping car had been taken from the train because of an emergency. Your ticket called for a lower berth, but the conductor had no space to give you except an upper berth in another car. Now that you have arrived home, write the company, requesting a refund of the difference between the price of the lower berth and that of the upper. Explain the matter courteously.

B. You have just bought a history textbook at a downtown bookstore, paying the current list price of the book. When you arrived at school, your teacher told you that the class was to use a later, revised edition. Write a letter to the bookstore asking for an adjustment.

C. Write a letter to a mail-order house which made an error in filling an order that you have just received.

D. Your monthly bill from a department store contains an item which you did not receive. Write a letter asking for a correction.

E. A pair of gloves which you purchased recently at the same department store has proved defective. Write a letter to the store, asking for an adjustment.

THE LETTER OF PAYMENT

One of the most frequently used types of business letters is the letter of payment. Ordinarily the bill, with the check or money order clipped to it, is all that is necessary. But, if an accompanying letter is necessary, it should be brief, stating why the money is sent, how much money is sent, and in what manner the money is sent.

```
                                    828 Justice Place
                                    El Paso 8, Texas
                                    February 2, 19__

The Community Grocery and Meat Market
181 Pensacola Avenue
El Paso 2, Texas

Gentlemen:

I am enclosing a check for $1.85 in payment of the
grocery order which was delivered Saturday while I
was away from home.

                                    Yours very truly,

                                    Susan Wigmore
                                    Susan Wigmore
```

THE LETTER OF REQUEST

A letter of inquiry is a request for information. For this reason it must be brief but specific. Inquiries about goods or services should clearly and courteously explain what is wanted.

Routine inquiries, such as requests for catalogues, price lists, and other already prepared material, should be short and to the point. The request, unaccompanied by explanation or comment, is sufficient.

                                        Rural Route 4
                                        Hays, Kansas
                                        October 7, 19__

Jenkins Supply Company
1315 Grand Avenue
Kansas City 7, Missouri

Gentlemen:

Will you please send me the new Fall Catalogue
which you mention in your advertisement in the
Farmer's *Friend* of October 2, 19__.

                                   Very truly yours.

                                   John Blaine
                                   John Blaine

   Nonroutine inquiries about goods or services should contain definite
questions to which the reader can refer in his reply.

                                        Minden, Nebraska
                                        January 4, 19--

Philco Distributors, Incorporated
445 North Lake Shore Drive
Chicago 11, Illinois

Gentlemen:

I have studied the radio section of your Winter Catalogue. Before I make my decision, I should like to
have the answers to the following questions:

  1. Which Philco models are immediately available?
  2. Does the quality of the wood vary in the table
     models?
  3. Are the radios guaranteed? If so, for how long?

I want the radio to stand on a walnut end table.
Please recommend the model you think would be most
appropriate.

                                   Yours truly,

                                   Sarah Chambers
                                   Sarah Chambers

Letters that request favors must take several facts into account. They must explain why the information is needed, they must not request confidential information, and they must be courteous. The nonsales inquiry should be written so that it is easy to understand and easy to answer. Because granting the request will require some of the reader's time, the writer should try to point out some of the advantages to be gained by complying with the request. A considerate gesture would be to enclose a stamped, addressed envelope.

FOR PRACTICE AND APPLICATION

A. Write a letter to a local radio station requesting tickets for a special broadcast that you would like to attend. *Be sure to proofread your letters for capitalization, punctuation, and sentence sense.*

B. Write a letter to a music supply house requesting that you be placed on its mailing list for announcements of new records.

C. Write a letter to a railroad company asking for a current timetable. Be specific in your request.

D. Write a letter to your Congressman asking him to send you a copy of the *Congressional Record* containing one of his speeches.

E. Write a letter to one of your senators asking him for his voting record on a bill in which you are interested.

TELEGRAMS

At some time or other you may be called upon to send a telegram, either by telephone or by messenger. Some skill is required to write a telegram in such a way that the meaning is made entirely clear without the use of unnecessary words, since the cost of a telegram is based on the number of words used beyond the minimum charge for the first fifteen words. Economy in the use of words should not, however, interfere with normal courtesy of expression. The word *please* may cost a few cents extra, but it is usually worth more than it costs.

Punctuation marks are sent as individual words and are therefore not usually employed in telegrams except to avoid misunderstanding. In the following message a period proved indispensable:

HAVE EMPLOYED JOHNSON HAGGERTY AND TOD JAMES PERIOD PERKINS UNSATISFACTORY

"THIS IS A TELEGRAM — RUN FAST!"

In the following telegram, which a businessman sent to his secretary, every word is necessary for the full understanding of the message:

    MISS JOSEPHINE WISHWELL
    ACME PUBLISHING CO CHICAGO ILL
    TRAIN RUNNING FOUR HOURS LATE PLEASE REVISE
      APPOINTMENT SCHEDULE
                              FORRESTER

FOR PRACTICE AND APPLICATION

Rewrite the following messages so that they would be suitable to send as telegrams.

1. I regret that I shall not be able to attend the board meeting as I had planned. Please extend my best wishes to all who will be present.
2. Uncle Bob was suddenly taken ill last night. His condition today is serious. I will keep you informed of developments.
3. The cold is too severe to permit open-air meetings. What do you suggest?
4. The price of beef has gone up five cents since I left the office. Do you still want me to buy?
5. I am applying for a position with the Webster Steel Company. Will you be good enough to send a recommendation for me to Mr. Josiah Boyce, the president of the firm? Thank you very much.

ADVERTISEMENTS

Writing commercial advertisements is an art requiring much training and experience. Often, however, it may be necessary to insert brief, noncommercial advertisements in the newspaper. When you do so, state your facts clearly and fully. Omission of important details in a lost-and-found advertisement, for example, may lead to a great many unnecessary letters and telephone calls. If the want ad department of the newspaper is efficient, it will call attention to obvious omissions, but of course it cannot be responsible for the inclusion of essential facts.

Economy of words is another important factor. Writing an advertisement is in this respect very much like writing a telegram. Notice that most want ads in newspapers attempt to combine brevity and persuasiveness.

FOR PRACTICE AND APPLICATION

A. Write an advertisement for the lost-and-found column telling about a dog that you have found.

B. Write an advertisement asking for a position that you would like.

C. Write an advertisement announcing a new service that you are planning in the distribution of newspapers, mowing lawns, answering telephones, or something more original.

D. Write an advertisement announcing the loss of your brief case. Be sure to give full description and approximate location at time of loss.

E. Write an advertisement offering a used article of furniture for sale.

THE JOB INTERVIEW

To obtain a position, it is frequently necessary to pass the test of the job interview.

Assume that you have been invited by a prospective employer to come in for such an interview. You may have been recommended by your school or by a friend who knows the employer, or you may have written a successful application letter. In any case, the job is not yet yours; perhaps a dozen or more candidates are to be interviewed. You are eager to prepare yourself in every way you can to be the successful candidate.

It is a help to realize that the principles behind a successful job interview are the same as those behind a good application letter. A good first impression, a clear and well-organized presentation of your qualifications, and an attitude of courtesy, tact, and self-respect are the main requirements.

Before going to the interview, find out all you can about the business in which the firm is engaged. Search business reference books and trade papers not only for information about the general field but also for specific items about the objectives and achievements of the firm to which you are applying. This preparation will help you to meet the interviewer on his own ground.

The head of the vocational and educational department of the New York Board of Education has stated that of twenty boys who apply for a job, it is quite possible that ten will be disqualified because of their appearance. It is not necessary (for most jobs it is not even desirable) that you have the features of a movie star, but it is necessary that you appear healthy, rested, and well groomed. Be sure that you have had a recent bath and that your hair and nails are well cared for. Wear business clothes, conservative in style and preferably of a dark color. See that your clothes are well pressed and brushed and, of course, spotless. Girls, wear a hat (not a scarf) and stockings, and be sure that your stocking seams are straight.

Knowing you look your best will help you to feel comfortable and poised when the interview begins. Unless a secretary has announced you, it will be necessary for you to give your name to the interviewer and say that you have come at his suggestion to apply for the position; do this as briefly as possible, looking straight at the interviewer. You should also look straight at him frequently during the interview, but not so frequently as to embarrass him. From the introduction on, let the interviewer take full charge of the conversation. Do not offer to shake hands; do not sit down unless you are invited to do so; stand or sit still; and do not chew gum.

The interviewer will ask you questions about your training and experience and perhaps about your general attitudes and interests. If you did not write a letter of application for this job, it is a good plan to bring with you a neatly typed summary, in tabular form, of your qualifications. The summary should include education, previous experience, and personal details such as age and marital status. When the interviewer asks the first question about one of these points, answer it; then hand him the summary, saying, "This will give you a brief view of the whole picture."

If further questions are asked, answer clearly and fully even though the desired information is given in the summary: one purpose of the questions is to give you an opportunity to talk. It is well to have memorized a short statement about your education and experience (with dates) so that you will not flounder in trying to recall precise details. Speak distinctly and as though you mean what you say. Do not ramble. Show that you understand the requirements of the job and concentrate on proving that your training and experience fit you to fill it. The employer is interested in hiring a person who will be useful to him rather than in giving you a chance for advancement; therefore, emphasize what you have to offer him rather than what you hope to gain for yourself.

The interviewer may be of the expansive type: he may spend considerable time in describing his business to you or even in recounting his personal achievements. In that case, all that is necessary is to listen attentively and show that you understand what he is talking about. Or he may be a man of few words and may ask only a few searching, even blunt, questions. Do not try to lead such a person to talk about his business (he may think it is not your affair), but ask any questions necessary to make sure that you understand what will be expected of you.

The interviewer will usually indicate by a pause in his remarks that the interview is over. At this point, rise and prepare to leave promptly. The interviewer may ask you to telephone, or he may say that he will inform you by letter of his decision. If he does not do this, it is proper to say, "May I call in a few days to find out what you have decided?" Then thank him for seeing you, say good-by, and leave quietly.

When you reach home, it is a good idea to write a brief note thanking the interviewer for the time he gave you and reminding him of any points brought out in the interview which you thought made a particularly good impression on him.

FOR THE CLASS TO TALK ABOUT

A. In answer to an invitation from the employer, you go to apply for a position. The secretary directs you to the door of the employer's office. The door is closed. Should you (1) knock, (2) walk right in, (3) ask the secretary whether you should enter, (4) sit or stand outside until someone gives you further instructions?

B. When you enter the office, the interviewer is busy at his desk. He does not look up or greet you. Should you (1) wait; (2) say, "I am John Blank. I've come to apply for the clerical position which is open in your firm"; (3) sit down and light a cigarette; (4) back out of the office; (5) cough to attract his attention?

C. Some interviewers have devised "tests" which they use on applicants for positions. Some of the tests are peculiar and even unfair. One of these is to leave a wad of paper in a conspicuous position on the floor near the door by which the applicant enters the office. The test turns on whether the applicant picks up the paper or not. One interviewer may think it shows neatness and willingness to oblige if you pick it up; another may think the same action shows officiousness or meddling. If confronted with this situation, how should you act?

D. The interviewer asks why you left your last position. As a matter of fact, you were discharged. What should you say?

E. The interviewer asks what experience you have had. You have never worked in an office before. What should you say?

F. The interviewer inquires whether you smoke. You do, and you do not know what his attitude is. What should you say?

G. The interviewer asks you to be seated and then looks you in the eye for several seconds without speaking. What should you do?

H. The interviewer asks you a question about your race, religion, nationality, or marital status. You have reason to fear that a truthful answer will mean your rejection. What should you say?

I. The employer asks what salary you would be willing to accept. What answer will you give?

J. On your first day at work, your employer has given you a task and then abandoned you to your own devices. He has not introduced you to anyone. No one has told you where to find the rest room. What should you do?

K. When lunch hour arrives, everyone hurries out of the office, leaving you to wonder where you can go to lunch. What will you do?

L. On your first day at the office, you have worn the same conservative clothes that you wore to the interview. You notice that most of your co-workers are in shirt sleeves. Is it better to imitate them or to retain your more formal dress?

M. A friend calls you at the office to make a social engagement. You answer the telephone, which is at your employer's elbow. How can you end the conversation quickly and tactfully, and how can you prevent such incidents from occurring often?

N. One or more of the employees take it upon themselves to "warn" you against another employee on the ground that he is a talebearer. How will you respond?

O. You notice a slight error in another employee's work. Should you (1) call the employee's attention to the error, (2) inform your supervisor, (3) inform the head of the firm, (4) say nothing about it?

APPENDIX

Conjugation of TO TAKE

Principal Parts

Present: take   *Present Participle:* taking
Past: took   *Past Participle:* taken

Indicative Mood

ACTIVE VOICE   PASSIVE VOICE

Present Tense

SINGULAR	PLURAL	SINGULAR	PLURAL
1. I take	we take	I *am* taken	we *are* taken
2. you take	you take	you *are* taken	you *are* taken
3. he * takes	they take	he *is* taken	they *are* taken

Past Tense

1. I took	we took	I *was* taken	we *were* taken
2. you took	you took	you *were* taken	you *were* taken
3. he took	they took	he *was* taken	they *were* taken

Future Tense

1. I *shall* take	we *shall* take	I *shall be* taken	we *shall be* taken
2. you *will* take	you *will* take	you *will be* taken	you *will be* taken
3. he *will* take	they *will* take	he *will be* taken	they *will be* taken

Present Perfect Tense

1. I *have* taken	we *have* taken	I *have been* taken	we *have been* taken
2. you *have* taken	you *have* taken	you *have been* taken	you *have been* taken
3. he *has* taken	they *have* taken	he *has been* taken	they *have been* taken

Past Perfect Tense

1. I *had* taken	we *had* taken	I *had been* taken	we *had been* taken
2. you *had* taken	you *had* taken	you *had been* taken	you *had been* taken
3. he *had* taken	they *had* taken	he *had been* taken	they *had been* taken

Future Perfect Tense

1. I *shall have* taken	we *shall have* taken	I *shall have been* taken	we *shall have been* taken
2. you *will have* taken	you *will have* taken	you *will have been* taken	you *will have been* taken
3. he *will have* taken	they *will have* taken	he *will have been* taken	they *will have been* taken

* *She* and *it* and *singular nouns* are used just as *he* is.

Subjunctive Mood

ACTIVE VOICE	PASSIVE VOICE

Present Tense

if I, you, he take | if I, you, he *be* taken
if we, you, they, take | if we, you, they *be* taken

Past Tense

if I, you, he took | if I, you, he *were* taken
if we, you, they took | if we, you, they *were* taken

Present Perfect Tense

if I, you, he *have* taken | if I, you, he *have been* taken
if we, you, they *have* taken | if we, you, they *have been* taken

Past Perfect Tense

if I, you, he *had* taken | if I, you, he *had been* taken
if we, you, they *had* taken | if we, you, they *had been* taken

Imperative Mood

take | *be* taken

Infinitives

Present: to take | to *be* taken
Perfect: to *have* taken | to *have been* taken

Participles

Present: taking | *being* taken
Past: taken | taken
Perfect: *having* taken | *having been* taken

Gerunds

Present: taking | *being* taken
Perfect: *having* taken | *having been* taken

The Verb TO BE

Principal Parts

Present: be | *Present Participle:* being
Past: was | *Past Participle:* been

Indicative Mood

Present Tense

SINGULAR	PLURAL
I am	we are
you are	you are
he is	they are

Present Perfect Tense

SINGULAR	PLURAL
I have been	we have been
you have been	you have been
he has been	they have been

Past Tense

I was	we were
you were	you were
he was	they were

Past Perfect Tense

I had been	we had been
you had been	you had been
he had been	they had been

Future Tense

I shall be	we shall be
you will be	you will be
he will be	they will be

Future Perfect Tense

I shall have been	we shall have been
you will have been	you will have been
he will have been	they will have been

SUBJUNCTIVE MOOD

SINGULAR — PLURAL

Present Tense

if I *be*	if we *be*
if you *be*	if you *be*
if he *be*	if they *be*

Past Tense

if I *were*	if we *were*
if you *were*	if you *were*
if he *were*	if they *were*

Present Perfect Tense

if I *have been*	if we *have been*
if you *have been*	if you *have been*
if he *have been*	if they *have been*

Past Perfect Tense

if I *had been*	if we *had been*
if you *had been*	if you *had been*
if he *had been*	if they *had been*

IMPERATIVE MOOD

The imperative mood has only one form: *be*, and one person: *second*.

INFINITIVES

Present: to be
Perfect: to have been

PARTICIPLES

Present: being
Past: been
Perfect: having been

GERUNDS

being

having been

INDEX

A

A, an, the, 52
  capitalized and italicized, 153, 158
  correct use, 58–59, 65
  disregarded in card catalogue, 254
Abbreviations, 154–56
  in footnotes, 274–75
  when not to abbreviate, 154, 333–34
About and *around,* 77
Abstract noun, 25
Abstract words, 127–28
Accept and *except,* 196
Action in narrative, 242
Active voice, 12, 117–18, 119
Ad, colloquial abbreviation, 196
Address. *See* Letter writing
Adjective, 51–60, 64–71
  as objective complement, 52, 56
  classification, 51–53
  comparison, 57–60
  compound, 55–56
  compound direct, hyphen with, 152
  dangling elements, avoid, 67
  defined, 51
  fraction as, hyphen with, 152
  infinitive as, 9, 53, 55–56
  irregular, 57–58
  numeral as, 52
  participial phrase as, 53, 56, 84
  participle as, 8, 53, 56, 59
  possessive noun as, 52
  predicate adjective, 7, 52, 55–56, 64
  pronoun as, 52, 59
  redundant, avoid, 65
  using correctly, 57–59, 64–70
  vivid adjectives, using, 54, 71, 116
Adjective clause, 89–90, 93–95, 97, 98
  to subordinate ideas, 107–8
Adjective phrase, 52–53, 55–56, 62, 71, 84
Adjustment letter, 332, 347–48

Adverb, 60–71
  as conjunction, 86, 143
  comparison, 61
  compound, 60, 63
  confusion with adjective, 61, 64
  dangling elements, avoid, 67
  defined, 60
  formation, 61
  infinitive as, 9, 61
  irregular forms, 61
  kinds, 60–61
  misplaced, avoid, 112–13, 115
  modifying an infinitive, 61
  modifying a participle, 61
  prepositional phrase as, 61
  redundant, avoid, 65–66
  using correctly, 64, 65–66, 67–68, 69–70
  vivid adverbs, using, 62, 71, 116
Adverb clause, 90–92, 93–95, 97, 98
  comma with introductory, 141
  distinguished from nominative absolute, 91
  elliptical, 91, 95
  to subordinate ideas, 106–7
Adverbial objective, 61, 65
Adverbial phrase, 61–62, 71, 84
Advertisements, writing, 352
Affect and *effect,* 196
Aggravate and *annoy,* 196
Agreement
  of pronoun with antecedent, 41–44, 59
  of verb with subject, 10, 46–51
Agree to, on, or *with,* 205
Aim at or *to,* 205
Ain't, avoiding, 21
Allegory, 190–92, 242
Alliteration, 193, 240, 242, 243
Allow, correct use, 20
All ready and *already,* 196
All the farther, all the faster, 68
All together and *altogether,* 196
Allusion, illusion, delusion, 197

359

Almost and *most*, 64
Alright, misused for *all right*, 197
Also, misused as conjunction, 78
Alumni and *alumnae*, 197
Among and *between*, 74
And, misuse of, 75
And's, and so's, avoiding, 104
Antecedent of pronoun, 40, 41–44, 59, 110–11
Antonym, 121, 309
Anxious and *eager*, 197
Any, followed by *other*, 58, 113
Anyway, not *anyways*, 68
Anywhere, not *anywheres*, 68
Apostrophe, 150–51, 164
Apostrophe, figure of speech, 190–92
Application blank, employment, 345
Application letter, 341–45
Appositive, 28, 31, 33–34, 37, 39
  adjective, 52
  aid to expression, 123, 309
  case of, 28, 39
  comma with, 139
  dash with, 148
  dependent clause as, 92, 96
  gerund as, 35
  infinitive as, 35, 37
  to subordinate ideas, 108–9
Apt, liable, likely, 200
Argumentation, 239–42
As—as and *so—as*, 69
As, as how, misused for *that, who*, 73
As, as if, like, 73
At about, misused for *at* or *about*, 78
At and *in*, 77
At and *to*, 73
At, by, with, correct use, 74
Ate or *eaten*, not *et*, 199
Attacked, not *attackted*, 197
Attention line in letter writing, 334, 339
Attributive adjective, 52
Autobiography, 242
Auxiliary verb, 7, 19, 23
Avocation and *vocation*, 197
Awful, awfully, misused, 64
Away, not *way*, 70

B

Bad and *badly*, 64
Badly and *very much*, 69

Balance, colloquial usage, 197
Bar graph, 124
Because, misused for *that*, 79, 113
Because of and *due to*, 79
Become ill, not *take sick*, 22
Behind and *in back of*, 77
Being as, being that, misuse of, 76
Beside and *besides*, 73
Between and *among*, 74
Bibliographies for reference, 261
Bibliography, 263–67, 276–77
Biographical dictionary, 187–88, 259–60
Biography, 242
Blame on, misused for *blame*, 78
Blew or *blown*, not *blowed*, 197
Block form, for a letter, 330, 332, 337
Bodily communication, 281–82
Body of letter, 335–36
Boldface type, how indicated, 82
Books of facts, 258–59
Books to read, choosing, 306
Borrow and *lend*, 19
Bound and *determined*, 197
Brackets, 149
Breathing, improving, 283–84
Bring and *take*, 19
Brought, not *brang* or *brung*, 197
Business letter. *See* Letter writing
Burst or *broken*, not *busted*, 197
But, misuse of, 66, 75
By, misused for *at*, 74

C

Cacophony, 193
Calculate, correct use, 20
Call number, 255–56
Call slip, 255
Can and *may*, 23
Cannot help but, 66
Capitalization, rules for, 156–58
Card catalogue, 254–55
Cardinal number, 52
Caret, when to use, 172
Cartoons, aid to expression, 124
Case
  after *as* and *than*, 40
  defined, 27
  nominative, 27–31, 38–40
    after linking verbs, 28, 39

Case—*Continued*
  objective, 27, 32–37, 39–40
  possessive, 27, 32–33
    apostrophe, use in forming, 40, 150
    time and measurement, 44, 150
    with gerund, 39
    with inanimate objects, 44, 150
    pronoun, 38–40
    with appositives, 28, 39
Cause was . . . , 76
Censor and *censure,* 197
Central idea, 211–19, 237–38
Characterization in narrative, 239, 242
Character sketch, topics for, 225
Christmas and *Xmas,* 154
Ciphers, using, 155
Circle graph, 124
Circumlocution, 209
Clarity of expression, 194, 242
  See also Ideas, expressing clearly; Sentence style, improving
Clause, defined, 85
  See also Adjective clause; Adverb clause; Dependent clause; Elliptical clause; Independent clause; Noun clause; Subordinate clause
Cliché, 190–92, 206–8
Climax, 117–19, 242
Climbed, not *clumb,* 197
Closed punctuation, 332–33
Coherence, in paragraph, 211–19, 222, 242
Collective noun, 25, 48, 164
Colloquial usage
  adjective and adverb forms, 64–65, 68–70
  confused expressions, 196–202
  defined, 5
  noun and pronoun forms, 44–45, 110
  preposition and conjunction forms, 77–80
  verb forms, 18, 21–22, 23–24
Colon, 144–45, 147
Comma, 137–143
  aid to expression, 123
  defined, 137
  following parenthesis or bracket, 149
  rules, 138–39, 140–41
Comma fault, 103–5
Common gender, 27
Common noun, 25, 158
Communication, tools of, 280–90
Comparative degree, 57, 61

Compare to or *with,* 205
Comparison
  aid to expression, 121–22
  avoid double, 58
  avoid incomplete, 76
  defined, 6
  figurative, 121–22, 128, 237
  within group, 58
Comparison of adjectives, 57–60
Comparison of adverbs, 61–62
Complected, misuse of, 59, 197
Complement
  objective, 33, 34, 52, 56
  predicate, 33, 37, 39
Complete predicate, 82–83, 87
Complete subject, 82–83, 87
Complex sentence, 89–97
  defined, 89
Compliment and *complement,* 197
Complimentary close of letter, 336
  capitalization, 158
  comma after, 138
Compose and *comprise,* 198
Compound-complex sentence, 97–99
  defined, 97
Compound elements
  adjectives, 52, 55–56
  adverbs, 60, 63
  dependent clauses, 89, 95
  direct objects, 32, 34, 37
  errors with pronouns in, 39
  indirect objects, 32
  objects of preposition, 32, 52
  order of pronouns, 43
  predicate nominatives, 28, 31
  prepositional phrase, 55–56
  subjects, 27, 30, 82
    agreement of verb with, 48–49
  verbs, 8, 30, 82, 86
Compound noun, 25, 150
Compound number, hyphen in, 152
Compound personal pronoun, 26
Compound sentence, 85–88
  comma in, 141
  conjunctions in, 86
  defined, 86
  distinguished from compound verb, 86
  use of semicolon in, 86, 143
Compound word, hyphen in, 152, 188
Conclusion of speech, 301

Concrete noun, 25
Condition and *shape,* 201
Conflict in narrative, 239, 242
Conjugation
  defined, 6
  verb *to be,* 357–58
  verb *to take,* 356–57
Conjunction, 71–80
  adverb as, 86
  capitalization in titles, 158
  co-ordinate, 72, 76, 86, 106, 141, 143
  correlative, 72, 78, 86
  defined, 72
  in compound sentence, 86
  kinds, 72
  subordinate, 72, 89, 90, 106–7
  using correctly, 73–74, 75–76, 77–79
Conjunctive adverb, 86, 143
Connectives, 26, 219, 242
Connotation of words, 194–95, 284
Consensus, correct use, 78
Considerable, misuse of, 68
Contact, correct use, 24
Contemptible and *contemptuous,* difference between, 198
Context clues, 129–32, 308–9
Continually and *continuously,* 198
Contractions
  avoid confusing possessive pronouns, 40
  using apostrophe in, 151
Contrasted elements, comma to set off, 138
Conversation, 291
Co-ordinate conjunction, 72, 76, 86, 106, 143
Co-ordinate modifiers, comma between, 141
Copulative verb. *See* Linking verb
Corrections and insertions, 172
Correct usage, 14–25, 38–51, 57–60, 64–71, 73–81, 194–210
Correlation with other classes, 50, 60, 69, 77, 80, 90, 92, 105, 109, 112, 115, 119, 121, 128, 132, 140, 143, 160, 170, 209
Correlative conjunction, 72, 86
  correct placement, 78
Creative writing
  appeal to reader's senses, 227
  argumentation, 239–40, 241
  being good observer, 226–27, 251
  defined, 223
  description, 237, 241
  essay, 237–38, 241

Creative writing—*Continued*
  evaluation, 231–36
  exposition, 237, 241
  glossary of terms for, 242–44
  letters of opinion, 229–30
  personal letters, 228–29
  poetry, 240, 241
  short story, 238–39, 241
  topics for composition 223–26, 230–31
Credible, creditable, credulous, 198
Crisis in narrative, 242
Criticism, defined, 242
Cunning, colloquial usage, 198
Cute, colloquial usage, 198

D

Dangling elements, avoiding, 67–69, 111–12
Dash, 123, 148, 149
Data, plural of *datum,* 198
Date, 138, 155
Debate, 296
Decimal point, period as, 135
Decimal, use figures for, 155
Declarative sentence, 81, 134
Declension
  defined, 6
  pronoun, 38
Definition
  aid to expression, 120, 309
  avoid using *when* and *where,* 76, 113
Delusion, allusion, illusion, 197
Demonstrative pronoun, 26, 52
Denotation of words, 194–95, 284
Dependent (subordinate) clause, 89–99
  as adjective modifier, 89–90, 93–95, 97
  compound, 89
  as adverb, 90–92, 94
  as noun, 92–94, 96–97
  defined, 85
  elliptical, 91, 95
  verb tense in, 17
Derivation of words, 178–82
Description
  defined, 242
  guides for writing, 237
  sense appeal, 237, 242, 244
  topics for, 225
Descriptive adjective, 52
Details, aid to creative writing, 226–27

Determined and *bound*, 197
Dewey Decimal System, 256
Diagramming
  adjective clause, 94–95, 97
  adjectives, 55–56, 63–64, 83, 88, 94–95
  adverb clauses, 95, 97, 99
  adverbs, 63–64, 83, 88, 94–95, 99
  appositive, 31, 34, 37, 96
  complex sentence, 94–97, 99
  compound-complex sentence, 99
  compound sentence, 88
  conjunctions, 30–31, 34, 37, 55, 63, 88, 94–96, 99
  dependent clauses, 94–96, 99
  direct object, 34, 36–37, 55, 56, 63–64, 83, 88, 94–96, 99
  elliptical clauses, 95
  gerund, 36–37, 56, 63–64
  independent elements, 30–31, 81, 96
  indirect object, 34, 37, 56, 63–64, 95–96
  infinitive, 36–37, 55–56, 63–64, 95
  interjection, 81
  nominative absolute, 96
  nominative case, 29–31
  nominative of address, 31
  noun clauses, 96
  objective case, 34, 36–37
  objective complement, 34, 56, 96
  object of participle, 56, 63–64
  object of preposition, 55–56, 63–64, 96
  optional use of, 29
  participial phrase, 56, 83
  participle, 56, 95
  possessive noun, 55
  predicate adjective, 55–56, 63–64, 95
  predicate complement, 37
  predicate nominative, 31, 36, 37, 55–56, 94–96
  prepositional phrase, 55 56, 63, 83, 95, 99
  retained object, 34, 96
  steps in, 30
  subject of infinitive, 37
  there, 30
  to analyze sentence structure, 29–31, 34–37, 55–56, 63, 81, 83, 88, 94–96, 99
  verb and subject, 30–31, 34–35, 36–37, 55–56, 63–64, 83, 88, 94–96, 99
Diagrams, aid to expression, 124
Dialectal words, explained, 187
Dialogue, 239, 243

Diction, 175–210
  characteristics needed for good diction, 194
  colloquialisms, 5, 24–25, 39, 42, 44–45, 64, 69–70, 73–74, 77–81, 110, 196–201
  defined, 194
  reference books for, 178
  See also Words
Dictionary, 185–89
  kinds of, 178, 185, 240, 258–59
  types of information, 186–88
  using, 58, 130, 156, 163, 167, 168, 169, 182, 185–89, 195, 290, 310
Didactic writing, 243
Did not, not *never*, 70
Didn't go to, misused for *didn't mean* or *intend to*, 21
Differ from, about, over, or *with*, 205
Different from, not *different than*, 73
Diminutives, 179
Direct address. *See* Nominative of address
Direct object, 32, 33, 34, 35, 36, 37, 39, 55–56, 63–64, 83–84, 88, 94–96, 99, 144
  compound, 32, 34, 37
  dependent clause as, 92–94, 96–97
  gerund as, 35–36
  infinitive as, 35, 37
  of a gerund, 35
  of a participle, 53, 56, 63–64
Direct question, punctuating, 136
Direct quotation. *See* Quotation, direct
Discussion, 294–98
Disinterested and *uninterested*, 198
Disremember, misused for *forget*, 21
Distance or *way*, not *ways*, 65
Documents, source of information, 252–53
Doesn't and *don't*, 46
Double comparison, avoiding. 58
Double negative, avoiding, 66
Double subject, avoiding, 42
Dragged, not *drug*, 198
Drew or *drawn*, not *drawed*, 198
Drowned, not *drownded*, 198
Due to, misused for *because of*, 79

E

Each, agreement with, 48, 49, 59
Eager and *anxious*, 197
Editorial, 243
Effect and *affect*, 196

363

ei or *ie*, 166
Either, agreement with, 48, 59; of *two,* 45
Eligible and *illegible,* 198
Ellipses, 135, 158, 269
Elliptical clause, 91, 95
Elliptical expression, dangling, avoid, 67
Elliptical questions, punctuating, 136
Else's, 40
Emigrate and *immigrate,* 199
Eminent and *imminent,* 199
Empathy, 282
Emphasis
   (force) in paragraph, 211–22, 243
   using dash for, 148
   using italics for, 153
Emphatic forms of verb, 11
Enclosures, indicating, in letter, 337
Encyclopedias, 257–60
Enervating and *invigorating,* 199
Enthuse, correct use, 24
Envelope, 338, 339
Epithets, capitalize, 157
Esq., when to use, 154
Essay, 226, 237–38, 243
Etc., not *and etc.,* 75
Etymology, 178
Euphony, 193
Evaluate, not *size up,* 201
Evaluating motion pictures, 325
Evaluating radio and television, 320–24
Evaluating speech, 302–3
Evaluating writing, 231–36
Every, agreement with, 49, 59
Everybody, using *they* with, 42
Everywhere, not *everywheres,* 68
Exact language, aid to expression, 127–28
Except and *accept,* 196
Exceptional and *exceptionable,* 199
Except, misused for *unless,* 76
Except, outside of, 77
Exclamation mark, 136–37, 147
   after interjection, 81
Exclamatory sentence, 81
Expect, correct use, 20
Explanatory expressions, 143, 148
Expletive, 30, 47, 81, 82
Exposition, 237, 243
Extempore speech, 298
Eye span, in reading, 311

F

Family names, 157, 179
Famous and *notorious,* 200
Farther and *further,* 199
Faulty expressions, 196–203
Feminine gender, 27
Fetch, use of, 19
Fewer and *less,* 58
Fiction, 243
Figurative comparison, 128, 190, 237
Figurative language, 189–92, 240, 243
Figures (numbers), 152, 155
Figures of speech, 190–92, 243
Filing
   bibliography cards, 263, 276–77
   by subject, 269
   card catalogue, 254
   systems for library books, 256–57
Finished, not *through,* 23
Flashback in narrative, 243
Flat statement, avoiding, 227
Folks, colloquial usage, 199
Following, misused for *after,* 79
Footnote, 274–75
   aid to expression, 122
Force
   in paragraph, 211–22, 243
   vocal force, 284
Forget, not *disremember,* 21
Formally and *formerly,* 199
Fragment of sentence, 8, 9–10, 29, 54, 92, 100–2, 105
   types of, 101
From, not *off* or *off of,* 74
Ful and *full,* 166

G

Gender, explained, 27
Gent and *guy,* 199
Gerund, 35–37, 56
   dangling, avoid, 67
   defined, 9
   object of, 35, 36, 56
   possessive case with, 39
Gerund phrase, 35–36
Gestures, 282
Get, correct use, 23

Glossary
  of faulty expressions, 196–203
  of terms used in creative writing, 242–44
Good and *well*, 64
Good at or *for*, 205
Grammar
  defined, 6
  guides for studying, 5
Grand, colloquial usage, 199
Graphs, aid to expression, 124–26
Great deal, misused for *many*, 70
Grew or *grown*, not *growed*, 199
Group comparison, 58
Guess, correct use, 20
Guidebooks for reference, 261
Guides
  argumentation, writing, 239–40
  bibliography, compiling, 266
  conversationalist, how to be good, 291
  description, writing, 237
  essays, writing, 237–38
  exposition, writing, 237
  figures of speech, recognizing, 190
  grammar, studying, 5
  interview, conducting, 292
  interviewing, 252
  job interview, 292
  letters of opinion, writing, 229
  library books, obtaining, 255
  manuscript form, correct, 170
  notes, taking, 269
  poetry, writing, 240
  proofreading, what to look for in, 133
  radio and television
    appearing on, what to remember in, 293
    standards of selection, 322
  report, preparing final draft, 277
  short stories, writing, 238–39
  spelling, 163
  studying, 313
  syntax, solving problems in, 83
  telephoning, what to remember in, 291

H

Hackneyed expressions, 206–8
Had of, *would of*, avoiding, 19
Had ought, 19
Handwritten copy, 170–71, 339, 345
Hardly, in double negative, 79

Heading, letter, 332–33, 336
Healthy, healthful, wholesome, 199
Himself, not *hisself*, 42
His or *one's*, 45
History of words, 178, 180
How, misused for *that*, 73
Hyperbole, 190–92, 238
Hyphen, 152, 166, 169, 188

I

I and *me*, 39
Ibid., explained, 274–75
Ideas, expressing clearly
  comparisons, 121–22
  context, helpful, 129–32, 308–9
  definition, explanatory, 120
  footnotes, 122
  illustrations, 124–26
  interpolated expressions, 123
  language, exact and concrete, 127–28
  language, simple, 126–27, 227
  meanings of words, correct, 175–92
  parentheses, 122
  quotation marks, 122
  sounds of words, 193
  summarizing expressions, 132
  synonyms and antonyms, 121
  underscoring, 122
  usage of words, 194–210
  See also Sentence style, improving
Ideas, ways to subordinate, 107–9
Idiomatic usage, 204–5
ie or *ei*, 166
If, misused for *whether*, 79
Illegible and *eligible*, 198
Illiterate usage. *See* Words
Illusion, allusion, delusion, 197
Illustrations, aid to expression, 124–26
Imagery in writing, 243
Immigrate and *emigrate*, 199
Imminent and *eminent*, 199
Impatient with, of, or *at*, 205
Imperative mood, 13
Imperative sentence, 81, 134
Imply and *infer*, 19
Impromptu speech, 298
In and *into*, 74
In and *at*, 77
In back of and *behind*, 77

Indefinite pronoun, 26
  as adjective, 52
  as antecedent, 42
    agreement of verb, 48
  avoid *you, it, they* as, 44
  gender, 42
  number, 42
  one's and *his,* 45
  possessive case of, 40, 150
Indented form, for a letter, 330
Independent clause, 86–99
  defined, 85
Independent elements, 30–31, 47, 81, 91, 123
Indicative mood, 13
Indirect object, 32, 34, 35, 39, 61
  compound, 32
  dependent clause as, 92–94, 96–97
  gerund as, 35
  of a participle, 53
Indirect question, period with, 135
Indirect quotation, 17, 147
Infinitive
  as adjective, 9, 53, 55–56
  as adverb, 9, 61
  as appositive, 35, 37
  as direct object, 35, 37
  as object of preposition, 35
  as predicate nominative, 35
  as subject, 35–36
  dangling, avoid, 67, 111–12
  defined, 9
  modified by adverb, 61
  modified by adverb clause, 90, 95
  object of, 32, 39
  predicate complement, 33, 37, 39
  subject of, 32, 35, 37, 39
  when *to* is omitted, 35
Infinitive phrase, 36, 53–54, 61
  to subordinate ideas, 109
Inflection, grammatical, 6
Inflection of voice, 285
Information, sources of, 250–67
Ingenious and *ingenuous,* 200
Initials, 135, 157, 337
Inquiry, letters of, 348–50
Inside address of letter, 332, 334
Inside or *inside of,* misused for *within,* 77
Instance, instant, incident, 200
Intensive pronoun, 26, 44
Interjection, 81, 84, 140

Interpolation, aid to expression, 123
Interrogation point. *See* Question mark
Interrogative pronoun, 26, 38, 52
Interrogative sentence, 81
Interview
  guides for, 252
  how to conduct, 292
  job, 292, 352–55
  personal, 251–52
In the worst way, misused for *very much,* 68
Into and *in,* 74
Intransitive verb, 12
Introduction
  of speaker, 302
  of speech, 301
  social, making and acknowledging, 293
Invigorating and *enervating,* 199
Irony, 190–92
Irregardless, misused for *regardless,* 200
Irregular verb, 11, 14–16
Italics, 82, 153, 171
Its and *it's,* 40

J

Job, securing
  application blank, 345
  application letter, 341–45
  interview for, 292, 352–55

K

Key words, in reading, 312
Kind of and *sort of,* 69
Kind of a, sort of a, type of a, avoiding, 70
Kind, sort, type, singular, 59
Knew or *known,* not *knowed,* 200

L

Later and *latter,* 200
Latin word elements, 180, 182, 310
Lay and *lie,* 15–16
Learn and *teach,* 19
Leave, not *lief,* 68
Lecture-forum discussion, 296
Lend and *borrow,* 19
Less and *fewer,* 58
Let and *leave,* 20
Letterhead, business, 330, 333, 336

Letter writing
  addressing the envelope, 339
  block form, 330, 332, 337, 343, 346, 348, 349
  business letters, 340–50
  diagnostic test (pretest), 329–30
  enclosures, indicating, 337
  folding, 338
  general appearance, 330
  heading for second page, 336
  indented form, 330
  initials, dictator's and transcriber's, 337
  mastery test, 340
  opinion letters, 131, 229–31, 319, 323
  parts of letter
    body, 335–36
    complimentary close, 336
      capitalization, 158
      comma after, 138
    heading, 333
    inside address, 334
    salutation, 334
      business letter: colon after, 144, 334
      capitalization, 158
      social letter: comma after, 138
    signature, 336–37
  personal letters, 220, 228–29
  punctuation, open and closed, 332–33, 337, 339, 343–44, 346, 348, 349
  semiblock form, 330–31
  stationery, 330, 333, 336
Levels of usage. *See* Usage
Liable, likely, apt, 200
Library, 253–67
  card catalogue, 254–55
  classification of books, systems, 256–57
  reference books, 178, 185, 240, 257–63
Library of Congress system, 256–57
Like, as, as if, 73
Limiting adjective, 52
Line graph, 124
Linguistics, 178
Linking (copulative) verb, 7, 12, 28, 52, 64
Listening
  being a good listener, 326–27
  to radio and television, 319–24
  to yourself, 284–90
Locate and settle, 200
Looking
  at motion pictures, 324–26
  at television, 283, 319–24

Lose and *loose,* 200
Lots, misused for *very much, very,* 70
Loudness of voice, 285–86
Luxuriant and *luxurious,* 200

M

Magazines, reading, 314–16
Main clause. *See* Independent clause
Maintenance activities
  follow-up, 21, 41, 44, 50, 60, 65, 66, 69, 102, 119, 140, 160, 168, 208, 241, 283, 290, 316
  review, 24–25, 46, 50–51, 71, 80–81, 161–62, 209–10
Man and *guy,* 199
Manuscript form, 170–71
  correction symbols, 172
Many, not *great deal,* 70
Map graph, 125
Margins for manuscript, 170
Masculine gender, 27
  with indefinite pronouns, 42
May and *can,* 23
May be and *maybe,* 200
Me for *I,* 39
Messrs., Misses, Mmes., use of, 165, 334
Metaphor, 190–92, 243
Metonymy, 190–92
Mighty, for *very,* 70
Monosyllables, 165, 169
Mood in writing, 243
Mood of verb, 13, 18
More, not *worse,* 68
Most and *almost,* 64
Motion pictures, viewing, 324–26
Myself, correct use, 44

N

Narration, defined, 243
Neither, agreement with, 48, 59; of *two,* 45
Neologisms, 182
Never for *did not,* avoiding, 70
Newspaper, 311, 314, 316–19
Nice, colloquial usage, 200
No and *yes,* comma with, 140
Nohow, avoiding, 68
Nominative absolute, 91, 96, 109
Nominative case, 27–31, 38–40

Nominative of address (direct), 28, 31, 138
Nonfiction, 243
Nonrestrictive clause, 89–90, 139
  aid to expression, 107–8, 123
Nonrestrictive phrase, 123, 139
No sooner than, 79
Notes, taking, 252, 268–70, 273
Notorious and *famous,* 200
Noun, 25–51
  as appositive, 28, 31, 33–34, 37, 39
  as adverbial objective, 61, 65
  as direct object, 32, 33, 34, 39, 55–56, 63–64, 83–84, 88, 94–96, 99, 144
  as indirect object, 32, 34, 35
  as objective complement, 33, 34
  as object of infinitive, 32, 35
  as object of preposition, 32, 52–53, 55–56, 61, 71
  as predicate complement, 33
  as predicate nominative, 7, 28, 31, 47, 56
  as retained object, 33, 34
  as subject, 27–31, 82, 84
  as subject of infinitive, 32, 35, 37
  case, 27–35
  classification, 25
  defined, 25
  gerund as, 9, 35–37, 39, 56
  infinitive as, 9, 35–37
  number, singular and plural, 26, 164–65
  possessive, as adjective, 52
  properties of, 26–28, 32–33
  strong nouns, using, 116–19
  using correctly, 39–40, 42–43, 44–45, 46–49
  we and *us* used with, 39
Noun clause, 17, 92–94, 96–98
Novel, 243
Nowhere near for *not nearly,* avoiding, 68
Nowhere, not *nowheres,* 68
Number
  of nouns and pronouns, 26, 38, 41–42
  of verb, 10, 114–15, 198
  plural, use of apostrophe, 151
Numbers (figures), 52, 152, 154–55

O

Objective case, 27, 32–40
Objective complement, 33, 34
  adjective as, 52, 56
  dependent clause as, 92–94, 96–97

Object of infinitive, 32, 39
Object of participle, 53, 56, 63–64
Object of preposition, 32, 35, 39, 52, 55–56, 71
  compound, 32, 52
  dependent clause as, 92–94, 96–97
  gerund as, 35
  infinitive as, 35
Object of verb. *See* Direct object
Observation, 226–27, 250–51
Off or *off of,* misused for *from,* 74
Of, misused for *have,* 19, 73
On account of, misuse of, 76
One's or *his,* 45
Only, in double negative, 66
On, misused for *for,* 74
Onomatopoeia, 193, 240
Op. cit., explained, 275
Open punctuation, 332–33, 337
Opinion letter, 131, 229–31, 319, 323
Oral and *verbal,* 202
Order letter, 345–47
Ought, 19
Outline
  for discussion, 295
  for speech, 301
  kinds of, 271–72
  note cards, arranging to fit, 273
  punctuation, 135, 271–72
  See also Report
Outside of, misused for *except, except for,* 77
Overrun by or *with,* 205

P

Panel discussion, 296, 318, 321, 323
Panel-forum discussion, 296
Pantomime, 283
Paragraph, 211–22
  central thought, 211–19
  coherence in, 211–19, 222
  concluding a paragraph, 221
  defined, 211
  development, types of, 215–17
  force or emphasis in, 211–22, 243
  for each change of speaker, 146, 214
  quotation marks, where to place, 146
  single-sentence, 222
  topic sentence, 212–14
  transitional, 220
  unity in, 211–19, 222

Parallel structure, 17, 76, 114–15, 271–72
Paraphrase, 268–70, 273, 275
Parentheses, 135–36, 148–49
  aid to expression, 122
Parenthetical elements, 138, 148
Participial phrase, 53–54, 56, 84, 336
  to subordinate ideas, 109
Participle
  as adjective, 8, 53, 56, 59
  dangling, avoid, 67, 111–12
  defined, 8
  indirect object of, 53
  modified by adverb, 61
  modified by adverb clause, 90, 95
  object of, 53, 56, 63–64
Parts of speech
  defined, 6
  See also Adjective; Adverb; Conjunction; Interjection; Noun; Preposition; Pronoun; Verb
Party, misused for *person*, 201
Passive voice, 12, 117–19
Patronymics, 179
Payment letter, 348
Penmanship, improving, 170–71
Per cent, spell out, 155
Percentage, use figures for, 155
Period, 134–36, 147, 154
Periodic sentence, 117–19
Persecute and *prosecute*, 201
Person of nouns and pronouns, 27, 41–43
  order of pronouns in compounds, 43
  shifts, avoid, 45, 114–15
Personal letter, 220, 228–29
Personal pronoun, 26, 38–40, 44–45, 52
Personification, 158, 190–92, 243
Philology, 178
Phrase, 108–9, 139–40
Picture graph, 125
Pie or circle graph, 124
Pitch of voice, 285
Plagiarism, 243
Plenty, colloquial usage, 201
Plot, 239, 243
Plumb, colloquial usage, 201
Plural, 10, 26, 38, 41–42
  rules for forming plural nouns, 164–65
Poetic words, 188
Poetry, 240–41, 243, 287, 290, 303
  capitalization, 158

Poorly, incorrect use, 69
Positive degree
  adjective, 57–58
  adverb, 61
Possessive case, 27, 32–33
  apostrophe, use in forming, 40, 150
  time and measurement, 44, 150
  with gerund, 39
  with inanimate objects, 44, 150
Possessive noun as adjective, 52
Possessive personal pronouns, 40
Posture, 282
Practical and *practicable*, 201
Predicate
  complete, 82–83, 87
  See also Verb
Predicate adjective, 7, 52, 55–56, 64
Predicate complement, 33, 37, 39
Predicate nominative, 7, 28, 31, 39, 47, 56, 144
  dependent clause as, 92–94, 96–97
  gerund as, 35, 37
  infinitive as, 35
Prefix, 166, 180–82, 310
Preposition, 71–80
  capitalization, 158
  defined, 71
  idiomatic usage, 204–5
  list, 72
  object of, 32, 35, 39, 52, 55–56, 71
  phrasal, 72
  redundant, avoid, 74
  to end a sentence, 79
  using correctly, 73–74, 75–76, 77–79
Prepositional phrase
  as adjective, 52, 55–56, 62, 71–72, 84
  as adverb, 61, 72
  compounded with noun, 152
  defined, 52, 72
  to subordinate ideas, 108–9
Principal and *principle*, 201
Principal parts of verbs, 11, 14, 188
Progressive verb, 11
Projection of voice, 286
Prolixity, 209
Pronominal adjective, 52, 59
Pronoun, 25–51
  antecedent, 40–44, 59, 110–11
  appositive, 28, 33, 39
  as adjective, 52, 59
  as direct object, 32, 34, 39, 88, 95–96

Pronoun—*Continued*
  as indirect object, 32, 34, 39, 61, 63
  as objective complement, 33
  as object of infinitive, 32, 39
  as object of preposition, 32, 39, 52, 55–56
  as predicate complement, 33, 37, 39
  as predicate nominative, 28, 31, 39
  as retained object, 33
  as subject of infinitive, 32, 37, 39
  as subject of verb, 27–28, 30, 31, 36–37, 39, 56, 63, 94–96, 99
  case, 27–28, 38–40, 150
    with *to be,* 28, 31, 33, 37, 39
  classification, 26
  declension, 38
  defined, 26
  faulty reference, avoid, 43–45, 110–11, 115
  gender, 27, 41–42
  illiterate forms, 42
  number, 26, 38, 41–42
  person, 27, 41–43
    order in compounds, 43
    shifts, avoid, 45
  properties of, 26–28
  redundant, avoid, 43
  using correctly, 38–51
    agreement of verb with subject, 46–49
    agreement with antecedent, 41–44
    case of pronouns, 38–40
    miscellaneous pronoun faults, 42–45
Pronunciation
  aid to spelling, 163, 166–68
  dictionary indicates, 187
  difficult because of word divisions, 169
  elements of correct, 289
  words often mispronounced, 290
Proofreading, 133–72; guides, 133
  abbreviations and numbers, 154–55
  capitalization, 156–62
  corrections and insertions, 172
  final check in report, 278
  manuscript form, 170–71
  punctuation, 134–56
  spelling, 163–68
  syllabication, 169–70
Proofreading written work, 102, 105, 119, 131, 140, 143, 160, 170, 228, 230, 241, 278, 316, 326
Propaganda, 253
Proper adjective, 52

Proper name, 154, 178–79
Proper noun
  capitalized, 156–57
  compounds ending in, 152
  defined, 25
  family names, 179
  forming plural of, 165
Prose, 244
Proven, for *proved,* 24
Proverbs and quotations, outworn, 206
Providing, misused for *provided,* 79
Punctuation, 134–56
  external, 134–37
    exclamation mark, 81, 136–37, 147
    period, 134–35, 147, 154
    question mark, 136–37
  internal, 137–45
    colon, 144–45, 147, 334
    comma, 52, 81, 89, 137–43, 147, 149
    semicolon, 86, 143–44, 147
  open and closed, 332–33, 337
  pairs of punctuation marks, 145–49
    brackets, 148–49
    dash, 148–49
    parentheses, 135, 136, 148–49
    quotation marks, 135, 136, 145–48, 243, 264, 269, 273
  special marks, 150–52
    apostrophe, 40, 150–51
    hyphen, 152, 166, 169, 188
  See also Italics; Underlining

Q

Quality of voice, 285
Question mark, 136–37
Quiet and *quite,* 201
Quotation, direct, 138, 145–46, 158
  in notes, how to incorporate, 268–69
  in report, how to incorporate, 243, 273, 275
Quotation, indirect, 147
Quotation marks, 145–48
  aid to expression, 122
  used on bibliography card, 264
Quotations and proverbs, outworn, 206

R

Radio, 293, 319–24
Raise and *rear,* 20

Raise and *rise*, 15
Rather, not *some,* 64
Readers' Guide, 261
Reading, 304–19
   in thought phrases, 286–87, 303, 311
   poetry, 240–41, 243, 287, 290, 303
   speech from manuscript, 299
Real, for *very* or *really,* 64
Reason . . . because, misused, 113
Reckon, correct use, 20
Recommend, colloquial usage, 201
Redundance, 208
   avoiding, 43, 65–66, 74
Reference books
   bibliographies, 261
   books of facts, 258–59
   defined, 257
   dictionaries, 178, 185, 240, 258–59
   encyclopedias, 257–60
   guidebooks, 261
   guides to periodicals, 261–62
   special reference works, 259–60
Reflexive pronoun, 26, 42, 44
Regardless, not *irregardless,* 200
Relative pronoun, 26, 38, 43, 52
   agreement of verb with, 49
   to introduce adjective clause, 89
   to subordinate ideas, 107–8
Remainder and *balance,* 197
Report, 246–78
   bibliography, 276–77
   final draft, 277–78
   first draft, 273; revising, 276
   footnotes, 274–75
   originality, 278
   outline
      final, 270–71
      preliminary, 249–50
      working, 267–68
   paraphrases, 273, 275
   proofreading, 278
   quotations, 243, 273, 275
   sources of information, 250–67
   subjects for, 248–49
   table of contents, 278
   title page, 278
Reports, oral, 125–26, 183, 246–47, 262–63
   preparing speech, 298–301
Request letter, 348–50
Research, 245–78

Respectively and *respectfully,* 201
Restrictive clause, 89
Retained object, 33, 34
   dependent clause as, 92–94, 96–97
Reverend, use of, 201
Review practice. *See* Maintenance
Right as adverb of degree, avoid, 68
Round-table discussion, 295
Run-on sentence, 102–105

S

Said, misused as modifier, 201
Saint, abbreviation for, 154
Same, incorrect as pronoun, 45, 201
Says, misused for *said,* 17
Scarcely, in double negative, 79
Schedule, time, for students, 305, 307–8
Seldom ever, incorrect use, 65
Self, compounds with, hyphen with, 152
Semantics, 129–32, 195
Semiblock form, for a letter, 330–31
Semicolon, 86, 143–44, 147
Sentence
   analysis of, 82–99
      method of procedure, 84
   comma fault, 103–5
   defined, 81, 100
   kinds (meaning), 81
   kinds (structure), 82–99
   loose construction, 117–19
   periodic construction, 117–19
Sentence outline, 271–72
Sentence style, improving
   forceful sentences, using, 116–19
   phrasing, 36, 53, 119–32
   reference, establishing clear, 110–15
      dangling modifiers, avoid, 67–69, 111–12
      illogical constructions, avoid, 113–15
      misplaced modifiers, avoid, 67, 112–13, 115
      parallel structure, maintaining, 17, 76, 114–15, 271–72
      pronouns, 43–45, 110–11, 115
      verbals, 111–12, 115
   relating ideas within sentences, 102–10
Sequence of tenses, 17, 114–15
Series, words in, 140, 144
Set and *sit,* 14–15
Setting of narrative, 244

Settle and *locate*, 200
Shall and *will*, 23
Shape and *condition*, 201
Short story, 238–39, 244
Should and *would*, 23
Show up, colloquial usage, 201
Sic, bracketed, 149
Signature of letter, 336–37
Simile, 190–92, 243, 244
Simple predicate, 7, 29, 54, 82–83
Simple sentence, 82–84, 86
  defined, 82
Simple subject, 82–83
Size up. Slang for *evaluate, understand*, 201
Skimming, in reading, 312
Slang, 184
Sneaked, not *snuck*, 201
So—as and *as—as*, 69
Some for *rather* or *somewhat*, 64
Somewhere, not *somewheres*, 68
So, misused for *so that, exceedingly, very*, 202
Sort, kind, type, singular, 59
Sort of a, kind of a, type of a, avoiding, 70
Sort of and *kind of*, 69
Speaker, introduction of, 302
Specie and *species*, 202
Speech, 279–303
  discussion, 294–98
  evaluating, 302–3
  informal activities, 291–93
  introducing a speaker, 302
  making a speech, 298–301
  rate of speaking, 286
Spelling, 163–68
  when to spell out numbers, 155
  words often misspelled, 167, 196–202
Squinting modifier, 67–69
Standard English usage
  changing language, 177–85
  defined, 5
  world language, 175–77
  See also Words
Stationery for letters, 330
Stole or *stolen*, not *stoled*, 202
Stop and *stay*, 202
Studying, guides to better, 313
Subject
  agreement of verb with, 10, 46–49, 51
  avoid double, 42
  complete, 82–83, 87

Subject—*Continued*
  compound, 27, 30, 82
    agreement of verb with, 48–49
  dependent clause as, 92–94, 96–97
  gerund as, 35
  infinitive as, 35–36
  of infinitive, 32, 35, 37, 39
  shifts in voice and subject, avoid, 20
  simple, 82–83
Subject for a report, 247–50
Subject for speech, 299–300
Subjunctive mood, 13, 18
Subordinate conjunction, 72, 89–90, 106–7
Subordinate (dependent) clause, 85
  avoiding shifts from verbal to, 114–15
  See also Dependent clause
Subordination, defined, 106
Substantive, 25, 82
Suffix, 180–81, 310
  rules for adding, 165–66
Superlative degree, 57–61
Superscript, defined, 274
Sure and *surely*, 64
Suspense, 117–19, 244
Suspicion, misused for *suspect*, 22
Syllabication, 152, 169
Symposium, 296
Synonym, 309
  aid to expression, 121, 189
Syntax, 6, 82–83

T

Table of contents, research paper, 278
Take and, avoiding, 22
Take and *bring*, 19
Take sick, misused for *become ill*, 22
Tautology, 208
Teach and *learn*, 19
Telegrams, writing, 350–51
Telephoning, what to remember in, 291
Television, 293, 319–24
Tense, 10–11, 17, 114–15
Testing program, explained, iv, 6
That, not *where*, 73
That or *which*, not *what*, 43
Them, misused as demonstrative, 42, 59
There as expletive, 30, 47, 82
These (or *those*) *kind* or *sort*, avoiding, 59
They with *everybody*, using, 42

This here, that there, avoiding, 42, 65
Threw or *thrown,* not *throwed,* 202
Through, misused for *finished,* 23
Till and *until,* 202
Till, until, misused for *when,* 76
Time, 44, 145, 150, 154–55, 157
Title, 239, 249
Title page, research paper, 278
Titles, writing
  capitalization, 158
  for persons, 154, 157, 165, 334
  quotation marks with, 147
  underlining, 153
To and *at,* 73
Too to modify past participle, avoid, 70
Topic outline, 271–72
Topic sentence, 212–14
Topics, 225–26, 248–49, 324, 326
Transition in writing, 219–20, 244
Transitive verb, 12, 32
Transposed elements, comma with, 139
Trite expressions, 190, 192, 206
  in business letters, 335
  in conversation, 206–8
Try to, not *try and,* 79
Type, kind, sort, singular, 59
Type of a, kind of a, sort of a, avoiding, 70
Typewritten copy, rules for, 171

U

Underlining, 122, 153, 171, 264–65
Understand, not *size up,* 201
Uninterested and *disinterested,* 198
Unity, 103–5, 211–19, 222, 244
Unless, not *except* or *without,* 76
Usage, correct, 14–25, 38–51, 57–60, 64–71, 73–81, 194–210
Usage, levels of, 5
  colloquial, 18, 21–24, 44–45, 64, 65, 68–70, 77–80, 110, 196–202
  illiterate, 17, 19–22, 42, 59, 64–66, 68–70, 73–76, 196–202
  standard English, 14–15, 17–24, 38–49, 57–59, 64–70, 73–79, 190, 192, 196–202, 204–8, 335
Us and *we,* used with nouns, 39
Used to could, avoid, 22
Using English in all classes.
  See Correlation with other classes

V

Verb, 7–25
  agreement with subject, 10, 46–49, 51
  as simple predicate, 7, 29, 54, 82–83
  auxiliary, 7, 19, 23
  compound, 8, 30, 82, 86
  defined, 7
  distinguished from verbal, 8–9
  emphatic forms, 11
  intransitive, 12
  irregular, 11, 14–16
  linking, 7, 12, 28, 52, 64
  misused as noun, 22
  mood, 13, 18
  more than one word, 7–8
  number, 10
  of action, 7–8, 10–11
  of condition, 7–8, 10–11
  omitting *ed* from past tense, 20
  one word, 7
  person, 10
  principal parts, 11, 14, 188
  progressive forms, 11
  properties of, 10–13
  regular, 11, 14
  repeated if different form needed, 23
  repeated to make sentence clear, 19, 20
  shifts in person, number, voice, tense, avoid, 114–15
  strong verbs, using, 24, 60, 62, 116–19
  tense, 10–11, 17
  transitive, 12, 32
  troublesome, 14, 19
  using correctly, 14–15, 17–24
  voice, 12–13, 117–19
  with separated parts, 8
Verbal
  as adjective modifier, 8–9, 53
  infinitive, 9, 53, 55–56
  participial phrase, 53–54, 56, 84, 109, 336
  participle, 8, 53, 56, 59
  as noun gerund, 8–9, 35–37, 56
  as noun infinitive, 9, 35–37
  confusion with verb, avoid, 8–9
  defined, 8
  faulty reference, avoid, 111–12, 115
  shifts in, avoid, 114–15
  See also Gerund; Infinitive; Participle
Verbal and *oral,* 202

Verbal phrase, 35–36, 53–54, 56, 61, 84, 336
  comma with, 141
  verb tense in, 17
Verbosity, 209
Verb phrase, 7–8, 13
Very much, not *in the worst way*, 68
Very much, not *lots*, 70
Very, not *so*, 202
Very or *really*, not *real*, 64
Very to modify past párticiple, avoid, 70
Viewing
  motion pictures, 324–26
  television, 283, 319–24
Vocabulary, 175–210, 318. *See also* Words
Vocation and *avocation*, 197
Vocative, 28, 158
Voice, 283–90
  and meaning, 284–85
  controlling the breath, 283–84
  defined, 283
  improvement, 287–89
  inflection, 285
  projection, 286
  vocal factors, 285–87
Voice of verb, 12–13, 117–19
  avoiding shifts in, 20, 114–15

W

Way, misused for *away*, 70
Ways, misused for *way* or *distance*, 65
We and *us*, used with nouns, 39
Well and *good*, 64
What as relative pronoun, 43
What, misused for *that* or *which*, 42
When, not *till* or *until*, 76
When, *where*, misused in definition, 76, 113
Where, misused for *that*, 73
Whether, misused for *if*, 79
While, misuse of, 79
Who and *whom*, 39
Who is and *who's*, 40
Wholesome, *healthy*, *healthful*, 199
Who, *which*, and *that*, 42
Will and *shall*, 23
Within, not *inside* or *inside of*, 77
Without, misused for *unless*, 76

Words
  aid to expression, 126–32
  alliteration, 193, 240, 242, 243
  archaic, 188
  cacophony, 193
  changed meaning, 177
  confused as to spelling, 167, 196–202
  connotation and denotation, 194–95
  derivation, 178–82
  dialectal, 187
  etymology, 178–80
  euphony, 193
  family names, 179
  faulty expressions, 196–203
  figurative, 189–92, 240, 243
  foreign, 153, 180–82, 187, 189
  Greek elements, 181–82, 310
  history of, 178–180
  idiomatic, 204–5
  in groups, 311
  key, in reading, 312
  Latin elements, 180, 182, 310
  localisms, 187
  mispronounced often, 290
  neologisms, 182
  obsolescent, 187
  obsolete, 187, 189
  poetic, 188
  provincial, 187
  recognizing new, 308–10
  semantics, 129–32, 195
  slang, 184
  sounds of, 193
  specific, 127–28
  trite expressions, 190, 192, 206–8, 335
  variation in American and British, 175–76
  vivid verbs, nouns, adjectives, adverbs, 116
  wordiness, 208–9
Worse for *more*, avoiding, 68
Would and *should*, 23
Would of, *had of*, avoiding, 19
Wrote or *written*, not *writ*, 202

Y

Yes and *no*, comma after, 140
You are and *you're*, 40

Dance photograph on the cover courtesy of "The Silver Spurs," teen-age Western exhibition dance group, Spokane, Washington.